Melville and Women

Melville & Women

EDITED BY

Elizabeth Schultz

and

Haskell Springer

The Kent State University Press

KENT, OHIO

© 2006 by The Kent State University Press, Kent, Ohio 44242
ALL RIGHTS RESERVED
Library of Congress Catalog Card Number 2005034829
ISBN-10: 0-87338-859-3
ISBN-13: 978-0-87338-859-7
Manufactured in the United States of America

10 09 08 07 06   5 4 3 2 1

LIBRARY OF CONGRESS CATALOGING-IN-PUBLICATION DATA
Melville and women / edited by Elizabeth Schultz and Haskell Springer.
    p. cm.
  Includes bibliographical references and index.
  ISBN-13: 978-0-87338-859-7 (pbk. : alk. paper) ∞
  ISBN-10: 0-87338-859-3 (pbk. : alk. paper) ∞
1. Melville, Herman, 1819–1891—Characters—Women. 2. Women in literature. 3. Melville, Herman, 1819–1891—Relations with women. 4. Novelists, American—19th century—Biography. I. Schultz, Elizabeth. II. Springer, Haskell S.
PS2388.W6M45 2006
813'.3—dc22   2005034829

British Library Cataloging-in-Publication data are available.

Dedicated to Friendship

Contents

I. Introductory
   Melville Writing Women/Women Writing Melville 3
   ELIZABETH SCHULTZ AND HASKELL SPRINGER
   Melville and the Women in His Life 15
   LAURIE ROBERTSON-LORANT

II. Melville Reading Women
   Women Reading Melville/Melville Reading Women 41
   CHARLENE AVALLONE
   "Piazza to the North": Melville Reading Sedgwick 60
   PETER BALAAM
   "Bartleby" and "Uncle Christopher's": Sites of Wage Slavery
   and Domestic Abuse 82
   ELIZABETH SCHULTZ
   "Tender Kinswoman": Gail Hamilton and Gendered Justice
   in *Billy Budd* 98
   WYN KELLEY

III. Readings of *Pierre* and Women
   Melville and Isabel: The Author and the Woman Within
   in the "Inside Narrative" of *Pierre* 121
   WENDY STALLARD FLORY
   Women, Ownership, and Gothic Manhood in *Pierre* 141
   ELLEN WEINAUER

IV. Women in the Fiction and Poetry
    Island Queens: Women and Power in Melville's South Pacific   163
        JUNIPER ELLIS
    "Suckled by the Sea": The Maternal in *Moby-Dick*   181
        RITA BODE
    Of Cuttle-Fish and Women: Melville's Goneril in
    The Confidence-Man   199
        BEVERLY A. HUME
    When Silence Speaks: The Chola Widow   213
        MARIA FELISA LÓPEZ LIQUETE
    Circassian Longings: Melville's Orientalization of Eden   229
        TIMOTHY MARR

Bibliography   252

Contributors   271

Index   273

Part One

Introductory

Melville Writing Women/ Women Writing Melville

Elizabeth Schultz and Haskell Springer

Women in Melville's Life and Writing

Herman Melville's life (1819–1891) and writings spanned the nineteenth century. Witness to its political, economic, and social upheavals, he recorded his responses to this tumultuous history, including its shifts in gender roles for both men and women, in his novels, stories, and poems. While his position as breadwinner for and torchbearer of a distinguished family, following the untimely deaths of his father and older brother, as well as his years on male-dominated sailing vessels, led him to be keenly conscious of his society's demands on "manhood," most of his life was spent in the intimate company of women.

Surrounded by his mother, sisters, wife, and daughters, he was dependent upon them for copying and proofing his manuscripts, for organizing his social life, and for companionship. He also found himself embarrassingly dependent on his wife, Elizabeth (Fig. 1), and her eminent and successful family for financial support. Following the death of their first son, tensions emerged between him and his wife that have become the subject of debate by several Melville biographers. His relations with his daughters also appear to have been painfully conflicted. However, as Melville became increasingly reclusive in the last decades of his life, his relationship with Lizzie mellowed, and his granddaughters came to idolize him. Throughout his long life, he enjoyed regular correspondence with female friends as well as with women relatives in his extended family.

Cognizant of the limitations placed on the family women by the Cult of True Womanhood, which prescribed a life of purity, piety, domesticity, and submission, Melville was also aware of nineteenth-century women's transgression of these boundaries. Living for many years in New York City, Melville attended both the theater and opera and would have seen the nineteenth century's great women performers as well as become familiar with their roles. He admired the works of Madame de Staël and was personally acquainted with several prominent women writers, including Catharine Maria Sedgwick (Fig. 2) and Alice and Phoebe Cary (Fig. 3). The arguments for women's equality made by his bold contemporaries Margaret Fuller, Elizabeth Cady Stanton, Susan B. Anthony, and Lucy Stone are not directly reflected in his writings, but in them he reveals a consciousness of powerful and self-actualized individual women as well as of women's sexuality, of women's disempowerment, and of working women's lives.

Women appear in Melville's writings from the very beginning (the two "Fragments from a Writing Desk" [1838]), and they continue to do so as a gender, as individuals, and by allusion through to the end (*Billy Budd* [1891]). Probably the best-known Melvillean woman is Fayaway of *Typee* (1846), beautiful, kind, exotic—the iconic Pacific island woman, portrayed even late in the century by artist John LaFarge. Both the mysterious Isabel and virginal Lucy of *Pierre* (1852) have major roles, while to a short list of Melville's canonical female dramatis personae we might add the sorrowful Hunilla ("The Chola Widow" of "Sketch Eighth" of "The Encantadas") (1856), and Urania, the astronomer of "After the Pleasure Party" in *Timoleon* (1891). With these few exceptions the women are, in traditional terms, "minor characters" or less; but their significance far exceeds the number of words expressly concerning them or their apparent insignificance as literary characters. These heterogeneous women are realistic, allegorical, symbolic, and mythic. In his prose and poetry alike, they often express or reflect the author's, narrator's, or protagonist's psychology and biography. They imply Melville's literary goals, embody his dreams and ideals, and exist as critiques of religious, political, economic, and social realities in the United States, as well as of cultural conditions more generally.

In fictions long and short, Melville inserts—both with and without commentary—unnamed women, often in groups. They include, for example, the immigrant women suffering through their voyage to America in *Redburn* (1849). In *Moby-Dick* (1851) appear the widows at Father Mapple's service, and the young Pacific island women aboard the homeward-bound *Bachelor*. In

Pierre (1852) Melville includes the rural sewing circle and the mob of urban prostitutes. "Benito Cereno" (1855) features the African slave women aboard the *San Dominick*. "The Paradise of Bachelors and the Tartarus of Maids" (1855) presents the silent, chilled, exploited "maids" of the title. Sometimes women in these groups are named and specifically characterized, as they are, notably, in three short fictions where the narrator's household includes his wife and two daughters and their servant, Biddy: "Jimmy Rose" (1855), "I and My Chimney" (1856), and "The Apple-Tree Table" (1856).

Women also come into play in Melville's writings in interpolated stories. In *Typee* the islanders strip a missionary wife of her clothes; Mrs. Pritchard, wife of the British consul, defies French orders to take down the British colors; and the queen of Nukuheva drives off the French with a shocking display. In *Omoo* a missionary wife abuses two native men, treating them like draft horses. In *The Confidence-Man* appears the story of the ostensibly freakish Goneril. In other works women are mentioned, seemingly only in passing, but they subsequently haunt the reader's memory. This is the case in *Redburn* (1849) with the young sailor's description of an anonymous woman, the starving mother in a Liverpool cellar. Contrarily, though, little or no emotion attaches to the wife of Israel Potter, with whom he has eleven children but who exists in the novel in only one dependent clause.

Throughout his work, Melville also cites specific women from history, literature, and myth. In a seminal 1990 dissertation, "Women, Marriage, and Sexuality in the Work of Herman Melville: A Cultural/Gender Study," Fred Pinnegar points out that an examination of Melville's marginalia in the books in his library reveals his "fascination with all kinds of women" (31). The mock-gothic tale "The Apple-Tree Table" alludes to "the Fox girls" (famed and derided spiritualist sisters) as well as to Ann Radcliffe, author of the gothic *Mysteries of Udolpho*. In *Moby-Dick* he mentions Queen Elizabeth I, Queen Anne, Tanaquil (Tarquin's wife), and Benjamin Franklin's grandmother, Mary Folger, née Morrel. Even in *White-Jacket* (1850), a novel that tells us to leave "our women and children behind" before entering its "man-of-war-world," the narrator is free to allude to women, ranging from Lady Hamilton (mistress of Lord Nelson) to the prophet Mohammed's first wife, Kadija.

That Melville was impressed by Sir Walter Scott's female characters is evident, for example, from his references to *Ivanhoe*'s Rebecca (in "Fragments from a Writing Desk" and "Paradise of Bachelors") and to the White Lady of Avanel from *The Monastery*. He also presents likenesses to Danae and to Beatrice Cenci in *Pierre*; compares Billy Budd to Georgiana, victim of her husband's hubris in Hawthorne's "The Birth-mark"; and ends *Moby-Dick* with the biblical Rachel, after having earlier alluded to Shakespeare's Queen

Mab and the goddess Isis. For so allusive an author as Herman Melville, it is no surprise to find him—in narration, description, and figurative language—glancing at Euridice, Persephone, Semiramis, Lot's wife, Lady Macbeth, and many others.

Women are scattered unevenly through Melville's poetry, sometimes even coming unmediated before the reader's eye. For example, in the war poems of *Battle-Pieces* (1866), America is a woman. Human women, though far from the scene of battle, influence the action, as in "On the Slain Collegians," where—as always in wartime—they "incite" the young soldiers who, in their ignorance about war, march off to die. More directly, a poetic response to an Elihu Vedder portrait, "Formerly a Slave," draws a "sybilline" old black woman who looks on the celebration of victory that has won the freedom of her descendants, while in "The Scout Toward Aldie" a brave, mysterious Southern woman defies Union cavalry. And in the epic-length *Clarel* (1876) Melville created, among others, the Jewish Rebecca, loved by the eponymous hero. In *Timoleon* (1891) Lamia sings directly in "Lamia's Song," while "the turbulent heart and rebel brain" that Melville assigns to Urania, his female protagonist in "After the Pleasure Party," might well be a portrait of himself as artist.

Women in Melville Scholarship

One of the last half-century's dominant literary-historical narratives is that the great male Artists of an American Renaissance found their works ignored by a readership too preoccupied with the domestic and sentimental "scribbling" of popular women writers to take note of the great literature available to it. Complementing this narrative is another indicting the canonical writers of the American Renaissance for holding women's writings in disdain. Both narratives have effectively perpetuated the legend that the male writers of the nineteenth century, with Melville leading the pack, were misogynistic, reinforcing limited and derogatory stereotypes of women at worst and indifferent to women and their lives at best. Only Hawthorne, who created both the excoriating term "scribbling women" and the remarkable Hester Prynne, has barely escaped these condemnations. An 1888 essay by his son, Julian, placed Melville's works beyond the pale of women's interest, classifying them initially as "Man-Books." He denigrated them further, claiming that Melville "wrote books that were certainly not meant for women; but they were not exactly man-books either . . . they were books of adventure—boys' books" (Leyda, *Log* 2: 810). Contemporary scholarship by both men and women suggests, however, that male and female authors of the mid-nineteenth century were regularly reading one another's works and writing in multinuanced response to them.

From the Melville Revival on, influential male scholars of the American Renaissance continued to read Melville's writings as misogynistic. Lewis Mumford's important 1929 biography, for example, contends that "all Melville's books about the sea have the one anomaly and defect of the sea from the central, human point of view: one-half of the race, woman, is left out of it. Melville's world, all too literally, is a man-of-war's world" (137). According to Pinnegar, the misogynistic position of such early Melville scholars as Raymond Weaver, Newton Arvin, and Richard Chase was grounded in a Freudian reading of Melville's biography—in their interpretation of "a female- or mother-damaged Melville" (13)—which they then applied to his writing. As recently as 1980, Charles Haberstroh, in *Melville and Male Identity*, claimed that Melville's "fear and distrust of females" resulted either in his omitting women from his texts or in his representing them as man-traps (66). Although her 1982 essay on Melville in *American Novelists Revisited* reasserts Melville's "hatred of" and "disinterest in" women, Gene Patterson-Black also credits the perception of women's absence in his works to the construction of a Melville academic canon that "crystallized around works in which women do not figure, thereby producing a distorted concept of Melville's work as a whole and producing a general reading public that assumes that Melville did not write about women" (107–8).

During the latter part of the twentieth century, however, in part due to the increase in scholarship written by women, the picture of Melville as a misogynistic writer has been steadily under revision. With the rise of feminist literary criticism in the 1970s, scholars such as Ann Douglass, Joyce M. Warren, and Wilma Garcia, in reexamining nineteenth-century American canonical literature from an explicitly feminist perspective, turned their attention from Melville's indifference to women and their absence in his work to his representing women (as they perceived it) only in terms of degraded gender stereotypes. Warren, for example, maintains that "when women do appear in his works, they are either little more than animated memories—traditional images of femininity as conceived by men—or overpowering nightmare figures who threaten the autonomy of the male self" (115). In their discussions these early feminist critics are quick to identify Annatoo (*Mardi*) and Mrs. Glendinning (*Pierre*) as termagants; like *Mardi*'s Hautia and Yillah, *Pierre*'s Isabel is read as the "prototype of evil . . . an emasculating witch-woman who uses all of her powers to subjugate man to her will" in opposition to Lucy, who is read as "the prototype of good . . . a softly yielding, angelic maiden with no will of her own and totally dependent upon man for her protection, even for her existence" (117). Despite their legitimate feminist concern that Melville projects male fantasies rather than fully developed, individual woman characters, early feminist Melville critics failed to consider the strengths of such characters, in prose and poetry, as Hunilla and Urania; to recognize Melville's understanding of women's victimization; or to perceive, as does Dilek Direnç in her essay "What Do These Women Want? *Pierre* and the New World of Gender" (1997), that Melville's representation of his women characters is often ambiguous.

Although the significance of women in the Melvillean literary and ideational landscape was slow to register, since the 1930s women scholars have participated fully in the flourishing critical examination of Melville's works, thereby speeding that recognition. In view of the general paucity of women scholars active in the first decades of the twentieth century, it is not surprising that none participated in the Melville Revival of the 1920s. However, since Constance Rourke's commentary in *American Humor* on Melville's works in 1931, women have contributed in increasing numbers to the critical and biographical interpretation of these works. Through the forties and fifties and into the sixties, they looked at Melville's works through the lens of New Criticism, as did men. Therefore, New Critical essays written by women on Melvillean works that more recently have been illuminated by applying to them a feminist perspective focus on the male narrator's experience rather than on the situation of women. They include those published in the sixties in *American Literature* by Judith Slater ("The Domestic Adventurer in Melville's Tales") and Beryl Rowland ("Melville's Bachelors and Maids: Interpretation Through Symbol and Metaphor"). Women's research during the 1940s, 1950s, and 1960s, however, has proven seminal and indispensable for Melville studies. With her edition of Melville's *Journal of a Visit to London and the Continent, 1849–1850* (1949) as well as *Herman Melville: Cycle and Epicycle* (1953), Eleanor Melville Metcalf provided valuable information regarding her grandfather's life in relation to his work. In addition, the pioneering research and editorial work of Nathalia Wright on Melville's use of the Bible in 1949 and of Elizabeth Foster on *The Confidence-Man* in 1954 continue to be cited. Such significant work has been carried on by Mary K. Bercaw Edwards on Melville's literary sources, Gail Coffler on Melville's use of classical sources and his allusions to religion, Lea Bertani Vozar Newman in her guide to Melville's short stories, Kathleen Kier in her Melville encyclopedia, and Lynn Horth and Alma A. MacDougall in their editorial contributions to the scholarly Northwestern University–Newberry Library editions of Melville's writings.

Since the 1960s, women scholars have been engaged in discussing a range of issues in Melville's writings from diverse perspectives and theories. Newman's

1986 essay on "The Bell-Tower," which she labels "a story of female revenge" and interprets as describing "a revolt against an exploitative male-dominated culture" (11), was among the first critical works to explore Melville's response to women's powerlessness and to locate that concern in his short fiction. Often drawing on New Historicism, women scholars have significantly advanced understanding of Melville's works in relation to nineteenth-century attitudes toward gender as it is entwined with sexuality, domesticity, sentimentality, and labor conditions. Full-length studies such as Sheila Post-Lauria's *Correspondent Colorings: Melville in the Marketplace* (1996) and Wyn Kelley's *Melville's City: Literary and Urban Form in Nineteenth-Century New York* (1996) exemplify the usefulness of New Historicism in illuminating Melville. In recent years women have led Melville scholarship in their attention to orientalism (Dorothee Finkelstein), war (Joyce Sparer Adler), labor (Cindy Weinstein), race (Eleanor E. Simpson, Carolyn Karcher, Toni Morrison, Dana Nelson), nature and the visual arts (Elizabeth Schultz), queer studies (Eve Kosofsky Sedgwick), politics (Myra Jehlen, Wai Chee Dimock, Clare Spark), domesticity (Gillian Brown, Wyn Kelley), and gender (Nancy Fredericks, Camille Paglia, Robyn Wiegman). Certain essays by contemporary women scholars have become canonical in Melville studies, such as two on *Billy Budd* written for *Herman Melville: A Collection of Critical Essays,* edited by Myra Jehlen: Sedgwick's "*Billy Budd:* After the Homosexual" and Barbara Johnson's "Melville's Fist: The Execution of *Billy Budd.*"

Contemporary male writers have also contributed substantially to an understanding of the position of women in Melville's life and writing. For example, Pinnegar focuses on marriage and sexuality, Michael Paul Rogin on the intricate tangle of the women in Melville's family with those in his fiction, Leland Person on creativity as feminine in Melville's fiction, and Dennis Berthold on the ambiguity of Medusa in Melville's works, while Hershel Parker's monumental two-volume biography provides extensive, detailed accounts of Melville's multiple and diverse relationships with the women in his family—his mother, aunts, sisters, wife, daughters, granddaughters, sisters-in-law, friends, and cousins. In contrast to the early biographical and critical studies of Melville written by men, with their Freudian orientation, recent studies by Elizabeth Renker and Laurie Robertson-Lorant emphasize the significance of gender in reading Melville's life, paying special attention to his changing relationship with his wife. Elizabeth Hardwick's brief reading of Melville's life and writing is at once lyrical and rigorous but is focused more on his relationship with Hawthorne than with women.

The number of women attending Melville conferences, claiming membership in the Melville Society, serving as officers in the society, and participating in its ISHMAIL listserve, in addition to the number of women actively engaged in Melville scholarship—both in the United States and abroad (with significant scholarship being published by Turkish, Japanese, French, Canadian, and Danish women)—suggests that the appeal of Melville's works has deepened for women scholars and readers. Their contributions denote their commitment to the study of Melville's writings and to the promotion of them nationally and internationally. Melville's works can no longer be said to be either "Man's Books" or "boys' books"—they are equally illuminating to men and women readers and as illuminating about female as about male gender.

Melville and Women: *An Overview*

Melville and Women treats works from Melville's earliest to his last using a variety of theoretical approaches. Laurie Robertson-Lorant provides a general biographical overview of Melville's life, pointing particularly to the diversity of his social and intellectual connections with women as well as the changing relationship with Lizzie. Recognizing him as the most accomplished author of his age who wrote in multiple genres, *Melville and Women* illuminates his novels, short stories, and poetry. Reaching beyond those texts proper, it probes their unexpected relation to now marginalized writing of his day and also reveals new evidence about Melville's audience. The results add to his known reading of nineteenth-century women's work and their reading of his.

These essays are not only newly written but often new in their approaches to specific subjects. The result is an illuminating defamiliarizing of familiar texts. Juniper Ellis, Wendy Flory, and Tim Marr, for example, argue for alternatives to traditional classifications of women in Melville's works. Beverly Hume and Rita Bode break ground in applying ecofeminism to Melville, while Hume also extends the traditional boundaries of androgyny and Bode widens the subject of "mother" in Melville. As Charlene Avallone, Peter Balaam, Elizabeth Schultz, and Wyn Kelley argue for connections and influences between Melville and women writers of his time, they shift the ground on which particular Melvillean works have been understood to stand. In addition, Ellen Weinauer examines the gothic mode in relation to nineteenth-century law; Balaam biographically and thematically resituates ideas about American architecture; Kelley and Schultz continue the critical project of legitimizing sentimentality.

Several of the most innovative of these new essays point to specific women authors, not only suggesting a much more widely read Melville but further steering us away from critical androcentrism toward scholarly inclusiveness, greater accuracy. Avallone makes a detailed historical analysis of Melville's familiarity with women's writing as well as of the extension of women's reading beyond sentimental fiction. The result permits Avallone to challenge conventional gender assumptions regarding nineteenth-century male and female audiences. *Pierre*, which draws on Catharine Maria Sedgwick's *The Linwoods*, exemplifies Melville's complex response to women's fiction, while Elizabeth Elkins Sanders' *Remarks on the "Tour around Hawaii"* represents the impact his writing, in this case *Typee*, may have had on women writers. Balaam reveals how the intertextuality of Sedgwick's 1821 novel *A New-England Tale*, featuring a mournful madwoman, and Melville's late tale, "The Piazza" (1856), with its ever-mourning Marianna, invalidates traditional caricatures both of Sedgwick as scribbling blue-stocking and of Melville as aloof, godlike artist. Schultz newly probes gender and class questions by examining "Bartleby, the Scrivener" in comparison to the superficially dissimilar story by Alice Cary, "Uncle Christopher's," both written in 1853. The resulting clarification also suggests a link with Melville's "The Paradise of Bachelors and the Tartartus of Maids" a year later. Kelley considers gendered justice in *Billy Budd, Sailor*, implying that Melville was familiar with the concept through an essay by Gail Hamilton (Fig. 4), a well-known author read by Elizabeth Melville. Hamilton wrote on the infamous *Somers* mutiny case, long known to be a source for *Billy Budd*, but Kelley's discussion of her 1889 essay is the first in relation to Melville's last work of fiction.

At the heart of four essays are female characters. Hume looks at the odd and elusive Goneril in *The Confidence-Man*—a cold, snaky, slippery woman—a wife but a trickster in literal or metaphoric drag. Hume reconsiders her in relation to recent ecofeminist and ecocritical discussions of the human-nonhuman continuum. She finds Melville linking the environmental and cultural degradation of his mid-nineteenth-century America to an androcentric reinvention of the natural world. Postcolonial theory shapes Maria Felisa López Liquete's essay on Hunilla, the Chola Widow in "The Encantadas," a tale of a mixed-race woman's mournful silence under the questioning, appropriative gaze of Western men: the author, the narrator, and the male characters in the story. Liquete explicates Melville's understanding of the mestiza's fortitude in the face of pain, violation, and repression. Ellis, on similar theoretical foundations, constructs the formidable South Pacific island queens in *Typee, Omoo,* and *Mardi*. Although earlier critics have made passing references to these queenly figures, Ellis establishes their political and narrative importance in Melville's Pacific islands narratives. Flory sees the four women of *Pierre* as psychologically symbolic characters personifying dimensions of Melville's mind. This perspective allows a revaluation of Isabel, Pierre's half-sister, as the difficult muse of both Pierre and Melville himself. The consequence of her argument is a coherent *Pierre*.

Using theory in several ways, Bode considers the maternal element in *Moby-Dick*. Relying on close critical reading, the thought of Luce Irigaray, and ecofeminist theory, she establishes the maternal both as presence and absence, contending that Melville expresses a destructive loss and imbalance in his whaling world while offering an alternative to the aggressive whale hunt paradigm. Contextualizing Melville historically, Weinauer revalues the gothic mode of *Pierre*, considering how changes to the laws of "coverture" (under which a married woman's property was considered to be her husband's) are reflected in its gothic picture of manhood. Like Flory, though on different grounds, she finds coherence in this fascinating but puzzling novel. Finally, Marr probes Melville's use of the nineteenth-century concept of the Circassian woman. Seeing in much of Melville's work, most especially his late poetry, its evocation of women as heavenly muses of artistic beauty and inspiration, he reveals the sometimes exotic sources and products of Melville's generative vision of woman as an angelic Eve symbolically connected to the freshness and youth of creation.

While these illuminating essays indicate new directions in the study of women in Melville's works, in so doing, they implicitly call attention to areas and subjects in his oeuvre that are not treated here but that we hope will be addressed in the future. Missing from discussion in our collection are Melville's domestic short stories of the 1850s as well as the twinned tales "The Paradise of Bachelors and the Tartarus of Maids," with the latter's famous, allegorically biological depiction of suffering factory women. Mentioned in these pages but not explored are the newspaper pieces "Fragments from a Writing Desk," spoken by men but entirely taken up with women. Similarly, just touched on are important poems such as "After the Pleasure Party," largely spoken by an intellectual woman painfully questioning her life of the mind that has rejected physical passion. The women in the epic-length *Clarel* are also absent from our essays. The subject of sexuality does not have its own essay, nor does the female body. Mentioned but unexamined is the intriguing issue discussed by Melville biographers: the probably discarded "Story of Agatha," focusing on a faithful, patient woman abandoned by her bigamous husband.

Despite more than eighty years of intense Melville scholarship and criticism, this collection is the first full-length study of Melville and women. The essays here open new venues for reading Melville's works in relation to nineteenth-century women's writing, ecofeminism, cultural studies, feminist studies, gender studies, and women's lives. We hope that *Melville and Women* will prompt continued work on Melville's changing, ever ambivalent and complex, but always challenging inscription of women's lives.

Beyond Melville and Women

Melville's writings, perhaps more so than those of any other American author, have been subject to often astonishing reinterpretations by diverse artists and commercial entrepreneurs. In 1992 Joyce Sparer Adler published dramatizations of three of Melville's works—*Moby-Dick,* "Benito Cereno," and *Billy Budd*. Increasingly artists have come to *Moby-Dick,* the novel perceived by critics as Melville's most relentlessly masculine, with a feminist orientation. From Ann Wilson's abstract quilt (1955) to Abby Schlachter Langdon's *Queequeg in Her Coffin* (1997; Fig. 8) and Aileen Callahan's two series of oil paintings, *The Birth of Moby Dick* (2000–2001; Fig. 5) and *Moby Dick's Mouth* (2003–2004), numerous women visual artists have identified the feminine in *Moby-Dick*. Two men, Gilbert Wilson in his 1949 operatic dramatization of *Moby-Dick* and Orson Welles in his 1965 *Moby-Dick Rehearsed,* insisted on women having roles in their productions, and in the closing decades of the twentieth century even more women were called for in new stagings and revisions of *Moby-Dick*—Patty Lynch's 1987 *Moby-Dick*-inspired drama, *The Wreck of the Hesperus;* a 1992 British rock-musical set at a girls' prep school; as well as Bill Peters' drama *Hunting for Moby Dick* (1996).

The stunning re-creations of *Moby-Dick* by performance artists JoAnne Spies (1997), Ellen Driscoll (1998; Fig. 6), and Laurie Anderson (1999) emphatically insisted on a space for women. In addition, Sena Jeter Naslund's 1999 bestselling novel *Ahab's Wife* opened a national discussion of women's position in *Moby-Dick,* contributing to what might even be called the feminizing of Melville's novel. Rinde Eckert's evocative opera, *And God Created Great Whales* (2000), builds on the relationship between a man and a woman, each of whom takes several roles from *Moby-Dick*. That *Moby-Dick* continues to appeal to women artists is indicated by the recent work of weaver Aimée Picard (Fig. 7), installation-creator Sharon Butler, and bookmaker Margo Lemieux. While artists of both sexes seem determined to claim *Moby-Dick* for women in diverse ways and through diverse media, apart from this novel other works by Melville have to date resisted feminist or women-centered visual interpretations. Leos Carax's 2000 film *Pola X,* based on *Pierre,* for example, reinscribes the novel's stereotypes: woman as victim, temptress, and termagant.

Debased representations of Melville's multiethnic cast of characters in illustrated children's editions of *Moby-Dick* sell alongside other children's editions with illustrations representing these characters in individualistic and complex ways (Schultz, "Visualizing Race"). A similarly bifurcated attitude continues to exist in popular conceptions regarding Melville's response to women. Gene Patterson-Black claimed in 1982 that Melville's disinterest in women was reciprocated by the disinterest of women readers in Melville (108); and in a 2001 *Prairie Home Companion* performance at Tanglewood, spoofing the nineteenth-century writers living in the Berkshires, Lizzie Melville tells her husband that "women are not going to read an endless saga of men and the sea." At the Melville Society meeting at the Modern Language Association Meeting in 1985, however, a panel on "Women in Melville's Art" indicated the increasing scholarly interest in the subject of Melville and women. In introducing this session, Joyce Sparer Adler quoted Charlene Avallone as stating that Melville was "frequently more sympathetic to women's rights and problems, more cognizant of full female humanity, and more imaginative in suggesting changes in the status quo than he is generally credited with being" ("Introduction" 3).

The increasing number of women scholars, members of the Melville Society, visual artists, performance artists, poets, and musicians, all illuminating Melville's life and writings, suggests that women are not only continuing to read Melville's sagas of men and the sea but that they have also come to identify women's positions in these sagas. The increased attention of scholars, artists, and readers—both men and women—to the presence of women in Melville's life and writings reflects cultural developments in our times as well as Melville's own arduous commitment as a writer to grasping the always ungraspable complexities of the lives of men and women.

Melville and the Women in His Life

Laurie Robertson-Lorant

When I completed my dissertation on Melville and race in 1972, I could not have said how many brothers and sisters, wives and children Melville had (Lorant). We were taught that information about a writer's life was irrelevant, and given the current appetite for spicing up pretentious critical theories with scandalous biographical revelations, there was some wisdom in that point of view. As *New York Times* critic Michiko Kakutani has observed, biography is "a blood sport" these days.[1]

Particularly bitter controversy characterizes biographers' representations of Melville's attitudes toward women, especially regarding his treatment of his wife, Elizabeth. According to several letters discovered by Dr. Walter Donald Kring in the archives of All Souls' Church, New York, Elizabeth Shaw's stepbrother Sam, a Boston attorney, and her pastor, Dr. Henry Whitney Bellows, discussed kidnapping her to get her away from Melville in May 1867 because they thought he was insane.[2] Publication of Donald Yanella's and Hershel Parker's *The Endless, Winding Way: New Charts by Kring and Carey* (1981) made what were once vague and unsubstantiated rumors that Melville drank heavily and physically abused his wife sound more plausible, but to dismiss Melville as a wife-beater, as Elizabeth Renker does in "Herman Melville, Wife-Beating, and the Written Page" and *Strike Through the Mask: Herman Melville and the Scene of Writing*, is to reduce a long and complex marriage to little more than a case study.

When I was in graduate school, Walker Cowen's 1965 dissertation on Melville's allegedly misogynistic marginalia was cited as proof that Melville hated women, and the erasures someone had tried to make as proof that Lizzie was trying to suppress this awful truth. No one considered that Melville himself or someone other than Lizzie might have made them. Perhaps the "methodological misogyny" of Melville scholars like Cowen and biographers like Edwin Haviland Miller says less about Melville's biases than their own.[3]

Early Melville biographers either ignored or denigrated the women in Melville's life. They portrayed Melville as an Olympian isolato surrounded by unintelligent women whose presence was a cross he had to bear. Because his early fiction was based on his sea voyages, the temptation was to *biographize* Melville from his six first-person sailor-narrators and his novel *Pierre* (1852), whose protagonist seems to be a psychological portrait of its volatile, troubled, angry author.[4] They describe Elizabeth Shaw as a poor choice as a wife for the adventurous sailor who had dallied with naked whihinees in the South Seas and his mother and sisters as dull, pious women who could not possibly have appreciated Melville's books.

I remember being told that Lizzie Melville was a homely woman who suffered from a "rose cold" and that Melville's dedicating "Weeds and Wildings, with a Rose or Two" to her at the end of his life was proof that he hated her. This alleged hatred then became proof that Lizzie was a thorn in the great man's side. From the available evidence, it would be just as easy to argue that because her allergies prevented him from giving her real roses, Herman wanted to present her with a bouquet of "roses" she could enjoy. The truth is that by the time the Melvilles moved back to New York in 1863, Lizzie had learned that her malady was hay fever, which left Herman free to plant a rose garden at their house on 104 East 26th Street. He was evidently proud of his roses, as he dried the petals and sent them to women friends and relatives such as his cousin Kate Gansevoort.

Materials preserved in various archives and private collections provide information about the women in Melville's immediate family and the lives of his woman friends and relatives in Albany, Lansingburgh, Pittsfield, Boston, and New York. As the family correspondence demonstrates, Melville depended on the women in his family all his life. In the prime of his life, he and his wife shared their home with his sisters and their domineering mother. That he found this difficult and at times resented it is not hard to imagine, especially since he was never able to earn enough money from his writing to make life comfortable for his family. Even so, for every bit of evidence that he was restless and dissatisfied with domestic life, other evidence shows that he enjoyed the company of his women friends and relatives and found support and eventual solace in his marriage.

Melville knew both of his grandmothers. During summer epidemics of typhoid and cholera, his mother took her children upriver while her husband remained at his business in Manhattan. At his mother's home in Albany, Melville got to know his Dutch grandmother, Catherine von Schaick Gansevoort, a depressed but strong-willed widow who defied convention by traveling "alone" with a black servant (or slave) named Chris—something respectable female members of the Dutch aristocracy of New York State did not do.[5]

When Melville was eight, he spent part of the summer with his paternal grandparents in Boston. His grandmother, Priscilla Scollay, suffered from rheumatism and spent most of her waking hours sitting very stiffly in a straight wooden chair doing needlework. His grandfather, Major Thomas Melvill, was a colorful character who still wore the cocked hat and satin knee britches of the Revolutionary era and liked to chase fire engines and watch fires. He kept a glass vial on the mantel to show visitors the tea leaves he had found in his boots the night he and his cohorts dumped the British tea in the harbor. Years later, in *Redburn* (1849), Melville described the miniature glass ship they kept in their parlor and the spell it cast on his imagination.

Melville's mother was a powerful presence in his life. A communicant of the Dutch Reformed Church, she kept two Bibles by her bedside—one in English, the other in Dutch, her mother tongue. As a girl, she played the piano but was not allowed to read nondidactic poetry or fiction. Maria was obsessed with good penmanship, as good penmanship was a sign of good character, and good character was a sign of a proper upbringing. Both she and her husband considered the robust, apple-cheeked Herman slow in comparison with his glib and priggish older brother, Gansevoort. Herman never mastered penmanship, and he once told his sister Fanny he thought his mother hated him.

Melville was the third oldest of eight children, with an older sister and brother and five younger siblings, three of them girls, and some two dozen cousins, most of whom remain comparatively obscure. When he was six, his sixteen-year-old cousin Anne Marie Priscilla, the only surviving daughter of his uncle Thomas Melvill's French wife, Françoise Lamé-Fleury, came from Pittsfield to New York to attend school and to help Melville's mother with the younger children. As a child, Herman was fascinated by her occasional dreaminess, which he interpreted as sorrowful longing for her French mother, and she seems at least partly to have inspired the character Isabel in *Pierre*.

Following the horrific death of his father when he was in his early teens, Melville spent several summers working on his Uncle Thomas Melvill's Berkshire farm, where he and his cousin Julia Maria, who was a year younger than he, seem to have enjoyed a close relationship. A bright, intellectually curious girl who felt "very much in debt to the *Phoenicians* for the invention of wrighting [sic]," Julia pronounced her cousin Herman's sketches of seashells "very axeptable [sic] indeed."[6]

As an adult, Melville enjoyed bandying words and flirting with his Albany cousin Catherine Gansevoort. Twenty years younger than Herman, Kate married Abraham Lansing, a Dutch businessman whom she had known all her life, when she was thirty-four. Herman welcomed her husband as an ally in teasing her. "Poor Abe," she wrote her new husband in 1873, "even Cousin Herman says if you are not happy it will be *my fault*,—how cruel always to blame we poor women!!!"[7] Although judging from the lighthearted tone of her letter, Kate did not take offense at her cousin's teasing; later, however, she took seriously Lizzie's references to Melville's depressive, misanthrophic moods and supported Lizzie's efforts to keep her temperamental husband on an even keel.

Women were the Melville family historians and chroniclers; it was their job to spin a web of correspondence capable of holding families and friends together. Although their letters paint a vivid picture of domestic life, writing about intimate matters was taboo. The women were prolific letter-writers, but they left almost no diaries or journals. When Kate Gansevoort made the Grand Tour in 1860, for example, she took along a leatherbound day book to record her experiences, but most of its pages are blank.[8]

There is much we do not know about Melville's relationships with women. We know very little about his pre-Pacific relationships with the belles of Lansingburgh, other than that the young schoolteacher read Tennyson and Byron to Harriet Fly and Mary Ellen Parmalee on the banks of the Mohawk River and that he may have been the author of five anonymous love poems that appeared in the local newspaper around this time.[9] Young sailor Melville's sexual history remains a mystery, but it was an open secret that young men who sailed for the Pacific looked forward to a polymorphous sexual initiation in the South Seas. Even so, we do not know whether Melville engaged in sexual activities aboard the "blubber-hunters" and "wooden Gomorrahs" of the deep or whether he had sexual encounters of any kind on land or sea before he married Elizabeth Shaw in 1847.

Contrary to what biographers of earlier generations thought about Melville's attitude toward women, he appears to have enjoyed the company of his sisters, and they idolized him. His older sister, Helen Maria, boarded for a year at Elizabeth Sedgwick's school in Lenox, Massachusetts, where even the youngest girls studied Latin. By the time they were ten, most could speak French like Parisians. "By some sort of unknown alchymy [sic], Mrs.

Charles transforms all the common minds under her charge into geniuses: I cannot say that she has been equally successful with me, but certainly her other pupils are 'past the common,' as the Irish say."[10] Although she loved Mrs. Sedgwick's school, Helen missed her family, so Gansevoort and Herman drove over to Lenox on the weekends to take tea with their sister and her classmates at the school. Mrs. Sedgwick's sister-in-law was Catharine Maria Sedgwick, the celebrated novelist whom Herman would meet in August 1850. Helen, an avid reader, pronounced Miss Sedgwick's novel *The Linwoods* (1835) her best book so far.[11]

Once Helen finished her course at Mrs. Sedgwick's, she spent as much time as she could visiting her friends in Boston. She preferred that quaint old city to Lansingburgh, the village across the river from Albany to which her mother had moved after being forced to sell some of her furniture to pay off her late husband's debts. She enjoyed going to plays and parties with Jane Dow and Jane's cousin Elizabeth Shaw, the daughter of Allan Melvill's old friend Lemuel Shaw, chief justice of the Massachusetts Supreme Judicial Court. When the Shaws took the girls to see the celebrated British actor William Macready as Macbeth, all Helen could think of the entire evening was how much Herman would enjoy the show, especially his favorite scene, where the witches stir "eye of newt and toe of frog" into a "thick gruel" while chanting spells over a "cauldron of Hell-broth."[12] She was devoted to Herman and later served as his copyist for *Redburn* (1849), *White-Jacket* (1850), and parts of *Moby-Dick* (1851).

A great admirer of Charles Dickens, Helen wrote Augusta that she had shaken the hand of "the great Boz" when he visited Boston in 1842, and she would never wash that hand again.[13] Although a childhood illness left her with a limp that cramped her dancing style, Helen attended teas and dancing parties in hopes of meeting an eligible Boston bachelor. Her letters give a lively picture of those visits, from the customary after-dinner *tableaux vivants* to the sleet storm that forced Lizzie and Helen to grip the iron railing in front of the State House and "stoop like frogs"[14] so as not to lose their footing on the icy sidewalk. Despite her energetic efforts to find a suitable husband, Helen was thirty-six when she and Boston attorney George Griggs married in January 1854; sadly, their only baby was stillborn.

Augusta, who was two years younger than Herman, wore spectacles and during their childhood kept a pet bird. She was such a sober, pious girl that Herman referred to her as the "Sad One," and when she was only fifteen, people in Pittsfield mistook her for "a middle-aged widow."[15] A Sunday school teacher, she collected cast-off clothing and worn Bibles to send to the "heathen" in the South Seas—the same "savages" her brother considered far more civilized than the missionaries dispatched to convert them to Christianity and "the blessings of civilization." Augusta had a self-described "literary thirst," but it's hard to imagine her approving of *Typee* (1846), which scandalized those who reviewed it for the denominational magazines.[16]

In her youth, the bookish Gus was courted by Stephen van Rensselaer, and although at one point she became engaged to Anthony Augustus Peebles, the son of her mother's cousin, for some reason the engagement was broken. Augusta seems to have shied away from romantic relationships with young men, and it's not difficult to imagine her settling into a "Boston marriage" with another woman, but she never did. She devoted herself to teaching Sunday school, to proofreading and copying *Mardi* (1849) and portions of *Moby-Dick,* and to preserving hundreds of family letters that give a vivid picture of the Melvilles' life at Arrowhead.

Herman's sister Catherine and two of their Gansevoort cousins were called Kate, the name Herman proclaimed "the most engaging I think in our whole family circle."[17] When Catherine Melville was twenty-seven, she married John Hoadley, a widowed engineer who invented a portable engine, wrote passable poetry, and read Melville's *Battle Pieces* (1866) and other poems appreciatively. Melville visited the Hoadleys in Lawrence, Massachusetts, fairly frequently, so during the war years, when Hoadley was in charge of the New Bedford Copper Rolling Mill, Melville may have visited them and their three children following their move to a stately home at the corner of Madison and Orchard Streets, near New Bedford's millionaires' row more often than the surviving records show.[18]

Frances Priscilla, or Fanny, Melville's youngest sister, was a "hellion," according to her cousin Julia: "Aunt Maria will not own her when she goes home she has grown so wild & turned out so dreadfully."[19] Although it seems Fanny cut loose when she visited her aunt and uncle's Berkshire farm, she never quite cut the umbilical cord. She became pathologically shy and sensitive as an adult and never married. Even though Herman teased her unmercifully at times, she loved books and reading and looked up to her author-brother, whose Civil War poems she thought grand.

The most important woman in Melville's adult life was his wife, Elizabeth Shaw, a clever, well-educated, self-assured young woman whose mother had died giving birth to her. Several years later, her father, Lemuel Shaw, married Hope Savage, a loving woman who treated Lizzie and her brother John as kindly as her sons Lem Jr. and Sam Shaw. Lizzie called her "Mother" and thought of her as her best friend.

The Shaws brought Lizzie up to be as smart as she was good. By the time she was seven, she could read and write and cipher and play the piano. In

Boston she studied at a strict monitorial school similar to the one Herman attended in New York. She then boarded at the Uxbridge Classical Academy, a girls' school, for two years. At twelve she entered the School for Young Ladies, founded by George B. Emerson, a second cousin of Ralph Waldo Emerson, who believed young women should receive as rigorous an education as young men. In his opinion, it was not enough for them to be "good daughters and sisters, good neighbors, good wives, and good mothers" (Puett 25). To equip women to be educated citizens, he offered courses in English, Latin, arithmetic, science, and history that were the equivalent of the college preparatory course for young men; graduates of the school could go on to study at either the Mount Holyoke Female Seminary or Oberlin College in Ohio.

For some reason, Lizzie decided not to attend college, perhaps because she had fallen in love and could not bear to go away. According to Joyce and Frederick Kennedy, Lizzie had two beaux while Melville was in the Pacific. One was her childhood friend John Nourse, the son of Melville's aunt Lucy's second husband, Amos Nourse; the other was Daniel McIlroy, a Harvard Law School graduate. John Nourse died suddenly in 1844, and Judge Shaw opposed her marrying McIlroy because he was a Roman Catholic Irish Nationalist ("Elizabeth and Herman" 2: 3–8).

Shortly after Melville returned from the Pacific in October 1844, Helen invited Elizabeth Shaw to Lansingburgh, and it fell to Herman to squire Miss Shaw around for several weeks. After Lizzie returned home, Herman began visiting the Shaws in Boston more frequently than usual, and soon he was courting Miss Shaw in earnest. He splurged to buy her the lavishly illustrated *Floral Tableaux*, a book on the language of flowers very popular with New England girls, and he had trouble concentrating on his writing.

Melville must have found Elizabeth Shaw a refreshing change from the girls who were pursuing the sailor-author who had written a racy travel book. Lizzie was a down-to-earth, honest Yankee woman—practical, modest, well educated, and capable of total loyalty. She loved hearing Melville expound on books and ideas as much as she loved hearing about his adventures in the South Seas, but she did not dote and fawn over him as did other girls. Like Desdemona, she loved him for the dangers he had passed; and like Othello, he loved her for her unaffected charm and for the image of himself as an attractive young man of the world that he saw reflected in her admiring eyes. Both young people had lost a parent early in life, so their bond was based on grief as well as joy. It may have been this bond that saved their marriage two decades later.

Shuttling back and forth between Lansingburgh and Boston while courting Lizzie, Herman found it difficult to concentrate on his work; behind the scenes his mother was wielding a "steering oar"[20] to guide him into the harbor of marital bliss as soon as possible. *Typee,* which he dedicated affectionately to Judge Shaw, and *Omoo* (1847), which he dedicated to his uncle Herman Gansevoort, were enjoying a measure of success, so the way was clear to propose marriage and set the date.

Gossip columnists predicted that once Melville married Miss Shaw, he would find more happiness in civilization than in the romantic Marquesas. Fanny Longfellow offered the opinion that Lizzie was a "peculiar choice"[21] for Melville after his dalliance with the whihinees of the South Seas. Abolitionist Edmund Quincy remarked snidely that Miss Shaw appeared to have inherited her looks from her "distinguished father," but Gus's friends Millie Van Rensselaer Thayer and Augusta Whipple Hunter thought Lizzie a lovely woman, kindhearted and gay.[22]

Shortly before the wedding ceremony on August 4, 1847, Herman found a four-leaf clover, and legend has it that each year on their anniversary he found another and presented it to Lizzie in remembrance of their wedding day. The couple's honeymoon journey took them by train, stage, and canal boat through the White Mountains to Quebec and Montreal and then back through Vermont and across Lake Champlain on a crowded canal boat. In her spirited account of the trip, Lizzie described how she crawled "like a bug" onto a jerry-rigged upper shelf in the women's quarters to avoid sleeping on the floor, while Herman spent the whole night on deck "chilled and half-frozen with the fog and penetrating dampness" to avoid the crowd in the gentlemen's apartment.[23]

Once they settled down in Lansingburgh, Lizzie had time to reflect on the fact that she was now a married woman. "I'm afraid no place will ever seem to me like dear old crooked Boston," she wrote her stepbrother, but "with Herman with me always, I can be happy and contented anywhere." All the same, when he came into her sitting room without knocking to bring her "a button to sew on, or some such equally romantic occupation,"[24] she began to suspect marriage was not as "ethereal" as her unmarried friends imagined it must be.

Lansingburgh soon proved to be so confining for Melville that he and his brother Allan, a New York lawyer who had recently married socialite Sophia Thurston, pooled their money and bought a brownstone at 103 Fourth Avenue that was big enough for the two men, their wives, mother, sisters, and, eventually, an infant or two. Once Melville established a daily routine that allowed him to write without interruption, Lizzie's main job was attending to household chores and being available when her husband needed her. One of her letters to her mother gives a vivid picture of her early married life:

We breakfast at 8 o'clock, then Herman goes to walk, and I fly up to put his room to rights, so that he can sit down to his desk immediately on his return. Then I bid him good bye with many charges to be an industrious boy, and not upset the inkstand, and then flourish the duster, make the bed, &c in my own room. Then I go downstairs and read the papers a little while, and after that I am ready to sit down to my work—whatever it may be—darning stockings—making or mending for myself or Herman—at all events, I haven't seen a day yet, without some sewing or other to do. If I have letters to write, as is the case to-day, I usually do that first—but whatever I am about I do not much more than get thoroughly engaged in it, than ding-ding goes the bell for luncheon. This is half past 12 o'clock—by this time we must expect callers, and so must be dressed immediately after lunch. Then Herman insists upon my taking a walk every day of an hours length at least. So unless I can have rain or snow for an excuse, I usually sally out and make a predestrian tour a mile or two down Broadway. By the time I come home it is two o'clock and after, and then I must make myself look as bewitchingly as possible to meet Herman at dinner. This being accomplished, I have only about an hour of available time left. At four we dine, and after dinner is over, Herman and I come up to our room, and enjoy a cosy chat for an hour or so—or he reads me some of the chapters he has been writing in the day. Then he goes down town for a walk, looks at the papers in the reading-room &c, and returns about half past seven or eight. Then my work or my book is laid aside, and as he does not use his eyes but very little by candle light, I either read to him, or take a hand at whist for his amusement, or he listens to our reading or conversation, as best pleases him. For we all collect in the parlor in the evening, and generally one of us reads aloud for the benefit of the whole. Then we retire very early—at 10 o'clock we all disperse. Indeed we think that quite a late hour to be up.[25]

Melville's friend Evert Duyckinck, editor of the *Literary World,* thought Melville's situation was idyllic: "Melville has got into a happier valley than the Happar not far from here and the wife and I have looked in at the Ti—two very pretty parlors odorous of taste and domestic felicity."[26]

Duyckinck's observation notwithstanding, marriage could not have been easy for young couples subjected to the Victorian era's puritanical sexual ideology. Medical experts and self-styled sexual gurus like Sylvester Graham (the inventor of the eponymous cracker) prescribed rigid rules for adult sexual behavior. They admonished men to refrain from intercourse more than once a month, lest their vital fluids be depleted, and to avoid masturbation. "Spermatic economy" was considered an investment in the future of America, rather like stocks and bonds (Baker-Benfield 267). Doctors and ministers condemned contraception and abortion as detrimental to the expansion of the Republic; as a result, effective birth control was not available in America. Each act of intercourse, then, could result in pregnancy. As a result, the sexual energies of many men and women were either savagely repressed or guiltily indulged. Caught between the Scylla of serial pregnancy and the Charybdis of abstinence, many men and women suffered from neuraesthenia and various other chronic complaints. Some couples abstained from sex once they had several children; others practiced companionate marriage or cultivated same-sex friendships to fill the void; still others must have ignored these repressive theories.[27]

Young couples such as Herman and Lizzie also had to contend with a bevy of gender role stereotypes: men could not control their sexual urges; women were sexless angels, temptresses, or bovine drudges; marriage was a bower of bliss, a cage, a prison, an ethereal paradise. Women covered their bodies completely and wore whalebone corsets in public, and most married couples did not see each other naked, even while making love.[28] In the South Seas, Melville had seen naked men and women and had undoubtedly encountered sexual behavior unmentionable in middle-class homes and sentimental novels, but we have no way of knowing to what extent Victorian attitudes affected his intimate relations with his wife.

In the early days of their marriage, Melville was writing *Mardi* (1848) and reading it aloud to Lizzie and the other women in his family at the end of the day. The literature of the day was replete with hackneyed references to henpecked husbands and nagging wives, so in *Mardi* the new husband drew on stock characters for the termagent Annatoo and her long-suffering husband, Samoa. Although some critics have assumed that their violence reflects Melville's relationship with Lizzie, their Punch-and-Judy-like fights seem designed to make readers laugh. Melville read the manuscript aloud to the women every evening, probably both to tease them and to solicit their approval. Although we don't know how he intended these passages to affect them, or how the women in the family reacted, his description of the contentious couple ends on a mellow note that seems almost a foreshadowing of his future relationship with Lizzie: "But now grown wise by experience, they neither loved overkeenly nor hated; but took things as they were; found themselves joined without hope of a sundering, and did what they could to make a match of the mate" (84).

The few times Melville went away on business, he missed "the idol of his heart,"[29] and with her husband away, Lizzie had time to reflect on married life: "I think both men and women miss it who marry at an early age because they only anticipate the happiness which would be just the same to them after enjoying years of pleasure and freedom from care, which otherwise they lose—I am very, very happy now, more so than ever before, but still I'm very glad I waited as long as I did before entering into the 'married matrimonial state'—for I feel as young now as ever I did, whereas if I'd 'done it' at 18 or 20 years old, as some girls do, why I might have been quite an elderly matron now, and looked back to my school days as something that happened before the flood."[30]

The company of a wife who appreciated his writing and adapted to his moods gave Melville the emotional anchor he had never had; their relationship was the safe harbor from which he could risk venturing into forbidden territory in his fiction, knowing there was a mooring to which he could return. Melville's genius was unfolding daily as he was writing *Mardi*, and he was creating a very different kind of book from his first two. He believed *Mardi* would bring him real literary recognition, not just the distinction of being known as a writer of travel narrative. But his writing at a white heat from early morning to midafternoon in their crowded townhouse must have been stressful for Lizzie, who was busy making the fair copy of the three-volume South Sea saga for the printer.

In August 1848 Herman took Lizzie for a vacation at the Melvill House in Pittsfield, which cousin Robert and his "very quiet, timid, little wife" had turned into an inn. Relieved to escape the heat and dirt of the city and the presence of so many other people in the house, Herman and Lizzie began to discuss moving to the Berkshires.[31]

Mardi, unfortunately, was a complete flop with readers and reviewers, and Lizzie, for the first time, had a disappointed, angry author on her hands. With no profits in sight from the book he thought would be greeted as a masterpiece of political satire and philosophical insight, Melville decided to knock off two potboilers to make money. While he was writing *Redburn* (1849) and *White-Jacket* (1850), which are definitely not potboilers, the Melvilles' first child, a boy, was born in February 1849. Not long after this, Allan and Sophia had their first child, Maria Gansevoort Melville, who they called Milie.

This cameo of domesticity appears in *White-Jacket* after a paragraph describing some of the "pleasurable sights and sounds" that can keep a man in a good mood:

> But of all the chamber-furniture in the world best calculated to cure a bad temper, and breed a pleasant one, is the sight of a lovely wife. If you have children that are teething, the nursery should be a good way upstairs; at sea, it ought to be in the mizzen-top. Indeed, teething children play the very deuce with a husband's temper. I have known three promising young husbands completely spoil on their wives' hands by reason of a teething child, whose worrisomeness happened to be aggravated at the time by a summer complaint. With a breaking heart, and my handkerchief to my eyes, I followed those three hapless young husbands, one after the other, to their premature graves. (46)

Readers who assume that Melville is dismissing women as the "furniture" of a man's abode are missing his mock-sentimental tone and overlooking Lizzie's probable enjoyment of the implied comparison of domestic life to life aboard a brutal man-of-war. Lizzie often felt the lash in Mother Melville's caustic criticisms of her housekeeping, and, as Wyn Kelley argues in "'I'm Housewife Here': Herman Melville & Domestic Economy," it is possible to see Herman and Lizzie as co-conspirators in a rebellion against the "oppressive ideology" of domesticity exemplified by Melville's mother (7–10).

By July 1850, Melville had started on his "Whale," as he referred to the book he was writing about the sperm whale fishery, and the New York townhouse was getting too hot and crowded, so, leaving Allan in the city, Herman packed up Lizzie, Sophia, and the two babies and took them all to the Berkshires. This sojourn in the Berkshires marked the beginning of a new phase of Melville's social and writing life because, by the end of the summer, he would decide to buy a farm near the old Melvill place and settle down in the Berkshires. From 1850 to 1863, Melville lived in Pittsfield, where he fathered three more children and wrote some of his greatest books. Here he became acquainted with novelist Catharine Maria Sedgwick as well as Nathaniel Hawthorne and Sarah Morewood, who were kindred spirits.

On August 5, during a hike up Monument Mountain with literary lions from New York and Boston, Melville met Hawthorne, an event that was as catalytic for him as his first meeting with a tattooed Marquesan chief. In the older writer Melville found a mentor and friend, one whose own dark romances inspired the "ontological heroics" of *Moby-Dick*.

That week he also met Sarah Morewood, whose husband, Rowland, a conservative businessman, worked in New York during the week. Sarah was an avid reader and a gregarious party-thrower. On August 9, the Morewoods hosted a magnificent costume ball. Herman came as a Turk in a turban and long robe, Lizzie dressed as a flower girl, and Sophia wore an old-fashioned hat and a black dress with a train that made her look like royalty. The following day the indefatigable Mrs. Morewood scooped up Herman and Lizzie, Allan and Sophia, and Herman's guests, New York literati Evert and George Duyckinck and Cornelius Mathews, and they all set off for Constitution Hill in Lanesborough in wagons, plus two saddle-horses. At one point Lizzie was riding one of the horses when Allan and Sophia's wagon bumped into her horse, and she was thrown to the ground. An experienced rider, Lizzie was wearing a short skirt, so when Herman saw her fall, he leaped from his horse in a dramatic display of heroism designed to protect her modesty. As the two of them rolled through the grass, Sophia screamed so hysterically that Herman ordered Allan to take her home.[32]

After a summer that combined picnics and parties with work on his whaling book and long talks with Nathaniel Hawthorne, Melville bought Doc Brewster's farm on Holmes Road. He moved into the house with his wife, baby son, mother, and unmarried sisters Helen and Augusta in October. Lizzie now had on her hands a toddler, a husband obsessed with a white whale, and an imperious mother-in-law who disapproved of the way "Yankee girls" kept house and admonished Lizzie every time the grocery bill was too high or stains appeared on the upholstery.

At Arrowhead (so named because he found arrowheads in the pasture) Melville was surrounded by women who adapted to his schedule and catered to his needs. He rose early to feed his horse and cow before eating breakfast, then he wrote feverishly when he wasn't looking out the window of his study at Mount Greylock. Meanwhile Lizzie did the mending and wrote letters to family and friends in addition to joining Helen and Augusta in the arduous task of making fair copies of Herman's manuscripts. Without assistance from Lizzie, Helen, and Augusta, it is doubtful Melville would have been able to publish six books in six years. As if copying books as long and complicated as *Mardi* and *Moby-Dick* were not demanding enough, Melville insisted on adding his own punctuation, which meant that his copyists had to anticipate the punctuation but not make the actual marks—at best a tedious and irritating task.

After he was done writing, Melville ate his midday dinner and went for a ride in the wagon or the sleigh, depending on the season. He usually took one or more of the women with him, and sometimes he drove Lizzie to her sewing circle, which perhaps inspired a scene in *Pierre*. In the winter it was already dark by the time Melville finished his dinner, and his mother and Augusta grew impatient waiting for him to finish writing and eating so they could visit their friends. Eventually they persuaded him to teach them how to drive the carriage so they could go out on their own.[33]

Lizzie often stayed behind while Herman and other members of the family went on excursions with Sarah Morewood and their friends, perhaps because she had one or more small children at home and suffered every summer from allergies that sapped her energy. Although Lizzie apparently did not accompany Herman on many of Mrs. Morewood's outings, we have no real evidence that Herman and Lizzie were not happily married during these years. Tensions undoubtedly existed, but given the demands of a temperamental husband, a growing family, and the presence of an overbearing mother-in-law and three household servants, Lizzie may just have wanted some time to herself once in a while.

Melville enjoyed an especially close friendship with Sarah Morewood, with whom he exchanged books and little gifts. In notes to her, he adopted a mock-chivalric tone, calling himself "the humble Knight on the Hill" and Mrs. Morewood the "Ladyship of Southmount." An account of the overnight hike Melville and his family and friends made to Greylock in August 1851 describes Melville climbing a tree and hacking off branches with an axe to make a fire. While the others slept, he and Sarah sat up talking and laughing, swatting insects and reciting Shakespeare.[34]

It would not be hard to imagine a flirtation between Melville and the reigning "goddess" of the "Paradise" of Broadhall. It seems safe to say that these neighbors who frolicked together during picnics, excursions, hikes, and costume balls and discussed books such as Hawthorne's strangely erotic novel *The Marble Faun* (1860) were kindred souls. Before a picnic in Pittsfield's State Forest, Sarah placed a music box beneath the Balance Rock so that when Melville and the others arrived, they would hear "mysterious and enchanting music" emanating from the boulder. Might Melville have been thinking of Sarah Morewood's music box when he described Isabel's haunting music in his scandalous melodrama *Pierre*?

Even though Mrs. Morewood loved books and had eclectic tastes, when *Moby-Dick* was published, Melville issued her a jocular warning: "Dont you buy it—dont you read it, when it does come out, because it is by no means the sort of book for you. It is not a peice of fine feminine Spitalfields silk—but is of the horrible texture of a fabric that should be woven of ships cables & hausers [sic]. A Polar wind blows through it, & birds of prey hover over it. Warn all gentle fastidious people from so much as peeping into the book—on risk of a lumbago & sciatics."[35] Sophia Hawthorne, a very perceptive reader of *Moby-Dick*, praised the chapter on the spirit-spout and grasped the symbolic nature of the book. Although he preferred talking "ontological heroics" with her husband, Meville appears to have enjoyed Sophia's company as well. Sophia, for her part, found Melville "very agreeable and entertaining.... A

Laurie Robertson-Lorant

man with a true warm heart & a soul & an intellect—with life to his fingertips—earnest, sincere & reverent, very tender & *modest*."[36] Although she considered Melville a "boy" compared to Mr. Hawthorne, Sophia suspected Melville might be as great a man as her husband some day.

Although Melville poured his heart and soul and mind into *Moby-Dick*, few readers or reviewers appreciated it, and his next book, *Pierre*, was soundly trounced by reviewers, including one who called Melville "crazy." The Melvilles by now had two children, and Herman was not earning enough money to pay the mortgage on the farm, so he began writing for two magazines that paid well for stories and sketches, *Harper's New Monthly Magazine* and *Putnam's Monthly Magazine*. The stress and strain of working the farm and writing for hours took their toll both physically and mentally; he began drinking heavily, which is not surprising given the high rate of alcoholism among the Melville men. In the mid-1850s, Melville suffered attacks of sciatica and rheumatism that drove him to summon his neighbor, Dr. Oliver Wendell Holmes Jr., and to use alcohol as a painkiller in conjunction with the medicine Dr. Holmes prescribed.

Melville was a volatile personality, given to mood swings. He could be kind and considerate one minute, cold and cruel the next. Rumors that he pushed Lizzie down the back stairs have circulated in Melville circles for decades, causing controversy and dissension. Much of this depends on how different people interpret surviving texts—for example, the letter Herman and Lizzie wrote Sarah Morewood from Boston on December 2, 1860. In that letter, Melville tells Mrs. Morewood he plans to return to Arrowhead without Lizzie and the children "to get matters in readiness for them—putting up the stoves, airing the bedding—warming the house, and getting up a grand domestic banquet," and Lizzie adds a closing comment: "The order of things is completely reversed, since Herman is going on to Pittsfield to get the house ready for *me*—that is, to get Mr. Clark to put the stoves up, and get it *warm* for me to go to work in—A new proverb should be added 'Wives propose—husbands dispose'—don't you think so?"[37]

Although this joint letter sounds like typical married couples' banter, those searching for clues to family secrets might wonder why Melville did not write Mr. Clark directly and ask him to get the house ready so the family could return to a warm house together. Was Mr. Clark illiterate, so that Sarah Morewood had to relay this information to him, or did Melville have a secret reason to want Sarah to know he would be coming home ahead of Lizzie and the children? We know very little about the Melvilles' relationships with the cooks, handymen, and nannies who worked for them (except that Herman badgered successive cooks about the strength of his coffee and the consistency of his oatmeal), and, as far as we know, Herman's relationship with Sarah Morewood was entirely platonic. So we have to assume Melville simply wanted to protect his wife and children from coming back to a cold house.[38]

This Morewood letter is a small indication of the kinds of problems biographers face. Surviving documents probably constitute only a fraction of those actually written by members of the Melville family, friends, and associates. We know Melville burned many of his papers before moving back to New York City in 1863, but we do not know exactly what he destroyed, or why. Family members may have suppressed unpleasant information about Melville's treatment of his wife; they were proud and clannish people who closed ranks when threatened. In 1856, after *Putnam's* folded, depriving him of a steady income and the belated respect of educated readers, Melville was despondent. He had four children to support by this time, and Lizzie's family thought he was having a breakdown, so they were very relieved when Herman decided to travel to Europe and the Holy Land. After he returned to the United States in 1857, Melville tried but failed to gain a consular post in the Lincoln administration, made three lecture tours that earned him little money, and wrote a volume of poems about the Civil War that received respectful reviews but, again, made very little money for their author. In 1866 he obtained a job as a customs inspector in the Port of New York, a position that earned him four dollars a day and left him some free time to write poetry.

The following year, the tensions between Herman and Lizzie erupted into a full-blown crisis, perhaps exacerbated by tensions between the Melvilles and their elder son, Malcolm, who was now seventeen. In May 1867, Lizzie's stepbrother Sam, a Boston lawyer, decided Melville was insane and so dangerous that Lizzie had to get away from him. Sam, who in his younger days had played ball with Melville and raced him up and down the Berkshire Hills, wrote Henry Whitney Bellows, Lizzie's pastor, for advice. Dr. Bellows advised Sam that the family should kidnap Lizzie and take her forcibly to the family home in Boston so she would not be charged with desertion.[39]

In the end, Lizzie decided to stay with Herman against her family's wishes. Was this because under the laws of New York State women could not own property, and so everything was in Herman's name? Did her minister agree it was her wifely duty to stay? Did she still love Melville? Or could she simply not face life outside of marriage? Probably a combination of factors she could not herself have analyzed at this point convinced her to stay. Lizzie found solace in religion, and in the end she seems to have found solace in her marriage, too. In a letter to Dr. Bellows, she prays for strength to meet any trial and "submission and faith to realize the sustaining power of the Master's love, and to approach His table in the very spirit of His last commands."[40]

According to the domestic ideology of the times, women were "angels in the house," responsible for controlling the "beast" in men and, if possible, improving their character and behavior. Perhaps, after all, Lizzie took the ideology of domesticity to heart, and perhaps in the end "the angel in the house" did manage to tame the savage beast. In an edition of poems by the Portuguese writer Luis de Camöens, Melville underscored the line "Woman was to him as a ministering angel, and for the little joy which he tasted in life, he was indebted to her."[41]

Melville's relationships with his children were tense and tender, even terrible at times. The ecstatic letter Herman wrote his brother Allan on the occasion of Malcolm's birth seems hyperbolically brilliant when first read but manic and egotistical when read a second time; in hindsight, Augusta's jocular observation that Herman would "devour" Malcolm seems eerily prophetic.[42] Although he was a devoted, playful father for many years, once Malcolm grew up and had a steady job, Melville resented his son's independence and tried to assert control while his son was still living at home by imposing a curfew. Malcolm naturally resented his father's attempts to control him; he began staying out later and later, evidently going to nightclubs and drinking with his friends.

Despite Lizzie's attempts to act as a buffer between her husband and her older son, eighteen-year-old Malcolm shot himself with his service revolver in October 1867. His death was initially ruled a suicide, but under pressure from the family, the verdict was amended to say it was an accidental death. Malcolm's younger brother, Stanwix, was traumatized by his brother's suicide, as he knew Malcolm kept a pistol under his bed pillow, and he went deaf, perhaps as a psychosomatic reaction to the gunshot. Unfortunately, Melville's relations with Stanwix and his other children were also dysfunctional once they became young adults. Wracked with guilt over his brother's death, Stannie never settled into job or family life and died of TB out west when he was only thirty-five, plunging his mother into inconsolable grief.[43]

Daughters Elizabeth and Frances had mixed feelings about their father. As birthday presents, he selfishly gave the girls esoteric books that he needed for his research, and he woke them up at night and made them proofread *Clarel* (1876), his 18,000-line poem about the Holy Land. Bessie contracted rheumatoid arthritis and became virtually crippled by the time she was twenty-six. Fanny married a young man named Henry B. Thomas, with whom she had two daughters in quick succession and two more later. Melville knew only the first two granddaughters, Eleanor and Frances. The third, Katherine Gansevoort Thomas, was not even one year old when Melville died in 1891; the fourth, Jeannette Ogden Thomas, was born the following year. Lizzie, who lived until 1906, knew all four girls.

Melville and the Women in His Life

Although Melville's treatment of his granddaughters was less threatening than his treatment of his daughters, Eleanor and little Fanny had equally mixed feelings about him. Both girls loved their grandmother, but their feelings toward their grandfather seem to combine fascination and affection with some fear. Whenever they visited their grandparents' home on 26th Street, they could hear their grandfather pacing back and forth in his study composing poems. They would wander upstairs to see whether the china butterfly on his desk had flown away or to listen to the Aeolian harp he kept in the window. Melville let Fanny make houses with the big blue books stacked on the study floor (his set of Schopenhauer's writings), and sometimes he would draw up chairs and tell them stories (Metcalf 282–83). As soon as the girls were old enough, Melville took them along on walks, but they could barely keep up with his long strides or understand the long words he used, and he apparently had very little patience with their slow pace. Once he took Fanny to Madison Park to see the tulips and absentmindedly walked home without her while she was playing. Horrified, Lizzie ran, and Bessie hobbled, to the park expecting the worst, only to find little Fanny walking blithely home (Doenges 11–12).

Some afternoons Melville would sit in the comfortable chair in Lizzie's room to read, and Eleanor would clamber into his lap and hold on to his whiskers to steady herself while he told stories of his adventures in exotic lands. His was "no soft silken beard, but tight curled like the horse hair breaking out of old upholstered chairs, firm and wiry to the grasp, and squarely chopped," and he didn't object to her squeezing it during the most exciting of his "wild tales of cannibals and tropic isles." Only years later did she realize that her grandfather was himself the hero of these adventures and that he was "reliving his own past." Although Melville feared his grandchildren would turn against him as they grew older, Eleanor later said she thought of him with "nothing but a remembrance of glorious fun, mixed with a childish awe, as of someone who knew far and strange things" (Osborne 184).

During the 1870s, Herman and Lizzie lost a staggering number of close relatives and friends to illness and old age, but Lizzie inherited a few small legacies that made life materially easier for them. After Melville retired from the customs house in 1885, Lizzie began giving him an allowance of twenty-five dollars a month to spend on books and prints. Occasionally, he received a royalty check, but it was so small that it served as little more than a painful reminder of his failure to earn money from his writing all those years. He and Lizzie were now an old married couple who had weathered the storms of life as stoically as the old couple in Melville's poem "The Figure-Head," whom he describes as buffetted by "iron-rust and alum sprays" with nothing left but the "tears in their eyes, salt tears not few" (*Collected Poems* 197).

In his last years, Melville wrote poetry or worked on *Billy Budd* during the day and went for a stroll when he was done, stopping to browse in book and print shops along the way. In the evenings he and Lizzie played backgammon or read before the fire.[44] In several of the poems in *Timoleon* (1890) and in his last prose work, *Billy Budd*, which was published posthumously in 1924, Melville worked through his troubled relationships with his mother, his brother Gansevoort, and his sons. On the flyleaf of his copy of *The Divine Comedy*, Melville repeated Dante's anguished cry, "*tu asperges me*" ("forgive me"), which must have been his plea for absolution for the sufferings he had inflicted on Lizzie and his children, especially Malcolm, whose suicide was as tragic as the death of Billy Budd.[45]

Not long before his death on September 28, 1891, Melville put aside the draft of *Billy Budd* to finish another volume of poetry, and Lizzie once more made the fair copy for the printer. In these poems, phallic and vulvic images, the scimitar and the rose, meet in a kind of orientalist mating dance. Initially he had planned to call the book "roses without thorns, eternal ones, the roses of St. Elizabeth of Hungary," but he scrapped that unwieldy title for the humbler *Weeds and Wildings, with a Rose or Two*. In the tradition of the troubadours and courtly love, he dedicated the privately published volume to "Winnefred," an allusion either to "Winifreda," who represents happy marriage in Percy's *Reliques,* or to Saint Winifreda, the patron of bakers. Lizzie enjoyed baking and was especially proud of her pies and gingerbread, and Melville's use of the soubriquet "Winnefred" recalls his habit of calling her pet names such as "Dolly" and "Oriana" when they were first married (*Weeds and Wildings* 60).

In the dedicatory epistle, the poet reminds "Winnefred" of their shared affection for the clover that grew in the fields at Arrowhead, especially the red clover. In a playful vein that evokes the flower language of their courtship, he explains that he loves the clover not because they were "living in clover" in those days, or even because the clover reminds him of the "happy augury" he found on their wedding day—the four-leaf clover—but even more because "this little peasant of flowers" is hardy and accessible to all (*Weeds and Wildings* 5). In *Weeds and Wildings*, Melville portrays himself as a "Rose-Farmer" in the garden of "truant Eve," who, like all women, has inherited "more of the instinct of Paradise" than men, and, finally, as another Rip Van Winkle, a "goodhearted good-for-nothing" old "idler" like Irving's Rip, nostalgic for the idyllic early days of marriage when he and his "winsome bride" could dally in their "nuptial bower." Reminiscing about his wife's garden, he remembers the lilac he once planted. Years later, he returns and discovers that the lilac has crowded out the "immemorial willow," and the whole region has become an edenic "Lilac Land" that will bloom for his "children's children" (*Weeds and Wildings* 27).[46]

These poems are a last bouquet from a man who yearned for a tranquil domestic life even as the tensions of art and sexuality tore him apart and sometimes made him lash out at those closest to him. Like Lear, Melville could be egotistical and cruel to those who loved him, but he reached the end of his life's journey purged of his "great rage" and ready to face his inevitable death. He did not achieve this victory alone, however; whatever peace he gained late in life was the product of relationships with friends and relatives, especially Lizzie.

Melville lived in a culture, in a century, that saw the emergence of modern America, and in his writings he responded brilliantly and prophetically to the conflicts and issues of his life and times. He lived in a family that was to some extent dominated by stable and capable women. At no little cost to her own comfort and security, Lizzie Melville kept her sanity and self-respect intact and kept her husband's literary legacy alive after his death in 1891. She was as heroic in her way as he was in his, and in the end she understood him best and took whatever secrets she had with her to the grave. Carved into the back panel of her writing desk are these wise and poignant words: "To know all is to forgive all."[47]

Notes

1. See also Philip Weiss.
2. Yannella and Parker 11–15.
3. Markels 119. Early biographers did not have access to Jay Leyda's incomparable *Melville Log* or to all the letters and documents available today. The *Log*, reprinted with supplementary material in 1969, is the work on which Leon Howard based *Herman Melville: A Biography*. Edward Haviland Miller's *Melville* is an impressionistic psychobiography focused on Melville's allegedly homoerotic relationship with Nathaniel Hawthorne. Dr. Henry A. Murray worked on a biography of Melville for many years but never finished it; the manuscript is among the Murray Papers in the Harvard University Archives.
4. The *Log* and studies such as Charles Robert Anderson's *Melville in the South Seas* and William H. Gilman's *Melville's Early Life and Redburn* make it much easier to separate fact from fiction.
5. Caty, as she was known, may have found some solace in alcohol; she ordered a prodigious amount of liquor for the family to celebrate baby Herman's christening. Most, if not all the Melville men were alcoholics. See Robertson-Lorant, *Melville*.
6. Julia Maria Melvill to Augusta Melville, 26 June 1837, Melville Family Papers, New

York Public Library (hereafter MFP/NYPL). These letters, which Augusta Melville saved and stored in a trunk at the home of her uncle, Herman Gansevoort, were discovered in 1983 when a neighbor showed them to John De Marco of the Lyrical Ballad Bookstore in Saratoga Springs, NY. Recognizing their importance, De Marco contacted the New York Public Library, which purchased the collection.

7. Catherine Gansevoort Lansing to Abraham Lansing, 14 Nov. 1873, Leyda 2: 735. Her charming eccentricities are described by Eleanor Melville Metcalf (210–11).

8. Gansevoort-Lansing Collection, NYPL. As far as we know, Melville himself kept only three journals in seventy-two years: 1849–50, 1856–57, and 1860 (see *Journals*). He did not keep a journal during his summer cruise to Liverpool in 1839 or during his whaling voyage to the Pacific and his passage back aboard the frigate *United States*, though he based six fictionalized narratives on those two voyages. We don't know if he actually tried to save a woman and her children from starving to death while he was in Liverpool, as Redburn does in a novel based on Melville's maiden voyage, nor do we know if he ever had a tattooed "cannibal" as a bedfellow or a Marquesan maiden as a lover, much less whether he fathered a son in Polynesia, as he later bragged to his barber in Glen Falls, NY, according to Ferris Greenslet. See Ferris Greenslet to Willard Thorp, 22 Nov. 1846, Melville Collection, Newberry Library, Chicago; Sealts, *Early Lives* 217n.75. Mary K. Bercaw Edwards, "Herman Melville's Whaling Years" (*Moby-Dick* Marathon, New Bedford Whaling Museum, New Bedford, MA, 3 Jan. 2004), argued that so much of *Typee* is fictionalized that even though we know Melville was in the Marquesas, we cannot be sure he actually visited the Typee valley.

9. Mysteries such as the identity of "the particular lady acquaintance" uptown who read the draft of *Omoo* and persuaded him to take out three chapters critical of missionaries will probably never be solved (Herman Melville to Evert Duyckinck, 8 Dec. 1846, *Correspondence* 66–67). New York State Library archivist Warren F. Broderick of Lansingburgh, NY, discovered five poems signed "H." in the *Democratic Press and Lansingburgh Advertiser*, 15 and 22 Sept. 1838, 16 and 23 Mar. and 6 Apr. 1839, two of which appear to have been addressed to Mary Parmalee, whom Melville courted (13–16).

10. Helen Melville to Augusta Melville, 8 Oct. 1835, MFP/NYPL.

11. Ibid.

12. Helen Melville to Augusta Melville, 27 Nov. 1843, MFP/NYPL.

13. Helen Melville to Augusta Melville, 16 Feb. 1842, MFP/NYPL.

14. Helen Melville to Augusta Melville, 14 Jan. 1844, MFP/NYPL.

15. Herman Melville to Evert Duyckinck, 13 Dec. 1850 and 12 Feb. 1851, *Correspondence* 172–74, 181.

16. Augusta Melville to Fanny Melville, 17–20 Mar. 1854, MFP/NYPL.

17. Herman Melville to Catherine Melville, 20 Jan. 1845, *Correspondence* 27.

18. Peggi Medeiros of New Bedford, MA, hopes to uncover evidence that Melville visited the Hoadleys while they were living in that city.

19. Julia Maria Melvill, Saturday, n.d., 1836, MFP/NYPL; Puett 25.

20. Metcalf 42.

21. Fanny Appleton Longfellow to Nathan Appleton, 3 Aug. 1847, Leyda 2: 916.

22. Edmund Quincy to Caroline Weston, 2 Jul. 1847, Kennedy "Additions" 4–8; Millie van Rensselaer Thayer to Augusta Melville, 22 Dec. 1845?, MFP/NYPL; Augusta Whipple Hunter to Augusta Melville, 6 Oct. 1847, MFP/NYPL.

23. Elizabeth Shaw Melville to Hope Savage Shaw, 28 Aug. 1847, Metcalf 46–47.

24. Elizabeth Shaw Melville to Samuel Hay Savage, 12–18 Sept. 1847, Kennedy, "Elizabeth and Herman" 1: 7.

25. Elizabeth Shaw Melville to Hope Savage Shaw, 28 Aug. 1847, Metcalf 48–49.

26. Evert Duyckinck to George Duyckinck, 15 Nov. 1847, Leyda 1: 264.

27. See Barker-Benfield for information on Rev. John Todd and Dr. Augustus Kinsley Gardner, who specialized in obstetrics and insanity. Some have speculated that Gardner became the Melville family doctor when they moved back to New York, which is a frightening prospect, as Gardner treated almost all female complaints with a knife. It is hard to know how widely birth control was used in nineteenth-century America, but Todd and Gardner and the other male experts on female reproduction opposed its use. Todd gave strict instructions to couples about when and how often to have intercourse (Barker-Benfield 297). This same John Todd was chosen to officiate at the ceremony celebrating the completion of the transcontinental railroad. Blessing the gold wedding rings exchanged by representatives of the two coasts, Todd extolled the driving of the golden spike as a symbol of the penetration of the "virgin" continent by robust pioneers. For detailed discussion of companionate marriages, see T. Walter Herbert and Joan D. Hedrick.

28. Metcalf writes that her mother, Melville's daughter Frances, had "contemporary ideas on the subject of modesty," which makes her much more liberal than her Aunt Fanny, Melville's sister, who rebuked Eleanor "for leaving her own well-boned undergarment on the back of a chair in her own bedroom, for fear her own husband might see it!" (Metcalf 197).

29. Herman Melville to Anne Maria Priscilla Melville, 3 Apr. 1848, MFP/NYPL.

30. Elizabeth Shaw Melville to Samuel Hay Savage, 3 Apr. 1848, Kennedy, "Additions" 9.

31. Herman Melville to Fanny Appleton Longfellow, 23 Jul. 1848, Leyda 1: 279.

32. Sophia Thurston Melville to Augusta Melville, 11 Aug. 1850, MFP/NYPL.

33. Augusta Melville to Helen Melville, 14 Jan. 1851, MFP/NYPL.

34. J. E. A. Smith's "That Excursion to Greylock," *Taghconic* (1852) and Evert Duyckinck to Margaret Duyckinck, 13 Aug. 1851, Leyda 1: 424.

35. Herman Melville to Sarah Morewood, ? Sept. 1851, *Correspondence* 206.

36. Sophia Hawthorne to Elizabeth Peabody, 4 Sept. 1850, Leyda 1: 393.

37. Herman Melville and Elizabeth Shaw Melville to Sarah Huyler Morewood, 2 Dec. 1860, Leyda 2: 944.

38. Novelist Larry Duberstein describes an intimate and tender relationship between Melville and Sarah Morewood plausibly and with taste, sensitivity, and discretion, but at no time does he claim the relationship is fact not fiction.

39. Both of Melville's granddaughters, Eleanor Melville Metcalf and Frances Cuthbert Thomas Osborne, are very circumspect in their veiled references to family troubles. In an 1856 letter to his mother and Lemuel Shaw, Sam Savage makes reference to "ugly attacks," but it is not clear whether he is referring to attacks of sciatica that laid Herman low or attacks Melville inflicted on Lizzie. After writing two more novels and a dozen or so stories and sketches in five years, Melville was nearer a breakdown than financial solvency (Sam Savage to Lemuel Shaw and Hope Savage Shaw, 27 Aug. 1856, Kennedy, "Additions"; see also Puett 226n.53). More than a decade later, Hope Shaw was still worried about Lizzie, but the exact nature of her concern is not clear. In a fragment dated 1868 she describes a visit from Melville's sister, Helen Melville Griggs, who had "a full and plain discourse with her about not writing to Mrs Melville, & giving her sympathy for her distress relating to her husband when all Mrs M asks [is] a little sympathy from her friends" (Hope Savage Shaw fragment, 14 Sept. 1868, Leyda 2: 701).

40. Elizabeth Shaw Melville to Henry Whitney Bellows, Yannella and Parker, 15.

41. Leyda 2: 686.

42. Augusta Melville to Helen Melville, 31 Dec. 1850, MFP/NYPL. Renker cites Edwin S. Schneidman's theory that Malcolm kept a gun handy to shoot his father if he physically abused

his mother in one of his crazy or intoxicated states, but there is no real evidence for this theory (52). See also Cohen and Yanella.

43. Helen Melville Griggs to Catherine Gansevoort Lansing, 5 May 1856, Leyda 2: 798. My hunch is that Stanwix was gay, which the late Paul Metcalf thought highly plausible given his dandyish appearance.

44. The references to backgammon come from notes scribbled in pencil by Dr. Titus Munson Coan made during an interview with Elizabeth Melville a year after her husband's death (file folder marked "Miscellaneous," Coan papers, New York Historical Society).

45. Lea Newman 305–38. See also Robertson-Lorant, *Melville*.

46. See also Milder, "Old Man Melville"; John Bryant, "Ordering the Rose"; and Evans, "Inaccuracies and Discrepancies."

47. This desk can be seen at the Berkshire Athenaeum in Pittsfield, Mass.

Part Two

Melville Reading Women

Women Reading Melville/ Melville Reading Women

Charlene Avallone

> The ladies were shocked at [*Typee* and *Omoo*]. . . . Hardly reading that would commend itself to Lowell mill-girls, to the Warner sisters, or the Carys, or the myriad readers of *The Wide, Wide World.*
> —Fred Lewis Pattee, *The Feminine Fifties* (1940)

> [Melville] was out of harmony with a predominantly female fiction-reading public.
> —William Charvat, *Studies in Bibliography* (1959)

> Melville had no interest in women writers.
> —James Wallace, *American Literature* (1990)

Perhaps neither the Warner sisters nor many factory "girls" got around to reading much of Melville, just as he may not have read much of their literary output. Contrary to longstanding critical notions, however, contemporary women in the United States did read Melville's writing, and Melville did read some women's writing as well. Since the modern revival of Melville cast his work as a catalyst in the project of "masculinizing American culture," ascendant critical assumptions have presupposed a male readership for his work as well as a male-authored (largely canonical) library as the inspiration behind it (Lauter 216). Neither the "renaissance" thesis of high American literature nor the "feminization" thesis of middle-brow culture has lent itself to questioning received wisdom about Melville and women as readers (see, for example, Reynolds, Douglas, Gilmore). Even the "revolution" in Melville study that Robert Milder predicted from new theoretical trends in reader-response criticism and hermeneutics has largely bypassed considerations of women (4). Although a hypothetically "feminine" readership has been much disparaged for Melville's disappointments in seeking popularity, little has been written about his actual female readers (Pattee 29; Charvat, "Common Reader" 41; Douglas 290–313; Gilmore). What small attention has focused on his reading of women writers promotes Melville's status by crediting him with satirizing their presumptively limited, sentimental perspectives from a remote position of intellectual and aesthetic superiority.[1] Critics have yet to ask in any systematic way what in Melville's writings may have engaged contemporary women, what in women's writings might have engaged Melville.

Studying Melville's imbricated relations with women readers and writers of his time shows that women found manifold significance in his work, as various as men did, and that Melville found women's texts compelling in a number of ways. More importantly, such study can contribute to questioning the critical paradigms that truncate cultural history in consigning male and female writers to separate spheres or women to positions beneath men.[2]

Recent criticism has developed models of reading more sensitive to actual readers than are the modernist variations on separate spheres. The progression of reader-response criticism in general away from theorizing text-based constructs of readers and toward such sensitive models calls into question studies that would maintain gender-divisions with conclusions about antagonisms between "Melville and the Common Reader" yet cite not a single common reader, female or male (Charvat 42, 43). While some critics still reiterate separate-sphere distinctions with theories that categorize critical readers as male and privilege them as a source of data—subsuming women into the category of popular readers and even there erasing their voices as not representative (Machor 83n.23; see 63–64)—the shift toward historical approaches more often entails increasing attention to women readers and their acts of reading.[3] Such study demonstrates that gender appears to have been less significant a determinant of what women read than it was a factor in how they might read. Individual women often read diverse texts in diverse ways, showing, among other things, that there were not necessarily different readers for different sorts of writing—say, completely separate audiences for what the nineteenth century called standard and fugitive writings or for serious books and ladies' magazines or for other matter later categorized as men's reading and women's reading.[4] Nor have women necessarily read in ways that critics assumed, some preferring affiliation with heroes or "plots of adventure and social responsibility" rather than identification with heroines of the romance plot (Sicherman, "Sense and Sensibility" 212; and see Radway). This essay builds on this scholarship to offer an alternative understanding of Melville's relations with his audiences and his reading. To that end, it details historical and biographical context, presents evidence of women reading Melville and Melville reading women, and analyzes an example of each of these phenomena.

To begin, it is necessary to question some assumptions about nineteenth-century women's limited literacy and limiting gentility that underlie critics' sense that Melville's work was both too serious and too sensational for women, while their writing was too conventional to interest thinking men, especially Melville. Neither paradigms nor practices of reading in Melville's time made such gender distinctions among readers as rigidly or extensively as later critics would. William Charvat represents the nineteenth-century "fiction-reading public" as "predominantly female" yet on the same page acknowledges that contemporary critics did not observe such a distinction. Still, Charvat's gendered model of audience has proven more influential than his conclusions from reviews that Melville's early writing "was offered to an undifferentiated audience of men, women, and children among whom there was ... a fantastic range of sophistication and seriousness" ("Common Reader" 41).[5] The relatively small gender profiling of presumed readers discernible in contemporary criticism, despite the separate spheres ideology appearing in critical vocabulary, bears out Charvat's observation of an "undifferentiated" readership. A midcentury journal might on the same page recommend to "the public" both Sarah Ellis's *Hearts and Homes* and Melville's *Redburn* (*U. S. Magazine and Democratic Review* 25 [Dec. 1849]: 575). When categories such as "lady readers" do appear, they often evoke such contradictory notions of readership and taste as to suggest that they functioned more as an ideological or marketing strategy than as any indicator of actual audiences.[6] Some empirical study suggests that actual readers, in any event, did not often reflect critical categories (Zboray and Zboray 166). Further, the distinction between a serious reader and a "superficial skimmer" is often ungendered in nineteenth-century criticism, as it is in Melville's evocation of the distinction ("Mosses" 251). Women writers cited differences between "superficial" and insightful readers to inspire or mark their intended audiences, at least partially female (Graves iv). A female literary association invoked "Dame

Fashion" for support of the observation that "she who superficially skims over the surface" presents a less "interesting character" than the woman whose reading renders her "distinguished for intellectual and moral worth."[7] Here, as elsewhere when women readers were singled out from men, the aim often was to diminish differences in reading methods and subjects. Even the higher moral standard propounded for women did not invariably constrain their reading. Women read *Jane Eyre* and the novels of E. D. E. N. Southworth for erotic pleasure (Karcher 325; Harris, *19th-Century* 19, 22–23). Some read proscribed writers and risqué novels. At the same time, others, especially writers and teachers, deployed the rationale of moral elevation to promote ever more advanced literacy for women.

From at least the mid–eighteenth century, new emphases on what was called "female education" in British and American advice literature, education, literary criticism, and journalism helped women's reading to become increasingly thoughtful and stressed genres considered serious, especially history (including biography) and travels. In this vein, Hester Chapone's *Letters on the Improvement of the Mind* (1773)—one of the few books surviving from the library of Maria Gansevoort (Herman's mother), passed on through daughter Augusta—became one important model for American women conduct writers, whose work, burgeoning in the 1840s, urged serious reading. By the time Melville's sisters and wife were being educated, schooling instituted the suggestions of such writers in pedagogical practice, along with rhetorical training (often including literary criticism). Ideologies of companionate marriage and true womanhood reinforced the training of women as readers, competent at least to engage husbands in literary conversation, direct children's education, and grace the social circle, while more progressive notions of gender equity and religious tenets of spiritual development alike encouraged higher levels of female literacy and oralcy (see, for example, G. Emerson, *Lecture* 338, *Reminiscences* 144–45). If such widely circulated tracts as Hannah More's *Strictures on Women's Education* (1799) mocked the notion of educating women to be critics (2: 23–24), and Sarah Hale's monitory tales satirized the blue-stocking's excessive discussion of her reading, women writers and teachers (including Hale) nonetheless promoted complex models of both appreciative and critical reading that we are only beginning to recover.[8]

Herman's sisters would have been taught to read seriously for purposes of familial and social conversation, as well as composition, at the Albany Female Academy, where *salonière* Anne Lynch studied and then taught (see *Memoirs of Anne C. L. Botta* 36–37). Helen Melville also studied at Elizabeth Sedgwick's Lenox school, where sister-in-law Catharine Sedgwick informally inculcated the principles of advanced female literacy that inform her conduct writings and fiction. From Augusta Melville's correspondence, Wyn Kelley sketches a portrait of her as an analytical, "avid reader within a highly literate society." Augusta herself praised sister Fanny's "literary communications" (now lost) with "comments upon the books of the day . . . [as] almost equal to reading the books themselves" (W. Kelley, "Thirst" 48, 49). From 1835 to 1841, Elizabeth Shaw attended the school of George B. Emerson, noted pioneer in female education and theorizer of reading for conversation, and she may also have attended the Sedgwick school in 1837 (Robertson-Lorant 153; Howes 30). Women privileged to such education, if—like Herman himself—lacking the advanced classical literacy of the university-man, would have been more literate readers than the majority of men, who received little schooling. Nor did the extension of public schooling, in which Herman participated as a teacher, advocate distinctions between girls' and boys' literacy, except in reminders of differential application in private and public adult life.

Further complicating distinctions between men's and women's literacy, antebellum ideology promoted models of familial and social relations that encouraged discursive exchanges based in reading for mutual intellectual and moral culture. Augusta's brother Gansevoort may have intended to shape her understanding of advanced female literacy along with her own reading practices with his gift of *Memoirs of the Literary Ladies of England* (Sealts 175, no. 202a), and the book would have enabled her to discuss women's literacy practices with her brothers, as both her education and cultural milieu would encourage. Herman presumed to prompt Helen's reading beyond conventional limits even after her marriage. If Helen apparently favored fiction over Plutarch (*Correspondence* 640), she nonetheless approached reading with informed taste and may have influenced her brothers' reading as well, as when still a schoolgirl she recommended Sedgwick's latest novel as her "best" according to critics (cited in Parker 1: 100).

Also blurring gender differences in literacy, men's reading extended to social performance in conversation even as women were said to be more adept at such practice. Herman participated in family "loud" readings of both female and male writers (largely British, if survivals from the family library and letters are representative) and joined in literary recitations with the mixed company at Anne Lynch's New York soirées and on country excursions.[9] Practiced by men or women, social reading in myriad forms could encompass intellectual or analytical pursuits. Even *tableaux vivants* might be construed as thoughtful interpretation of literature and history (Tuthill, *Lady* 101–5; Robertson-Lorant, *Melville* 129). Women, like men, made social reading coextensive with writing in a variety of ways, some of which, such as Fannie Osgood's poetry performances at Lynch's salon, counter stereotypes that define nineteenth-century women in opposition to the intellectual, aesthetic, and erotic (see Dobson). Contemporary report held that the composition of *Typee* grew out of the reading and discussion practices of the Melville family circle, a fact Sheila Post-Lauria explains as enabling Melville successfully to tailor his text for a large readership of both men and women (29–30; see Leyda 1: 188). Merrell Davis speculates that the addition to the family circle of Lizzie Shaw's reading influenced the composition of *Mardi*. Yet the impact of social reading on Melville's writing and audience remains largely unexplored.

Recent empirical studies of antebellum audiences additionally challenge a neat gender divide. Statistical analysis "points away from the idea of strictly separated intellectual spheres," showing that women did read travels, history, and fiction of sea adventure, for example, while men read books classed as "sentimental," including books by women, and likely made equally avid novel readers (Zboray 164). Women's personal and published writings, long ignored in literary history, likewise challenge stereotypes of readership. Some women's recording of their "*private* opinion" of texts shows complex reactions against fiction whose advocacy of conventional marriage disappointed their erotic fantasies, a fact that invites reassessment of indiscriminate labeling of women readers as a "sentimentalized," "domesticated" audience.[10] A woman might neglect to read *Typee* not because the book shocked feminine sensibilities or she favored domestic fiction, but rather because she was too busy reading history and the classics (see Robertson-Lorant 178). Susan Warner, that paradigmatic sentimentalist, preferred "the fine naval characters and doings" in Cooper's adventure tales over Sedgwick's novels of domestic manners (Warner 317; see 305, 313), while Louisa Tuthill, through her model young lady's preference for Cooper in *The Boarding-School Girl*, endorsed his historical fiction as holding superior moral and intellectual appeal for female readers. Such expansive reading patterns among women show up in reviews as well, including some written by women and others aimed at a female audience.

Melville, on the other hand, sometimes fell prey to the sort of generalities that sustain gender formulae ("as a general thing, women have small taste for the sea") and occasionally figured reading in stereotypes dismissive of "boarding-school misses" or a wife undertaking a "new course of history."[11] Yet he also evidenced appreciation of some women's reading acumen. Most famously (though some read it as tongue-in-cheek), he credited Sophia Hawthorne's creative interpretation of *Moby-Dick* with first acquainting him with "subtle significance" he had not noted (*Correspondence* 219). He teased Sarah Morewood that this novel was not a "feminine" enough text for her refined taste, yet he assumed that they shared the same reading method ("for a fine book is a sort of revery to us—is it not?") and expressed gratitude for the novels that she selected for him (*Correspondence* 206). Perhaps more significantly, Melville maintained a longstanding friendship with Ellen Gifford, his wife's cousin, that turned on reading. He sent Gifford his writing; she left him her membership in the New York Society Library; but little of their correspondence survives to suggest how she read his work (*Correspondence* 490–99, 513). Although not much appreciation of women readers makes it into Melville's published writing, cousin Cherry in "Hawthorne and His Mosses"—like Aunt Mary Melvill who gave Herman his copy of *Mosses from an Old Manse*—is reader enough to know, unlike the essay's male narrator, that Hawthorne's sketches and tales afford summer reading superior to Timothy Dwight's *Travels in New-England*. If Melville imagined a series of male readers—first Dana, then Hawthorne—as his ideal audience, finally he made no gender distinctions in despairing that "an author can never—under no conceivable circumstances—be at all frank with his readers" (*Correspondence* 149, 160, 213).

Herman could likewise alternately welcome and reject active, sometimes "literary" responses from his female associates in the family who copied his writing and read that of others to him. It seems more promising for future study to consider the probability of their having made a significant impact on his writing—that is, to admit the evidence and arguments supporting what Julian Markels calls "the literary intelligence of the Melville women" (119)—rather than to extend the long tradition dismissive of the notion that these women could have made any serious contribution (see, for example, Arvin, *Melville* 126–28; Howard 90, 123; Parker 1: 805).[12] That the foremost expert on Melville's reading could not distinguish whether it was Herman or Lizzie who marked the copy of William Ellery Channing's *Works* that survives from the family library, for instance, invites revisiting the evidence on her reading and that of the Melville sisters as a step toward rethinking how far apart Melville's reading habits and thought were from theirs (Sealts, personal letter, 13 June 1983; *Melville's Reading* 164, no. 130). Reviews of Melville's writings, backed by readers' comments and library records, can begin to establish a contemporary female audience whose multiple approaches to reading Melville's work may offer hints for reconsidering the female readers closest to him.

"Everybody ought to read Typee," the *Home Journal* dictated ("Singular Development," 25 July 1846), and white women were in the many audiences who did.[13] The variety of their responses can offset a recent biography's unfortunate casting of the representative female reader of *Typee* as an antebellum groupie star-struck by the author "as sex symbol" (Parker 1: 930; see 413, 464–65, 485). Margaret Fuller recommended the book to two female audiences, to missionary sewing societies for its account of abuses in foreign missions, and to rural sewing societies for its adventure and romance. Missionary Clarissa Chapman Armstrong appreciated that Melville was committed to telling "a good story" in *Typee*, even as she objected to his and other "scandalous" writing against the Hawaiian government and the ABCFM missions (quoted in Broderick 16). Contemporary report held that the romance delighted seamstresses equally with lawyers and mechanics (Post-Lauria 64). Grace Greenwood testified to her conviction of the book's "truth," questioned in some reviews (cited in Leyda 1: 220), and Anne Lynch's review of *Los Gringos* defended *Omoo* along with *Typee* from that book's "unreliable . . . gossip" (*The Literary World* [27 Oct. 1849]: 356). Later, Greenwood demonstrated how closely she attended to *Typee*'s style and themes by parodying them, honing the racy style that made her a professional journalist at nineteen. She rewrites Melville's racial and sexual subtexts, however, focusing her fantasy not on the author of *Typee* but on a "voluptuous" native poet, whom she imagines as "a veritable Polynesian Tom Moore," and "the female part" of his audience. The Polynesian's recitation evokes "poetical enthusiasm" with an erotic edge that inspires women to dance with one another and the more "lady-like Fayaway," with "heaving bosom," to crown her compatriot with her lei (294–95). Lydia Maria Child, too, invoked Fayaway in her story "The Hindoo Anchorite," suggesting that more of "the female part" of *Typee*'s audience were interested in the possibilities of sexual and social freedom figured in that female character than in sexual fantasies about the author or his hero.

A general female public borrowed *Typee* from the library and, along with women closer to literary men, recorded responses in journal entries and letters that parallel professional responses ("very sprightly & amusing, but of doubtful veracity," "golden splendor & enchantment glowing before the dark refrain constantly brought as a background—the fear of being killed & eaten").[14] Whether from the family circle or the editorial chair, women pronounced critical judgments on Melville's writings that attest to discriminating reading and differing perspectives. Fanny Appleton Longfellow, reading aloud with her husband, concluded, as later critics agree, that *Typee* is superior to *Omoo* (Parker 1: 540), but Caroline Kirkland liked *Omoo* for its lack of respectability, enough to puff the book in the *Union Magazine* (1 [Aug. 1847]: 96). Women readers can be found even for *Pierre*, a work some reviews claimed had no readers at all. Elizabeth Oakes Smith's account of an excursion to Niagara quotes Sarah Whitman citing *Pierre* to support her agnostic position on spiritualism: "'From without,' says Herman Melville, 'no wonderful effect is wrought within ourselves, unless some interior, corresponding wonder welcome it'" (462). Recorded responses suggest that women read Melville's later and earlier books alike from a number of motives and toward a variety of ends. The variety of their responses further suggests the inadequacy of privileging Melville's texts as educating readers, or men's reviews as superior data for studies of reading.[15]

Even as antebellum women's reading expanded to include Melville, institutions structured by masculinist authority—familial, religious, literary—could exert complex, sometimes contradictory expectations linked to gender. When Emily Dickinson's father discovered her reading a book that scholars suspect was *Typee*, he "advised wiser employment and read at devotions the chapter of the gentleman with one talent," she reported, believing that "he thought my conscience would adjust the gender." The incident testifies to conflicting notions of what a woman might "profitably" read as well as to expectations that women would develop the ability to read texts written by and about men and form interpretations relevant to themselves, even as patriarchal authority exerted pressures on the making of meaning and the choice of texts (quoted in Sewall 634). While women might resist ideologies intended to shape their reading, in choosing disapproved matter, for example, or interpreting didactic fiction against its own moralizing (see Harris, *19th-Century* 28; Zboray and Zboray 161–62, 165–66), such pressures extended into controls on women's more public acts of reading. Had editorial policy permitted extensive criticism in the journals likely to publish women's reviews, Kirkland would have written more on *White-Jacket*, for "a few glances showed [her] that it was such a capital thing, and the young people seized upon it with such avidity" (Roberts 263).[16] Men in authority—whether editors, fathers, writers, publishers, husbands, or teachers (as well as women socialized to a masculinist perspective)—might presume to direct women's reading and response, urge time be better spent or the moral sense be engaged in interpretation, or assume that women would interpret texts to have application to themselves even when written by and for men. But such expectations did not always cohere and were not systematically brought to bear, nor did women readers categorically comply when gender expectations were evoked. Instead, such expectations only contributed, sometimes by contrariety, to the complex motivations of what and how women read (see Nichols). If Augusta Melville internalized a sense that a "spare half hour" belonged to family obligations "& [she ought] not selfishly spend it in reading," that did not prevent "three weeks . . . almost given up to reading & reflection" (quoted in W. Kelley, "Thirst" 49).

Journals known to have served wide female readerships published appreciative notices of Melville's work, including some by female journalists. While male reviewers considered to be addressing a general or male public were attacking his writings for licentiousness and other immoralities, the *Mother's Assistant and Young Lady's Friend* endorsed *Omoo* as holding exceeding interest for its readers, and the *Ladies' National Magazine* recommended *Typee*'s humor as a good antidote to the blues and illness. Although magazines with a female audience preferred *Redburn* to *Mardi,* anticipating later critical judgment, *Peterson's,* a journal described with some accuracy as "a fashionable ladies' magazine" (Charvat, *Profession* 244), declared *Mardi* would reward "the skimmer" with its imagination and the deeper reader with its thought, satire, allusiveness, and style. *Godey's Lady's Book* skimmed over the sailor's perspective on Polynesia to enthuse over *Omoo*'s "sketches of character" equal to Dickens and judged *Moby-Dick* "worthy" of Melville's international reputation for originality. While male reviewers charged *Pierre* with unintelligibility, even madness, the *Lady's Book* detected satire and parodied the text's nihilism and precious style. That magazine, whose large readership shows it among the most astute in negotiating women's (and men's) varied tastes, prematurely announced Melville as a contributor, perhaps hoping for sketches that would be at home in its pages, perhaps sentimental sketches like those in *Redburn* or didactic ones like those in *White-Jacket*.[17] Had Melville, like Hawthorne and Poe, published there, he might have found yet more appreciative female readers.

One appreciative reader of Melville's work, Elizabeth Elkins Sanders, was among the writers whose tradition of criticizing missionary imperialism he carried on in *Typee* (1846) and *Omoo* (1847). Sanders, aged eighty-seven, at the end of two decades of writing against missions and the displacement of indigenous peoples, reprinted three of her essays in *Remarks on the "Tour around Hawaii"* (1848), including two that generously defend Melville's apprentice novel, *Typee,* against what she viewed as attacks by "the missionary party" (34). By contrast with her progressive positions on issues of political and cultural imperialism, Melville's criticisms of missionaries in his early work often appear muddled and contradictory. Indeed, despite denouncing missionaries, *Typee* replicates their view of Hawaiians as unregenerate savages—a fundamentalist stance that informs *Typee*'s defense of the 1843 British takeover of island government as much as it informed the missions' evangelical project. In the Appendix account, even the celebration following restoration of the Hawaiian government to King Kaui'keaouli vindicates the takeover, for Melville claims a "heathenish uproar" took place that showed the "true colors" of Hawaiian character, which he figures—in the theological discourse of the missionaries—as licentious, "depraved and vicious" and which, he argues, requires the force of Lord Paulet's "sway" over native government (258, 254).

Sanders, more insightfully than Melville, narrates the specific material, moral, and cultural devastation of Hawaiians in the wake of the missions, recognizing "the native urbanity and domestic affection common to these Islanders" as a resource for their own regeneration as well as for reform of U.S. social relations—if Americans, including the missionaries, brought home efforts to realize the cultural ideals that they instead attempt to impress on others (15). Melville's early romances, despite criticism of missionaries strong enough to prompt complaints from conservative reviewers, circulated oppressive stereotypes of Hawaiians and accommodated hegemonic views sufficiently to advance his literary reputation first in England, then in the United States,[18] whereas Sanders' uncompromising exposé of the missionaries and of misrepresentations of Hawaiians helped ensure her work's lesser circulation and subsequent erasure from the circuits of influence that build literary status.

Sanders had her readers, however. Sometime after *Omoo*, Melville changed his views of Hawaiians. In his South Seas lectures (1858–1859), he reportedly argued against American annexation of the islands "until we have found for ourselves a civilization morally, mentally, and physically higher" (*The Piazza Tales* 420). Sanders' agenda of domestic reform echoes here, indicating that the Melvilles' habit of collecting notices of Herman's work likely brought him under the influence of this woman reader and writer, an influence that a literary history organized by dividing writers into separate spheres or elevating subversive men over submissive women cannot chronicle.

Melville likely had begun reading women writers early. There is no reason to think that he skipped over the selections from Joanna Baillie, Caroline Bowles, Charlotte Smith, and Jane Porter that appear in *The London Carcanet*, his prize at the Albany Academy in 1831 for "ciphering books" (we would say "interpreting texts"), or that he avoided (unless "desperate" for reading matter, as one biographer claims) volumes by women available in the libraries of the Albany Young Men's Association and in the vessels that he shipped aboard.[19] Indeed, strains of sentimental and religious discourses in his romances suggest an engagement with writers in those modes that may relate to such early reading.[20] It could also be instructive to consider the possible impact of early reading on the distance between the overheated style and Poesque sensationalism of the sketches that Melville published before boarding the *Charles and Henry* in 1842 and the "cozy, person-to person style of the journalism of the forties" that critics remark characterizes much of the short fiction he wrote in the fifties (Charvat, "Common Reader" 42). Works by women who pioneered this American colloquial magazine style, including Child, Sedgwick, and Eliza Leslie, were aboard this first ship on which the aspiring author of the "Fragments from a Writing Desk" sailed (see Heflin). Later, in his journal, Melville registered appreciation of Kirkland, the "spirited, sensible, fine" author of *Holidays Abroad*, whose "unsentimental" reflections on the shortfall of Roman "grandeur" from expectations anticipates similar musing in *Moby-Dick* (*Journal* 8; *Holidays* 2: 16); and in marginalia he registered wonder at Germaine de Staël's linking "so feminine & emotional a nature" with such "penetration of understanding" in *Germany*, concluding her to be "greater" than even Mrs. Browning (in Cowen II: 114).

Melville read different women writers to different purposes and with varying degrees of engagement. Some of his reading appears to inform his developing sense of audience as well as his writing style. He seems to have "read a little in Mrs Kirkland's European book" primarily as entertainment and guidance for his first grand tour (*Journal* 8). He shows deep interest in the thought of *Germany*, where his marginalia empathize with Staël's literary and philosophical discussions, and his comments enter the critical debate over the possibility of reconciling femininity and intellectuality, apparently agreeing with defenders of her androgynous "feminine genius" (Cowen II: 2, 114). Such responses would reward scrutiny beyond the scope of this essay, as would the multiple parallels between *Corinne* and *Pierre* which suggest that Staël provided hints for the structure of his romance (both episodic texts are divided into books and chapters and incorporate strains of romance, *künstlerroman*, melodrama, and psychological fiction) as well as for the exploration of relationships among Romantic conceptions of creativity, suffering, and domesticity through the dark (Corinne/Isabel) and the "celestial," light (Lucile/Lucy) ladies of romance tradition (Staël 317). Criticism tends to downplay internal and external evidence of Melville reading women, however, instead speculating on hypothetical analogues made to conform to critical paradigms of female sentimental authorship, such as the writing of "Mrs. [Susannah] Rowson and her imitators," Mrs. Sigourney's tales and "bestsellers cranked out by women like Mrs. E. D. E. N. Southworth," or Warner's *The Wide, Wide World*.[21]

Although Melville, with few exceptions, reserved his deepest reading for European authors, whether women or men, an American writer presents one interesting example of his critically neglected reading of women. Paradigms of American literary history, regional culture, and sentimental/domestic fiction alike have been inadequate to register connections between Melville and his literary neighbor in New York and the Berkshires, Catharine Sedgwick. Melville studies render Sedgwick so insignificant that a recent biography misnames the work that Edgar Allan Poe and Margaret Fuller judged her "best book" as "*The Lintons.*"[22] The single strand of criticism that proposes Melville knew Sedgwick's writing reinforces a hierarchical gender paradigm, presuming that the intellectual, aesthetic male author satirized the shallow, sentimental female scribbler.[23] An examination of *The Linwoods* and the sketch "The Country Cousin" as pretexts informing *Pierre,* however, can show a more complex dynamic of reading. If the thirty-one-year-old Melville did, as he stated, intend *Pierre* as his first "regular romance," what better exemplar than his sixty-one-year-old Berkshire neighbor whose romances had helped put American writing on the international literary map and were already being issued as "standard" works definitive of American literature (*Correspondence* 226)?[24] And what better text than "Country Cousin," honored with inclusion in the first collection of American short fiction, and the historical romance that, as Melville's sister Helen reported from the Sedgwick school, critics "unanimously pronounced as Miss Sedgwicks [sic] best work" (quoted in Parker 1: 100)?

Indeed, in 1849 when Putnam's American Authors Series reissued several of Sedgwick's novels along with works by Irving and Cooper, the *Literary World,* under Melville's promoters, the Duyckinck brothers, worked to represent her writings as feminine and passé rather than canonical—"domestic" fiction, "a class which the modern improvements in fiction have rather elbowed out of popularity" (6 Oct. 1849, 297). But by the time Melville began his foray into literary domesticity two years later with *Pierre, The Wide, Wide World* would make it clear that the class was not to be "elbowed aside" just yet. Then the *Literary World* instead tried to enlist Sedgwick's place as American author to promote Melville's and Hawthorne's reputation by association with her: A squib placed the men in Berkshire—where "Miss Sedgwick, as is well known to all readers of American literature, is" (27 Sept. 1851). Sedgwick may have appeared worthy of emulation to the younger writer still aspiring to literary status and at the moment rethinking his relation to popularity and to the publishers (Harpers) he shared with Sedgwick.

In drafting his first "regular romance," Melville need not have looked far for names for his female characters; Lucys appear commonly enough in antebellum fiction, Isabels even more often (as in *The Linwoods*). Yet the pairing of Lucy and Isabel in the romance roles of light and dark ladies occurs, so far as I know, only in *Pierre* and in Sedgwick's "The Country Cousin," given widespread currency by republication in Mary Russell Mitford's *Stories of*

American Life (1830).[25] Melville's characterizations echo Sedgwick's attribution of American associations, meekness, and rural simplicity to her Lucy and to Isabel, by contrast, Old World identification, pride, and cosmopolitanism. Melville's novel, like Sedgwick's story, features a passionate, ambitious young hero, "early steeped in the military spirit of chivalry," who defies his worldly, widowed mother; and both texts present this hero ambivalently through alternating satire and commendation ("Cousin" 108). Both texts plot a shift of affections from the light to the dark lady and a "private marriage" undertaken to evade parental disapproval that nonetheless results in parental repudiation. Both explore the limits of martyrdom to filial duty and the priority of the sibling bond over romantic attraction ("duty to [a] father, and love to [a] sister," as Sedgwick puts it [124], although her siblings are sisters). Thematics in *Pierre* further parallel Sedgwick's story, including its fascination with mystery, "mysterious visitations," and destiny ("Cousin" 99). Both narratives display something of the didactic intent of an object lesson. Meville's linking of Christianity with American republicanism is more unfavorable than Sedgwick's, but both satirize "the false notions and artificial distinctions of fashionable society" and sentimental conventions of representing a heroine ("Cousin" 105). Both writers also reverse romantic conventions of nature's influence on thought and emotions, and they exploit tensions between earthly passions and celestial attractions. Sedgwick's tale finally punctures notions of supernaturalism and romantic idealism to opt for domestic stability, while Melville's novel yearns toward the transcendent even in the act of denying its possibility as well as the viability of domestic or romantic idealisms. The multiple correspondences between the two texts suggest that although the two writers end up with different conclusions, reading Sedgwick may well have served to prompt Melville's thinking and narrative art rather than merely the derision that criticism has posited as his sole response to her.

Pierre shows even more extensive parallels with *The Linwoods*. Both texts explore socially imposed limits on sororal/fraternal love, seek to sort out thematic ambiguities through angelic and "terrestrial" women, mock readers' expectations of romance conventions in representing the light heroine, exploit melodrama and the stereotype of the matchmaking, worldly mother for humor as well as thematics, represent family history as paradigmatic of national history, consider the mutable significance characters attribute to nature, and dismiss romantic idealizing of the country while yet exhibiting a Jeffersonian distrust of the city. Both writers plot their fiction through the same Shakespearean antecedent, developing maddened characters on the models of Ophelia (Sedgwick) and Hamlet (Melville). Further, both writers resist conventional narrative forms and romance plot: they stretch the sentimental romance genre to its limits with melodrama and digressive episodes and challenge romance audiences with occasional coy narrative poses.

While Sedgwick largely returns her romance to a middle-class conventionalism from its forays into deviance, Melville ends not in satirizing Sedgwick, but rather his own protagonist's immature efforts to transcend conventionalism; Pierre's attempt to write a "Mature Book" produces instead a "reeking pile" of bathos he spits upon, and the triple "fool of Truth, . . . of Virtue, . . . of Fate quits . . . forever!" his ménage à trois (or à quatre, counting Delly), vowing to "skate to [an] acquittal!" absurdly "hate-shod" on letters from his publishers, cousin, and Lucy's brother (302, 357–58). Melville's romance finally is unable to sustain unconventional alternatives for his characters and ends in melodrama, as the defiance that the narrator earlier celebrated conduces only to personal dissatisfaction, outlawry, and obscure death for them all.[26] Critics of both *Pierre* and *The Linwoods* objected to the romances' rejection of proprieties, particularly to their sympathetic representation of crazed characters, as a violation of conventional mores.[27] Despite the unconventionality of *The Linwoods* and publishers' concern lest its serious matter make the novel "heavy," Sedgwick succeeded in shaping a fiction that garnered readers (M. Kelley, *Private Woman* 205). Melville did not.

Melville's fiction registers a wide range of responses to Sedgwick's writing. *Pierre*, in delineating the doom of a "Democrat" descended from a "richly aristocratic" and "proudly patriotic . . . line," does appear to satirize Sedgwick's depiction of American democratic nobility (13, 12, 5). *Pierre* likely burlesques the episodes in *The Linwoods* that show the chivalric heroism of Jasper Meredith and Herbert Linwood in saving women from horses. Parody might begin to account for the bizarre scene in which Pierre crawls about under his horses in an "equestrian performance" that promotes his heroic status through an image of horses' drool "epauletting his shoulders" (22). As the parallels detailed above suggest, however, Melville appears to have found Sedgwick's work compelling enough that he reached back more than a decade and a half not merely for an easy target to satirize but also, as he did with the works of male writers, for stimulus to thought and models for writing. If his "Poor Man's Pudding" (1854), published two years after *Pierre*, parodies her *The Poor Rich Man, and the Rich Poor Man,* published nearly two decades earlier, Melville's choice of target may suggest just how far back he was looking to Sedgwick, a pioneer of the sketch form, to see how popular literature about serious economic issues might be written.

. . .

It would not do to imagine that Melville read primarily women writers or that his readers were primarily women, of course. But careful examination of available evidence and future uncovering of more can lead to subtler, less misogynistic understandings of his audiences and a less wholesale dismissal of the thoughtful contemporary female audience for his works, as well as to new views of his writing and its reception. Attention to Melville's reading of women and women's reading of Melville makes less tenable the old critical paradigms of separate or hierarchical cultural spheres. Whatever the intent of the author, or the work that his texts have been made to perform in reinforcing an androcentric and misogynist American culture, the uses to which women put Melville's writings are varied, surprising, and instructive for readers yet to come.

With thanks to Wyn Kelley for her generous editorial suggestions.

Notes

1. See Arvin, "Gothic Novel" 33, 47; Bickley 81–82; Douglas 300; Reynolds 58; Colatrella 184; Silverman. So entrenched are presumptions linking sentimentality with the feminine and the feminine with women that they inform even efforts to revise this critical tradition. Paul Lewis's fine essay, for example, argues that scholarship now appreciates Melville's "dialogue with [women], including Catharine E. Beecher, Lydia Maria Child, and Catharine Maria Sedgwick," yet cites as evidence only Elizabeth Schultz's study of the sentimental in *Moby-Dick,* which treats Dickens, not women writers. Carol Colatrella insightfully questions whether categories such as "women readers" encompass individuals "necessarily alike in their base assumptions, reading strategies, or outcomes of their readings" (3), yet her study privileges what she sees as the intended reader of Melville's "theory of reading and interpretation" with its "inevitably" determined positions and does not escape arguments that treat women writers only as lesser than Melville (4, 5, 6). But see essays in this volume by Peter Balaam and Wyn Kelley. Scholars have begun to attribute agency and insight to later women's reading of Melville; see Cahir.

2. See especially Douglas and Reynolds. For critiques of these models, see Romero and Avallone.

3. Machor's argument "for the superiority of reviews as data" over evidence of actual women reading elides the agency women exercised in negotiating "reading codes, ideological assumptions . . . , and the textual construction of audience," values professional reviewers' notions of women over "common" women, and appears to assume that the categories of women readers and reviewers are mutually exclusive (83n.23, 61). The changing focus from Steven Mailloux's *Interpretive Conventions* to *Rhetorical Power* is symptomatic of the shift away from constructions of ideal, intended, or inscribed readers and toward history. So, too, is the recent flourishing of studies of early U.S. women readers that builds on the work of such scholars as Louise Rosenblatt (whose model of transactional analysis moved away from formalists' text-focused models to account for the active, varied role of readers in making meanings) and, especially, of Janice Radway and Cathy N. Davidson (whose work investigates actual women's acts of reading in historical context). See also Batsleer et al.; Harris in Machor; Sicherman in Davidson, Zboray, Zboray and Zboray; and Ryan and Thomas.

4. For one example see Scott in Ryan and Thomas; also see Batsleer et al. 141; Harris, *19th-Century American Women's Novels* 13; Sicherman, "Sense and Sensibility" 208, 216; "Reading and Middle-Class Identity" 150; M. Kelley, "Reading Women/Women Reading" 71 and "A More Glorious Revolution"; Hall 351.

5. See also Charvat, *Profession* 242, 305–6; Romero 13. Ronald Zboray's empirical research challenges representations of a predominantly female audience for fiction (162).

6. For an example see Baym 47–54. Such contradictory stereotypes of women readers as sensation seekers and as prudes anticipate presumptions informing later criticism's dismissal of women as readers of Melville.

7. Mrs. M. L. Hinkson, inaugural address as president of the Edgeworthalian female debating society, Bloomington, Indiana, 28 Jan. 1842 (in Wheeler 193–94). See also Augusta Evans Wilson, cited in Harris, "But is it any *good*?" (50–51); and Louisa May Alcott, cited in Reynolds 708. Hannah Foster's popular narrative warns young ladies against superficial reading.

8. Catharine Sedgwick's "Old Maids" (1833) teaches a woman-centered hermeneutics in reading Walter Scott, for instance, and Foster's novel critiques misogyny in Alexander Pope. Emma Willard cites the misogyny of the British canon (which she illustrates in readings of not only Pope but also Joseph Addison, Lord Byron, Tom Moore, and John Milton) as evidence of the superiority of American literature and American female education (in which she, presumptively, taught the critical reading method she details). Such evidence shows that some nineteenth-century models of reading anticipated Judith Fetterly's argument that to read as a woman requires refusal of a text's inscriptions of misogyny, whether through strategies of "resistance" such as she describes or through appropriations of texts to women's own purposes. Susan K. Harris notes women readers' "tendency to question their inscription in texts" (*19th-Century* 28). Christina Zwarg discusses Fuller's paradigms of reading. George Emerson taught a reading practice for "improving and elevated conversation" to make a woman "a charming companion and . . . a blessing to the circle of which she is the ornament" (*Reminiscences* 144–45). Because "the history of women's struggle for literacy, especially advanced practices . . . , has only begun to be written," we can anticipate learning much more about varieties of women's reading and literacy pedagogies (Hobbs 1). See the essays in Hobbs as well as M. Kelley, "Reading Women" and "More Glorious Revolution."

9. See Elizabeth Melville letter in Leyda 1: 266; W. Kelley, "Thirst" 50; Robertson-Lorant, *Melville* 175–76, 178; Parker 1: 855. Little criticism has followed up Sealts's suggestion that family readings constituted a possible influence on Melville (66). Drawing conclusions about reading or taste in the Melville family based on library survivals requires caution, as many books were given to the women by men and many books were sold away from the library; see Sealts 45, and e.g., 150, #6. Assumptions that Melville was "lured" or "command[ed]" to attend Lynch's Saturdays both diminish the importance of her gatherings as a literary institution traversing separate sphere distinctions and discredit women's cultural power by fetishizing their personal power (Arvin, *Melville* 124; Parker 1: 584). Female journalists who publicly responded to his work (Fuller, Greenwood, Kirkland, Lynch, and Oakes Smith) and the writers that Mansfield and Vincent find he engaged in *Moby-Dick* (Oakes Smith, Sedgwick, and Fanny Forester) alike moved in the salon circles that Melville has been depicted as visiting reluctantly (see *Moby-Dick,* ed. Mansfield and Vincent xlviii, 632–33, 725–26).

10. Lydia Maria Child, cited by Karcher 325; Douglas 291; and see Harris, *19th-Century* 19.

11. *Correspondence* 219; marked in Lady Shelley's *Shelley Memorials,* see Cowen 10: 69, cf. *Confidence-Man* 70; "I and My Chimney" in *Piazza Tales* 361–62. Melville's marking in William Godwin's letter to Shelley (*Shelley Memorials*) suggests agreement that "a true student is a man seated in his chair, and surrounded with a sort of intrenchment [sic] and breastwork of books. It is for the boarding-school misses to read one book at a time. . . . True reading is

investigation—not a passive reception of what our author gives us, but an active inquiry, appreciation, and digestion of his subject." Melville's markings in a Mary Shelley letter appear to agree, too, that women's "material mechanism makes [them] quite different creatures; better, though weaker, but wanting in the higher grades of intellect" (Cowen 10: 97). On Sophia Melville (Herman's sister-in-law) as a reader of history, see Parker 1: 464.

Romero includes Melville with contemporaries (Cooper, Hawthorne) who protested women's hegemony as both producers and consumers of culture but cites no supporting evidence (12–17). Had Melville completed the "Burgundy Club" sketches, would he have clarified his own position in the dialogue between his fictional poet/editor/narrator who has not given a thought to "the ladies" and his fictional journalist who claims that popular publication depends upon "conciliating the suffrages of the ladies, and in marked preference to those of men" ("House of the Tragic Poet" in Sandberg 68)?

12. See, for example, Melville's inscription in Lizzie's copy of *Timoleon,* cited in Robertson-Lorant 607; see also 180. Robertson-Lorant's biography is the first to begin questioning the tradition dismissive of women in the Melville family.

13. I have found no evidence that women of color read Melville.

14. Journal of Charlotte Brooks Everett, 30 June 1846, cited in Zboray and Zboray 151; Sophia Hawthorne cited in Metcalf 91; and see Zboray 173.

15. See, for example, Charvat, *Profession* 247; Douglas 307; Machor 83n.23.

16. Roberts speculates that Kirkland's notice appeared in *Holden's Dollar Magazine* 5 (May 1850): 314–16. Both Kirkland's response and the popularity of *White-Jacket* undermine arguments claiming exclusive hegemony for a feminized popular audience that preferred sentimental narratives and ignored Melville.

17. See Horace Greeley, "Up the Lakes," *New York Weekly Tribune,* 26 June 1847, and George Washington Peck, rev. of *Omoo, American Whig Review* 6 (July 1847): 36–46, rev. of *Moby-Dick, United States Magazine* 25 (July 1849): 44–50; *Mother's Assistant* (Oct. 1847): 95; *Ladies' National Magazine* 12 (July 1847): 40; see Higgins and Parker 142; *Godey's* 35 (July 1847): 56, and 44 (Feb. 1852): 166; *Peterson's* 15 (June 1849): 219; *Godey's* 45 (Oct. 1852): 390. For the announcement of Melville's contribution, see the advertisement at back of *Godey's Lady's Book,* Dec. and Jan. 1851; *Correspondence* 171, 603.

18. Charles Anderson, although requiring revision by more accurate historians, remains salient on Melville's rhetorical situation (336).

19. *Albany Argus* in Sealts 194; Parker 1: 233. By the 1848 catalog (the earliest I have been able to obtain), the Albany Association indexed women writers under the rubrics of "Polite Literature," travels, history, and biography. Heflin treats the library aboard the *Charles and Henry.* Parker discusses the library on the *United States* only in the context of what he calls the "manly" love of reading (273; see 267–73). Sedgwick's works (including *Home,* apparently on the *Charles and Henry*) developed tropes of libraries and reading, tropes later featured in *Mardi* and *White-Jacket. Home* should be added to the Unitarian writing aboard the ship that Heflin notes as likely to interest Melville. Brother Gansevoort Melville took women's writing seriously enough to note in his commonplace book his reading of Jane Porter's historical fiction, one title of which (*Thaddeus of Warsaw*) survives, signed by Augusta, from the family library (see Gilman 72; Sealts 206, no. 406).

20. See Post-Lauria, esp. 30, 40, 127–28; Schultz, "Subtext"; Heflin 16.

21. Charvat, *Profession* 251–52 and cf. 276; Douglas 312; and see Braswell; *Pierre* 369; Post-Lauria, esp. 128–30.

22. Parker 1: 100, 936; Poe 1201; and see Fuller "American Literature" 388. Although literature anthologies now include Sedgwick, studies continue to misname her ("Maria" Sedgwick,

58   *Charlene Avallone*

"Catherine Sedwick") and relegate her, following Douglas, to "a notable list" of women who were attracted to W. E. Channing (Winslow and Wojnar 2; Young 18).

23. See Bickley 81–82; Douglas 300; Silverman. Widmer notes that Sedgwick's *Redwood* may have influenced "the trope of the Virginian" in the *Mosses* essay, but he discusses only her brothers as significant participants with Melville in the Young America movement, and her works do not appear in his bibliography (263n.92). Mansfield and Vincent argue *Hope Leslie* influenced Melville's naming of the Pequod (*Moby-Dick* 632–33).

24. Putnam's American Authors Series reissued *Clarence* and *Redwood* in 1849 and *A New-England Tale and Miscellanies* in 1852. Harpers, Sedgwick's publisher beginning in 1830, continued to issue *Hope Leslie* and *The Linwoods,* her most critically acclaimed texts, into the 1870s. See Damon-Bach 300–301, 298, 296–97. Critics collapse the generational difference between Sedgwick and Melville, further promoting Melville as more progressive. Both writers, however, may be viewed as progressive in certain regards or contexts, conservative in others.

25. Mitford's collection also includes "The Indian Hater," a known analog for *The Confidence-Man.*

26. Not only Sanders imagined reformed domesticity. Other now-neglected women writers were imagining unconventional domesticities in ambiguous narratives of psychological and stylistic complexity, such as Caroline Chesbro's *Isa.* That *Pierre* cannot finally sustain the trope of incest as an alternative to either conventional marriage or literary composition complicates interpretations that claim Melville eclipses sentimental women writers in his satirizing the limits of their vision or in offering a superior model of family and writing (see Silverman 356, 358).

27. See reviews of *The Linwoods* in the *North American Review* 42 (Jan. 1836): 160, and *Boston Pearl* 5 (12 Mar. 1836): 207.

"Piazza to the North"

Melville Reading Sedgwick

Peter Balaam

𝒲ithin a few miles of each other in 1850, the eminent novelist Catharine Maria Sedgwick and her new neighbor, Herman Melville, added piazzas to their old-fashioned houses outside adjacent Berkshire towns. Andrew Jackson Downing's *The Architecture of Country Houses* appeared the same year, identifying the piazza (or veranda) as among the "most valuable" (32) features for Romantic-style American houses in rural settings.[1] According to Downing, proper emphasis on architectural features unique to dwellings such as the bay window and the piazza could soften and relieve the symmetry of older Georgian and Greek-revival styles or the unadorned plainness of the workingman's cottage to harmonize a house visually within its setting of rural grounds and landscape (47, 119–22). Because a piazza expressed more clearly than other forms of ornament its inhabitant's freedom from merely utilitarian concerns and a dignified love of pleasure, it became his program's requisite feature: "The moment [a] dwelling rises so far in dignity above the merely useful as to employ any considerable feature not entirely intended for use, then the verandah should find its place"; for to "decorate a cottage highly, which has no verandah-like feature, is, in this climate, as unphilosophical and false in taste, as it would be to paint a log-hut, or gild the rafters of a barn" (120).[2]

Catharine Sedgwick was an avid supporter and close friend of Downing; she made extended visits to his Newburgh, New York, estate along the Hudson River. Like his, her later works struck a popular chord in their promotion of a reform-minded domesticity that ran counter to the dominant economic ethos of the late antebellum era.[3] Sedgwick's illustrious family had long been associated with the civic life of Stockbridge and Lenox, but in 1850 the vogue in scenic views made the prospects from surrounding hills more attractive than the constraints of the village. Mary Dewey's 1872 biography of Sedgwick describes how her brother Charles's house, in which she occupied an entire "wing," was moved in 1850 "from the somewhat cramped position it occupied in the village of Lenox to a charming situation at a little distance, on the brow of the hill, and commanding a vast and beautifully varied prospect. Here Miss Sedgwick's 'wing' received still farther additions, notably that of a broad and well-inclosed piazza, looking to the south over twenty miles of valley, meadow, lake, and hill, to the blue Taghkonic range in southernmost Berkshire" (329).

Just a few miles to the north, recently arrived in Pittsfield from New York, Herman Melville—the author of *Typee* and lately of *White-Jacket*—was at work on a new book of whaling adventure when he likewise undertook several projects to expand and spruce up "Arrowhead," the 1780s Federal-style farmhouse he had just purchased. Renovations included the addition of a piazza that, unlike Sedgwick's and against convention in the cool Berkshire climate, faced north. As his first summer at Arrowhead began, Melville wrote Hawthorne (also in Lenox) describing his rustic and writerly activities: "Since you have been here, I have been building some shanties of houses . . . and likewise some shanties of chapters and essays. I have been plowing and sowing and raising and painting and printing and praying,—and now begin to come out on a less bustling time and to enjoy the calm prospect of things from a fair piazza at the north of the old farm house here" (*Correspondence* 195).

One of Downing's principles in *The Architecture of Country Houses* is that a dwelling's visual effect will inevitably express the spirit or character, the "truth" of the life, of its inhabitants (24–25). Something of this idea is operative in these two accounts of Berkshire piazzas, which, particularly in their degree of conformity to contemporary ideals of genteel domesticity, construct quite different visions of rural householding. In its celebration of Sedgwick's new living arrangements, Dewey's biography emphasizes the piazza as the particular site where the great novelist's writerly and domestic skills seamlessly intertwined. Sedgwick is recalled as thriving in various idealized bucolic roles—gardener, harvester of fruit, brilliant talker, thoughtful hostess—through which she produced on her piazza the joy of "Arcadian repasts" and achieved in her person the noted effect of her fiction: the transmission to her guests of "unconscious inspirations of health and happiness" (329). This picture of domestic self-sufficiency and fulfillment is consistent with Downing's vision of the most opulent type of American dwelling, the rural "villa," to which, he notes, we may look for "the happiest social and moral development of our people," for it is in the villa that "the social virtues are more honestly practiced, . . . the duties and graces of life have more meaning, . . . [and] the character has more room to develop its best and finest traits than within the walls of cities" (258). By contrast, in his letter to Hawthorne, Melville foregoes the dignity supposedly available to rural authors and inhabitants of country houses. In identifying recent progress on the house and his new book as the construction of "shanties"—the utilitarian and impermanent shelters of the poor—he emphasizes the restless striving and futility inherent to rural life. His piazza offers respite from toil and "a calm prospect of things," but a catalog of chores—"plowing and sowing and raising and painting and printing and praying"—drains the picture of the grace that country living was thought to guarantee.

The fact that Melville built a piazza onto Arrowhead at all would hardly reward our scrutiny were it not that he drew so much attention to it as a coveted and crucially expressive architectural feature in "The Piazza," his fictional introduction to *The Piazza Tales* (1856). The narrator's special fondness for piazzas "as somehow combining the coziness of in-doors with the freedom of out-doors" echoes Hawthorne's notions of romance as a "neutral territory" or median zone of synthesis between fantasy and reality, and, as readers have long noted, "The Piazza" seems intended to probe the ethics of literary romance.[4] The narrator's desire to retire to the quiet and repose of a country house develops into an ironically restless search for a proper seat, the optimal location, orientation, or point of view from which to take in the scenery around his house. When the addition of a piazza also fails to cure his restlessness or shield him from disillusionment, he suddenly departs on a quest to lay eyes on the "queen of fairies" or "glad mountain girl" he believes to be the source of an alluring gleam of light from nearby hills. Flush with romantic expectations of receiving a healing vision or an opportunity for heroism, the narrator is brought up short in his encounter with the woman he actually finds, the despairing and sleepless seamstress Marianna, who spends long days alone in a rotting house cheering herself with visions of the happiness that must reside in the distant sun-gilded house she sees—the narrator's own. A brief denouement describes the narrator's failed attempt to deny his knowledge of Marianna's misery and to return to the imaginative safety of the piazza.

Through his narrator's failed quest and the bad faith of his denial, Melville seems to be expressing wariness about imaginative literature itself, in both the writer's creation of pleasing artifice and the reader's act of complacent consumption. Given such ambivalence, it is no surprise that within the tale a piazza should be the site of both private repose and public contention. The narrator recalls with amusement the mutual disdain that erupted between him and an established neighbor when he began to build his piazza on the north side of his house in the cool, inland climate. Borrowing the names Dives and Lazarus from the parable of "the rich man and the beggar"—with which Luke's gospel makes the case for the spiritual advantages of poverty in this life—the narrator tells of the pleasure with which, from the conventional warmth of a south-facing piazza, his neighbor Dives scoffed as he himself had his piazza built to the north. In this comedy of unneighborly competitiveness, Melville combines the balances of the parable's social vision—in which the rich enjoy their reward in this life while the poor look forward to comfort in the next one—with Downing's sense of the piazza as guarantor of its inhabitant's dignity. What results is the idea of the piazza as gauge or indicator of the ultimate righteousness of an individual's householding. Melville's narrator, for instance, covets a piazza for its being "so pleasant to inspect your thermometer there" (1). Meanwhile (though in winter Dives laughs at the sight of Lazarus shivering on his frigid northern piazza) the very poverty and departure from custom the latter willingly undertakes in building his piazza to the north become his salvation in the trying heat of August; then, "in the cool elysium of my northern bower, I, Lazarus in Abraham's bosom, cast down the hill a pitying glance on poor old Dives, tormented in the purgatory of his piazza to the south" (1–3).

The schadenfreude between Lazarus and Dives becomes clearer when we realize that in Dives Melville alludes to his enviably prominent neighbor, Miss Sedgwick. This cryptic reference is part of a multilayered joke at the expense of the Berkshire "squireocracy" of which Sedgwick was arguably the most prominent member.[5] The joke, embedded in Dives's narrow sense of convention in the placement of piazzas, is that the Berkshire region's notorious reputation for religious orthodoxy and intolerance had only shifted in several decades of liberalizing reform from matters of religious doctrine to issues of literary and domestic style. The joke entails as well Melville's application of the reversals of fortune suffered by a rich man and a beggar to the careers of authors in the antebellum literary marketplace, by which he prophesies from Dives-Sedgwick's comfortable, this-worldly success an August purgatory of future obscurity and from Lazarus's austere but principled poverty a promise of his own future reception. If as popular writer Sedgwick played the wealthy squire to Melville's late-coming squatter, his play with the parable enabled him to depict Sedgwick's popular success as the temporary status and comfort of a "poor rich man" and to exalt his own current lack of honor as the sign of the righteous patience and promise of a "rich poor man."

Melville Reading Sedgwick 63

The topsy-turvy of this moral vision was of course not Melville's at all but Sedgwick's; such were the compensating reversals of fortune and status envisioned in her popular 1836 book, *The Poor Rich Man and the Rich Poor Man*, which Melville had already satirized in "Poor Man's Pudding, and Rich Man's Crumbs" (1854).[6] Melville's subversive engagement with Sedgwick's work in "The Piazza" almost certainly extends as well to his narrator building his piazza to the north in order to better take in the sunset illumination of Mt. Greylock, an event he identifies as "the coronation of Charlemagne" (2). This otherwise unaccountable reference to the eighth-century Holy Roman Emperor is a nod to *Le Bossu* (1832), Sedgwick's romance of filial rebellion in the court of Charles the Great. The resolution of *Le Bossu* involves Charlemagne's defeat of rebel factions led by his illegitimate son, Pepin, and the latter's evasion of official punishment by exiling himself to rural life on an island in Lake Constance to the north of the Alps and far from the court at Aix. At this remove Pepin lives in disguise as a priest, builds a rural chapel, and performs for the local peasants regular services to honor and effectively prolong the reign of his father, the emperor Charlemagne (108).

These veiled references to Sedgwick haunt the opening paragraphs of Melville's tale because, as an examination of the truth status of fiction and wary comment on the vogue for genteel fiction from the borderlands, "The Piazza" draws on and revises the first Berkshire novel, Sedgwick's *A New-England Tale* (1821).[7] Despite the obvious differences between these writers' styles and intended audiences, it is important to see that just as Melville accepted the convention of a domestic piazza but built his to face the north, so rather than turn entirely away from the conventional fiction of a successful writer such as Sedgwick, he drew on such writings for his own purposes. Like its predecessor, "The Piazza" is set in the wooded uplands of Berkshire County, a region widely associated—in part because of Sedgwick's books—with picturesque scenery. Both of these works examine the ethics of the picturesque in their protagonists' discovery, behind the veil of lovely scenery, of suffering women abandoned in mountain huts and barely sheltered from the wasting effects of time and nature. Because they drew on picturesque discourse at different points in its trajectory through U.S. literary history, Melville and Sedgwick saw quite differently the meaning of this landscape and the suffering women it houses.

Sedgwick's novel uses the picturesque to depict the Berkshire woods as a mixed setting, one that naturally accommodates bright and dark elements in a single composition.[8] This vision of nature as a varied and inclusive canvas enables Sedgwick's novel to critique and pass beyond the classical moral symmetry of local Calvinist orthodoxy and to envision new and

Arminian forms of virtue. Thirty years later, Melville's depiction of the Berkshire uplands emphasizes the threat of moral complacency inherent in the picturesque that had itself become classical in the popular fiction of the time. Sedgwick's picturesque is primarily a transitional mode; if her novel relies on female figures of suffering and ruin to sponsor its heroine's moral education in sympathy, it expends little anxiety about such victims of its plot. By contrast, in "The Piazza" Melville attempts a radical fidelity in narrative form to the rupture and disturbance inherent in the picturesque and so refuses the smooth symmetries normally called for in the denouement of a romance. Accordingly, his tale's ending turns conventional revelations, recognitions, and expectations of marriage "to the north" and leaves the ethics of represented pain unfinished in the narrator's sense of being haunted. Implicit in this inconclusive account of a male hero's moral education is a quiet tribute to the reality of Marianna, the alienated and despairing woman his plot depends on but refuses to sacrifice.

Because Melville tends to be associated with masculine shipboard worlds such as those aboard the *Neversink*, *Pequod*, and *Bellipotent*, and with dramas of male individuation in which young men confront psychic "fathers," it is instructive to note the degree to which his work could also be interrelated with that of a popular domestic writer and literary "mother" such as Sedgwick. In its alert exposition of the power relations implicit in patriarchal society and aesthetic theory such as that surrounding the picturesque, "The Piazza" offers insights into how Melville saw himself in a professional neighborhood dominated by the example and force of Sedgwick as woman, competitor, and precursor and into the degree to which a sense of "women's wrongs" held for him a prophetic authority.

Born in 1789, Catharine Sedgwick was a generation older than Melville. She was from one of interior New England's most illustrious families, a hardly needed reminder of the status Melville's family had lost during his youth. Sedgwick never married and was supported in her career by considerable inheritances and her four notable brothers, a situation very unlike that of Melville, who was sole breadwinner at Arrowhead for a household that included a pregnant wife, young child, mother, and three sisters. Though she had not published a major work since the 1830s, Sedgwick had been one of the most respected American authors of Melville's childhood. Her most recent works, including *Home* and *The Poor Rich Man*, had been written in a consciously didactic style intended for the majority of American readers. For better or worse, that majority had responded with an enthusiasm that had made Sedgwick a feather in the cap at Harper's, Melville's publisher as well since *Omoo* (M. Kelley, *Private* 13). Resigned as Melville was that he could not or would not build his writerly piazza facing south and write what he called "the other way" (the way that would pay), he would have had cause to wonder at if not resent his neighbor's security and success (*Correspondence* 191).[9]

Sedgwick's cultural authority in antebellum literary culture is nowhere clearer than in the fact that scholars credit the plot of *A New-England Tale* with having established the "trials and triumph" paradigm for nineteenth-century American "woman's fiction." Following Sedgwick's *ur*-plot, scores of American novels written by and for women tracked the progress of a marginalized young girl on her way through difficulties en route to the middle-class triumph of relative autonomy within enlightened marriage (Baym, *Woman's* 12, 54). Reading Sedgwick, Melville may have felt that in trials life could in fact be too like a romance for comfort, with metaphors of triumph painfully slow to arrive. Like Sedgwick's young heroine, Melville had experienced as a boy the ruin and sudden death of a father amidst revelations of fiscal irresponsibility and deceit and had found his way into young adulthood in psychic struggle with his immediate family's genteel and Calvinist codes of behavior and models of reality (Tolchin xi). The fact that he drew on Sedgwick's work in composing "The Piazza" reinforces the common impression of Melville as one whose muse was stimulated by skeptical and parodic assimilation of the work of other writers. Just as he altered conventions to suit himself in building a genteelly fashionable piazza to frame a view to the north rather than collect the warmth available in the south, so also he frequently found his own voice in parodic reply to others' works (Moore 45; Breinig 270).

In contrast to Sedgwick's, Melville's fiction's relatively male orientation in character, theme, and intended audience is hardly contestable. Beginning in the early 1850s, though, his work shows a preoccupation with female characters in whose suffering, patience, and uncomplaining defiance Melville locates an arresting vision of human dignity. None of Melville's women thrive, and none is the subject of an empowering narrative of domestic self-fashioning. Indeed, these characters tend to be victims of abandonment about which they can do little other than wait and wield in either protest or despair the scraps of some kind of faith against the wasting forces of time and nature. Notably, not all of these women are women; their original progenitress may be the defiant sovereign within Ahab, whose interiority is described late in *Moby-Dick* (1851) as the realm of a "queenly personality . . . [who] feels her royal rights" (507). The hero of *Pierre* (1852) exhibits a guilty sensitivity to "women's wrongs" when he rapidly overthrows his rights, privileges, and sense of identity as the male scion of Saddle Meadows to concede authority to his illegitimate and unacknowledged half-sister, Isabel. Joyce Carol Oates notes a similar cross-gender sensitivity in the feminist political vision of "The

Tartarus of Maids" (1855), citing Melville's "appalled sympathy with the fates of girls and women condemned to factory work ... and ... to being female in a wholly patriarchal society." Oates describes Melville's sympathetic vision as the rare feat of a male writer's "trying to see from the perspective of the 'other sex' ... [and] in a way highly critical of the advantages of masculinity" (3–4). Melville's female characters arrive with the end of the ambitiously public phase of his career, and their proliferation suggests his discovery in the ruin, mourning, and speechlessness of women a means to both express and distance himself from his own loss, doubts, and resignation.[10]

The abandonment that strands and immobilizes Melville's female characters is always linked to the contrasting social advantages his male characters typically enjoy: exuberant camaraderie, economic autonomy, mobility, and verbal self-possession. After *Pierre,* Melville was engaged with "the story of Agatha," to which he was drawn by "the great patience, & endurance, & resignedness" he found in the story of a Nantucket woman abandoned and deceived by her mariner husband (*Correspondence* 232). Though he apparently destroyed the Agatha book when Harper's rejected it, it is reasonable to wonder whether Agatha's remains are not legible in Hunilla of "The Encantadas" and Marianna of "The Piazza," in whom any Griselda-like patience once praiseworthy in Agatha has darkened to an exotic, insistent but futile faith (Sattelmeyer and Barbour 399). Melville's women, including the queenly being at Ahab's core, suffer from an ontological divide between the genders in which all acknowledged forms of power, all mobility, expression, and autonomy are on the side of males. If he does not present ready solutions to these social arrangements, Melville surely treats this terrain in his work to protest it. If his male protagonists are officially empowered citadels of social advantage, such conventional power tends to render them sanguine innocents, literal readers ready to mistake their own warm feelings of goodness and sympathy for proof of a cosmos incapable of real harm. While none of them triumphs, Melville's women, like their feminized male counterparts, Bartleby and Benito Cereno, are granted a consciousness of power relations that their privileged male interlocutors entirely lack. A male writer's skepticism about the social advantages of masculinity constitutes an assault from the citadel of social power on that citadel itself—and so recalls the mediating function of the Romantic-era aesthetic known as the picturesque.[11]

The notoriously unstable picturesque, with its origins in eighteenth-century British landscape aesthetics, has served a wide array of architectural and aesthetic programs but, according to Martin Price, has always arisen in "response to the severity and uniformity of an established ... style" (260, 261).[12] Sidney K. Robinson describes the landscape architectural origins of the picturesque within greater mid-eighteenth-century economic shifts from feudal "estate culture" to metropolitan "Bourgeois culture." It arose as a specific response to the need to see the visual composition of grounds and landscape in a way other than the tyrannical imposition of order. The picturesque was meant "to reconcile, at least momentarily, a passing world based on nontemporal, static classification with an emerging one that emphasized transformation." The increased complexity and mobility of ideas and resources "required a level of abstraction and placelessness that the specifics of [British landscape] could no longer support," and so it was the mediating role of picturesque style to find a way for the country house or estate to "tell us about mobility" rather than permanence (143). Without an established estate culture to modify, the picturesque appeared in post-Revolutionary U.S. travel writing as a novel form of appreciating North American scenery. The picturesque rejected the clear dualism inherent in the Puritan dread of wilderness and offered a response to nature that could "balance the conflicting claims of wildness and disorder, on the one hand, with those of civilization and order on the other." It provided early-nineteenth-century painters, writers, and botanizers with an organized, cool aesthetic that restrained exaggerated emotion and framed one's view of rude nature with the artistic perspective of the landscape painter. The picturesque thus allowed even the wildest scenery to blend moral lessons with visual and emotional pleasure and provided Americans with a congenial, respectable, eminently civilized standpoint from which to study and enjoy the wilderness (Berthold, "Charles Brockden Brown" 63, 69).

Sedgwick's use of the picturesque in *A New-England Tale* evinces these trends precisely. Early in the novel the Lloyds, a Quaker couple from Philadelphia, leave the city in search of more healthful environs, journeying north up the Housatonic River valley in Connecticut. Putting seaboard farms and towns behind them, they enter the wooded hills of southern Berkshire and take increasing delight in the scenery for its beauty and abundant moral lessons. The childlike "turbulence" of a "noisy stream dash[ing] impetuously" along with them begets their bemused tolerance; "delightful to the imagination," the stream "reminds [them] . . . of the joy of untamed spirits, and undiminished strength" (29). But if the picturesque enables Sedgwick to affirm wild and untamed elements in the landscape, it does so ultimately only to more firmly establish traditional forms of social stability. The heights of aesthetic and moral rapture such as the Philadelphians enjoy along the Housatonic are unavailable to a lame Yankee mountaineer in whose hut they wait out a thunderstorm. Behind the mixture of inspiration and amusement the Lloyds draw from the comical stoicism of the Yankee is the sense that such encounters with the picturesque poor enliven and amuse because, if they bring together members of different classes, they also effectively reinforce the naturalness of given social hierarchies. The novel ennobles the Lloyds to readers not only when they admire the mountaineer in his independence and ingenuity but also when they hold their noses before the hut's "want of neatness and order" (32). As if in answer to the impertinent stream they admired in the landscape, a freshet flows (with impetuousness harder to read as morally uplifting) right through the house. The travelers note the pale looks and haggard faces of the mountaineer's family. As the storm passes and they prepare to depart, Mr. Lloyd asks the mountaineer what plans exist to divert the flow of the water from the house. In an act of spontaneous largesse as he is stepping out the door he vanquishes the mountaineer's indifference by giving him ten dollars.

The travelers' appreciation of the picturesque mountaineer thus serves to prove their own moral worth and magnanimity. Such positive valuation of the unkempt en route to reassertions of a familiar sense of social order is emblematic of Sedgwick's use of the picturesque. Back on the road, their focus has shifted. They remain devotees of the landscape but no longer for its wildness; now they admire its stabler, more civilized qualities. "I, too, prefer this scenery," Mr. Lloyd agrees with his wife. "It has a more domestic aspect. There is, too, a more perfect and intimate union of the sublime and beautiful. These mountains that surround us, and are so near to us on every side, seem to me like natural barriers, by which the Father has secured for His children the gardens He has planted for them by the river's side" (33). Thus a Berkshire clearly designated for domestic settlement is arrived at by a day's rough passage through the forest, and what began as a series of openings to the attractive moral expansiveness of natural wilderness ends in visions of settlement in which the very "natural barriers" of the landscape delineate divinely backed property ownership.

Like the piazza's architectural effect of relaxing the straight lines and plain surfaces of Greek revival structures, the popular "women's fiction" for which Sedgwick was known can be seen as mediating cultural shifts away from the authority of religious doctrine to that of sentiment and sympathy. Sedgwick began writing what became *A New-England Tale* as a tract to illustrate the soul-warping moral effects of the Calvinism that she had abandoned in converting to Unitarianism. The resulting novel offended the local orthodox but struck a popular chord in its confident depiction of virtue informed by individual responsibility and human moral perfection (M. Kelley, *Private* 2).[13] Jane Elton, the heroine of Sedgwick's Cinderella-like plot, suffers the deaths of her genteel parents and passes into the custody of an orthodox aunt, Mrs. Wilson, whose domesticity and parenting are determined by her opportunistic reliance on doctrines of divine sovereignty and unconditional election. In struggle against the passivity and self-deception such doctrines foster in her aunt, Jane figures forth a morality exemplified by her pluck, intelligence, and commitment to ethical action. Jane's training in this new morality comes most notably through the novel's most picturesque figure, Crazy Bet, a homeless transient who plays the role of gadfly, village idiot, designated mourner, and impassioned advocate of feeling among the sober and dignified Calvinists of the village. Living among the tombs of local graveyards, Bet pierces with a prophetic sense of outrage the hypocrisies and sloth of established Calvinists such as Mrs. Wilson. Despite Sedgwick's claim that Crazy Bet is the single "sketch of a real character" in her novel ("Preface" 7), she was clearly composed along the lines of marginal prophets from John the Baptist and Shakespeare's wise fools to Meg Merrilies, the sybilline gypsy of Sir Walter Scott's *Guy Mannering*.[14] Like the picturesque aesthetic she embodies, the "poor crack'd body" Bet is an irritating, colorful figure in the landscape, an irreverent outlaw against decorum, and an image of human understanding in noble ruins (79). Unchecked by windows and walls, she magically appears when and wherever she may storm the citadel of unfeeling order on which the social power of the novel's Calvinists depend.[15] That order can read only as "crazy" a person whose mainsprings are grief, outrage, and feeling. It is Bet who guides Jane out of the paralyzing rigor of her religious training and awakens in her a robust awareness of the link between natural beauty and nature's God-backed "law" of the heart, sympathy.

The novel's need to move Jane beyond the moral restrictions of her aunt's house calls for her exposure to dark and uncivilized sources of power and insight. This initiation takes the form of a midnight tour through the Berkshire mountains that Melville would re-create thirty years later in his narrator's quest beyond the piazza into "fairy land." Having made a hasty promise to help a stranger in trouble, Jane sneaks out of the house in the middle of the night to meet Crazy Bet at a spot in the woods called "Lucy's grave" (83). Though initially afraid of the dark and full of remorse for acting with unaccustomed stealth, Jane soon responds to the serene magic of the forest, her way lit by reveling fireflies and a waning moon that "shed its mild lustre over the peaceful scene." She makes of an uprooted tree a "rude passage" over a stream and comes upon Bet awaiting her in alarming disarray, flowers and vines woven through her hair. Dressed in ritual garb for an occasion Jane knows nothing of, Bet refuses Jane's request that she compose herself and then further disturbs her by speaking reverently of the need to await the onset of "Lucy's hour," when the spirit of an Ophelia-like suicide walks the forest (79, 83–84). Jane softens in sympathetic response to the story of the dead woman's suffering and then, Lucy's hour arriving and releasing them to proceed, follows her mad guide on a manic tour through the ancient rock-strewn chaos of the Berkshire woods:

> They now entered a defile, which had been made by some tremendous convulsion of nature, that had rent the mountain asunder, and piled rock on rock in the deep abyss. The breadth of the passage . . . was walled in by the perpendicular sides of the mountain . . . Her wayward guide pressed on, heedless of the difficulties of the way. She would pass between huge rocks, that had rolled so near together, as to leave but a very narrow passage between them; then grasping the tangled roots that projected from the side of the mountain, and placing her feet in the fissures of the rocks . . . she would glide over. . . . They were sometimes compelled . . . to prostrate themselves and creep though narrow apertures in the rocks . . . and Jane felt that she was passing over immense masses of ice, the accumulation perhaps of a hundred winters. . . . Till they came to an immense rock, whose conical and giant form rested on broken masses below, that on every side were propping this "mighty monarch of the scene." (87)[16]

This passage through the jagged sublimities of the Berkshire landscape—from the narrow gorge known only to "the wild bird and the wild woman," to that ready Romantic icon of upended hierarchies, a toppled monarchic boulder—swiftly catches up all the associations of cataclysm and waste that the outmoded Calvinism of Sedgwick's upbringing had seen in the vast North American wilderness (Moore 7). Bet leads Jane on this forced passage through the woods because Sedgwick must give the girl—as through her novel she would give her audience—a picturesque, morally positive reading to a natural landscape that had formerly carried only the threat of calamity and destruction. Heeding Bet's command to remain below, Jane observes as Bet leaves her and reappears at the top of the immense boulder where, in a state of religious and aesthetic transport, waving a stick high above her head, the mad woman sings an impassioned stanza from the mad poet Christopher Smart's "A Song to David" (1763). The lines paint Bet as a female Moses on Sinai responding to the divine charge: "Tell them, I AM." The material earth, listening in dread, is "smitten" like the rock-strewn defiles of the Berkshire landscape, and from the smitten rock flows nature's assent, "O Lord, Thou art!" (86–88).[17]

From this scene of transformational violence, its riot of intertextual echoes rupturing established paradigms, emerges the key to a new domestic morality. Sedgwick confidently underscores the iconography of changing dispensation, from orthodox legalism to domestic grace, by putting an end to Bet's rapture with the descent of a bird that alights on her staff. Like the Baptist she recalls in her rough appearance and role as herald of the new, Bet has prepared the way for Jane, baptized her in this Jordan of picturesque sights and feeling, and now announces it time for the girl to "do [her] earthly work" (88). That work begins with a test of Jane's capacity to read human misery with an eye retrained by the picturesque and freed from orthodox moral sanction. Entering the tree-shrouded hut of a poor mountaineer called John of the Mountain, Jane takes in the sight of Mary Oakley, victim of her cousin David Wilson's libertinism, sitting on a bed "fixed as a statue" with a stillborn child in her arms. While the sight of this woman might formerly have prompted judgment or withdrawal, Jane notes with approval the beauty of Mary's glossy black hair "in confusion, and clustered in rich masses over her temples and neck," and the poignancy of a tear suspended as if frozen on Mary's downcast eyelash. Thus absorbed in the sculptural details of this rough Berkshire *pietà,* Jane shows her training in the picturesque by wondering internally "that any thing *so wretched could look so lovely*" (93; emphasis added). In fact Jane has arrived too late to be of help to poor Mary Oakley, who dies as she watches, but Mary's suffering and death contribute lavishly to Jane's (and Sedgwick's readers') moral education. The novel quickly moves our attention beyond Mary's demise in staging Jane's next lessons in which John and Bet admonish Jane to apprehend the woman's death not in speculation into the likelihood of her soul's election but simply as the release of pent tensions, a welcome end to earthly imperfection and pain (93–95).

How would Melville, reading Sedgwick, have responded to these picturesque negotiations? While architectural styles considered picturesque were at the height of their popularity during the 1850s (O'Malley ix), the picturesque in literature was in the same era generally coming to be associated with a "want of moral depth and earnestness."[18] Melville himself has been described as more aware than most Americans of his era of the "poverty and power implicit in British countryside" and the aesthetic traditions it helped to theorize.[19] John Bryant argues that while it is widely assumed that Melville was critical of the picturesque as reflecting "America's shallow optimism," his attacks on it were meant "to clarify its deeper ethical and aesthetic potentials" ("Toning" 145, 146). Quoting Martin Price, Bryant explains the effect of the picturesque interpenetration of optimism and anxiety in Melville's prose as fostering neither love nor fright but a piqued state of curiosity, an "intensity of awareness" that is "primarily moral" (146, 148). Knowledge of his attraction to the picturesque will help us to grasp his intent in giving voice to a character who introduces himself in cheerfully admitting his desire to seek comfort in part by regarding external reality as merely "a picture":

> When I removed into the country, it was to occupy an old-fashioned farm-house, which had no piazza—a deficiency the more regretted, because not only did I like piazzas as somehow combining the coziness of in-doors with the freedom of out-doors, and it is so pleasant to inspect your thermometer there, but *the country round about was such a picture*, that in berry time no boy climbs hill or crosses vale without coming upon easels planted in every nook, and sun-burnt painters painting there. A very paradise of painters. (*Piazza Tales* 1; emphasis added)

Typifying his view as a paradise *for* painters would adequately commend the beauty of the spot; the phrase he uses, "paradise *of* painters," suggests play on the word "picturesque," which, with its source in the Italian *pittoresco*, derives from the word not for picture but for painter (*pittore*). The phrase thus conveys the narrator's comfort in relying on the painters he finds in the landscape as visible proof of his view's picturesqueness. In this sense the painters nicely occupy the foreground of his canvas as do the bandits and gypsies—colorful figures whose outlaw status underscores the wild ethos of broken landscape—in paintings by Salvator Rosa.[20] Similarly, the exposure of these "sun-burnt" painters inevitably prefigures Dives in his August purgatory and Marianna blinded by the sun at her window. In the pleasure the narrator takes at others' exposure, Melville characterizes him as one whose resources and security—like Jane Elton's calm sense of aesthetic mastery while registering the loveliness of the wretched Mary Oakley—enable him to benefit from sights of misfortune and ruin when they come at no risk to himself (Robinson 11).

The sensibility Melville exposes in such passages anticipates what John Ruskin critiqued as "the modern feeling" of the picturesque, "perhaps the most suspicious and questionable of all the characters distinctively belonging to our temper, and art" (11). Ruskin distinguishes in the fourth volume of *Modern Painters* between the "nobler picturesque," which depends on a properly restrained depiction of "unconscious suffering," and the "surface" or "shallow picturesque," typified by an apparently "heartless" "delight in ruin" (16–17, 11). This distinction is helpful in understanding Melville's use of the picturesque and its differences not only from Sedgwick's use of it but from the attitudes of his own narrator, whose delight in the ever-changing Berkshire landscape Melville brings down into awareness of a woman whose poverty, isolation, and exposure make her defenseless against such change.

According to Ruskin, the lover of the surface picturesque goes forth into the world "in a temper as merciless as its rocks. All other men feel some regret at the sight of disorder and ruin. He alone delights in both; it matters not of what. Fallen cottage—desolate villa—deserted village—blasted heath—mouldering castle—to him, so that they do but show jagged angles of stone and timber, all are sights equally joyful" (20). In just this mode, with his hungry eye and his style blithely juxtaposing calamitous literary, classical, and biblical allusions, Melville's narrator gorges himself on the ruinous grandeur of a fallen world and revels in the sight from the house

> when the turned maple woods in the broad basin below me, having lost their first vermilion tint, dully smoked, like smouldering towns, when flames expire upon their prey; and rumor had it, that this smokiness in the general air was not all Indian summer—which was not used to be so sick a thing, however mild,—but, in great part, was blown from far-off forests, for weeks on fire, in Vermont; so that no wonder the sky was ominous as Hecate's cauldron—and two sportsmen, crossing a red stubble buck-wheat field, seemed guilty Macbeth and foreboding Banquo; and the hermit-sun, hutted in an Adullum cave . . . did little else but . . . just steadily paint one small, round, strawberry mole upon the wan cheek of northwestern hills. (4)

While the narrator excuses these observations with their gratuitously apocalyptic effects as products of "a mad poet's afternoon," they embody the heartless aspect of the picturesque in the evident thrill with which the narrator projects judgment, guilt, sickness, stealth, and stain onto the landscape. Though stirring, such grandiose landscape description gains its authority from the distance it reinforces between the narrator in repose and the heat of the "far-off" fires.

Rather than establish the privilege of this point of view, as Sedgwick does in *A New-England Tale*, Melville's plot undermines its ground by submitting the plenitude and ease the narrator has projected in his rural domesticity to a series of trials. These include bouts of illness and despondency that keep him indoors for weeks at a time, the wormy infestation of the china-creeper that twines up his piazza post, and the outcome of his quest to locate a woman on the mountain, the sight of whom he believes will "do [him] good, it will cure this weariness, to look on" (6).[21] To convey his narrator's quest into fairyland, Melville uses an old-fashioned periodic sentence that compulsively piles up clauses of forward movement in an "on . . . on . . . on" pattern that mimics the way Bet compels Jane through the same terrain. As the rock-strewn sublimity of nature in Sedgwick's novel was the dark inversion of Jane Elton's tidy morality, so here nature is revealed as the obverse of the controlled achievement in the narrator's intended domesticity. As the china-creeper petals, peeled back, "showed millions of strange, cankerous worms" the same color as the blooms, so what appeared from the piazza as a distant "gallery" of gorgeous, ever-changing verdure (2) reveals on closer inspection a realm of defunct and abandoned human enterprises, wrecks, traces, and dying echoes that molderingly tell a story of general futility and change:

> A winter wood road, matted all along with winter-green. By the side of pebbly waters . . . on I journeyed—my horse and I; on, by an old saw-mill, bound down and hushed with vines, that his grating voice no more was heard; on, by a deep flume clove through snowy marble . . . where freshet eddies had, on each side, spun out empty chapels in the living rock; on, where Jacks-in-the-pulpit . . . preached but to the wilderness; on, where a huge, cross-grain block, fern-bedded, showed where, in forgotten times, man after man had tried to split it, but lost his wedges for his pains—which wedges yet rusted in their holes; on, where, ages past, in step-like ledges of a cascade, skull-hollow pots had been churned out by ceaseless whirling of a flint-stone—ever wearing, but itself unworn; on, by wild rapids pouring into a secret pool, but soothed by circling there awhile, issued forth serenely; on, to less broken ground, and by a little ring, where, truly, fairies must have danced, or else some wheel-tire been heated—for all was bare; still on, and up, and out into a hanging orchard, where maidenly looked down upon me a crescent moon, from morning. (7)

Though Melville's voyager reverently welcomes the "maidenly" sight of a "crescent moon" as a sign of his passage at dawn into the female realm of the fairy queen he seeks, the catalog of futile projects to which he has been exposed during the night extends to his encounter with the actual Marianna. Sitting down next to this polite but pallid, silent, and unremarkable woman, he first takes in how wrong he was in his expectations: "This, then, is the fairy-mountain house, and here, the fairy queen sitting at her fairy window" (9). His realization of the distance between his expectations and Marianna's reality leads quickly to a second insight: that the hazy atmosphere distorts what Marianna sees as well. The "far-off, soft, azure world" he comes from is hard to recognize; when he manages to identify his own house through the haze, it appears "less a farm-house than King Charming's palace" (9).

Melville Reading Sedgwick 75

The scene carries Melville's suggestion that, despite the narrator's and Marianna's differences in gender and economic class, and the access to resources and mobility theoretically determined by such differences, this man and woman are essentially united, not only in their isolation, sleeplessness, and despair but in their dependency on nurturing illusions. If the narrator's privilege as viewer has depended on his difference from what he sees, on his being sheltered while others are exposed, then the discovery of his sameness with a lonely mountain woman and her cultivation of shadows violates the principles of his visual pleasure and safety. That through the haze the narrator's farmhouse seems a palace and Marianna's cottage the dwelling of a fairy queen brings us back to Andrew Jackson Downing, whose illustration of a "Bracketed Veranda from the inside" (122) graphically suggests the unlikely regressive fantasies of feudal social organization that lay behind his vision of reformed domestic taste. In an era riven by political uncertainties and economic changes, Downing proposed the cultivation of domesticity itself as a cure for the "feverish unrest" that plagues humanity even on republican American soil.[22] When the narrator tries to engage Marianna with such genteel domestic ideology—"You must find this view very pleasant," he coaches her—it falls flat. Not only does the view no longer please her but she blames herself for the fact. Surely she must walk happily up here, the woods being so wide? "And lonesome," Marianna replies, "lonesome because so wide." But her rural hearth must be a cheery place for nurturing reveries? Not exactly, she replies, though it's true one can "better feel lone by hearth, than rock" (9). The disenchanted realism of Marianna's answers suggest that she has already tried such promises as Downing's that "the occupations of the country are full of health for both soul and body, and for the most refined as well as the most rustic taste" (258). The narrator and Marianna both invest with the power of a restorative charm their wish to glimpse the happy being each projects as the apotheosis of the view, revealing their shared adherence to contemporary ideologies of picturesque landscape and rural householding. It was a basic tenet of Downing's works that the civilized felicity of country living was legible not only in the "spirit" of a house but in the "faces" of its inhabitants: "higher and deeper than either proportion or decoration is that beauty of expression which indicates the spirit that lives within the country house. You may never have investigated it, but you have nevertheless tacitly recognized, that a spirit of frankness or reserve, a spirit of miserly care or kind hospitality, a spirit of meanness of generosity, a spirit of system or disorder, a spirit of peace or discord, may be found in the expression of every house, as well as every face in the country" (260).

The irony of the mountaintop scene of "The Piazza" generally stems from the idea that the narrator is revealed as being as dependent on illusions as is Marianna. What most disturbs him about Marianna's existence is that, in his version of it, for her "shadows are as things" (11). But her finding pleasure in the play of shadows on the floor of her cottage is a grim version not only of what Downing commends as the "desirable play of shadows, broad and deep," the "softening" and "humanizing" effects of light one can cultivate domestically with a vine-covered trellis or piazza (114), but it is arguably the same kind of diversion the narrator has sought in tracking the landscape's shifting play of light and shadow from his piazza.[23] Marianna's cultivation of relationships with shadows matters in another way as well, though. In the narrator's encounter with Marianna, Melville reworks the mountain enchantment of "Lucy's hour," the scene in which Sedgwick's Jane Elton is initiated into awareness of wider reality and learns to let feeling flow toward those wronged by misfortune. Accordingly, Melville's narrator is set to the challenge of Tray's hour, in which this inveterate looker finds himself the object of another's gaze. "Tray" is the name of a dog-shaped shadow on Marianna's floor whose head turns with the movement of the sun during the time the narrator spends in her hut. "Don't you see him? His head is turned toward you. Tray looks at you," she says. "This is his hour" (10–11).[24]

The narrator's undergoing Tray's scrutiny is of course only a version of the ethical perplexity confronting him in the need to respond to the claim on him made by Marianna's projections of a happy savior for herself onto the owner of his house. Given her failure to recognize him as the happy being she sought, none of his options in replying to her can be the heroic action or flattering response he sought in her, but the reply he does offer has the virtue of being the tale's most considered utterance. Citing the limits of his knowledge, he confesses that he is not (as of course he isn't) "that happy one of the happy house you dream you see." Because he sees that the truth can only remove a mainstay of her faith, his denial seems intended to carefully, perhaps even ethically, preserve to Marianna the illusions that sustain her (12). In a different light, of course, his reply seems merely evasive, a bachelor's refusal of commitment in preference for the mobility and autonomy granted him by his gender and status. In thus tip-toeing around Marianna's ostensible need for sustaining illusions, he denies not only the possibility that his bachelor mobility is itself dependent on illusion. He denies as well any awareness of the psychic bond the two have shared. That each has projected onto the other's house a vision of a happy and powerful figure whose sight would vouchsafe a domestic existence otherwise threatened by futility, disappointment, and loneliness might in more conventional narratives signal that the two were meant for each other.

Like the role of the artist Melville is exploring here, the narrator's denial to Marianna is wonderfully freighted with contradictory motives in which the ethical and the deceptive, the realistic and the romantic, touch and interpenetrate. In the sustained juxtaposition of these clashing motives Melville extends picturesque asymmetry to romantic fiction's marriage plot and refuses to smooth the rough and unsettled by revelations, recognitions, and the realignment of energies in marriage. The vulnerable narrator's being "haunted" by Marianna's face "and many as real a story" suggests that Melville is cultivating in his readers the moral curiosity they will need to manage the ambiguities not only, as many have suggested, of the remaining *Piazza Tales* but of such fictions and representations as govern the subjectivity of everyday life as well. Unlike Jane Elton and Crazy Bet, Melville's Marianna submits to neither a saving marriage nor a morally instructive death but maintains her unarticulated though resistant otherness. Like a sphinx's riddle threatening readers at the gate of *The Piazza Tales* and anticipating their encounters with the untold stories and troubled faces of Bartleby, Hunilla, Babo, and Benito Cereno, Marianna enables Melville to infect with doubts his narrator's baronial fantasies of visual and narrative objectification. That Melville's male hero emerges from an interview in a hoped-for fairyland haunted by the face of an exhausted but strangely faithful, real woman suggests his sensitivity to social realities too troubling to be rendered pleasing in a picturesque mode. And in this wronged but visionary woman whose haunting face has the power to disturb all facile trust and complacency, Melville conveys a memorable image of the potential force he craved for himself and his own art.

Notes

This essay has been revised from a selection from *"Misery's Mathematics": Mourning, Compensation, and Reality in Antebellum American Literature,* by Peter Balaam. © 2004 by Routledge.

1. John Stilgoe describes these shifts in architectural style as paralleled by a general trend in middle-class city-dwellers' exodus from the "wilderness of bricks" in increasingly crowded cities to suburban "borderland" regions such as the Hudson River valley and the Berkshire hills of Massachusetts. The pleasing roughness of picturesque natural beauty in such borderland regions offered the backdrop for a supposedly civilizing ideology of rural domestic peace as antidote to modern urban overcrowding and instability (9).

2. Vicki Halper Litman describes Melville's evident familiarity with Downing in several short works and *Pierre.*

3. According to the Swedish domestic writer Fredericka Bremer, Sedgwick regarded Downing as "one of our best men" (46). Adam Sweeting's *Reading Houses and Building Books* describes Downing's friendships with and the importance of his aesthetic reforms to a group of "Genteel Romantic" writers who created a popular antebellum literature of idealized rural domesticity. Along with Sedgwick, the group included Washington Irving, Nathaniel Parker Willis, Donald Grant Mitchell, William Cullen Bryant, and George William Curtis (4, 9–12).

4. Cf. Bryant, "Toning" 146; Breinig 268; Bergmann 270. Hawthorne describes the writer's familiar room becoming "a neutral territory, somewhere between the real world and fairy-land, where the Actual and the Imaginary may meet, and each imbue itself with the nature of the other" (*Scarlet Letter* 36). As a piazza exists in and combines two realms of reality, the same is true of Marianna's hut "set down on the summit, in a pass between two worlds, participant of neither" (*Piazza Tales* 8).

5. Hershel Parker reconstructs Melville's awkwardness in the neighborhood as son of lapsed gentility and author of *Typee*—"the sensualist's handbook"—among the Berkshire gentry whose wealth and security he would have envied but whose politics he disparaged (*Biography*, 1: 761, 881; 2: 64, 220).

6. Several recent critics have suggested that Melville's 1854 tale parodies Sedgwick's book. See Douglas 362; Rogin 156; Reynolds 58; and *Biography*, 2: 220.

7. For William Cullen Bryant the publication of *A New-England Tale* was "the first time that the beautiful valleys of our county had been made the scene of the well-devised adventures of imaginary personages, and we all felt that, by being invested with new associations, they had gained a new interest" (Dewey 439; quoted in Birdsall 367).

8. On the central function of mixture to the picturesque, see Robinson 1–27.

9. Melville's depiction of Sedgwick as a disapproving figure of the past and obstruction to the progress of Berkshire literature is not unique to him. In a letter to his wife, Evert Duyckinck described his deflated exhilaration after a hike up Monument Mountain with a group of male writers when the cohort was stopped by "a tall Miss Sedgwick" who administered "a cross examination which I did not stand very well on Hope Leslie and Magawisca." In print a year later, though, Duyckinck referred with mild approval to Sedgwick's presence in Berkshire as guarantee of the region's growing literary associations: "Miss Sedgwick, as is well known to all readers of American literature, is there, and near by arose for the world, doubtless, first painted on the mists of the valley, the vision of The House with the Seven Gables. Herman Melville, in the vistas of his wood and the long prospective glance from his meadows to the mountains, blends the past and the future on his fancy-sprinkled page" (Leyda 1: 385, 428). Similarly, at the end of *A Wonder Book* (1851), Hawthorne's Pegasus-flight view of the environs of Tanglewood associates Melville and an unnamed Sedgwick again as neighbors and writers: "But, here in Lenox, I should find our most truthful novelist, who has made the scenery and life of Berkshire all her own. On the hither side of Pittsfield sits Herman Melville, shaping out the gigantic conception of his 'White Whale,' while the gigantic shape of Graylock looms upon him from his study-window" (169). Hawthorne's tone is ambiguous, but given the desirable latitude of romance, the epithet "most truthful" seems at least skeptical if not disdainful, and a potential critique of mastery and exclusivity lurks as well in Sedgwick's having made Berkshire "all her own."

10. Neal L. Tolchin reads Melville as creating in his fiction women "implicated . . . in the experience of bereavement" that Melville himself, owing to gender, religious codes, and his family's psychic complexity, could not complete after the death of his father in 1832 (33).

11. "Picturesque imitation is not usually made by those who are totally marginal. An attack by those who have never known life in the citadel is not carried out as skirmishes, but as

furious destruction. The picturesque . . . challenge is made by residents on vacation from the center who engage in a kind of shadow-boxing. As weekend vagabonds, . . . advocates of the picturesque enrich a dominant tradition, mix it with doubt, but do not undermine it totally" (Robinson 147).

12. Cf. also Berthold 66

13. David S. Reynolds regards the cultural mediation performed by such antebellum fiction as Sedgwick's as constituting a narrative genre he calls the "Moral Adventure," which "probed the turbulence and linguistic violence of frontier or city life but tried to uphold firm ethical values through the portrayal of a central hero . . . who sustains integrity and moral power" (183).

14. Sedgwick's crucial and unacknowledged source for Crazy Bet is Meg Merrilies, from whom she borrows her outlandish costume, several spoken phrases, and her thematic role as a colorful and kindly alternative authority figure. As Peter Garside has shown, contemporary reviews of *Guy Mannering* took particular note of Meg Merrilies as a visual figure, especially in the "wild pathos" of the "highly picturesque" scene in which the "heart-struck sybil" harangues Godfrey Bertram, the Laird of Ellangowan, from a bank above a road, for having evicted the gypsies from his estate (145). Sedgwick reproduces this scene in Crazy Bet's transport high on a rock in the wilderness but replaces Scott's strife between social classes with a transcendental nature worship that makes room for sympathy.

15. Cf. the scenes of Bet's interrupting the normal order: 16–19, 81–82, 83–94.

16. In the final words Sedgwick is quoting without attribution Walter Scott's description of the Thames in *The Heart of Midlothian* (1818). Such literary references, a common feature of her prose, suggest a source for the particular allusiveness of Melville's prose in "The Piazza."

17. I gratefully acknowledge my student Sophia Paraschos for pointing out the source of Bet's lines in Christopher Smart.

18. A contemporary review of *The House of the Seven Gables* complained that Hawthorne's romance exhibits the shallow morality of its picturesque mode, its preference for psychological over social and political investments; see Woodson 172.

19. Stilgoe cites *Redburn* (1849) and its hero's inland ramble out of Liverpool. Redburn finds "old" England in the country, but his excursion leads quickly to an encounter with the "man-traps and spring-guns" that protect private rural property (311n.7). For more recent readings of Melville's alertness to the political anxieties within antebellum landscape representation, see Angela Miller and Samuel Otter ("Eden").

20. Cf. Bryant, "Toning" 147. Christopher Sten identifies Salvator Rosa, alongside Murillo and Claude, as Melville's "favorite artists" (9).

21. Melville's evident source for the narrator's investment in his china-creeper is Downing's explanations of the architectural effect and meaning of climbing vines on a rural cottage (they "always express domesticity and the presence of heart"). See Downing 79–80, 206–7. Downing touches on insect infestation (208, 210) and, for its twining vigor, blossoms, and domestic charm, glowingly commends the hop (211, cf. *Piazza Tales* 12).

22. "Much of the feverish unrest and want of balance between the desire and the fulfillment of life, is calmed and adjusted by the pursuit of tastes which result in making a little world of the family home, where truthfulness, beauty, and order have the largest dominion" ("Preface" xx).

23. In "The Piazza" the narrator observes "troops of shadows" "routed by pursuing light" in "mirrored sham fights in the sky" (5).

24. With the name Tray, Marianna's shadow dog not only makes an eerie suggestion of an unexpected third party between them, but Tray is one of the three dogs (with Blanch and

Sweetheart) that Lear hears barking at him on the heath during the night of his ethical awakening: "Take physic, pomp; / Expose thyself to feel what wretches feel" (*King Lear* III.vi.61–62, iv.35–36). A dog named Tray is the loyal hearthside companion of the narrator in Ik Marvel's *Reveries of a Bachelor* (1850), another popular work by another genteel romantic, Donald Grant Mitchell, from which Melville clearly borrows in "The Piazza."

"Bartleby, the Scrivener" and "Uncle Christopher's"

Sites of Wage Slavery and Domestic Abuse

Elizabeth Schultz

*W*all Street, the urban setting for Herman Melville's "Bartleby, the Scrivener," and Clovernook, the rural setting for Alice Cary's "Uncle Christopher's," are separated only geographically. Published in 1853, both stories reveal the effects of power on the powerless—women and children, the poor and the silenced—in a lapsed Christian democracy and in an aggressively emerging capitalistic economy. Although a decade later Melville and Cary would become friends in New York,[1] at the time of the stories' publications, Cary had only recently moved from rural Ohio to the city, whereas Melville was still living in the Berkshires in rural Massachusetts.

Examining Melville's story in relation to Cary's suggests their emphatically shared concern with class inequities and with wage slavery engendered by capitalistic production; such examination also reveals that Melville, no less than Cary, recognizes the degradations of domestic abuse. Such a comparison provides a catalyst for considering gender as a significant issue in "Bartleby" and for understanding Melville's scrivener's position, in particular, as similar to that of both women and children in antebellum American culture. Although Melville's recognition of the oppression to which industrialization and the market economy in the antebellum period subjected women does not become fully apparent until his account of women operatives in "The Paradise of Bachelors and the Tartarus of Maids," written in 1854, the year following "Bartleby's" publication, "Bartleby," read in relation to Cary's story with attention to gender, can be perceived as anticipating his later revelations regarding the debilitating conditions for working women.

A comparison of "Bartleby" and "Uncle Christopher's" also provides a catalyst for interpreting and appreciating Cary as a writer whose social concerns extended beyond the rural and midwestern locale of her stories. It could be argued that in "Uncle Christopher's" she appeals explicitly to an elite, urban audience with values resembling those of the lawyer-narrator of "Bartleby." As Judith Fetterley maintains, citing from Cary's preface to *Clovernook,* her story collection in which "Uncle Christopher's" appeared, "The readers Cary imagines for her work are not the inhabitants of her region, on whose sympathy she might rely, but are rather 'the inhabitants of cities, where, however much there may be of pity there is surely little of sympathy for the poor and humble, and perhaps still less of faith in their capacity for those finer feelings which are too often deemed the blossoms of high and fashionable culture'" ("Entitled to More" 105). For Bartleby, the scrivener, as well as for "Uncle Christopher's" "poor and humble" characters, who have a feminine capacity for "finer feelings" but who are caught in a changing economic and social system, mid-nineteenth-century society had finally little sympathy and no faith in their capabilities and desires.

While "Bartleby" illuminates the impact of changes in modes of production in the nation's largest city and in the urban workplace, "Uncle Christopher's" suggests their national ubiquity by indicating how they played out in Ohio, in rural areas, and in domestic arenas in antebellum America. Cary's preface to *Clovernook* argues that "there is surely as much in the simple manners, and the little histories every day reveals, to interest us in humanity, as there *can* be in those old empires where the press of tyrannous laws and the deadening influence of hereditary acquiescence necessarily destroy the best life of society" (Fetterley, "Preface" 3). While explicitly referring to feudal Europe, Cary subversively alludes to democratic America where the press of tyrannous laws was apparent in the South's chattel slavery and the deadening influence on humanity in the North's wage slavery, class inequities, and domestic abuse.[2]

Critics frequently note that the subtitle for "Bartleby"—"A Story of Wall Street"—alerts the reader from the story's beginning to the importance of its setting in the nation's financial capital in New York as well as in buildings whose inhabitants are oppressively surrounded by walls. The lawyer/narrator describes his quarters as having windows at either end, offering close-up views of walls: one set looks onto a white wall, "deficient in what landscape painters call 'life,'" while the other "commanded an unobstructed view of a lofty brick wall, black by age and everlasting shade" and, given the proximity of neighboring buildings, appeared to open into "a huge square cistern" (14). In the law office, Bartleby's desk is separated from the other desks in the office, screened off from his employer's, and placed before a small side window that gives "no view at all" (19); to his employer's consternation, he takes to standing here, as if mirroring his surroundings, in a "dead-wall revery" (29, 31). Although the lawyer believes the screen allows Bartleby and himself a combination of "privacy and society" (19), it is apparent to the reader that Bartleby's "society" must be found with himself alone. From the opening description of the law chambers to the closing description of New York's Halls of Justice and House of Detention, known as the Tombs, walls function in Melville's story to immobilize and isolate, to oppress and imprison individuals. "Uncle Christopher's" also opens with a painterly description of a still-life, one monolithically white:

> The night was intensely cold, but not dismal, for all the hills and meadows, all the steep roofs of the farm-houses, and the black roof of the barns, were white as snow could make them. The haystacks looked like high, smooth heaps of snow, and the fences, in their zigzag course across the fields, seemed made of snow too, and half the trees had their limbs encrusted with the pure white. (67) . . . All the shawls and muffs in Christendom could not avail against such a night—so still, clear, and intensely cold. The very stars seemed sharpened against the ice, and the white moonbeams slanted earthward, and pierced our faces like thorns—. . . yet the wind did not blow, even so much as to stir one flake of snow from the bent boughs. (68–69)

Although the setting soon shifts to the interior of Uncle Christopher's house, the freezing cold does not abate—its immobilizing persistence has a physical as well as an emotional effect—and life for some indeed proves dismal. On entering her uncle's house, the narrator finds herself in a large room "with a low ceiling, and bare floor, and so open about the windows and doors, that the slightest movement of the air without would keep the candle flame in motion, and chill those who were not sitting nearest the fire" (72–73). This is a house whose occupants move in darkness and in cold, with the light from its few candles and the warmth of its fire absorbed by its patriarch, Uncle Christopher. Abandoned by her father in this house, the narrator can only express her dismay: "I felt as if I were to be imprisoned" (75). Both the lawyer's office and Uncle Christopher's farmhouse, evoking sterility and confinement, prepare the reader for narratives where paralysis and oppression prevail.

Michael Paul Rogin, Michael Gilmore, and David Kuebrich have argued cogently that the lawyer's office in "Bartleby" reflects the changing modes of production in antebellum America, from a household system characterized by master-apprentice relationships, to a capitalistic enterprise characterized by hierarchical, impersonal relationships in which profit and property became dominant goals (Rogin 192–201, Gilmore 134–35, Kuebrich 385). Rogin, noting that the "lawyer's title, Master in Chancery, evokes the personal ties of dependence between master and apprentice," points out that antebellum employers and their supporters defended "workplaces as families" although the "routinization of work undermined the familially based set of master-apprentice relations" (194, 196). Melville's lawyer-narrator, perhaps acknowledging the absence of such familial associations that distinguished America's earlier office arrangements in his own workplace, recognizes that an office's lack of those "humanizing domestic associations" can lead a man to commit murder (36). Yet his social anxieties and ambitions repeatedly undermine his concern to introduce such "humanizing domestic associations" into the office and ultimately lead—if not to murder—then to Bartleby's untimely death. Although the workplace in "Uncle Christopher's" is a family farm, there is a complete dearth of any such "humanizing domestic associations." By demonstrating the devastation caused by substituting productivity for nurturing relationships in this setting, Cary harshly indicts the demand for industrial and capitalistic procedures.

The lawyer identifies himself as "an elderly man" (13), "somewhere not far from sixty" (15), and Uncle Christopher is described as "a tall muscular man of sixty or thereabouts" (71). These two men of similar age were socialized in an earlier, less industrialized time, but, as their narratives reveal, their behavior indicates their response to a class-conscious and capitalistic culture. From the second paragraph of "Bartleby," the lawyer informs the reader, by emphasizing the first-person pronoun, that he is master and owner of the workplace: "it is fit I make some mention of myself, my *employés*, my business, my chambers, and general surroundings" (13). Cary indicates Uncle Christopher's position on his farm from her story's title, emphasizing both his prominence and, through the title's open-ended possessive, the comprehensiveness of his ownership—the farm and all on it, both human and nonhuman, are ostensibly his property. His surname, Wright, suggests that he is, in the Oxford English Dictionary's definition, "an artificer or handicraftsman, especially a constructive workman." But as Cary emphasizes repeatedly throughout her story, not only does he believe he is the rightful master by legal, theological, and social right, but he has also ordained himself the righteous judge of and for all who exist on his property. In his immediate family's eyes and in his own eyes, he establishes the rites of the household; his is the right, and he is always right.

Throughout both stories, the lawyer and Uncle Christopher are represented as fathers, employers, and respectable men of society. In describing the treatment of the employees/family members by the employer/patriarch in the office/household, Melville and Cary reveal the full dysfunctionality in American relationships—among family members and between classes.[3] Managing others through a combination of implacable logic, sarcasm, and threats, neither the lawyer nor Uncle Christopher shows any knowledge of those beneath him in the hierarchy of relationships, and, more disturbingly, neither—until it is too late—shows any compassion.

Both men profess religious convictions, but their hypocrisy rapidly proves transparent and opprobrious. Melville's lawyer attends church on Sunday, but it appears he does so primarily "to hear a celebrated preacher," and he cannot resist dropping by his office on the way (26); he recalls Christ's injunction that "ye love one another," but with cynical logic and to his own satisfaction goes on to establish that only "self-love" prompts charity (36). Cary's narrator explains with grim satire that Uncle Christopher "was one of those infatuated men who fancy themselves 'called' to be teachers of religion, though he had neither talents, education, nor anything else to warrant such a notion, except a faculty for joining pompous and half scriptural phrases, from January to December" (73). The actions of both the lawyer and Uncle Christopher, motivated by narcissism, class-consciousness, and capitalistic goals, speak louder than their sanctimonious words, which serve mainly to promote their reputations.

The lawyer's apparent paternalistic attention to his employees' eating habits and his concern that Turkey be well clothed and that Bartleby not be reduced to vagrancy indicate that their employer attempts to maintain relationships in his office characteristic of earlier modes of production; it thus is possible to support Edwin Haviland Miller's position that on occasion the lawyer "acts as a nurturing parent to his clerks" (263). This parental position is contradicted, however, when he expresses his satisfaction at Bartleby's appearing "long famished for something to copy," at his not pausing "for digestion" in his work, and at his seeming "to gorge himself on my documents" (19). His ostensible paternal intent also seems primarily a concern for respectability. He reproves Turkey for his "indecorous manner" (15) and thinks well of Nippers for being "not deficient in a gentlemanly sort of deportment," for being "always dressed in a gentlemanly sort of way" (17). He wants his clerks to present themselves in respectable clothes so as to "[reflect] credit upon my chambers" (17). Complaining that Nippers consorts with "ambiguous looking fellows in seedy coats," he presents Turkey, whose coats he calls "execrable" and whose "hat is not to be handled," with one of his own cast-off garments, one that he still deems "a highly-respectable looking coat" (17). However, he subsequently cannot resist a condescending evaluation of Turkey in this second-hand apparel, in judging him as "insolent" and one "whom prosperity harmed" (18), though he fails to recognize the degree to which these judgments may apply to himself.

Early in his story the lawyer reveals his values through his idolatry of John Jacob Astor, whom Stephen Zelnick assesses as notorious "for monopoly power, for the destruction of the values of the community, for political corruption, for the emergence of an arrogant new aristocracy of wealth, for large-scale theft cloaked by the shrewd manipulation of the law, . . . and for the restructured social relations that reduced a significant portion of Americans to wage slavery and economic dependence" (75). The narrator "loves" the sound of Astor's name because it "rings like unto bullion," and he himself claims to have made "a snug business among rich men's bonds and mortgages and title-deeds" (14), a business that has, to his smug pleasure, permitted him to use the wealth of others to secure his own wealth and to separate himself from social responsibilities. He not only acknowledges the superior class and authority of Astor but also is susceptible to the opinions of his readers, with whom he identifies in the opening paragraph as "good-natured gentlemen" (13). In addition he is anxious regarding the effect Bartleby's bizarre appearance in his chambers might have on his "professional reputation" (38) and the possibility "of [his] being exposed in the papers" (40). Robert K. Martin summarizes Melville's lawyer's position succinctly: he is "too convinced of his own generosity to see the evil and inhumanity of the system in which he participates. His situation illustrates the sterility of a law divorced from morality. His dilemma is that of the 'good boss' whose integrity is inevitably compromised. He is a jailer who can never understand that even good treatment of a prisoner cannot alleviate the fundamental fact of imprisonment" (105).

Melville's respectable lawyer, perhaps because of his urban location, appears more sensitive to the judgment of others and the matter of class than does the more isolated, rural Uncle Christopher, for whom his own patriarchal authority is primary, with class being secondary. The narrator of "Uncle Christopher's," a young, unmarried woman whose own father pressures and manipulates her into leaving her comfortable home to journey out into the frozen landscape to visit her uncle and then abandons her at his farm, is understandably judgmental of patriarchal authority. She rapidly discovers on her arrival that

Uncle Christopher's attitude toward his six daughters, who, like herself, are all unmarried, and toward his two young wards, Mark and Andrew, is not that of a nurturing parent but of a repressive taskmaster and social arbiter. Using her representation of Uncle Christopher to question a self-absorbed individualism in relation to domestic ideology as well as the impact of rising class-consciousness and changing modes of production in rural America, Cary indicates that this self-reliant man is his own sole authority: "As a matter of form, Uncle Christopher always said, I will do so or so, 'Providence permitting'; but he felt competent to do anything and everything on his own account" (76). Though his wife may regard him "not only as the man of the house, but also as the man of all the world" (75) and worship his "gift" of words, the narrator reveals the narcissism behind his heinous sadism.

As a parent, guardian, and host, Uncle Christopher provides the bare minimum. Cary's narrator describes meals at Uncle Christopher's as occasions for him to dominate: "To the coarse fare before us we all helped ourselves in silence, except of the bread, and that was placed under the management of Uncle Christopher, and with the same knife he used in eating, slices were cut as they were required" (77). Mark, the youngest of Uncle Christopher's wards, returning late to the farm, finds that "the supper was served and removed, and not even the tea was kept by the fire for him. It was long after dark when he came, cold and hungry—but nobody made room at the hearth, and nobody inquired . . . what he had seen or heard during the day" (85).

The boys are dressed poorly, while the women are all dressed plainly and "precisely alike, in gowns of brown flannel, and coarse leather boots, with blue woollen stockings, and small capes, of red and yellow calico" (71). The narrator's description of Uncle Christopher's care for his own clothes and appearance, however, testifies to his personal vanity and fashion-consciousness: he was "dressed in what might be termed [a] stylish homespun coat, trowsers, and waistcoat, of snuff-colored cloth. His cravat was of red-and-white-checked gingham" (71). Although he greets the narrator by informing her that "earrings and finger-rings, and crisping pins" are "abominable" (72), he himself is much given to personal affectations, keeping a "long grizzly beard, which he wore in full" and combing his hair "straight from his forehead, and turn[ing it] over in one even curl on the back of the neck" (71). Although he judges women's pursuit of fashion as "foolish" and "unprofitable" (72), "much time and some money he spent in [the] vindication" (72–73) of his own mode of dress. If the lawyer signifies his authority in his office by his plaster-of-paris bust of Cicero, Uncle Christopher signifies it in his household not only by "monopoliz[ing] a good portion of the light, and all the warmth" but also by the "stout hickory stick" that he holds phallicly between his knees (71–72).

Both men, representatives of earlier business arrangements, have agreed to take on young apprentices, although Melville and Cary imply that these traditional arrangements are subverted through the masters' commitment to aggrandizing their own profit and status. Thus the twelve-year-old Ginger Nut, whose father, "a carman, ambitious of seeing his son on the bench instead of a cart . . . [sent him to the narrator's] office as student at law, errand boy, and cleaner and sweeper, at the rate of one dollar a week" (18), receives no instruction whatsoever from the lawyer. Instead, on his own, Ginger Nut learns to become an independent "cake and apple purveyor" to the other scriveners. Andrew and Mark, Uncle Christopher's wards, the former, "a relation from . . . Indiana, who, for feeding and milking Uncle Christopher's cows morning and evening, and [tending to] the general oversight of affairs, . . . enjoyed the privilege of attending the district school," and the latter, his grandson, regarded as "a wicked and troublesome boy, [who was being] subjected to the chastening influences of a righteous discipline" (76), become wage slaves in his household and learn only misery.

The lawyer claims he would have enjoyed Bartleby's being "cheerfully industrious" as he goes about the "dull, wearisome, lethargic" business of copying, but Bartleby, preferring not to be a happy wage slave, performs "silently, palely, mechanically" (20). Silence is emphatically maintained in Uncle Christopher's shop. As he "talked, and talked, and talked" (73), he determines when others may or may not speak. The narrator comments repeatedly on the prevalence of silence in this household and the absence of laughter. Declaring imperiously that "much speech in woman is as the crackling of thorns under a pot" (72) and that "it is better to dwell in the corner of the housetop, than with a brawling woman" (75), Uncle Christopher enforces silence from the women in his family in particular. His command to his wife—"Woman, fret not thy gizzard!" (81)—in response to her momentary lapse into sympathetic self-expression, might be considered comic were it not so vicious. In this household, words are not spoken but recited mechanically, and the mew of a kitten is regarded as an interruption. Uncle Christopher's voice thus becomes more than dominant here. The narrator, who finds that "the shut mouths and narrow foreheads of the seven women grew hateful," ultimately breaks the silence imposed on them all by telling their story and the story of this household.

To a degree, as indicated above, the lawyer accommodates his scriveners in managing his workplace. In consideration of Turkey's age, the same as his own, he retains him in service. It can also be argued that he paternally runs his office according to the humors of his two copyists, permitting Nippers' morning dyspepsia to balance Turkey's afternoon alcoholic paroxysms.

However, Melville demonstrates that the lawyer keeps his distance from his employees, removing himself from them by screening himself from Bartleby, by referring to his three long-time employees only by their nicknames, and by reducing Turkey to servility at the thought of his possible dismissal. Pleading his case by observing that he and the lawyer are the same age, Turkey introduces his claim three times with the phrase, "With submission, sir" (16), indicating his sensitivity to his employer's need to feel empowered as well as his own powerlessness. The lawyer confirms his conviction of his own superiority, control, and ownership of his employees by evaluating them in the degree that they are "valuable" (15) or "useful" (17, 23) to him.

As critics also frequently note, by accommodating his scriveners' humors, he guarantees the mechanical production of efficient, rapid, and uniform copies. In describing this procedure, the lawyer indicates that he runs his office with mechanical and military efficiency: "Their fits relieved each other like guards. When Nippers' was on, Turkey's was off, and *vice versa*." With self-satisfaction, he concludes that "this was a good natural arrangement" (18). Although his methods cause his office to malfunction, the lawyer fails to note that nothing at all "natural" exists in any of the arrangements in his workplace; and despite his ostensible attempts to accommodate his workers, he manages only to create a malfunctioning human machine in his office, transforming the labor of two men into that of one and depriving them both of individual dignity.

There is no degree of accommodation in the factory into which Uncle Christopher has converted his home. As patriarch and boss, he is, until the story's conclusion, a hard-driving, single-minded proto-capitalist, unlike the lawyer who occasionally expresses concern for his scriveners. Unstinting routinization, mechanization, uniformity, and silence, however, determine the lives of the inhabitants at Uncle Christopher's. Despite his proclamations of his competence and self-reliance, he is never shown as a "constructive workman." It is apparent that the women and children tend to the entire work of the household. We read that "in the genial warmth [of the fireplace] sat Uncle Christopher, doing nothing" (76), or "the family rose before daylight, and moved about by the tallow candles, and prepared breakfast, while Uncle Christopher sat in the great arm-chair, and Mark and Andrew fed the cattle by the light of a lantern" (84). The toll this work takes on the women of the household is evident as it consumes their individuality and humanity; on her arrival at the farm the narrator notes that they "so closely resembl[ed] each other, that one could not tell them apart; not even the mother from the daughters. . . . All seven were very slender, very straight, and very tall; all had dark complexions, black eyes, low foreheads, straight noses, and projecting teeth; . . . They had staid, almost severe, expressions of countenances, and scarcely spoke during the evening. By one corner of the great fireplace they huddled together, each busy with knitting, and all occupied with long blue stockings, advanced in nearly similar degrees toward completion" (71). While the indolent Uncle Christopher delivers "a homily on the beauty of industry" the morning after her arrival, the narrator observes the women in his family take up their tasks, "untwist[ing] seven skeins of blue yarn, which they wound into seven blue balls, and each at the same time beg[inning] the knitting of seven blue stockings" (78, 79). The seven women at Uncle Christopher's become parts of a smoothly functioning machine.

With the exception of Mrs. Wright and her youngest daughter, these women are denied any trace of individuality: they have neither names nor voices, with Uncle Christopher addressing his daughters in the collective as "maidens" or "the daughters of our house." Embodying all the primary virtues of the Cult of True Womanhood—piety, purity, submission, and domesticity—they become in Uncle Christopher's house not the angels who inhabit the houses of other antebellum writers but caricatures of womanhood. In this household, those who dare to express themselves are suppressed into conformity. Andrew, dismayed by Mark's ill treatment, reverts to a mechanical reading of dictionary definitions; Mrs. Wright conceals her instinct for kindness in "obsequious servility" (81) to her lord and master. The narrator, a guest in this stultifying household, feels pressured into working "diligently all the day, though [she] fail[s] to see the use or beauty of the work on which [she] was engaged" (79). Thus, as she notes, life here becomes a commitment to silent, mechanical, and uniform production: "There was no variableness in the order of things at Uncle Christopher's, but all went regularly forward without even a casual observation, and to see one day, was to see the entire experience in the family" (75).

All the wheels do not run smoothly, however, in the machinery of the lawyer's office and of Uncle Christopher's factory-household. The lawyer's office, in which two men do the job of one, clearly is not a model of efficiency. However, Bartleby and Mark, new additions to their workforces, reveal the more serious flaws of these proto-capitalistic sites to the reader. Bartleby ultimately prefers not to work and not to speak to the lawyer. Mark tells the narrator that he does not like his grandfather, and, as she observes, "he was, for the most part, sulky and sullen, and did reluctantly that which he had to do, and no more" (83–84). Though Bartleby is described as "a young man" (19) and Mark as a boy of ten or twelve, both seem old for their years. Cary's narrator, while repeatedly emphasizing the importance of play, laughter, and love in a child's life, informs the reader that Mark is forced into early manhood: he is described as acting "manfully" (70, 81); he is "thoughtful beyond his years" (74); and "in all ways he was expected to have the wisdom of a man—to rise as early, and sit up as late, endure the heat and cold as well, and perform nearly as much labor" (83). Slight in stature, both Bartleby and Mark border on physical starvation. Bartleby must feed himself but has little money for food, and in the last stages of his life, when food is placed before him, he chooses to eat nothing at all, whereas Mark is consistently deprived of nourishment.[4]

Initially both Bartleby and Mark seem determined to belong to the company team. They want to be considered respectable and to rise socially. On first meeting Bartleby, the lawyer notices that he was "pallidly neat, pitiably respectable, incurably forlorn" (19).[5] Bartleby's persistent defiance, to his employer's surprise, remains devoid of "uneasiness, anger, impatience or impertinence" (21). Whether understood in political, psychological, or philosophical terms, whether interpreted as a statement of self-assertion or passive resistance in the guise of deference, Bartleby's "I prefer not to," as much as Turkey's "With submission, sir," emanates from polite society. Acknowledging that Bartleby was "an eminently decorous person," the lawyer cannot imagine that his scrivener would "violate the proprieties" of Sunday by working—although he has no apparent qualms about doing so himself (27). However, as if to assure himself of Bartleby's respectability, the lawyer actually scrutinizes and itemizes his scrivener's pitiable attempts to keep up appearances: "Rolled away under his desk, I found a blanket; under the empty grate, a blacking box and brush; on a chair, a tin basin, with soap and a ragged towel" (27). Rooting more deeply among Bartleby's belongings, and justifying his voyeuristic actions by asserting, "the desk is mine, and its contents too" (28), the lawyer finds a savings' bank. Evidence of the scrivener's determination to survive economically and perhaps of his desire to rise socially, the bank would provide him the means for improving his "pitiably respectable" appearance. Yet the lawyer will later refer deprecatingly to Bartleby's belongings as "his beggarly traps" (33). Bartleby's endeavors to maintain a standard of social respectability the lawyer scorns by sarcastically referring to his "cadaverously gentlemanly *nonchalance*" (27), and when the gaoler at the Tombs suspects that Bartleby is "a gentleman forger," he is quick to disassociate himself from Bartleby, superciliously asserting that he "was never socially acquainted with any forgers" (44). This remark may have an ironic rebound in that copying originals, the work carried on by Bartleby and his fellow scriveners, is legal "forgery." In this sense, in dismissing Bartleby from his social register and from society at large, the lawyer is unknowingly critiquing himself and his profession even as he denies a relationship with his scriveners.[6]

While Bartleby at least initially manifests a commitment to maintain the appearance of respectability and to participate in a society organized by production, Mark actively attempts to pull himself up by his economic bootstraps into social respectability, with results as pitiable and futile as the scrivener's. Knowing that "money buys new things" (75), he struggles through chores and through small sales to earn a little, but he loses his earnings, once because of his own naïveté to some older boys and once because of his uncle's taking it from him as a fatuous and arbitrary moral lesson. Mark's disappointment in losing his hard-earned cash, as he explains to the sympathetic narrator, derives from the specific fact that "once he had enough money to buy ever so many clothes" (83). Appreciative of the linen the narrator hems, which he notes is "fine and pretty," and acutely sensitive to his own "homely and ill-fitting garments," he grieves that he cannot leave his present status because of his lack of appropriate and respectable dress (85, 83). In this rural setting, although Mark may express "those finer feelings which are deemed the blossoms of high and fashionable culture," that his desires are literally so dependent on fashion suggests their desperation and limitation. Unlike Cary's narrator, who has created art from her restricted surroundings, he chooses a much lower option.

Dependent on their economic and social superiors, both Bartleby and Mark are suppressed in their position of social inferiors; consequently emotional starvation shapes their psyches as physical starvation shapes their physiques. Though Bartleby does not suffer the sadistic extremes of physical cruelty from his boss that Mark does from his grandfather—isolation outside in freezing temperatures, deprivation of food, whippings, incessant verbal abuse and humiliation—he is, like Mark, subjected to psychological cruelty. Both Bartleby and Mark must know that they are evaluated in relation to property rather than as human beings. Thus, the lawyer not only perceives his scrivener as "a valuable acquisition" (26) and "a millstone" (32) but also tries to buy him off (33) and seeks to dislodge him by demanding, "What earthly right have you to stay here? Do you pay any rent? Do you pay my taxes? Or is this property yours?" (35). Mark, too, is conscious that his failure to produce income is directly responsible for his suffering. Because his earlier naïveté resulted in the loss of his earnings, he was punished by being sent to his grandfather. When he subsequently demonstrates his ability to earn money, however, his grandfather, instead of praising him, claims Mark's money for his own self-promoting and sanctimonious projects.

Melville and Cary also represent Bartleby and Mark in positions similar to those of women in antebellum America, thus challenging gender construction as well as domestic ideology. Melville's sisters, Augusta and Helen;

his wife, Lizzie; and for some of his later writings, his daughters, Fanny and Bessie, toiled to produce legible copy from his manuscripts. Melville, consequently, was familiar with the plaints of the women scriveners in his own household, engaged in the endless reproduction of his words, a point Elizabeth Renker discusses in *Strike Through the Mask: Herman Melville and the Scene of Writing*.[7] Even though, as Renker's argument implies, he might have understood the lawyer's frustrations with Bartleby's resistance, he writes in sympathy with the working women in *Pierre, or the Ambiguities*, his novel of 1852,[8] and with the women operatives in "The Paradise of Bachelors and the Tartarus of Maids," his story of 1855. In a single explicit reference in "Bartleby" to the lawyer's cleaning woman who lives in the attic over his chambers (26),[9] Melville also shows his sensitivity to the limitations imposed on lower-class women in his day. Reduced to subservient positions as domestics, poor women without families become nameless drudges and, like Bartleby, eke out solitary existences in their workplaces.

Both Patricia Barber in her neglected 1977 essay, "What If Bartleby Were a Woman?" and Gillian Brown in her 1987 essay, "The Empire of Agoraphobia," provocatively feminize Melville's scrivener, allowing readers to perceive him in the housebound context of antebellum American womanhood. Barber associates the passivity of Bartleby's resistance with a general concept of femininity,[10] whereas Brown explicitly identifies his immobility with a nineteenth-century agoraphobia associated with women's private sphere: "Reproducing the enclosure and stillness of home in the deportment of the individual, agoraphobia approximates domesticity, often proclaimed the nineteenth-century antidote to commercialism. . . . Bartleby presents an extreme version of such a model: in his 'long-continued motionlessness' he achieves an 'austere reserve,' the ideal of domesticity within Wall Street" (142). The silence that Bartleby maintains in the lawyer's presence may be interpreted as a response to the oppression of his work and of his environment as well as to the absence of communication in the office; it also mirrors the silence imposed on women in antebellum patriarchal households such as Uncle Christopher's.

In addition, Bartleby's habitual tidiness, in conjunction with his endeavor to set up housekeeping in the lawyer's office, displays the domestic inclinations expected by the dictates of the Cult of True Womanhood. When the lawyer inadvertently discovers Bartleby in "a strangely tattered dishabille" (26) at the door of his office, and apparently in charge and at home, he feels himself "unmanned" (27) and unable to answer Bartleby's mildness with the vigor—and possibly the violence—that he might use in responding to another man. This evident gender anxiety leads him not only to speculation about the possibility of Bartleby's appearing "in a state approaching to nudity" (27)[11] but also to his proprietary and voyeuristic investigation into his scrivener's paltry belongings. His masculinity thus threatened, the lawyer responds with gestures signifying his determination to categorize humanity by gender as well as by class and to dominate those his class consciousness authorizes him to deem beneath him—women and his employees. Although Melville would deconstruct gender categories in his creation of Bartleby, his narrator, in his anxiety, vigorously reconstructs them.

Mark's determination to progress socially and economically, in resembling that of other young men, differentiates him from the passivity of Uncle Christopher's daughters.[12] He is, however, aligned with the "finer feelings" of sentiment—a feminine gender attribute entirely repressed in them. Like Bartleby, he also exacerbates the desire of a powerful male to manage and control his life. Ostensibly attempting to eradicate the feminine in him and to make a "man" of him, Uncle Christopher literally seeks to freeze the boy's sensitivities; he treats Mark's frostbitten fingers and toes, cracked and bleeding from his ostracism in the barn, by sending him back out into the snow; he requires the destruction of the kitten Mark had tenderly placed in an old hat by the kitchen fire by demanding that he throw the creature into an old stone well. As Bartleby sabotages his boss's demands through feminine passivity and silence, Mark sabotages his master's demands, but through feminine action and sentiment. He saves the kitten with fierce resolve; acting maternally, he contrives the means of placing the creature, smaller and more defenseless than he, on a secure ledge in the well and shares his meager helpings of bread with it. Mark also circumvents his grandfather's insistence on ostracism and his command for silence. With Andrew and with the narrator, whose empathy and affection for the boys dissolves class and gender differences, and unlike the forlorn Bartleby, he discovers the "delight of communicating . . . his little joys and sorrows" (82), of sociability among those he trusts as they work together over domestic chores.

In challenging an oppressive economic, class, and gender system, both Bartleby's and Mark's protests are ineffectual in so far as their own lives are concerned.[13] Melville and Cary leave the nature of their deaths open-ended, allowing readers to consider the possibility that Bartleby and Mark finally choose suicide as the sole means by which they can ameliorate their situations. Betrayed by their surrogate fathers, their employers, and the men in their lives, they reject them unconditionally and die in the process. Bartleby dies in the cisternlike Tombs, "strangely huddled at the base of the wall, his knees drawn up, and lying on his side, his head touching the cold stones" (44). Mark, rather than the kitten, dies at the bottom of the stony farmhouse well. Only in their deaths do the men responsible for their well-being cross class and gender lines to reach out in gestures of love: the narrator touches Bartleby as he lies in what is clearly a fetal position, and Uncle Christopher "lifted the lifeless form of the boy into his arms, where he had never reposed before" (89).

When it is too late, when Bartleby and Mark are dead and imagistically infantilized, both Melville and Cary tug at the reader's sentimental chords. Through the sentimental words with which he concludes the scrivener's story—"Ah Bartleby! Ah humanity!" (45)—as well as through the penance of his telling the story itself, the lawyer may exorcise Bartleby's pale ghost and his own guilt.[14] Cary's Uncle Christopher—now "softened and contrite" (89)—is described as more overtly repenting; yet, ever conscious of his appearance, he ostentatiously orders the costliest of coffins for the poor boy's burial. The turn toward sentimentality in the conclusions of both "Bartleby, the Scrivener" and "Uncle Christopher's" does not dispel the inequities and oppressions generated by the development of a capitalistic production system and its accompanying domestic ideology. It does, however, suggest both Melville's and Cary's anxieties for what has been lost and what possibly may be retrieved: loving and respectful relationships among men, between parents and children, and between men and women—at home and at work.

Notes

1. Although Cary moved with her sister Phoebe from Ohio to New York in 1850, there is no evidence that she and Melville, who visited New York regularly during the 1850s, met during this decade. However, Melville moved his family to New York in 1863, and as Charles Hemstreet, editor of *Literary New York*, recorded in his memoirs, Melville attended the Carys' popular Sunday-evening salon in 1865, where he felt relaxed enough in their company to give a thrilling account of his seafaring days. See Leyda 2: 676–77; Robertson-Lorant 485–86; Fetterley, *Provisions* 218. It is also worth noting that the house Melville acquired for his family in 1863, formerly belonging to his brother whom he had visited regularly prior to his purchasing it, was on East 26th Street, as was the Cary home, making them fairly close neighbors.

2. Fetterley, citing the implications of this same passage, writes that "Cary's characters experience the press of tyranny not only from parents, to whom law and custom give authority over children, but also from a class system which ensures that some people will get more than others and which identifies certain desires as being out of bounds for certain persons" ("Entitled to More" 110).

3. Fetterley maintains that throughout the *Clovernook* stories Cary "identifies the primacy of class as an operative category in supposedly democratic America." She notes, in particular, that "in asserting the primacy of class as the organizing principle of social relations in America, ... Cary organizes the family as well, parents and children occupying in effect different classes" ("Entitled to More" 103).

4. Gillian Brown argues that Bartleby's refusal to eat is comparable to the behavior of an anorexic: "almost always a woman. . . . She maintains in her body the fantasy of domesticity Bartleby enacts: a perfect self-enclosure. While anorexia hardly seems an ideal condition, it is the fulfillment of the ideal of domestic privacy, a state in which complete separation from the demands and supplies of the world is attained" (145).

5. Remembering "the bright silks and sparkling faces I had seen that day, in gala trim, swan-like sailing down the Mississippi of Broadway"—a vision of wealth and style testifying to capitalistic success—the narrator expresses his own melancholy and alienation from society, thus momentarily identifying with Bartleby and concluding, "For both I and Bartleby were sons of Adam" (28). It is noteworthy, however, that although the sons of Adam, generically, are all men, of his immediate offspring, one was Cain.

6. See note 51 in Haskell Springer's hypertext edition of "Bartleby" at raven.cc.ku.edu/~zeke/bartleby.

7. Elizabeth Renker notes that "Bartleby" was copied by Augusta. More significantly, she discusses the stress that copying duties placed upon the Melville women, citing a letter from Lizzie to her stepmother dated 3 Aug. 1851: "I cannot write any more—it makes me terribly nervous—I don't know as you can read this I have scribbled it so" (*Strike Through the Mask* 64–65).

8. When Pierre moves to the city, in financial destitution, he becomes dependent on the services of three women—Delly, Isabel, and Lucy—even as they are dependent on him.

9. She may be connected to the mad women discussed in Gilbert and Gubar.

10. Barber asks her readers to imagine Bartleby as a woman secretary in a modern office and, subsequently, writes her essay with "Miss Bartleby" in mind (212–23).

11. Although Barber also calls attention to the erotic undertones in the story (217, 219), she completely skirts the issue of homosexuality, indeed giving a decided homophobic cast to her essay: "If little of this erotic quality seems apparent in the tale of the male Bartleby, there are, I think, two explanations—one, that the lawyer's propriety and language tend to lead us away from seeing that element, and two, the more important, that we simply do not expect to find a man having an erotic feeling for another man, no matter how familiar we are with Melville's scene of Ishmael and Queequeg in bed" (221–22).

12. Fetterley asserts that in *Clovernook*, "Being male or female does not give one more or less chance of escaping rustic circumstances" ("Entitled to More" 105).

13. Martin argues that "Bartleby the wage slave of meaningless work can only triumph by destroying himself" (105), and Rogin notes that "Bartleby punishes the lawyer by punishing himself" (195). Brown sees that "in the logic of anorexia's perfection of agoraphobia," Bartleby's death is "the best method of self-preservation" (148).

14. Barbara Foley maintains in "From Wall Street to Astor Place" that "the lawyer's irrational clinging to the scrivener—'him whom I had so longed to be rid of' (39)—takes shape not only as a subliminal recognition of his felt moral implication in the scrivener's fate but also, we may speculate, as a covert expression of the author's own implication in the fates of those who died at Astor Place" (109).

"Tender Kinswoman"

Gail Hamilton and Gendered Justice in *Billy Budd*

Wyn Kelley

*I*n the courtroom scene of *Billy Budd, Sailor* (1891), when Captain Vere rhetorically asks his officers if an "upright judge," even in an onshore trial, could admit the influence of a "tender kinswoman of the accused seeking to touch him with her tearful plea," Melville's reference to a weeping woman stands out in stark relief against the story's military and masculine field (111). The presence of a woman in the scene, even one invoked as a figure to be "ruled out," seems an intrusion. Yet during the same years in which Melville composed his story, Gail Hamilton, in her "The Murder of Philip Spencer" (1889), revisited the *Somers* affair of 1842, commonly thought of as a source for *Billy Budd*. And whereas Melville hesitated to introduce a loving kinswoman into his story of mutiny and murder at sea, Hamilton invited her readers to imagine Philip Spencer's mother brokenhearted and collapsing in grief. Her three-part narration appeared in *Cosmopolitan* magazine in the summer of 1889, while Melville was revising and expanding his manuscript. Although the two works differ noticeably in tone, style, and seeming intent, both take remarkably complementary stances in relation to vexing questions of justice, gender, and the instability of the texts that underwrite them. Examining *Billy Budd* next to Hamilton's treatment of the *Somers* mutiny suggests that Melville might have responded with considerable sympathy to a text radically different from his own. He may even have woven some of Hamilton's strands into his manuscript.

If he did, he would have complicated an already intricate text. Harrison Hayford and Merton M. Sealts Jr. unveiled *Billy Budd*'s many layers of complexity in their 1962 edition, and their painstaking reconstruction of Melville's writing, copying, and revision remains essentially unchallenged today.[1] In their widely accepted reading of the manuscript, they argue that Melville first wrote the ballad that now concludes the novella and then built the book in three main stages: beginning with Billy as the main character; developing his antagonist, Claggart, who accuses Billy of fomenting mutiny; and then bringing Captain Vere into the foreground as the morally troubled judge in Billy's trial for murdering Claggart with an unpremeditated blow. In the final pencil revisions, probably still going on at the time of his death in 1891, Melville continued to create doubts about Vere's judgment and handling of Billy's case. The ambiguities swirling around Melville's characterization of Vere have for many readers become the story's most debated points, the source of its enduring significance, and the clear manifestation of Melville's brilliance as a writer.

Without dislodging the Hayford and Sealts framework, I suggest that we still need to know not only *what* Melville did in the late stages of the manuscript but also *why*. Why did Vere become such an important character, and how does he evolve from a "straightforward" captain into a mysterious and conflicted one?[2] In particular, why does Melville make Vere so concerned with the morality of his decisions, taking pains to address the drumhead court's *feelings* about Billy, even if he plans not to consider them? Why does Melville have Vere evoke the sentimental figure of "some tender kinswoman of the accused" (111)? Why muddle the course of maritime justice by drawing attention to "the heart here, sometimes the feminine in man" (111)?

The answer, I believe, has something to do with the resurgence in public interest during the late 1880s in the *Somers* mutiny and in rethinking questions of justice and gender. Decades after the original events of 1842, when Captain Alexander Slidell Mackenzie hanged three crewmembers—one of them, Philip Spencer, the son of the U.S. secretary of war—for allegedly conspiring to mutiny, the case continued to draw sustained criticism and attention. As far as I can ascertain, however, in the large body of nineteenth-century commentary on the *Somers* mutiny Hamilton's "The Murder of Philip Spencer" is the only piece written by a woman. As no author had previously done, she emphasizes the figure of the pleading, interceding mother, as well as issues of childrearing and character, of gender and justice, to make Spencer's death appear not judicious execution of a criminal but murder of an innocent boy. Hers is therefore an energetic intervention into an already heated debate, one that plainly declares Spencer's innocence of the charges and Captain Mackenzie's blame for the unfortunate results. Furthermore, Hamilton's essay offers a striking model of feminist justice by which a reader may judge—and find offensive—the captain's actions. The internal evidence of Melville's much-revised text suggests that he might well have responded to Hamilton's powerful argument against the decisions of a rigid captain who, in her view, not only hanged a harmless youth but also distorted the records of his deeds.

It is important to establish at the start that one cannot prove that Melville read Hamilton's essay or incorporated it into his revisions. The manuscript evidence is tantalizing, however, and does not rule out such a possibility. Leaf 270, in which Vere's reference to the "tender kinswoman" appears, is among the large section of fair-copy pages that Hayford and Sealts identify as stage *Fa*, a late revision.[3] Although Hayford and Sealts explain that "Melville was doing more than his usual amount of revising and composing even while transcribing from the *X* draft to his *Fa* fair copy—that is he was copying even less directly than usual from his earlier version" (263), the leaf is relatively clean. But Melville did revise in pencil, at the stage Hayford and Sealts call "late" (quite possibly after Hamilton's article in 1889), and he did revise the sentence that follows his reference to the "tender kinswoman." The original line reads: "Well the heart here is as that pitious woman. The heart is the feminine in man, and hard tho' it be she must here be ruled out" (395). Melville crossed out the repetitive "The heart is the," circled the words "feminine in man," added a "sometimes the," and moved the whole phrase to its spot after "the heart here" to produce the sentence in Hayford's and Sealts's Reading Text: "Well the heart here, sometimes the feminine in man, is as that piteous woman, and hard though it be, she must here be ruled out" (111).[4] His blending of the brief, definite sentences and his introduction of the "sometimes" soften the rhythms and meaning while qualifying the association between the heart and the feminine in man. One could see this late revision, as John Wenke's argument permits, as introducing another ambiguity into the text. Melville might be saying that men's hearts are not always (only "sometimes") feminine; if so, then ruling out the feminine might be relatively easy, since the feminine was not there to begin with. Or he could be saying that men's hearts are only sometimes feminine and do not automatically plead for mercy. Either reading removes the earlier more categorical assertion that men have feminine hearts: "The heart is the feminine in man." If Melville had not read Hamilton's essay before making this change, one could argue, as Hayford and Sealts imply, that he is simply giving Vere more measured language to heighten the seriousness of the moment. If he had seen Hamilton's work, however—and one can identify a number of reasons why he might have—then he could be showing Vere's failure to acknowledge imperatives that Hamilton's article made clear were human, universal, and just. Contextualizing *Billy Budd* in relation to "The Murder of Philip Spencer" suggests that Melville could have deepened Hamilton's critique of the despotic captain by creating a character at once more sympathetic than Mackenzie and yet more deeply corrupted by his suppressing the feminine justice of the heart.

Did Melville know of "The Murder of Philip Spencer"? The case for Hamilton's influence on *Billy Budd* is old but flawed. Hamilton was first noted as a possible source in Charles Roberts Anderson's 1940 essay, "The Genesis of *Billy Budd*." Although Anderson did not look closely at the connection, his work certainly helped to establish the importance of the *Somers* affair in Melville's story. Melville mentions the mutiny directly in the courtroom scene:

> Not unlikely they were brought to something more or less akin to that harassed frame of mind which in the year 1842 actuated the commander of the U.S. brig-of-war *Somers* to resolve, under the so-called Articles of War, Articles modeled upon the English Mutiny Act, to resolve upon the execution at sea of a midshipman and two sailors as mutineers designing the seizure of the brig. Which resolution was carried out, though in a time of peace and within not many days' sail of home. An act vindicated by a naval court of inquiry subsequently convened ashore. History, and here cited without comment. True, the circumstances on board the *Somers* were different from those on board the *Bellipotent*. But the urgency felt, well-warranted or otherwise, was much the same. (113–14)

Melville had earlier referred to the *Somers* in *White-Jacket* (1850) and later in "Bridegroom Dick," written in the same period (1886–88) when he probably began *Billy Budd*. In his source study, Anderson reviews the facts of the mutiny, in which Philip Spencer was hanged at sea with two supposed confederates for planning to seize the ship, kill Captain Mackenzie, and embark on a career of piracy. Perhaps most significantly, the ship's first lieutenant, who conveyed the story of the plot to Captain Mackenzie, collected the evidence against Spencer, and led the drumhead court, was Melville's first cousin, Guert Gansevoort.[5] Melville might have written the *Somers* mutiny into his story, Anderson argues, because in June 1888 a Lieutenant H. D. Smith published an article, "The Mutiny on the Somers," in the *American Magazine;* according to Anderson, Melville commenced his narrative the following November, stirred by memories of the *Somers*.[6] Smith's 1888 article attempted to restore Mackenzie's good name long after it had been compromised by the court-martial verdict, which was deeply divided, and after the stream of criticisms of Mackenzie's actions, including James Fenimore Cooper's "Review of the Proceedings of the Naval Court Martial" (1844). It is unclear why Lieutenant Smith chose that particular moment to launch his defense, more than forty-five years after the events, but Anderson speculates that Smith's article might have inspired Melville to create in Vere a more fair and even-handed captain than Mackenzie, who in spite of Smith's attempts at restoring his character still bore the taints of earlier criticism. Says Anderson: "And so Melville determined to deal with Billy Budd's commander, whose conduct is pictured as blameless of all the villainy attributed to Mackenzie by Cooper, and possibly whispered in Melville's ear by Gansevoort or picked up from ship's gossip on board the frigate *United States* in 1843. This villainy he incorporated in another character, Claggart, in the much more complicated form of a sadism amounting almost to insanity" (340). In Anderson's reading, Vere is so much more rational than Mackenzie that he appears "blameless"; the insanity that writers like James Gordon Bennett of the *New York Herald* attributed to Mackenzie gets assigned to Claggart in order to resurrect the captain's good name and by implication Guert Gansevoort's.[7]

In this task—of responding to Smith's efforts to bring the *Somers* affair back into the public eye, perhaps of exonerating Gansevoort if not rehabilitating Mackenzie—Anderson suggests that Melville may also have drawn on what Anderson calls a "fictionized version" of the story, Gail Hamilton's "The Murder of Philip Spencer." It is unclear what Anderson means by calling Hamilton's treatment of the subject "fictionized"; her version is certainly less fictional than *Billy Budd*. Hamilton recounts events that would have been familiar to anyone who read the newspapers: the impassioned defenses of Mackenzie (by, for example, Richard Henry Dana), the attacks on him (most notably by Cooper) that followed the court martial, or the published proceedings of the trial, which included Mackenzie's long and fascinating report of the mutiny, including supposed transcriptions of Spencer's words and written statements.[8] Hamilton's account, which appears to rely on Cooper's review of the case and the documents from the court martial, might be called fictional only because it is lavishly illustrated, written in a lively style, and charged with satiric wit, but it is consistent, in its facts certainly, with other nonfictional renderings of the story from the 1840s. Anderson sees it, along with the Smith article, primarily as useful in jogging Melville's memory of events long gone, as "having been of considerable help to him" (340) in creating his characters.

But Anderson's judgment also depends on the sexist critical terminology of his day to stress Hamilton's emotionality and excess, her use of sentimentality to press her point. Perhaps he took exception to her essay because it works strenuously to subvert masculine authority. Whereas Smith seeks to exonerate Mackenzie, Hamilton attacks his decisions and behavior in forceful terms. Anderson calls her essay "melodramatic," rising "to rhapsody" (341) in its climactic moments. For Anderson, Hamilton's article makes the *Somers* affair "at best fit subject matter for melodrama" (345). His reading, by contrast, emphasizes that *Billy Budd* is tragedy; in his view, "Melville heightens the tragedy" of the events by choosing "a quieter, more Greek theme." Anderson's "tragedy," however, requires considerable reworking of Melville's plot: for example, he argues that "Billy Budd, the foundling of obviously noble descent, it is intimated, was the natural son of Captain Edward Fairfax Vere, who was thus faced with the historic dilemma of choosing between patriotic duty and paternal love" (345). Oddly, Anderson does not consider this fanciful reading of Vere as Billy's natural father as either "fictionized" or "melodramatic."

Although Anderson's essay gives one of the earliest considerations of the *Somers* affair as a source for Melville's work, Anderson himself disclaims the study of sources, concluding that "in *Billy Budd*, borrowing is reduced to a minimum, and imaginative invention counts for almost everything that makes it, as one critic declares, a masterpiece in miniature" (346). In spite of Anderson's disclaimer, however, his discovery of Gail Hamilton remains a tremendously important one that has not received sustained attention elsewhere except to be faithfully recorded in Mary K. Bercaw's *Melville's Sources* (146). Hamilton's reopening of the case (or response to Smith, if that is what she intended) does more than provide an intriguing footnote to *Billy Budd*; rather, it brings to bear a feminist ethic and sensibility wholly new in the *Somers* literature. Unlike James Bennett Gordon, who hastily labeled Mackenzie insane, Hamilton at great length and in painstaking detail shows his actions as arising out of a pattern of paranoid authority, high-handed manipulation, and craven panic.[9] Unlike Cooper, who moderated his attack so as not to be accused of professional spite—he and Mackenzie had earlier clashed in public over their different versions of naval history—Hamilton presses her case unstintingly against Mackenzie and his lieutenant, Gansevoort.[10] Indeed, in "The Murder of Philip Spencer," Hamilton's concerns come compellingly close to Melville's own in *Billy Budd*. When read together, Hamilton's and Melville's narratives bring into sharp focus the issue of justice and the extent to which justice is a matter of gender-biased ethical systems.

My framework here is built substantially on the work of Carol Gilligan and feminist moral theory.[11] Gilligan proposes a theory of ethical choice rooted in gender, a model in which a masculinist ethic is governed by rules logically and consensually arrived at through competition, and a feminist ethic operates according to networks of obligation and connection. Masculinist ethics grow out of experiences of vying for mastery, then creating laws by which others may avoid strife. Gilligan calls this system an ethics of justice. In feminist ethics, experiences of nurturance and relationship make maintaining central bonds rather than establishing logical boundaries of behavior the ultimate good. Gilligan identifies this as an ethics of care. Gilligan's work has been criticized because it seems to underwrite essentialist notions of gender identity, but as Wai-chee Dimock perceptively points out, the discovery of such shadings of difference in systems thought to be monolithic—law and science, for example—undermines the perception of them as objective ("Ethics" 513). One may argue over whether the law privileges masculinist logic over femininist responsibility, but once the argument begins, one has stopped recognizing the law as an absolute. Such a recognition of intervention into legal thought is critical for thinking about Hamilton and Melville, for both are concerned with conflicts between head and heart, justice and mercy, authority and love, and the gender implications of each.

If Melville read Hamilton's article, then, he might well have found it a provocative example of feminist ethics at work in a masculinist province—war—and indeed disturbing not only because of its strongly expressed opinions but also because of its closeness to his own personal concerns in writing *Billy Budd*. For Hamilton reminds her readers that no matter how badly Philip Spencer behaved, he should have been forgiven for two important reasons: first, the mutiny never in fact occurred; and second, he was a boy, only a boy, a boy with parents who cared about him. As the father of two sons who died before their time in unusual circumstances, Melville would surely have found this reminder painful.[12] And as someone writing about a boy in the middle of a war, he might have heeded Hamilton's words intently.

We still have no historical evidence, however, that Melville read the article, and before proceeding further with this line of argument, we need to address this difficulty. Anderson did not. He listed Hamilton as a likely source, as others have since, without considering whether Melville would or could have encountered her work. Although Melville was an avid reader of New York newspapers and journals, and especially of any material pertaining to his nautical experience, no evidence exists of his having read or subscribed to either the *American Magazine*, where Lieutenant Smith's article appeared, or the *Cosmopolitan*, source of Hamilton's.[13] And whereas one might assume that Melville would have read Dana's and Cooper's responses in the 1840s, since he knew both authors either personally or by reputation, no one since

1940 seems to have considered whether or not Melville knew Hamilton's work. Perhaps the question does not arise because Hamilton has little contemporary reputation to speak of. But in Melville's day she was a formidable author—widely published, influential, and just a bit scandalous—and he would have had ample opportunity to encounter her writing.

"Gail Hamilton" was the pseudonym of Mary Abigail Dodge (1833–1896), a precocious scholar, teacher, and writer from a large family in Hamilton, Massachusetts.[14] She resolved early in her life not to marry but to dedicate herself to her writing, although ironically such independence was earned by her living in other people's families—notably those of Gamaliel Bailey, editor of the *National Era* (and first publisher of Harriet Beecher Stowe's *Uncle Tom's Cabin*), and of the politician James G. Blaine. Caring for their children nevertheless left her time to write for newspapers on the subjects of gender roles, women's rights, religion, politics, and authorship. Her many books included a novel, *First Love Is Best* (1877); essay collections such as *Country Living and Country Thinking* (1862), *Gala Days* (1863), and *Women's Wrongs: A Counter-Irritant* (1868); biographies (of her mother and of Blaine); religious commentary; and children's books. She was known for her powerful mind, sharp wit, political acumen, and fearlessness in the fray. Fanny Fern called her "a lady, at whose mention stalwart men have been known to tremble, and hide in corners; who 'keeps a private graveyard' for the burial of those whom she has mercilessly slain; who respects neither the spectacles of the judge, nor the surplice of the priest; who holds the mirror up to men's failings till they hate their wives merely because they belong to her sex" (Coultrap-McQuinn, *Literary Business* 106). As feminist, satirist, political commentator, and advocate, she had few peers.

Melville would have had at least two opportunities to learn of Hamilton before "The Murder of Philip Spencer." In 1863 his wife, Lizzie, read Hamilton's magazine essay, "A Spasm of Sense" (later published in *Gala Days*) and pronounced it, in a letter to Melville's sister Fanny, "capital."[15] Hamilton's subject, the treacly inanity of religious tracts that recommend that young mothers sacrifice themselves mindlessly for their children, may have resonated with Lizzie, whose four children at that moment ranged between the ages of eight and fourteen. "Spasm" directly attacks the prevailing separate spheres ideology in the strongest possible terms, arguing that women need not martyr themselves to the home: "Women domesticate themselves to death already. What they want is cultivation" (290–91). And although Hamilton reinscribes the gendered spheres to some extent—"men are blockheads,—dear, and affectionate, and generous blockheads,—benevolent, large-hearted, and chivalrous,—kind, and patient, and hard-working,—but stupid where women are concerned" (290)—she also argues that separation of spheres hurts both genders: "A woman must make herself obvious to her husband, or he will drift out beyond her horizon.... I do not mean that they quarrel, but they will lead separate lives. They will be no longer husband and wife" (289). She calls on women to see through "false masculine notions" and to take responsibility for their welfare into their own hands, because "women have, or ought to have, a more subtle and intimate acquaintance with realities" (298). Characteristically, Hamilton also aims for an androgynous ideal of motherhood, an ethic that recalibrates traditional gender norms: "To be brave, and single-minded, and discriminating, and judicious, and clear-sighted, and self-reliant, and decisive, that is pure womanly. To be womanish is not to be womanly. To be flabby, and plastic, and weak, and acquiescent, and insipid, is not womanly" (298). Abjuring the Christian notion that women must suffer their lot in patient silence, Hamilton declares, "There is no use in suffering, unless you cannot help it; and a good, stout, resolute protest would often be a great deal more wise, and Christian, and beneficial on all sides, than so much patient endurance" (299). Her ideal mother, then, is brave, clear-sighted, and judicious, not teary, passive, and self-sacrificing. It is refreshing to think that Elizabeth Shaw Melville, a woman more thoroughly educated and socially successful than Herman Melville when she married him, but seemingly overwhelmed by her domestic duties afterwards, responded heartily to Hamilton's call for sense.

One should not assume, however, that Melville was wholly a "blockhead." Although Lizzie's breathless letters to her stepmother during her early marriage suggest a scene of generic Victorian domesticity,[16] life at Arrowhead required that the family divide up its tasks along less gender-specific lines. Melville occasionally had to care for his children when Lizzie visited her family; Lizzie and Melville's sisters Augusta and Helen took over the copying and editing of his manuscripts. As I have argued elsewhere in a reading of the cookbook that Melville gave his wife and of his stories of embattled women—especially "Poor Man's Pudding and Rich Man's Crumbs" (1854)—it is possible that Melville sympathized with his wife's ambivalence about domestic duties and oppressive gender roles. If, then, he read Hamilton's essay or absorbed his wife's comments on it, he may have responded to its call for more generous definitions of self than the current gender ideologies offered. It is, of course, possible that Lizzie and perhaps Herman experienced a shock of recognition in reading Hamilton's portrayal of the modern family as a battleground between the sexes: "Who does not know that the private history of families with the ordinary allowance of brains is a record of recurring internecine warfare?" (293). Only four years later their own household would be shattered by the death of their eldest son, Malcolm, most likely a suicide, an event that followed years of tension within the family.[17] Hamilton's portrait of the dangers of Victorian domesticity in "A Spasm of Sense" provides a sadly jarring counterpart to the Melvilles' family life.

Hamilton's career veered into Melville's orbit a second time during a conflict with her editor and Melville's acquaintance, James T. Fields.[18] Fields edited Nathaniel Hawthorne's books and was an enthusiastic participant in the authors' celebrated summer climbs to the top of Monument Mountain in the Berkshires in 1850 and 1851. Hamilton, however, was shocked to find out, after five years of amicable business and personal relations with Fields, that he had been giving her a lower-than-standard percentage of royalties. (Ironically, she discovered this fact because Sophia Hawthorne learned that Fields had apparently been underpaying her husband, too). Although Hamilton's exposé, *The Battle of the Books* (1870), made her little money, and the settlement she finally won was less than she had hoped for, she did succeed in some measure, for she "made a significant contribution to the history of professional (women) writers, and she exposed the Gentleman Publisher's market for what it really was: a relationship based on power, even when conducted as a friendship" (Coultrap-McQuinn, *Literary Business* 134). Likewise Fanny Fern's "fictionalized" version of the same hard truth in *Ruth Hall* (1854) and Melville's in *Pierre* (1852) garnered both authors more notoriety than acclaim. In the battle of the books, Melville could have perceived a spirit as independent as his own, a writer as dedicated to her craft and disillusioned with the publishing world as himself.

We can assume, then, that Melville would most likely have read or heard of an essay on the *Somers* mutiny printed in his own city in 1889 and might well have responded openly to one by the writer who inspired his wife's admiration and perhaps his own sympathy over two previous decades. But even without those historical connections, Hamilton's essay and Melville's story exhibit remarkable parallels in their themes and concerns. For example, although the pivotal figures for both narratives are the captain (Mackenzie or Vere) and the boy (Philip Spencer or Billy Budd), the mother in both accounts takes a secondary but vital role in defining the limits of masculinist justice. In "The Murder of Philip Spencer," Hamilton almost immediately, and in the charged rhetoric of reform and sentimental literature of the period, registers the impact of Spencer's death on his family, beginning with John C. Spencer, secretary of war: "more dreadful tidings never wrung a father's heart or convulsed a nation's capital." While paying tribute to the elder Spencer's "iron nerves" and the "clear mind" that allowed him to command himself and seek "not to avert, but to secure justice," Hamilton quickly makes the reader aware of the "heartbroken" mother, undone by the terrible news (133). Throughout her review of Mackenzie's testimony, moreover, she consistently reads the evidence from the mother's point of view. Young Spencer's "seduction" of and "tampering" with the crew, for example, which Mackenzie saw as a threat to shipboard discipline, Hamilton views as "the crude invention of a boyish fancy that had probably fed somewhat freely on the dime novels of the day" (136). What Mackenzie sees as a conspiratorial encounter between Spencer and shipmate Green, Hamilton dismisses as juvenile play: "Green was engaged in the piratical operation of tattooing love-devices on Spencer's arm—the ravaging arm which was to hew down some dozens of human beings before a week was out!" (136). Where Mackenzie detects a plotter buying off sailors with gifts of money and tobacco, Hamilton shows "a careless, generous boy, with a boy's interest in jack-knife curiosities, and a boy's lavish way of bestowing right and left whatever he had in hand" (137). For Spencer, Hamilton implies, the navy ship is not a sphere separate from the home; motherly anxiety and affection read Philip's actions perpetually in light of his youth and inexperience, which require maternal care rather than paternal discipline. Similarly, Melville's "Baby" Budd, though at twenty-one slightly older than Philip Spencer was at eighteen, seems the youngest and certainly the most naive sailor on both the merchant ship, the *Rights of Man*, and the warship, *Bellipotent*.

In contrast with Spencer's mother in Hamilton's narrative, however, the mother in *Billy Budd* is almost invisible, since as the narrator tells us, Billy has no mother, no family of any kind. "Billy Budd was a foundling, a presumable by-blow, and, evidently, no ignoble one" (52).[19] Whereas most of the other sailors "must have known a hearth of some sort . . . for Billy, as will shortly be seen, his entire family was practically invested in himself" (50). But Billy's mother, though unknown, is nevertheleless visible in Billy's beauty and charm, in "above all, something in the mobile expression, and every chance attitude and movement, something suggestive of a mother eminently favored by Love and the Graces" (51). Thus, although Billy lacks the guiding hand of a loving mother, her presence seems to protect him from within, showing itself in the feminine graces that enhance Billy and make him "a cynosure" (44). Lacking a mother's tuitions, Billy nevertheless seems to have feminine *in*tuitions that closely resemble an ethic of care. In the description of life on *The Rights of Man*, for example, Captain Graveling emphasizes Billy's ability to create a loving community out of the ship's "rat-pit of quarrels" (46). Although Billy finally responds to a series of insults with violence, giving Red Whiskers a "terrible drubbing" (47), he acts not according to logical systems of justice but defensively and childishly, striking at a bully. His sense of responsibility to and connectedness with his shipmates, however, makes him as much a leader as his physical prowess does. "They all love him" (47) and in loving him create an ideal of domestic harmony: "Some of 'em do his washing, darn his old trousers for him; the carpenter is at odd times making a pretty little chest of drawers for him" (47). The *Rights* resembles nothing so much as J. M. Barrie's Neverland in *Peter Pan* (1904), with the sailors as Lost Boys and Billy more a loving Wendy than an irresponsible Peter Pan. And like Spencer, Billy leaves this domestic sphere for a far more violent and volatile place, where an ethic of care has little agency.

Besides invoking an actual mother, Hamilton also uses a woman's point of view to challenge male choices and behavior on the *Somers*. In one interchange between Mackenzie and Spencer (taken from Mackenzie's report), the captain asks to see the paper containing the plan for the mutiny which he believes Spencer has rolled up and hidden in his neckerchief; Spencer, in Mackenzie's words, "with an air of deference and blandness," claims he has only his instructions for the day's work and that the odd storage place is "a convenient one." Hamilton, however, contrasts the commander's account of the episode, and in particular his incriminating language, with that of a midshipman witness who says that when Mackenzie remarks, "That is a singular place to carry a day's work; why should you carry it there?" Spencer "appeared embarrassed, and replied he 'did not know, except for convenience.'" Hamilton notes the differences in language and concludes, "The deference and blandness [in Mackenzie's words] are purely commanderly. The embarrassment and the 'don't know' [Spencer's] are thoroughly boyish." In the voice of motherly ridicule, she admonishes the captain: "What possesses that unaccountable but happily temporary organism which is called a boy, to carry everything everywhere that no one else ever dreamed of but himself?" (140).

Hamilton's tone becomes more serious when she challenges Mackenzie's claim that after Spencer's arrest, Lieutenant Gansevoort "ministered in every way to his comfort with the tenderness of a woman." As she drily comments, "It becomes instantly interesting to know what is the commander's idea of a woman's tenderness." In court, Mackenzie argued that Gansevoort wrapped the shackled sailor in his own grego to protect him from the rain and witnessed his penitent tears. Hamilton describes Spencer's being instead humiliatingly "bagged," confined in a sack with no air or light; "exactly how tenderly this was done we do not know, for the boy was hanged without any chance to give us his opinion of the operation" (140). Her ironic tone shows that Mackenzie and Gansevoort have no notion of care in their ministrations,

"Midshipman Spencer, being thus handcuffed, double-ironed, and bagged with womanly tenderness" (248).

In contrast to Spencer, Billy Budd is treated with a tenderness that is womanly in its care yet masculine—that is, overtly fatherly—in its meaning. From the moment Vere first touches Billy in the cabin, "laying a soothing hand on his shoulder" and urging him to take his time in answering to Claggart's accusations (99), Vere treats Billy with a gentleness that stands in utter contrast to Mackenzie's severity.[20] Whereas Mackenzie never gives Spencer a chance to face his judge and jury, Vere brings Billy into the courtroom and treats him with respect. When Billy affirms his patriotic fervor—"I am true to the King!"—Vere responds, "'I believe you, my man,' ... his voice indicating a suppressed emotion not otherwise betrayed" (106). And whereas Mackenzie errs in not taking into account Spencer's youth and immaturity, Vere sensitively detects when Billy cannot respond properly to a question—say, the question of *why* Claggart should have lied—because it is one "touching on a spiritual sphere wholly obscure to Billy's thoughts" (107), and hence he counsels Billy's silence. Even more striking is Vere's embrace of Billy after the verdict is announced. Although Melville's narrator offers only what *may* have happened, Vere "may in end have caught Billy to his heart, even as Abraham may have caught young Isaac on the brink of resolutely offering him up to the exacting behest" (115). As Eve Sedgwick has pointed out, Billy receives not only the captain's embrace but also the chaplain's kiss, a gesture that swathes these masculine caresses in the Christian ethic of care, a New Testament code of mercy that is associated explicitly with Christ and his mother, Mary. Thus, we might say that although mothers are absent on both Hamilton's *Somers* and Melville's *Bellipotent,* Hamilton's men fail to behave like women, whereas Melville's offer a pretty good imitation.

But only pretty good. Melville, like Hamilton, makes it clear that masculinist justice does not produce ethical results, and he does so through his references to an interceding female figure. Indeed, significantly at the crux of both narratives, such a figure intervenes, not directly to plead for the wayward boy but indirectly within the language to cast on men's justice the clear light of feminist ethics. The moral climax of Hamilton's narrative, for example, arrives at the moment of Philip Spencer's recognition, as he faces death, of what his actions will mean to his family: "the sudden presence of death stirred instantly in blood and brain his father's strength, his mother's love" (346). In her narration, quoting from the transcripts of the trial, Hamilton shows Captain Mackenzie writing down Spencer's last words at the boy's dictation, rather than giving him pen and paper. After leaving affectionate messages for his family and admitting to his wrongdoing, Spencer apparently said, "This will kill my poor mother" (348). Taken aback, Mackenzie writes, "I was not before aware that he had a mother" (348), although one of his reasons for hastening Spencer's execution was so that the erring son would not be rescued by his well-placed family on the ship's return: "for those who have friends or money in America there was no punishment for the worst of crimes" (348). Mackenzie, then, suggests that Spencer has friends who will intercede for him but appears to be staggered when the boy mentions a mother who would die of grief.

That same insensitivity to the mother reveals itself at the moral nadir of Hamilton's story. According to Hamilton, one of the worst violations Mackenzie commits, among many, is to rifle Spencer's locker and take Mrs. Spencer's letters into his possession. Mackenzie thought these letters, in which Mrs. Spencer begged her son to change his ways, would prove useful in establishing his case against Spencer. Publicizing them to the men, however, becomes in Hamilton's argument one of his most immoral acts: "Were anything wanting to complete the commander's infamy, it would be furnished by this testimony. Three days after Spencer's death, when no evidence is of any avail, letters officially searched for evidence of piracy, and found to contain no such evidence whatever, are publicly read to the ship's crew for the purpose of blackening the reputation of the man who has been three days dead: and a loving, anxious mother's tender, warning advice and exhortation to her boy are made by this fiendish hand to be the instrument of assail" (353). Mrs. Spencer's efforts to intercede for her son and turn him to the right path of conduct—written well before he is suspected of mutiny—become tools in the captain's attempts to justify executing him. In the end, Hamilton calls on her readers "in the name of every wife of an absent husband, every mother of a wayward son . . . to cleanse from our historic page the deepest stain that ever marred its purity" (354). Where Mrs. Spencer failed, then, to save her son, Hamilton uses her pen to intercede on his behalf and right the wrongs committed by abstract masculinist justice.

A similar image of female intercession, expressed in language more subdued than Hamilton's, but no less pathetic, appears in *Billy Budd* when Vere poses to the drumhead court the question that Hamilton raises for her readers: "But the exceptional in the matter moves the hearts within you. Even so too is mine moved. But let not warm hearts betray heads that should be cool. Ashore in a criminal case will an upright judge allow himself off the bench to be waylaid by some tender kinswoman of the accused seeking to touch him with her tearful plea? Well, the heart here, sometimes the feminine in man, is as that piteous woman, and hard though it be, she must here be ruled out" (111). Vere recognizes and honors the "tender" (Hamilton's frequent word) kinswoman, but then he rules her out. Unlike Mackenzie, he is not surprised by the figure of the interceding woman; he anticipates her presence and her attempts to "touch him with her tearful plea." Even, in fact, though Billy has no mother, Vere conjures up a female relative at the moment when she might be expected to appear. And Melville makes it clear that this tactic tests the men of the drumhead court to their utmost as they search vainly for ways to save Billy from his fate. That is not the kinswoman's last appearance in the story, however. As Billy lies in irons, he wears "something akin to the look of a slumbering child in the cradle when the warm hearth-glow of the still chamber at night plays on the dimples that at whiles mysteriously form in the cheek, silently coming and going there" (119). At this late moment in the story, Melville makes a reader see Billy, or Baby Budd, as a mother would. The effect, however, as it is in Hamilton's story, is to underscore the grotesqueness of masculinist justice in the face of feminist intercession.

It is clear, of course, that the effects of feminine intercession in the two stories are handled very differently. The sentimental touches that Anderson might call "fictionized" heighten Hamilton's melodrama, whereas Melville's references to a tender kinswoman are subdued and fleeting. Both accounts give highly "fictionized" versions of the *Somers* affair, however, and the passion of Hamilton's may well have captured Melville's imagination in a way her masculine sources, already familiar to him, might not. By forcefully revealing the melodrama and sentimental potential in the *Somers* mutiny, Hamilton's article might have given Melville the confidence to include sentimental touches of his own: Vere's embrace of Billy, the chaplain's kiss, the fleecy pink clouds attending Billy's death. But in a world constructed as masculine and martial, in a narrative identified as "no romance" (53), such melodramatic effects remain under strict control. Even with all the standard features of melodrama—an impossibly good hero and equally fantastic villain, the hero's uncertain birth and identity, a flawed figure of authority, the significant presence of music and song, even an eloquent mute[21]—*Billy Budd* contains its melodrama tightly. Ironically, Melville, who "fictionized" and sentimentalized sailors in *Billy Budd* much as he had in "John Marr" and "Bridegroom Dick," has been read as a more truthful chronicler of the *Somers* than Hamilton.

But although Hamilton and Melville clearly approach their subjects in very different ways, they also take up surprisingly similar themes in their parallel stories: the limits of masculinist justice, the power of feminist ethics, and the shock of motherhood as a rhetorical and emotional effect. They converge most closely, though, in a somewhat unexpected area, namely in the handling of texts. Here the gender issues do not seem so obvious as the intellectual and aesthetic ones. I am speaking of the ragged edges of writing.

Perhaps the most striking aspect of the *Somers* case, and the reason it nagged at both Hamilton and Melville so insistently, is the way it complicates itself as *text* or texts. As Hugh Egan has explained, "so much of the affair turns on the interpretation of texts—on codes, handwriting, dictation, translation . . . that its tensions *issue from* (as well as proceed into) the act of writing" (33). The tangled strands of the narrative seem to call for authorial intervention, for literary authority from outside: "From Spencer, through Mackenzie, Cooper, and Melville, the incidents of the 'mutiny' become increasingly counterfeited, fade into a tissue of commentaries that obscure the central act. In its place, authorship, the act of *writing*, at once capable of representation and distortion, is foregrounded" (34). Hamilton and Melville take up this imperative with profound ironic wit.

As we have seen, Hamilton's tactic throughout her essay is to hold Mackenzie's words up to common sense—not in a "spasm of sense" but in a steady stream—and keen ridicule. To do so she draws attention again and again to the instability of texts: Spencer's mutinous paper, for example, which turns out to seem more a form of boyish amusement than a serious threat. Mackenzie's "fertile imagination" (135) sees a piratical plot; the paper itself "shows that in a ship of one hundred and twenty persons the mutiny was confined to two boys of eighteen years,—one of whom was in foot-irons, hand-irons, and a bag!" (248). Spencer's "confession" is another such text. Mackenzie decides to write his last words for him rather than take the handcuffs off. Just as Billy is illiterate—even vocally disabled, since he stutters—Hamilton's Philip is made so by the captain's seizure of the text: "Thus Spencer could not write to his own father and mother a dying message." More tellingly, Hamilton remarks, Mackenzie fails even to write everything down at the moment of Spencer's dictation but constructs much of the record later, passing it off as a direct transcription: "He was in such haste to hang the boy that he could not even take that boy's tender words for his mother from his own lips, but hanged him first and jotted them down from memory afterward." But, says Hamilton, truth will out, even from the false paper: "Truth is so divine and eternal, so independent of effort to destroy or uphold it, that it can be *precipitated* from this hideous narrative, aided by the sinister and suppressed paper, almost as pure and clear as if truth had been the original intent" (347).

And Hamilton proceeds to extract that truth from Mackenzie's "stupid and silly invention" (348). In his most egregious falsehood, Mackenzie changes a single word in Spencer's statement, with diabolical results: "In the suppressed paper, which the commander wrote squat like a toad close at the ear of Spencer, he had written 'deserved death for this and other sins.' It was in his report, made up afterward at leisure on shore, that he changed sins to *crimes*. A sin is not a crime.... The father of lies put it into the commander's report" (348). Once again Hamilton reminds the reader of the importance of such distinctions: "He [Spencer] had sinned, not committed a crime, against his parents. He had been a wayward boy" (348). Mackenzie twists Spencer's remorse over his spiritual state into a confession of his guilty actions. The result, however, is a botch on all levels: "The writing was so 'hurried,' the commander was in such a panic, that much of the writing could not be made out by all the learning and leisure of the court-martial, and a good deal of what is made out is so higgledy-piggledy as to be incomprehensible" (350).

Not just texts but words themselves become pregnant issues in Hamilton's last scenes. Spencer's supposed co-conspirator, Elisha Small, turns to the crowd and says, "Shipmates, take warning by my example. I never was a pirate. I never killed a man; it's for saying that I would do it that I am about to depart this life. See what a word will do" (351). By now Hamilton's scathing irony has made it clear what words will do; she asserts, moreover, that every word in her account has the power to condemn and unmask Mackenzie's abuse of language. In another irony, Hamilton shows Spencer asking the captain to allow him to "give the word" at the fatal moment. Spencer's courage fails him, however, and he is unable to signal the executioner. "I am glad that he did not do it," says Hamilton. "Let the whole bitter burden of guilt rest on the commander, who could.... He gave the word, and the unspeakable crime was accomplished" (352). Again, Hamilton makes the reader aware of the ways Mackenzie's placing of words in Spencer's mouth have corrupted the youth and beyond that have corrupted language itself. Luckily for Hamilton the holes in Mackenzie's narrative, the places where his clumsy interventions become obvious, allow her to reveal the truth in his rotten text.

Hamilton's passionate defense of the truth, her heartfelt reverence for the word, suggest that justice is the responsibility of women because it is the responsibility of all human beings. Thus, although her narrative seems to separate the gendered spheres of justice, upholding maternal care over patriarchal violence, she uses an ethic of caring for language itself to raise her argument above gender differences. Strikingly, Melville too seems to be striving for a gender-neutral realm above the fray, a place where head and heart need not conflict and where the word can do its intended task. He finds such a realm in the spaces between, in the interstices of definition: "Truth uncompromisingly told will always have its ragged edges" (128). Like Hamilton, Melville emphasizes the unreliability of texts and words: Vere's ambiguous final speech, "Billy Budd, Billy Budd"; the self-serving official newspaper report, as false and twisted as Mackenzie's testimony; and even the sailors' ballad, which seems to speak for Billy but obscures the truth in a myth. Although Melville does not insist, as Hamilton does, that truth will emerge from these compromised words and texts, he makes it possible for the reader to make a judgment "by such light as this narrative may afford" (102). He shows that narrative itself can cast the light of truth on a corrupted text.

But like Hamilton, Melville, seemingly not satisfied with the ragged edges of truth, the corrupt texts of men, aims for a sublime utterance that can "preach Truth to the face of Falsehood!" (*Moby-Dick* 48). In this endeavor Melville, again like Hamilton, shows the danger in a masculinist justice that makes unequivocal statements. When Vere sees what Billy has done and delivers judgment—"Struck dead by an angel of God! Yet the angel must hang!"—Melville draws attention to the surgeon's "disquietude and misgiving" (101) to cast doubt on Vere's rapid conclusion. Yet unlike Hamilton's Mackenzie, Vere has the capacity to see another truth, even if he cannot act accordingly. Perhaps the most agonizing effect of his reference to the "tender kinswoman" is that it offers a brief and tangential glimpse of an ethic of care just beyond the reach of his jurisdiction. Melville's narrator, however, offers abundant examples of such care in the chaplain's tender ministrations, in the sailors' heartfelt tribute to Billy's courage, and most dramatically in Billy's final speech, "God bless Captain Vere!" (123). Billy's unequivocal statement, unlike Vere's, is uttered in a spirit that Melville does not hesitate to compare with Christian sacrifice and love. Remarkably, it endorses Vere's masculine authority at the same time that it intercedes tenderly on the captain's behalf. Within a ragged text that strenuously resists the authority of categorical pronouncements, Melville produces one clear statement of a truth that combines head and heart, justice and mercy, Law and Word.

We cannot ultimately know what Melville had in mind for the revisions and final form of *Billy Budd*. If, as Hayford and Sealts argue, Vere began as a frank, "straightforward" character and became progressively more conflicted and complex, one can imagine Melville evolving in his vision of the *Somers* affair as well. Perhaps Melville started, as Lieutenant Smith did, by trying to honor the captain, or more likely the suffering Guert Gansevoort, whose career was adversely affected by his morally ambiguous role in the affair. If Melville never read or heard of Hamilton's "The Murder of Philip Spencer," he might still have come to see that an "inside narrative" could tell more than one truth about the events, and he could have decided to change Vere accordingly.

If he did encounter Hamilton's article, however, Melville might have recognized in Hamilton a kindred voice, a voice speaking passionately for judicial reform, for an embrace of fluid notions of gender, and for a profound belief in the sacredness of the word of truth, which no text can render purely but which nevertheless women and men must try to write. If so, then he might have felt emboldened to speak, as Gilligan puts it, "in a different voice"—the voice of a feminist ethic. Melville's story, while never as direct and forceful as Hamilton's in making its intentions clear, is in its way an example of feminist justice; for it delays judgment while seeking to create relational bonds between the victim on trial (Billy) and his judges, the readers themselves. Melville, in letting a tender kinswoman into the story, opens up a small space for an alternative justice that transcends, as Billy does in his death, the limitations of gender and language.

Notes

1. "Editors' Introduction" in *Billy Budd, Sailor* 1–39; and *Billy Budd: The Genetic Text*. See also H. Parker, *Reading* Billy Budd.

2. John Wenke has recently given this issue sustained attention in one of the first rereadings of Hayford's and Sealts's *Genetic Text*. He argues that the late revisions emphasize the complexities in Vere's character and actions in order "that sane, judicious and well-meaning persons can reasonably take the same character, the same acts, the same words and draw radically antagonistic conclusions." See "Complicating Vere," 85, and "Melville's Indirection."

3. *Hayford and Sealts* esp. 260–63 and 395.

4. I am grateful to Dennis Marnon at the Houghton Library of the Harvard College Libraries for his help in reviewing this page of the *Billy Budd* manuscript in a conversation 7 Jan. 2004.

5. Anderson suggests that Guert could have been the inspiration for Claggart (338), an unlikely speculation, given the evidence of Melville's admiration for his cousin. See H. Parker, *Biography* vols. 1 and 2; and Robertson-Lorant. Melville writes admiringly of Guert in his poem "Bridegroom Dick." See Robillard.

6. Hayford and Sealts show, however, that Melville had already begun *Billy Budd* in 1886 (2) while he was writing *John Marr*, published in 1888. It is impossible to know from their evidence whether Smith's article inspired any details in *Billy Budd*.

7. McFarland 161.

8. For these documents and other materials and information on the *Somers*, see H. Egan; Hayford; and McFarland.

9. Hamilton's analysis of Captain Mackenzie much resembles Eve Sedgwick's of Captain Vere, especially in relation to the captain's paranoia and secrecy. See *Epistemology* 100–104.

10. On Cooper, see McFarland 210–11.

11. See also Kittay and Meyers; and Chodorow.

12. See especially Cohen and Yannella. Malcolm, the Melvilles' older son, died September 11, 1847, at home of a self-inflicted gunshot wound. Stanwix died February 23, 1886, in San Francisco after being estranged from the family for some years.

13. Neither Parker nor Robertson-Lorant mentions these newspapers. Bercaw includes them as sources, presumably on the authority of Anderson's article (54, 86, 120). On Melville's use of the *Somers* story and his reading of Smith and Hamilton, see also Howard 324–28; and

R. P. Warren 58–62, 82. Both Howard and Warren seem again to have relied on Anderson's article rather than finding new evidence of Melville's having read Smith and Hamilton.

14. See Coultrap-McQuinn, *Literary Business* and *Gail Hamilton: Selected Writings;* and Pulsifer.

15. Letter from Elizabeth Shaw Melville, May 1863, to Fanny Melville in the Augusta Papers, Gansevoort-Lansing Collection, New York Public Library. The full passage reads: "I saw 'the Atlantic Monthly' that you speak of in Boston and think the 'Spasm of Sense' *capital*—wish there was more such sense in the world." See Hamilton, "A Spasm of Sense" 407–20.

16. See, for example, Elizabeth Shaw Melville's letter to her stepmother, Hope Shaw, dated December 23, in Leyda 1: 266.

17. See Cohen and Yannella, Robertson-Lorant, Parker; also Renker, "Wife Beating."

18. See Coultrap-McQuinn, *Literary Business* 105–35.

19. It is curious in this regard that although we know nothing of Claggart's mother, Melville does refer to Vere's female ancestor, Mary Fairfax.

20. See Sedgwick's chapter, "*Billy Budd:* After the Homosexual," in *Epistemology* 91–130.

21. See Brooks 56–80.

Part Three

Readings of *Pierre* and Women

Melville and Isabel

The Author and the Woman Within in the "Inside Narrative" of *Pierre*

Wendy Stallard Flory

Melville's *Pierre; or, the Ambiguities* is unique among his works in the number and importance of its women. Among these, Isabel is clearly preeminent, and, in her role as symbolic character,[1] she is intimately related not just to Pierre, the struggling writer, but to Melville himself. In specifying her symbolic attributes and staging her interactions with Pierre, Melville was dramatizing his most urgent concerns at this difficult stage of his writing career. Important among these is his dilemma as an author who has a family to support but whose creative gift is ill-suited to the writing of popular, money-making fiction. In all the specifics of Isabel's detailed characterization, she personifies the creative imagination—and not just in some generalizing, allegorical way. She is carefully particularized as the Melvillean imagination, a powerfully dynamic, sinisterly coercive creative gift. For Pierre the consequences of being saddled with this burdensome gift are fatal.

To read Isabel, even in part, as a realistic[2] rather than a symbolic character is, almost certainly, to see Pierre's relationship with her as sexually passionate. In such a reading, he will appear to be overwhelmed by uncontrollable feelings and therefore weak. He will be seen as mistaking feelings of lust for a high-minded desire to be Isabel's protector and therefore self-deluded. But seeing Isabel as a symbolic character makes a radical difference in interpretation. Doing so changes our sense not only of Isabel but also of Pierre, of Melville's attitude toward both characters, of his main emphasis in this romance, of *Pierre*'s coherence, and of its success as a whole.

When Melville described *Pierre* to his publisher, Richard Bentley, as "calculated for popularity" and "a regular romance, with a mysterious plot to it, & stirring passions at work," he was describing the more superficial of the work's two levels (*Correspondence* 226). This is the one that might possibly allow *Pierre* to pass as a romantic novel (partly in the sentimental and partly in the sensationalist mode) that would appeal to a mass readership. *Pierre*'s "deeper," symbolic level had to be kept from Bentley, whose main concern was sales. Melville burdened Pierre with an even more extreme version of his own dilemma as a writer. The financial circumstances of both author and character require that they write a book that will sell well, though they know that, given the nature of their creative gift, the books that they are drawn to write will not appeal to popular taste. Melville has Pierre realize that "could he ... fall to on some shallow nothing of a novel ... then could he reasonably hope for both appreciation and cash" but that "the wiser and the profounder he should grow, the more and more he lessened the chances for bread" (305).

What Melville says of Pierre's book about Vivia can also be applied to that crucially important but largely disregarded "ambiguity" in *Pierre*, its two-level structure: "Two books are being writ; of which the world shall only see one, and that the bungled one. The larger book, and the infinitely better, is for Pierre's own private shelf" (304). As Pierre is still an immature writer, the "larger" book is being "writ down in his soul," but he cannot, especially under the pressures of his present circumstances, adequately translate it into words. In Melville's romance, his own "two books" are both present on the page. The "bungled" one is *Pierre* when read as though it were a realistic novel. The "larger" and cohering one is *Pierre* read as a symbolic romance, starring Isabel.

A reading that keeps a steady focus on *Pierre*'s symbolic "Inside Narrative"—the sustained level of symbolic significance over which Isabel presides—and on Isabel's symbolic role in particular can give the fullest sense of the work's overall coherence of plot, characterization, and style. A few critics have focused particularly on Isabel's symbolic meanings and have only missed identifying her as the imagination by assigning her a narrower significance or a more sweeping one. They have also incorporated interpretations that would only apply were she a realistically presented character.[3] The sustained symbolic reading that follows here differs significantly from these "mixed" readings in its account of Isabel's significances and of the coherence of Melville's romance as a whole.

Pierre's melodramatic excesses have made it a perplexing and often annoying book for its readers, evident in the contradictory comments of reviewers and critics in Melville's time and in our own. His contemporaries responded with ridicule at its overwrought style and with indignation at what they saw as its immorality. To critics from the Melville Revival on, *Pierre*'s mystifications are reflected in the wide range of differing theories about how it can best be interpreted.[4] In their responses, the original reviewers did not hold back: in addition to mocking and reproaching Melville, several accused him of insanity. Later critics are not angry at Melville, yet frustration at the perverse-seeming stylistic oddity of *Pierre* and at the difficulty of accounting for Melville's decision to write in this way often finds an outlet in very scathingly critical judgments of Pierre himself.

One important reason for Melville's extravagant style is that it suits his highly symbolic project. *Pierre* is so stylistically extravagant because it is so symbolic. As the relationship between Isabel and Pierre spirals downward to its tragic catastrophe, an "overwrought" style continues to be appropriate. In addition, the mode of melodrama allowed Melville to address an urgent personal dilemma in a symbolic and therefore veiled way. He must have hoped that he could explore his own, highly serious, metaphysically speculative, socially conscious, and prolifically imaginative bent, yet do so indirectly, without embarrassing self-revelation. He did this by creating the extravagantly symbolic Isabel as the personification of his own creative imagination and by representing his interactions with this imperious imagination through the relationship between Isabel and Pierre.

To see Isabel as the personification of Pierre's own Melvillean imagination, whose hold over him is preemptive and inescapable, is to see that Melville is emphasizing Pierre's plight more than his perversity. The Melvillean imagination, hyperbolically personified by Isabel, makes great demands and disrupts both "earthly household peace" (345) and literary reputation. Melville gives Pierre imaginative, intellectual, and temperamental qualities like his own—ones that greatly complicate a writer's life. Like Melville, Pierre has an extreme temperament that alternates between extravagant expansiveness and episodes of black depression.[5] Melville intimates his character's similarity to himself with the narrator's comment, "I am more frank with Pierre than the best men are with themselves" (108). Pierre's youth puts him at an additional disadvantage. Management of the difficult Melvillean mind requires the steadying influence of maturity. Pierre's mind is "youthful [and] as yet untranquilized by long habituation to the world as it inevitably and eternally is." Both author and character have "a mind fitted by nature for profound and fearless thought" that will "invariably" be led by "enthusiastic

Truth, and Earnestness, and Independence" into "Hyperborean regions" of thought that threaten to "confound" the "directing compass of the mind." When those with such minds do "advance to Truth" in some noticeable way, they become pariahs. They "leave the rest behind; cutting themselves forever adrift from their sympathy, and making themselves always liable to be regarded with distrust, dislike, and often downright . . . fear and hate" (165–66). Melville had recently seen these qualities in reviewers' hostile responses to *Moby-Dick*. Pierre's publishers will cut him off before he can even finish his book, reducing him to such poverty and despair that he sees suicide as his only option. Isabel, inevitably, dies with him.

Any reading of Pierre as drawn to Isabel by feelings of incestuous lust that he refuses to acknowledge for what they are will find him perversely self-destructive. General readings of Isabel as the dangerously sexual "Dark Lady" and Lucy as the virginal "Fair Maiden" (types often paired in the nineteenth-century romance) can produce very negative opinions of Pierre. Such readings, though, overlook many of the particulars of characterization. Isabel's dark hair and complexion, for example, symbolize more than sexuality or sinfulness: they show that she also personifies the depressiveness inseparable from the Melvillean creative imagination. This is the hereditary melancholia that ran through Melville's own bloodline[6] and that he calls in Pierre, the "black vein" of the Glendinnings (358). Isabel's "darkness" also symbolizes her role as revealer of the actuality of the dark world of Blakean "Experience." She initiates Pierre into an awareness of what she calls the world's "heartless usages and fashions" (64). When her letter makes known to Pierre his father's adultery and abandonment of his daughter, "Truth rolls a black billow through [Pierre's] soul" (65).

As the personification of Pierre's creative imagination, Isabel plays the role of Muse, but because of the connotations of that term, I will use it only sparingly and with the following proviso. The archaizing connotations of the term limit its usefulness as a designation for Isabel. "The Muse" connotes the allegorical, that is, a symbolic mode involving a set of significances preestablished by tradition. In contrast, Melville's personification of Pierre's creative imagination is highly dynamic, idiosyncratic, and particular to Melville's own personal situation as a writer. How original and independent of conventional allegorical representations Melville was in inventing his personification of the imagination is shown by the extent to which Isabel's role as Muse has been overlooked. And this despite her obtrusively symbolic characterization. The Muse as traditionally represented also has problematic connotations because it reinforces the gender stereotype of the woman "at the service of" the man—not herself the creative artist, but a presence that will help the male artist to fulfil himself creatively. Melville, however, makes Isabel a creative artist and the most powerful character in the story: her influence over Pierre and, through him, on others is irresistible and absolute. Melville also conceptualizes the creative imagination as beyond gender.

"Supernatural" as well as human, Isabel is associated with the timeless and the universal (112). In her fundamental nature Melville conceives of her as existing beyond the limitations of time or gender. She tells Pierre, "I have always been, and feel that I must always continue to be a child, though I should grow to three score years and ten." She also insists, "I am called woman, and thou, man, Pierre; but there is neither man nor woman about it. . . . There is no sex in our immaculateness." At their second meeting she graphically demonstrates what she means. Here she reveals her "profounder, subtler, and more mystic part" by changing from "unassuming maid" into "dark, regal being" (148, 149, 152). She stands before him "transformed," and Pierre, "bowing low over to her, owned that irrespective [i.e., independent], darting majesty of humanity, which can be majestical and menacing in woman as in man" (160).

Not only Isabel, but also the other women in *Pierre*—Lucy Tartan, Delly Ulver, and Mary Glendinning—are symbolically significant in ways that link them intimately to Melville himself. As symbolic characters they personify dimensions of Melville's mind and, in particular, those that determine both the kind of writer he was and the difficulties he was facing in his writing career. *Pierre* contains several important Keatsian allusions. "The Heart" and the "Imagination" in Keats's well-known phrase, "the holiness of the Heart's affections and the truth of Imagination" (*Letters* 1: 184), exactly gloss the symbolism of Melville's two main women characters. Where Isabel embodies the "Imagination," Lucy personifies "the Heart" or "the Heart's affections." At the beginning of the story, when she and Pierre are naïve and carefree young lovers, she is the embodiment of "Joy." Later, when she comes to live with Pierre, Isabel, and Delly in their increasingly desperate financial circumstances, she personifies "the Heart's affections" in the form of "Truth to oneself."

Mary Glendinning personifies what Melville calls "the prosperities" and "the proprieties" (89, 195). These are materialistic and "haughty" (4) attitudes about the value of wealth and social status that were inculcated in Melville as a child growing up in a family with socially prominent ancestors—such as his grandfather Peter Gansevoort, the model for Pierre's Glendinning grandfather. Delly, who has recently given birth to an illegitimate baby, obviously personifies sexuality. Her small part in the drama is a sign of the low priority of sexuality on the symbolic level of this story of the trials of authorship. Having dedicated himself to his Muse, Pierre must forego a sexual married relationship. Hence the never-married and now "unsexed" Delly lives in Pierre's household as servant to Isabel. Delly was only sexually active in the past. Now, her child is dead, and she leads a celibate life. In calling her Delly, Melville signals both her association with sexuality and her subsequent "unsexing." The only obvious derivation of "Delly" is "Delilah," but the diminutive, "Delly," has shed the obtrusive sexual connotations of "Delilah." Melville demystifies the theme of sexuality through his characterization of Delly. His mother, Propriety personified, reacts melodramatically to Delly's sexual "sin," but Pierre sympathetically and matter-of-factly takes Delly under his protection. He will not let her be abandoned as Isabel and her mother were. When he is "plunged into" a bewildering reverie about the "mysterious, inscrutable divineness in the world" by the news that Lucy is to join them, Delly's down-to-earth presence steadies him: "he felt overjoyed at the sight of the humanness of Delly" (317).

Delly's role as the embodiment of sexuality has been easy to overlook because Melville's borrowings from the conventions of the sensation novel appear to sexualize Isabel. Melville drops ambiguous hints that Isabel's relationship with Pierre may be a sexual one. Yet the story of Pierre and Isabel is much more than an overwrought melodrama of "forbidden passion" in the sensationalist mode. In presenting the inescapable and ultimately fatal control that Isabel has over Pierre, Melville dramatizes the struggle going on in his own mind. The desperation that this struggle generates is one of the important sources of energy that drives the writing of *Pierre*. The work's coherence comes from the urgency with which Melville, as he stages the drama of Isabel's preemptive demands upon Pierre, is articulating his own problems as an author. His strong, underlying identification with Pierre's desperate predicament undergirds the ornate superstructure of this byzantinely elaborated book. Once we are aware of the strength of this identification, we can see the book's structural soundness. Melville chose to dramatize his own present, difficult situation as a writer through Pierre's interactions with Isabel. The evidence is overwhelming that she personifies the creative imagination, and Melville was highly inventive in assigning to her attributes that announce this significance.

Melville, as he wrote *Pierre*, was exploring the question of how substantial his creative talent really was and whether, as he was beginning to fear, he was doomed to failure as a writer because of the *kind* of literary gift he had and the kind of books that it compelled him to write. The peremptory yet entirely dependent Isabel embodies, to the last detail, this idealistic, metaphysically speculative, and manic-depressively "extravagant" imagination, with the inexorable demands that it makes upon the artist to whom it belongs, who alone can put into verbal form the feelings and inchoate intimations that it "conjures up." Isabel's characterization is painstakingly consistent throughout, both in her symbolic status as a personified imagination and in her symbolic nature as a specific, "Melvillean" imagination. The subject of a writer's bedeviled career dominates both the realistic and symbolic levels of significance. That Melville's personal distress about the problematic circumstances of his own career strongly influenced his treatment of this theme is clear from the many similarities that Pierre shares with his creator.[7] That, unlike Melville, his hero goes down to utter ruin suggests the playing out of a "worst-case scenario," both as an overt act of protest against the market's rejection of the serious and truly original writer's works, and, psychologically, as an exorcising of Melville's own profound fears of professional failure and mental collapse.

Isabel personifies the imagination of a writer whose creative gift *is* authentic but whose lack of success with the public makes him doubt it. Melville dramatizes the strain of this uncertainty by having Pierre, at moments of greatest stress, question whether Isabel is his sister, yet these doubts pass quickly and his deepest intuitions persuade him "strong as death" (139) that she is. For example, Pierre had only seen a family resemblance between Isabel and a *portrait* of his father (rather than the image of his father's face as Pierre remembered it). When Pierre sees a similar resemblance between Isabel's face and the face in an anonymous portrait of a stranger, this seems to invalidate the "evidence" of the earlier resemblance. In wording that emphasizes Isabel's symbolic status as Pierre's imagination, Melville writes, "Of late to Pierre . . . the whole story of Isabel had seemed an enigma, a mystery, an imaginative delirium; especially since he had got so deep into the inventional mysteries of his book" (353–54). Now, recalling that "she did not even know that the sea was salt," Pierre doubts her story of her past, of which crossing the ocean was such an important part. Yet, right away, the three take a ferry across the bay and Isabel so obviously recognizes the motion of the waves from her childhood voyage that "it was impossible [for Pierre] altogether to resist the force of this striking corroboration of by far the most surprising and improbable thing in the whole surprising and improbable story of Isabel" (355).

That Pierre is, despite his misgivings, a "born writer" is conveyed symbolically by the relationship of a brother to an older sister. Pierre, the writer, and Isabel, his creative imagination, are related "by blood"—Pierre's creative gift is his birthright. Once Pierre, having moved beyond his juvenilia, discovers the deeper resources of his creativity, he is initiated through Isabel into an awareness of inhumanity, deceit, and suffering. Now he must write deep books if he is to be "faithful" to his imagination's bias toward metaphysical inquiry, concern for social justice, and exploration of individual psychology. "The devouring profundities, now opened up in him, consume all his vigor; would he, he could not now be entertainingly and profitably shallow in some pellucid and merry romance" (305).

Melville finds ingenious ways of making the details of Isabel's behavior, appearance, commentary, and past history into symbolic renderings of the workings of the creative imagination. Books 6 and 8, the "Story of Isabel" sections of *Pierre,* are set-pieces showing how deliberate and specific is this characterization. In them Melville skillfully dramatizes the process whereby unconscious intimations come into the conscious mind, either as feelings or as concepts apprehended by the intellect and then articulated in speech or writing. He characterizes Isabel as initially wholly unconscious and then describes the stages of the gradual growth of her conscious mind. At first Isabel, the Imagination, exists—as far as the requirement that she have a childhood will allow—in a completely unconscious state. The physical and emotional interactions with other human beings that foster the development of consciousness in a child have been, as far as possible, omitted from her experience. She can recall no contact with her mother: "I never knew a mortal mother . . . [my] lips . . . never touched a woman's breast; I seem not of woman born" (114). The old couple, the first guardians she can remember, show her no affection and avoid physical contact with her. Even though her experiences expand her consciousness, she remains fundamentally "of the unconscious." As she says to Pierre, "Scarce know I at any time whether I tell you real things, or the unrealest dreams. Always in me, the solidest things melt into dreams, and dreams into solidities" (117). She explains to Pierre that she was first able to register the idea of "humanness" from seeing a "beautiful infant." The consciousness of self that she was unable to learn in her own infancy, she could partly learn vicariously from watching a child's normal infancy: "this beautiful infant first brought me to my own mind, as it were; first made me sensible that I was something different from stones, trees, cats" (122).

While timelessness is characteristic of her fundamental, unconscious state, her initiation into consciousness begins to give her a sense of time and awakens in her the capacity for memory and desire. Made aware of her own humanness by the infant's, she becomes sensitized to the dilemmas of humanness in other individuals, seeing "all good, harmless men and women" as "human beings, placed at cross-purposes, in a world of snakes and lightnings, in a world of horrible and inscrutable inhumanities" (122). This development of a social consciousness is part of the process of her particularization as Pierre's individualized imagination, and it determines the idealistic bent of his future writings. As Isabel personifies creative inspiration that will find its form in an author's words, she is shown learning to read and write. As the primary mode of the unconscious is nonverbal, Melville has scrupulously excluded words, as far as possible, from her early life. "No name; no scrawled or written things; no book, was in the house" where she first remembers living. She recalls that the old couple there "seldom or never spoke to me" (115–16).

By having her kept for several years in a madhouse, in a room with a locked door, Melville can, concurrently, show her still cut off from communication with people yet also develop two themes: the difficulty of articulating unconscious intimations and the relationship between creative genius and insanity—or perceived insanity. Alluding obliquely to his own mentally unsettling preoccupation with ultimate questions, Melville includes Isabel's anecdote of the two "predestinarian opponents" in the asylum (121). The fact that this joking reference is out of character with Isabel's habitual seriousness is a sign that Melville is interjecting a wry autobiographical note and has in mind his concern about his extreme moods at the time he was writing *Pierre*.[8]

The kind of thought that comes naturally to Isabel is the spontaneous and unmediated upsurge of unconscious intuitions or inspirations. These find words for themselves, independently of her conscious efforts: "All my thoughts well up in me; . . . as they are, they are, and I can not alter them, for I had nothing to do with putting them in my mind . . . but when I speak, [I] think forth from the tongue, speech being sometimes before the thought; so, often, my own tongue teaches me new things" (123). In contrast to the effortlessness of this spontaneous expression, consciously finding words to express the circumstances of her own past and even recalling these circumstances are very effortful for her. The labored formality of her speech is Melville's way of rendering the fact that, in the province of conscious thought and deliberate speech, she is out of her element.

Only in her relationship with Pierre—the consciousness whose inspiration she is—does she need to try laboriously to communicate with conscious purposefulness. He is the first one to whom she has told her story. Long before she meets him, but in anticipation of the already-established blood-relationship between them, she first learns to read by studying his family name, Glendinning, on the handkerchief that their father had accidentally left on his last visit before his death. As she tells about meeting her father and learning to read by deciphering the word "Glendinning," Isabel, appropriately, speaks with an unaccustomed articulateness to which Melville draws particular attention (147).

While a musical instrument is a predictable attribute for a Muse, Melville inventively develops the symbolic meanings of Isabel's guitar. A counterpart to Isabel herself, it has a double significance, being associated with the conscious mind—the "human"—and with the unconscious—"mystery." When she plays the guitar at her first meeting with Pierre, it is an explicator of her past and of her previous experiences in the world of consciousness, as well as the medium for communications from the unconscious. As she says of it, "All the wonders that are unimaginable and unspeakable; all these wonders are translated in the mysterious melodiousness of the guitar. It knows all my past history. . . . Sometimes it strikes up in me rapturous pulsations of legendary delights eternally unexperienced and unknown to me" (125). When she begins to play, the sounds of "swarming sweetness, and . . . utter unintelligibleness, but . . . infinite significancies" create corresponding feelings of delight in him. Then Pierre hears a new sound, "Mystery! Mystery! / Mystery of Isabel!" It has a sexual resonance in that it is "wonderfully and abandonedly free and bold," and, as she plays it, Isabel sways in time to it "with a like abandonment, and suddenness, and wantonness." Yet its impact is also "cerebral" (of the creative mind), as Melville shows with his references to the "brows" of the brother and sister. Here, "a strange wild heat burned upon [Pierre's] brow" (126–27).

Pierre's full initiation into "The Mystery of Isabel," his irrevocable "cerebral" bonding with Isabel herself, takes place at their second meeting. As Isabel draws the guitar to her, veiling it in her "tent" of hair, Pierre finds "his whole soul . . . swayed and tossed by supernatural tides" at the sound of the music, so that he was "almost deprived of consciousness by the spell flung over him by the marvelous girl" (150):

> To Pierre's dilated senses Isabel seemed to swim in an electric fluid; the vivid buckler of her brow seemed as a magnetic plate. Now . . . was Pierre made aware of . . . an extraordinary physical magnetism in Isabel. And . . . a certain still more marvellous power in the girl over himself and his most interior thoughts and motions. . . . Often, in after-times with her, did he recall this first magnetic night, and would seem to see that she then had bound him to her by an extraordinary atmospheric spell—both physical and spiritual—which henceforth it had become impossible for him to break, but whose full potency he never recognized till long after he had become habituated to her sway. (151)

When Pierre arrives at his "unprecedented final resolution" to make Isabel his "wife," Melville describes him as having become the counterpart to Isabel's guitar: "The wonderful melodiousness of her grief had touched the secret monochord within his breast, by an apparent magic, precisely similar to that which had moved the stringed tongue of her guitar to respond to the heart-strings of her own melancholy plaints. The deep voice of the being of Isabel called to him from out the immense distances of sky and air, and there seemed no veto of the earth that could forbid her heavenly claim" (173).

Pierre as counterpart to Isabel's guitar is an Americanized version of the traditional imagery from British Romantic poetry of the writer as the "instrument" of the creative imagination. Pierre must put himself at Isabel's service as Shelley had asked his imagination, symbolized by the West Wind, to make him into a lyre "even as the forest is" (579). Melville alludes directly to the Romantic metaphor of the poet as "Eolian harp" in his first description of Isabel's face when, in apparitional form, it "peeps down" on Pierre as he listens to "the pyramidical and numberless, flame-like complainings of [an] Eolean pine" (41). A further, veiled allusion relates Isabel to a personification of the creative imagination in Coleridge's "Kubla Khan." Pierre says to Isabel, "thy all-abounding hair falls upon me with some spell which dismisses all ordinary considerations from me, and leaves me only sensible to the Nubian power in thine eyes" (145). Melville's use of "Nubian" here is a good example of the kind of stylistic excess in *Pierre* that, taken at face value, seems merely awkward but, read more searchingly, is entirely deliberate. To recall that Nubia was the earlier name for Abyssinia is inevitably to connect Isabel and her guitar to Coleridge's personification of his creative imagination, the "damsel with a dulcimer"—the "Abyssinian maid" (297) in "Kubla Khan."[9]

In characterizing Isabel, Melville several times alludes to Keats's representation of his own creative imagination. The farmhouse casement in which Isabel sits "enshrined" as she plays her guitar for Pierre echoes "a casement ope at night, / To let the warm Love in!" from "Ode to Psyche."[10] Isabel's description of the deep, mountainside pine woods surrounding her childhood home evokes Keats's description, from the same ode, of "some untrodden region of my mind, / Where branched thoughts new grown with pleasant pain, / Instead of pines shall murmur in the wind: / Far, far around shall those dark-cluster'd trees / Fledge the wild-ridged mountains steep by steep" (364–66). The lines "Ay, in the very temple of Delight / Veil'd Melancholy has her sovran shrine, / Though seen of none save him whose strenuous tongue / Can burst Joy's grape against his palate fine" (374–75), from the final stanza of "Ode to Melancholy," are alluded to, both generally, in the casement tableau, and conceptually and verbally in the "sacrament of the supper" episode. Here, below the distraught Delly in her upstairs room, "the low melodies of [Isabel's] far interior voice hovered in sweet echoes in the room; and were trodden upon, and pressed like gushing grapes, by the steady invisible pacing on the floor above" (118).[11]

Once Pierre is installed in the city and at work on his book, Isabel is particularly associated with the difficulties of writing, with the way in which the intimations of the imagination resist attempts to articulate them verbally. Melville writes that sometimes "when [Pierre's] day's work was done, [Isabel] sat by him in the twilight, and played her mystic guitar till [he] felt chapter after chapter born of its wondrous suggestiveness; but alas! eternally incapable of being translated into words; for where the deepest words end, there music begins with its supersensuous and all-confounding intimations" (282). Pierre says to her, "Any,—all words are thine, Isabel; words and worlds with all their containings, shall be slaves to thee, Isabel" (313), yet this does not lessen his difficulty in finding the words for his purposes. All words are hers to the extent that she is the inspiration that the writer is forced to "find words for," but she cannot herself provide the words or render the meanings she intimates. As she says to him later, "Thy hand is the caster's ladle, Pierre, which holds me entirely fluid. Into thy forms and slightest moods of thought, thou pourest me; and I there soldify to that form, and take it on, and thenceforth wear it, till once more thou moldest me anew" (324).

As his book becomes increasingly unsatisfactory, Pierre's impossibly demanding imagination comes to seem a sinisterly manipulative presence, as though he were a puppet under Isabel's control. On one occasion, "his flagging faculties seeking a momentary respite," he looks aside from his writing and the floorboard seams appear to him to be wires that "led straight from where he sat to the connecting door, and disappeared beneath it into the chamber of Isabel" (308). Isabel's symbolic identity as the embodiment of Pierre's creative imagination is made very clear at the point at which he finally gives up on his book. Pierre is finally overcome by self-distrust, "the most wretched distrust of all" (167). Now his book seems to him the work of a "coiner"—that is, both counterfeit and a project undertaken to make money—and he nails it to his desk. At this, Isabel "gave loose to a thin, long shriek" and then, transfixed, like the nailed-down book, "without the power to stir toward him, sat petrified in her chair, as one embalmed and glazed with icy varnish" (357).

To the reader who has not identified Isabel as the personification of the imagination of Melville the author, or who has not seen how this role supercedes her sexual significance, *Pierre* can appear to be a very unsatisfactory book. Even as eminent a Melville scholar as Hershel Parker continues to be distressed by what he sees as a radical flaw in the book as Melville published it. As he first explained in 1983 in "The Flawed Grandeur of Meville's *Pierre*" (co-written with Brian Higgins), he is convinced that Melville sabotaged his book in deciding to make Pierre an author, and one whose problems allow Melville to voice "sometimes embittered reflections on his own career." Parker claims that this emphasis on the theme of authorship "deprived Melville of a full sense of what he was doing . . . in the novel as a whole" and describes it as a "new obsession [that] drained off Melville's psychic and creative energies [so that] the original purpose was blighted." "One becomes anguished," Parker writes, "as Melville's genius goes tragically to waste" (Higgins and Parker 453–54). Not content with presenting this position on *Pierre*, Parker went on to demonstrate his thesis in a radical way. In 1995 he published his expurgated Kraken Edition of *Pierre*, having edited out the most obvious references to the theme of authorship, including three whole chapters and many shorter passages. Advertised as a "daring reconstruction" that "restores [*Pierre*] to its original, shorter form—before Melville added an extraneous subplot," Parker's editorial initiative was daring indeed, given the absence of any manuscript evidence to support it."[12] He presents this thesis yet again in his biography of Melville.

To focus on Isabel's symbolic significance is to see that making Pierre an author was not an afterthought but the whole point of Melville's project. That Parker should have seen Melville's focus on authorship as the problem with, rather than the point of, *Pierre* begs for some explanation. It strongly invites the question of why Isabel's specific symbolic significance, upon which the coherence of *Pierre* depends, should have been and still is so easy for critics to miss. Three reasons, in particular, suggest themselves. The first is the mind's tendency, when attempting to think consciously about material that has symbolic significances, to gravitate toward reading literally. In the case of Isabel, this takes the form of responding to some of her statements and actions as though she were not a personified imagination but an actual woman. Parker does this, for example, when he writes that "Melville portrays her almost as feral, repeatedly traumatized" (*Biography* 2: 61). Her power over Pierre is most likely to be seen as sexual seduction and his response to her as feelings of lust that he tells himself are simply a passionate desire to champion a wronged sister. If the bond between the two is not the entrapping tie between the Melvillean author and his impossibly demanding imagination, then it must be a sexual one—and if it is sexual, then it is also incestuous.

It is not surprising that Melville's contemporaries read *Pierre* as though it were a realistic novel and so emphasized its intimations of incest. By choosing to write *Pierre* in a melodramatic mode reminiscent of contemporary sensation novels, Melville was inevitably reinforcing the popular tendency to read sexually, expecting intimations of incestuous lust. Yet a twentieth-century reader, taking up the book after the Melville Revival—and increasingly so as the century progressed, and then turned—read it in the very different context of Melville's acceptance as a major author. This was a strong incentive to see beyond *Pierre*'s apparent flaws. Yet to do so required discovering a focus of more substantial concern to him than incest. This did not happen, and for a reason for which, in this case, Melville was not responsible. Freud's psychosexual hypotheses, which became increasingly well-known at the time the Melville Revival occurred, and which were to have so long-lasting an influence in literary studies, presented the strongest possible impediment to reading symbolically the apparently sexual.

The habit of reading psychoanalytically inevitably reinforced the reader's tendency not just to take Melville's sexual references literally but to see the bond between Pierre and Isabel as incestuous. Henry Murray's ninety-page "Introduction" to his 1949 edition of *Pierre* was enormously influential in determining subsequent views of the work. His position that *Pierre*, called by Murray "Melville's battle with the Kraken," was flawed in ways of which Melville was unaware, for example, established a strong precedent for the thinking that led Parker to undertake his Kraken Edition. Murray discussed Isabel partly in Jungian terms, but his reading of Pierre was heavily Freudian. He saw Pierre's "incestuous inclinations [as] more sinful than his father's amorousness" and strongly endorsed S. Foster Damon's position that "incest is 'the secret motivation of the whole moral knot of *Pierre*.'"[13] The approach to *Pierre* (and to the American romance in general) taken by Leslie Fiedler in his 1960 *Love and Death in the American Novel* was unswervingly oedipal. The influence of his intentionally sensationalist psychoanalytic readings persists even today. For Fiedler, *Pierre* is a "finally unsuccessful experiment" (459). Lucy is the paradigmatic "Fair Maiden"—he calls her "the incredible Lucy over whom Melville drivels in *Pierre* . . . so shamelessly" (58). Isabel is Hecate, Pierre's "lust for death," and her "darkness is the shadow of the incest taboo" (296–97). Fiedler finds "rage in Melville . . . anguish at the thought that there cannot be an immaculate love of brother and sister" and calls *Pierre* "the major attempt in the history of our fiction at making . . . great art" of the theme of "brother-sister incest" (424, 422).

More recent critical commentaries on the extravagances of *Pierre* are far more attentive to textual specifics. Culturally contextualized readings of *Pierre* in relation to nineteenth-century popular fiction by men and women have drawn attention to many new dimensions of the literary scene at the time of Melville's writing. As critics such as Charlene Avallone and Samuel Otter show, the relationship between the style of *Pierre* and of contemporary sensationalist, sentimental (and even sentiment-satirizing) popular writing is a fascinating and complex issue. They examine how Melville, in his rhetorical "effusions," is writing with an eye to the conventions and stylistic elaborations of sentimental or sensation writing of the time, including popular novels, magazine fiction, and essays on the picturesque. Some of these passages in *Pierre* are largely decorative, some are tongue-in-cheek parody, others (as Otter so perceptively detects) are means for implicit protest against American acts of dispossession against Native Americans and the landless poor.[14]

Yet, alongside the important cultural studies approaches to Pierre, the still strongly established habit of reading Freudianly persists, encouraging readers to give far greater weight to the idea of actual incest in Pierre than Melville could have anticipated. To take Pierre's incest theme too literally is to be distracted from the importance of symbolic "incest" to the story. The reader's sense of Pierre's coherence depends upon giving priority to its symbolic level, on which the "incestuous" relationship is between the author and his own creative imagination. Melville deliberately deconstructed his apparent references to actual incest so as not to eclipse Pierre's symbolically "incestuous" relationship with Isabel as a symbolic character. Freud's own symbolizing project, however, continues to get in the way of Melville's.

Pierre's "incest" references are among its most tricky "ambiguities." That actual incest is not at issue on the symbolic level of *Pierre* (and probably not on the literal level either) is strongly indicated by Melville's withholding of any definite evidence of incest between Pierre and Isabel and his problematizing of apparent incest references. Enceladus, Pierre's symbolic double, for example, though the "son and grandson of an incest" (347), is not himself incestuous. In the episode of the visit to the gallery of paintings, Melville links the portrait of the incest victim Beatrice Cenci ("so sweetly and seraphically *blonde* a being"), not to Pierre's sister, the black-haired Isabel, who stands transfixed at "the precisely opposite side of the hall" by another painting, but to Lucy, his virginal and golden-haired former fiancée (351). When, having just seen the image of Isabel's face in apparitional form in the Eolian pine tree, Pierre compares it to the face of Dante's Francesca (the lover of her brother-in-law), he immediately qualifies this: "Francesca's face—or, rather, as it had been Francesca's daughter's face" (42). Pierre's greatest fear is not that Isabel is his sister but that she is not. This would mean that the notions of Truth and Virtue that he has adopted under her influence are delusory. If his attempt to follow a "chronometrical" (idealistic) code of conduct is folly, then the actions it has led him to take are of no value and the sufferings he has inflicted on his mother and on Lucy in the process perversely destructive. This, of course, is how Pierre's thinking runs when he is overcome with self-distrust. If Isabel is not his sister, the kind of imagination that she embodies is not properly his.

The following passage would seem to offer the strongest evidence that Pierre's feelings for Isabel are incestuous:

> He held her tremblingly; she bent over toward him; his mouth wet her ear; he whispered it.
>
> The girl moved not; was done with all her tremblings; leaned closer to him, with an inexpressible strangeness of an intense love, new and inexplicable. Over the face of Pierre there shot a terrible self-revelation; he imprinted repeated burning kisses upon her; pressed hard her hand; would not let go her sweet and awful passiveness.
>
> Then they changed; they coiled together, and entangledly stood mute. (192)

Melville surely knew that his readers would be quick to read as an allusion to sexual intercourse a sentence as deliberately ambiguous and inconclusive as "Then they changed; they coiled together, and entangledly stood mute." However, even the apparently intimately physical phrase, "his mouth wet her ear," points beyond the physical to the work's symbolic level. Earlier, Melville had made a point of stating that, as Pierre waits for Isabel to break her silence and resume her account of her past, "his eyes fixed upon the girl's wonderfully beautiful ear, which chancing to peep forth from among her abundant tresses, nestled in that blackness like a transparent sea-shell of pearl" (119). Although the explicitness here holds the reader's attention, there seems to be little reason for Melville to emphasize the ear of a character who represents "the Imagination"—unless the reader identifies it as yet another allusion to Keats's "Ode to Psyche." In this ode, Keats's poet, addressing his own personified poetic imagination, asks "pardon that thy secrets should be sung / Even into thine own soft-conched ear" (364). It is easy to imagine that Keats's conch reference caught Melville's attention. It is certainly appropriate that the Muse of the author of stories of the South Seas should have a "sea-shell" ear.

Similarly, in the tableau in which Isabel and Pierre "changed . . . coiled together, and entangledly stood mute," Melville has provided a context that makes it fit also—and more fully—with the book's "deeper" theme of authorship. This is the theme of Pierre as the writer of a "deep" book whose inextricable bond to a demanding imagination subjects him to what Melville calls "the horrors of poverty in authorship that is high" (338) and represents as a "hellish" fate. In a passage at the end of Book 6 Melville pointedly prefigures the emphasis here on changing by coiling together: the image of Isabel's face is dramatically linked to a scene from the *Inferno* and so to Dante. In this earlier passage, Pierre, having just received Isabel's letter informing him that she is his father's daughter, is trying to establish some link between her face as he remembers it and his father's face in the "chair portrait" that was painted at the time of his rumored involvement with Isabel's mother. As Pierre thinks of what "was inexplicably mysterious" to him in the face in the painting and what "had been inexplicably familiar" in Isabel's face at their first encounter, these two faces "by some ineffable correlativeness . . . reciprocally identified each other, and, as it were, melted into each other, and thus interpenetratingly uniting, presented lineaments of an added supernaturalness" (85). Pierre now sees in his mind's eye the composite face formed from the "melting together" of these two faces, and he is transported into the realm of "Mystery" that is the proper world of Isabel as symbolic character. "The physical world of solid objects now slidingly displaced itself from around him, and he floated into an ether of visions." This is the world of "authorship that is high"—as high as can be, as Melville's invocation of Dante shows. As Pierre stared at the apparitional "transfixed face in the air," Melville writes: "he ejaculated that wonderful verse from Dante, descriptive of the two mutually absorbing shapes in the Inferno: 'Ah! how dost thou change, / Agnello! See! thou art not double now, / Nor only one!'" (85).

The passage from Canto 25 of the *Inferno* in which these lines, quoted by Pierre, appear describes the most extreme example of two bodies "coiling together." It continues (in the 1814 Cary translation that Melville owned): "The two heads now became / One, and figures blended in one form / Appear'd where both were lost" (86). The two faces that merge into one transformed face belong to the Florentine nobles, Agnello dei Brunelleschi and Cianfa dei Donati, who are condemned to Hell for being thieves, and it is not only their heads and faces that melt together. The lines that Melville quotes occur in the middle of an extended dramatic description of the fusing of their whole bodies. Before this happens, Agnello is in his human shape, but Cianfa is in the form of a "serpent with six feet" that coils itself around Agnello so inextricably that the two become one. "Ivy ne'er clasp'd / A dodder'd oak, as round the other's limbs / The hideous monster intertwin'd his own. / Then, as they both had been of burning wax, / Each melted into other, mingling hues, / That which was either now was seen no more" (86).

Melville focuses not on the fact that the two men were thieves but on their hellish predicament and on the imagery that Dante uses to describe it. Dante's Canto 25 is full of serpentine forms. In the context of Isabel's fatal binding of Pierre to her, Melville links Isabel to Dantean serpent imagery in its dual associations with vinelike (or ivylike) coiling and with poison. The power of the Isabel-imagination over Pierre-the-author is, ultimately, sinister and dangerous. As early as Book 2 and before Pierre's first glimpse of Isabel, Melville foreshadows this dangerousness when he has Lucy imagine the mysterious face that haunts Pierre's imagination as "a fixed basilisk, with eyes of steady, flaming mournfulness" (37). In Book 3, Section 2, after Pierre's first sight of Isabel's face, its "phantom" afterimage in his mind's eye has the power to reveal to him disorienting depths of mystery, both within himself and "underlying all the surfaces of visible time and space" (52). This phantom "seemed to have in it a germ of somewhat which, if not quickly extirpated, might insidiously poison and embitter his whole life—that choice, delicious life which he had vowed to Lucy" (53). Section 3 opens with Pierre recalling his earliest view of Dante as "the one who . . . had first opened to his shuddering eyes the infinite cliffs and gulfs of human mystery and misery" and whose "dark ravings . . . are in eternal opposition to [the] finespun, shallow dreams of rapturous or prudential Youth" (54). Isabel's claim on Pierre does, metaphorically, poison his life. She also provides the actual poison with which they will together commit suicide. The book's closing words reenact the "coiling together" passage that first made clear to Pierre how inescapably "wedded to" her he was. She drops the empty poison-vial that "shivered upon the floor; and her whole form sloped sideways, and she fell upon Pierre's heart, and her long hair ran over him, and arbored him in ebon vines" (362).

In this melodramatic final tableau, as in Pierre throughout, Melville shows how clearly he understood the source of his own troubles. Like his author-hero, he cannot disown his creative imagination, while he realizes that to "embrace her," on faith, is to deny himself both commercial success (that would allow him to provide for his family) and literary acclaim (that would reassure him about the possibility of lasting fame). The problematic woman in Melville's life was not, as Parker attempts to show (*Biography* 2: 795), Melville's wife, Elizabeth, but rather Isabel, the woman within. Melville seems to have anticipated that Pierre's (and therefore Melville's own) predicament would be misunderstood as being perversely self-inflicted—hence his choice of Isabel's dying words:—"All's o'er, and ye know him not!"

Notes

1. "Symbolic characters" have a sustained psychological-symbolic significance that gives them an important role in addition to the obvious part that they play on the work's "realistic" level. In detailing their symbolic attributes and presenting their actions and interactions with one another, the romance author creates a fully developed level of symbolic significance, one that stages a dramatization of the mind's unconscious workings. The critical context for this essay is my book manuscript, "Inside Stories: A New American Romance Criticism," which presents a "nonpsychoanalytic" approach to this psychological-symbolic dimension of the romance. I gave an early version of this reading of *Pierre* at the Melville Society meeting at MLA, 30 Dec. 1995. The abstract is included in *Melville Society EXTRACTS* 104 (Mar. 1996).

2. I use "realistic," as the opposite of "symbolic," for that level of significance that is generated when the characters of the romance are read as counterparts to actual people. "Literal," in that it is etymologically tied to the letter of the written word, applies less well to imaged forms.

3. E. L. Grant Watson's "Melville's Pierre" sees Isabel as a "soul-image" rather than as, specifically, the creative imagination, and so he considers the two chapters on the contemporary literary scene to be unrelated to Melville's main theme. Phillip Egan in "Isabel's Story" does identify Isabel with the creative imagination but sees her as personifying a specific set of ideas (a dangerously seductive Romanticism) rather than simply a mental faculty. Reading her, in part, as a realistically presented character, he describes her as suffering from hallucinations and paranoia. William Dillingham makes many good points about the symbolic dimensions of *Pierre*'s characters, but he assigns Isabel a very wide range of significances. For him she symbolizes Pierre's "gnostically oriented need for union with God"; his "pride, selfishness, and jealousy"; and his sexual appetites (230).

4. See Higgins and Parker for contemporary reviews of *Pierre* and for articles and essays to 1983. See also the "Historical Note" in *Pierre* (379–407). The notes for the *Pierre* chapters in Samuel Otter's *Melville's Anatomies* include summaries of more recent *Pierre* criticism.

5. Today Pierre's behavior might be identified as bipolar disorder or manic depression.

6. Pierre, who, like Melville, was twelve when his father "died a raver" (178), worries about his "hereditary liability to madness" (287). See the accounts of Allan Melvill's death in Parker, *Biography* 1: 57–59, and Robertson-Lorant 47–49.

7. See "Historical Note" in *Pierre* (375–79) and *Moby-Dick* (630–31, 692–98).

8. See Parker for Sarah Morewood's account of telling Melville that his extreme writing regimen, as he works on *Pierre*, creates "a state of morbid excitement which will soon injure his health." His response to her comment that "the recluse life he was leading made his city friends think that he was slightly insane" was that "long ago he came to the same conclusion himself" (*Biography* 2: 49).

9. Melville refers to Coleridge's "The Rime of the Ancient Mariner" in Chapter 42 of *Moby-Dick,* and the "Eolean pine" in *Pierre* also recalls his poem "The Eolian Harp."

10. Keats, *Poems* 366. In February 1849 Melville bought *Modern British Essayists,* which included Francis Jeffrey's review of Keats's *Endymion: A Poetic Romance* and *Lamia, Isabella, The Eve of St. Agnes, and other Poems* (Parker, *Biography* 1: 618). Both "Ode to Psyche" and "Ode on Melancholy" are included in this volume. As Mary K. Bercaw shows in *Melville's Sources,* critics have identified allusions in *Pierre* and earlier Melville works to six of Keats's poems, but none to "Ode to Psyche."

11. In his edition of *Pierre*, Henry Murray notes "echoes" of "Ode on Melancholy" in Book 4, Section 2 (453–54), but not this "pressed like gushing grapes" allusion in Book 6, Section 4.

12. That Melville expanded the manuscript that he brought to New York is not in question, nor that Book 17, "Young America in Literature," would have been one of the additions. The problem lies in Parker's insistence that the theme of authorship is an "extraneous subplot" and that his expurgated text is superior to *Pierre* as Melville published it. To justify his cuts, Parker argues that the original *Pierre* was written in a mood of intense exaltation at Hawthorne's praise of *Moby-Dick* and that *Pierre* could not have been about Melville's "failing or failed career" because his career did not fail until "after he brought the manuscript to town." Yet, as Parker's introduction itself shows, as Melville wrote *Pierre* he was deeply concerned about his plight as an author—about his woefully inadequate literary earnings and his increasingly desperate financial straits. (Even during the writing of *Moby-Dick* this was so, as the first of his June 1851 letters to Hawthorne dramatically shows.) When Melville added further material on authorship, he was elaborating rather than derailing the work's already established direction and momentum.

13. Murray xiv, xcii, lvi. Murray's "Introduction" is the victim of its own excesses. Combining intensive source-hunting with Freudian, Jungian, Christian, and myth-related readings in an attempt at an exhaustive commentary, Murray also presents himself as more astute about *Pierre* than Melville was. He calls *Pierre* "a literary monster" (xciii) and "the performance of a depleted puppeteer" (xiv) and is scathing about Pierre's weaknesses, which he sees Melville as unjustifiably "exonerating" (ci). Parker, although he dissociates his position on Melville from Murray's highly critical one, is like Murray in believing that he knows better than Melville how *Pierre* should have been written. Murray's strongly negative view of Pierre was also taken up by most subsequent critics, including Parker.

14. See Avallone, "Calculations for Popularity," and Otter, *Melville's Anatomies* 195–201.

Women, Ownership, and Gothic Manhood in *Pierre*

Ellen Weinauer

*I*n an 1852 review of *Pierre* published in the *Literary World*, the Duyckinck brothers—whose despairing dispraise of Melville's work, beginning with *Moby-Dick*, has become both well-known and infamous—draw on gothic images to tell the story of what they think has happened to their one-time critical darling. "The author of 'Pierre; or, the Ambiguities,'" they write, "is certainly but a spectre of the substantial author of 'Omoo' and 'Typee,' the jovial and hearty narrator of the traveller's tale of incident and adventure. By what *diablerie*, hocus-pocus, or thimble-rigging, 'now you see him and now you don't' process, the transformation has been effected, we are not skilled in necromancy to detect. . . . We would rejoice to meet Mr. Melville again in the hale company of sturdy sailors, men of flesh and blood" (qtd. in Higgins and Parker, *Critical Essays* 43). It is perhaps ironic to find, in a review so clearly intended to discredit *Pierre*, a key to the novel's central themes.[1] Yet, in highlighting what they see as Melville's transformation into a ghost of his former self, an authorial "spectre," the editors of the *Literary World* seem to draw, interestingly, on the trajectory of the novel itself. Like the once-substantial, "jovial and hearty" Melville, the eponymous author-hero of *Pierre* becomes similarly altered. Once a hale, "flesh and blood" youth, Pierre appears to be transformed, via his devotion to a new form of "truth-telling" authorship, into a nearly blind "states-prisoner of letters," a hungry, pale, vertigo-afflicted wraith that haunts the "utter night-desolation of the obscurest warehousing lanes" (340, 341). Like Melville in the Duyckincks' formulation, Pierre too has become a specter, his ghostly status ostensibly linked to his authorial commitments.[2]

In its use of gothic tropes and language to describe Melville's apparent metamorphosis, the *Literary World* points us to one of *Pierre*'s dominant narrative modes—the gothic—and to one of the novel's most insistent thematic concerns: the spectralization of white manhood in the antebellum United States, a spectralization that, the novel suggests, occurs largely at the hands of women. Although critics have long recognized the ways in which the gothic plays a role in many of Melville's fictions (*Moby-Dick*, "Bartleby the Scrivener," "Benito Cereno" among them), *Pierre* is generally viewed as manifesting Melville's most thoroughgoing use of gothic conventions. Brian Higgins and Hershel Parker note, for example, that in *Pierre* Melville "inherited a Gothic toybox stuffed almost as full as Poe's with mysterious family relationships, enigmatical recollections of long-past events, suspenseful unraveling of dark, long-kept secrets, and landscapes symbolical of mental states" (241). Yet readings of *Pierre*'s gothicism tend to understand the gothic as an ahistorical and/or a fundamentally puerile mode that Melville sets out to parody, to transform, or—futilely—to escape. Precisely such ideas are at work, for instance, in Higgins and Parker's formulation, which characterizes the gothic as a "trivial subgenre" (with its "toybox" of mere conventions) that Melville, at least in the novel's earliest pages, "converts" into an instrument of "profound psychological exploration" (248).[3]

But the novel's gothic retentions are instrumental, substantial, and historically relevant. In *Pierre* the gothic is neither trivial nor exclusively psychological in its thrust; rather, *Pierre*'s gothicism points to what Teresa Goddu, in her recent rehistoricization of the gothic, has called "sites of historical haunting" (10). In particular, Melville's novel, shot through with the language of ownership and proprietary dominion, registers the fact that antebellum manhood, underwritten as it is by what C. B. Macpherson has called "possessive individualism," is itself a "site of historical haunting." The antebellum man, *Pierre* suggests, is spectral and indeterminate precisely because he attempts to ground his identity in ownership—especially, for this novel, in his owning women.

Noting the form's emergence at a time when a nascent market society was generating new and seemingly less reliable forms of identity, Andrea Henderson has argued that the gothic's concern with "spectralization"—its obsession with people who appear less as people than as ghosts, shades, doubles, or indistinguishable substitutes—reflects the fact that, in society at large, "people themselves have taken on an indeterminate, spectral quality" (235). Such "spectralized" selves circulate throughout *Pierre*, as does the anxiety about "personhood" that those spectral forms encode. Notably, Pierre himself is frequently figured in spectral terms, even, significantly, *before* he commits himself to a life of truth-telling authorship: after he gets the first letter from Isabel (the most dangerously "dispossessing" of the novel's women), his body is described as merely "the embalming cerements of his buried dead within" (94). In many respects, in fact, one can read Pierre's project, both familial and authorial, as one of reconstitution and reconstruction. His story simultaneously records the "indeterminate, spectral" qualities of antebellum manhood—qualities that the women of the novel bring to the fore—and documents Pierre's ultimately futile, and finally self-incriminating, response to such spectralization.

Undermined by the incursions on his personhood enacted in particular by two formidable women, his mother and Isabel, Pierre turns not away from ownership (as readings of Pierre's willingness to disinherit himself often suggest) but rather *to* it in an effort to reground and restabilize himself, to author his way out of the gothic narrative of subjective indeterminacy. But the proliferation of gothic emblems in the novel's final scene (a moldering dungeon, a wheezing turnkey, "shadowy" figures, vials of poison, dead bodies, and the "ebon vines" of Isabel's hair, which "r[u]n over" and veil Pierre's corpse [362]) reminds its readers that the possessive male individual can never determine and secure his own boundaries. Pierre's personal drama thus functions as a cultural drama as well: in *Pierre*, Melville tells the (gothic) story of the "untrammeledly...ever-present self" (199), a self that is haunted precisely because it can never be either "untrammeled" or "ever-present." The novel dramatizes one man's doomed struggle to reinscribe the firm boundaries of antebellum selfhood, to fashion, through a literary fashioning, a repossessed male self protected from the gothic indeterminacy that has come to trouble it.

Pierre Glendinning is introduced as, above all, a descendant and a would-be proprietor, an "impassioned" youth (3) who stands to inherit a cultural narrative of ancestral reputation along with his property, and who inquires into the meanings of neither. We meet him "issuing from the embowered and high-gabled old home of his fathers" (3), a home nestled in a landscape whose "finest features" bear out "the proudest patriotic and family associations of the historic line of Glendinning" (5). All such "associations" are "full of pride to Pierre," who "stood heir" to the estate's "forests and farms" as well as the family's aristocratic reputation (6–7). Like Melville himself, Pierre has "a double revolutionary descent. On both sides he sprung from heroes" (20). As *Pierre* insists, over and over again, on such issues as "descent" and "birthright" (15), "historical line[s]," "ancestral kitchen hearthstone[s]" (12), "large estates, and long pedigrees" (11), we are reminded repeatedly of Pierre's identity as proprietor-to-be.

The novel's obsessive return to matters of lineage, familial reputation, and ancestral property reminds us not only of Pierre's status as heir but also of the literary gothic. And in the gothic, significantly, ownership is never uncompromised. Indeed, from its inception in Horace Walpole's 1764 novel, *The Castle of Otranto,* the gothic has been largely concerned with disputed legacies, usurped lands, and fights for proprietary dominion.[4] As is Hawthorne's *The House of the Seven Gables*—published just a year before *Pierre* and, Wyn Kelley has argued, a major influence on Melville's novel—*Pierre* is indebted to early gothics such as Walpole's, where the desire for property motivates a variety of sins and ancestral lines are corrupted by the crime of expropriation.[5] Like these gothic predecessors, both *House* and *Pierre* explore the rot at the heart of an apparently "noble" inheritance. Even as it reiterates Pierre's ancestral pride-of-possession, for example, Melville's novel shows that his birthright is compromised. Thus, we learn that the Glendinning estate was once Indian land; and although the Glendinnings hold "deeds" that "bore the cyphers of three Indian kings," we are led to question both the "nobility" *and* the validity of their proprietary claims (6), much as we come to question those of Hawthorne's Pyncheons.[6] As Brook Thomas asserts, "The Glendinnings' acquisition of Saddle Meadows mirrors the violence involved in the acquisition of land by the nation as a whole" (143).

Certainly Pierre's esteemed family "fathers" had few scruples about the Indians, or about anyone else. Pierre's grandfather's reputation as "the gentlest husband, and the gentlest father"—and "the kindest of masters to his slaves," the narrator asserts with biting irony—is tainted by the fact that he is known to have "annihilated two Indian savages by making reciprocal bludgeons of their heads" (29–30).[7] Unlike "this grand old Pierre" (to quote a phrase reiterated to the point of parody in the course of a few paragraphs [30–31]), the contemporary Glendinnings no longer hold slaves. But they, like many another proprietor of the "magnificent Dutch Manors at the North," keep their "thousand farmer tenants" in a form of enslavement to "haughty rent-deeds" that are written in "lawyer's ink unobliterable as the sea" (10–11).[8] Melville's reference to the antirent movement, which protested landowners' insistence that tenants were bound in perpetuity to leases made before the Revolutionary War, links the Glendinnings to the contemporary slaveholding South and establishes unequivocally the exploitativeness of their proprietary claims.[9]

While the novel, early on, points to several forms of corruption at the heart of the "historic line of Glendinning" (5), Pierre remains blissfully unaware of any taint in the family legacy until he learns, from Isabel, of his father's own violation of truth, duty, and family honor. Pierre's discovery of his father's relationship with Isabel's mother—and, perhaps more significantly, his ostensible abandonment of Isabel—causes Pierre's "inmost soul" to "[faint] with amazement and abhorrence" (138), and leads him, at last, to begin to question his birthright and, hence, the foundations of his identity. Yet, while Pierre is surely haunted by his father's betrayal, and by what that betrayal might signify for the family legacy as a whole, the novel suggests that the most significant taint in the Glendinning line, at least where Pierre himself is concerned, is the fact that the line itself has come under the ownership and control of his mother. A "haughty" widow, Mary Glendinning became the sole owner of "all the Glendinning property" when her husband's sudden "fatal sickness" prevented him from "framing a new will" that would make Pierre his beneficiary (179). By making Mary Glendinning a woman of property, Melville engages an issue that was much debated in the antebellum period: the extent to which women, particularly married women, should be granted improved rights of ownership under the law. Beginning in the late 1830s, the legal disabilities under which married women suffered came under increasing scrutiny and critique. Motivated by a variety of often conflicting concerns—economic (the desire to shelter family property from creditors in the wake of the Panic of 1837), procedural (the legal codification movements of the 1840s), and political (the effort to gain new rights for women)—states began passing revised marital property acts in 1839; by 1850, seventeen states had passed such laws.[10] Debates about these revisions were heated and took place in a variety of venues, from state legislatures and political conventions to mainstream magazines such as *Godey's Lady's Book* and the *United States Magazine and Democratic Review*.

The extent of the debate, and its vitriol, can be attributed not only to the economic and political stakes involved but also to the complex and more deeply seated issue of female (and, by extension, male) personhood that the question of marital property rights foregrounds. Women incurred a number of economic and procedural losses upon marriage, including the inability to own and/or devise any personal or real property, to claim their own wages, to sue, make contracts, or to execute a will. These losses emerged from the "doctrine of marital unity" in common law, the "presumption" that "the husband and wife were one person—the husband" (Basch 17). William Blackstone, whose *Commentaries on the Laws of England* (1765–69), became a kind of handbook for American legal practitioners, is cited almost ubiquitously for his exposition of this equation.[11] "By marriage," Blackstone writes, "the husband and wife are one person in law: that is, the very being or legal existence of the woman is suspended during the marriage, or at least is incorporated and consolidated into that of her husband: under whose wing, protection, and *cover*, she performs every thing; and is therefore called in our law-French a *feme-covert;* is said to be *covert-baron,* or under the protection and influence of her husband, her *baron* or lord; and her condition during her marriage is called her *coverture*" (1: 430).

Much of the anxiety surrounding the extension of property rights for married women seems to have emerged from the challenges to this model of female selfhood: the married woman with property came out from under the "cover" of her husband to assume independent, *feme sole* status. And her "free" agency looked, to many, like defeminization. A particularly salient example of this perception of the feme sole, and of the apprehension she provokes, appears in a "spicy debate" centering on an 1854 petition to the New York State Legislature in which nearly 6,000 people asked for a "review of the entire code of [New York's] statute laws" with an eye to improving women's status under the law (Stanton 612, 614). In February 1854, Elizabeth Cady Stanton gave a speech to the Joint Judiciary Committee of the New York State Legislature calling, among other things, for augmented property rights for married women. Stanton's speech was reinforced by the petition, which was presented to the Legislature just a few days afterward. With regard to marital property, the petition focused in particular on the right of married women to claim and control their own wages.

In response to a motion to refer the petition to a duly appointed committee, Jonathan Burnett, chairman of the House Judiciary Committee, asked that the motion be tabled. In a lengthy explanation of his request, Burnett referred repeatedly to the "unsexing" effects of the marital property rights for which the petition called. Burnett figures the petition as a "sacrilegious" "firebrand" that has been "cast . . . into our midst," an "unholy" document designed to degrade the "Divine law which declares man and wife to be one" (qtd. in Stanton 613). Like Stanton and other activists, in Burnett's estimation those who signed the petition "do not appear to be satisfied with having unsexed themselves, but they desire to unsex every female in the land, and to set the whole community ablaze with unhallowed fire" (qtd. in Stanton 613).[12] Bubbling beneath the surface of Burnett's rhetoric, of course, is apprehension about the ways in which a change in married women's relation to property will necessitate a shift in male identity as well. "God created man as the representative of the race," and woman was derived from him,

146 *Ellen Weinauer*

Burnett declares; by making husband and wife "one flesh and one being," with the husband as "the head," the "institution of matrimony" reaffirms the preeminence of man in God's creation (qtd. in Stanton 613). To grant women improved rights of property under the law is to challenge this matrimonial arrangement, along with the very constitution of male and female identity that the arrangement itself seems to affirm. Women are not the only ones who might be "unsexed," in short, by a revision in marital property laws—or so the note of hysteria in Burnett's speech would suggest.

Technically, of course, the issue of marital property does not apply to Mary Glendinning: as a widow, she is already a feme sole.[13] But the more general issue in the marital property debates—the relationship between female (and male) identity and the ownership of property—is at work in *Pierre* as well. Indeed, although she possesses great beauty, Mary Glendinning looks suspiciously similar to the monstrously "unsexed" and "unsexing" women depicted in political jeremiads such as the one Burnett delivered in 1854, just two years after Melville's novel appeared. For Mary Glendinning wields her power like a kind of phallic dominatrix, her peremptory treatment of those around her (Delly Ulver, or Pierre himself, when he violates her will) suggesting not the "beautifying influences of unfluctuating rank, health, and wealth" (4) but rather the corrosive effects of property ownership on women. In one particularly resonant passage in this regard, Mary Glendinning holds "grand old Pierre's" military baton. As she contemplates Pierre's eventual inheritance of this "symbol of command," she herself "swell[s] out" (20). Her tumescent response to the baton—a not particularly subtle indicator of her propensities for phallic authority—follows, significantly, on the heels of a passage in which she mentions Pierre's "sweet docility" (and the comforting "docility" of his betrothed, Lucy Tartan) not fewer than a dozen times (19–20). While Pierre will "prove a haughty hero to the world," he shall "remain all docility to me" (20), she declares, indicating her interest in maintaining feme sole authority over her son and his property, even when he comes into possession of the Glendinning lands. In this context, the fact that Pierre is the "only surnamed male Glendinning extant" (7) takes on new resonance. Maleness has been nearly bred out of the Glendinning line, which has "by degrees run off into the female branches" (7–8). It is thus no wonder that Pierre so fully resembles his mother. Indeed, so "striking" is the "personal resemblance between" Mary and Pierre that they are often taken for siblings—a misapprehension facilitated by the admittedly bizarre fact that they "were wont to call each other brother and sister" (5). "In the clear-cut lineaments and noble air of the son," the narrator explains, Mary Glendinning "saw her own graces strangely translated into the opposite sex" (5). In Pierre, then, Mary sees herself reiterated and her husband's genetic influence largely effaced. In this, she takes a "triumphant maternal pride" (5).

For Pierre, this now-matrilineal legacy is unnatural, unhealthy, and even dangerous. His inheritance is tainted not only by the crime of expropriation and exploitation but also by a kind of gender disorder necessitated by and reflected in the familial diversion into the distaff line. As a consequence of that diversion, Pierre is forced to function, Michael Rogin has suggested, as his mother's "phallus" (164). A nightmare version of the sentimental mother, Mary Glendinning possesses a virtually constitutive power over her son, who thereby becomes an empty sign by which his mother signifies.[14] In this, Pierre resembles not an ostensibly replete proprietor-to-be but rather, interestingly, a *feme covert*, his "very being . . . incorporated and consolidated into that of" his mother. Like the married woman, Pierre has become a kind of specter, a shadow self. As Rogin notes, Pierre "will have to free himself from [his mother] in order to acquire a self, sex, and power of his own" (164) and to recuperate the Glendinning legacy (one further compromised by his father's premarital transgressions) in the name of an uncorrupt(ible) and inalienable masculinity.

It would appear at first that Isabel offers such freedom and recuperative potential, as many critics contend. Isabel seems to free the heretofore conventional "youth" from his maternally inscribed past and to lead him into new, adult, autonomous realms of emotion, sexuality, and knowledge; she enables Pierre to begin his journey of ontological unfolding and remasculinization. Thus Phillip Egan argues that Isabel "revolutionizes" Pierre: she "pulls him loose from the fixities of his early life" because "she gets him to think unconventionally" (100). Richard Brodhead goes even further. From the moment Isabel appears on the scene, he asserts, she "begins to overthrow" Pierre's previous "sense of selfhood"; while this overthrow puts Pierre into a profound crisis, through it the "heroic Pierre is born" (*Hawthorne, Melville, and the Novel* 167–68). But, as Gillian Brown and Priscilla Wald have more recently suggested, Isabel and Mary Glendinning seem to function in many respects as analogues rather than opposites.[15] Like his mother's, Isabel's influence over Pierre "seemed to have in it a germ of somewhat which, if not quickly extirpated, might insidiously poison and embitter his whole life" (53). And, as with Mary Glendinning, that "germ" seems to have a great deal to do with ownership. Isabel too, and even more devastatingly, threatens Pierre's property in himself.

When Pierre sees Isabel for the first time, at the neighborhood sewing circle, he is captivated—indeed, he is dispossessed—by her. Having "entirely surrendered himself" to the passionate "curiosity" that her countenance evokes, he struggles to "regain the conscious possession of himself" (47). For two full days after Pierre first sees Isabel, her face "fully possessed him for its own" (51). "For those two days," we learn, "Pierre wrestled with his own haunted spirit," fighting to "regai[n] the general mastery of himself" (50). A dual discourse of possession, connecting liberal notions of self-ownership with occult renditions of spirit possession, proliferates as the narrator describes the effect that Isabel has had on Pierre. The face continues to "steal upon" Pierre with a "mystic tyranny" (53). Frustrated by his inability to reclaim himself, Pierre repeatedly turns to the language of ownership, of "rights," "shares," and theft: "The face!—the face!—. . . the face steals down upon me. Mysterious girl! who art thou? by what right snatchest thou thus my deepest thoughts? . . . Leave me!—what share hast thou in me?" (41). In an earlier ride with Lucy, Pierre offers a description of the *beau ideal* of marital relations that would please William Blackstone himself. "A god decrees to thee unchangeable felicity," he promises, "and to me, the unchallenged possession of thee . . . for my inalienable fief" (36). But Pierre's response to Isabel indicates that such a model of "unchallenged" male sovereignty over the female subject is illusory. With Isabel, Pierre is certainly no baron of an "inalienable fief." Extending the feudal metaphors, the narrator explains that Pierre is in "wild vassalage" to the face and to the "original sensations" it elicits from him (52). That this "vassalage" has disturbing gender consequences Pierre himself makes plain: "This indeed almost unmans me with its wonderfulness," he thinks, when he realizes that "escape the face he could not" (49).

In depicting Isabel's penetration into the "most withdrawn and subtlest region of [Pierre's] own essential spirit," Melville seems to come to the gothic point of *Pierre*. Many critics have noted that Isabel is a key element of *Pierre*'s gothicism. Taking note in passing of Isabel's transgender potential, Newton Arvin calls her "a perfectly legitimate descendant, if not of Pierre's father, then certainly . . . of a long line of betrayed and persecuted heroines *or even heroes* in Gothic fiction," a line beginning with *The Castle of Otranto,* whose own "persecuted heroine" is named Isabella (44; emphasis mine). Ken Egan has also addressed Isabel's gothic function in *Pierre,* arguing (by contrast with Arvin) that Isabel is not a gothic hero(ine) but rather the "quintessential Gothic 'monster,'" "truly other, truly uncanny, precisely because she *is* 'outside of culture'" (155). Certainly there is much in the text to situate Isabel in the way that Egan does, not least her own seemingly unbounded, indeterminate, and spectral nature. Having heard "The First Part of the Story of Isabel," for example, Pierre struggles to "condense her mysterious haze into some definite and comprehensible shape" (136). Yet, if Isabel is herself a kind of shapeless, spectral gothic "monster," so too does she render Pierre himself shapeless, spectral. Reversing the trajectory of her personal history (Isabel, of course, is herself propertyless, deprived of lineage, divested even of a coherent life story), the "dispossessed" Isabel comes to possess one thing: Pierre. As she does so, not surprisingly, she interrupts Pierre's sense of inalienable self-possession. Breaking down the boundaries between inside and outside, self and other, she reveals those boundaries to be contingent, endlessly shifting, and perpetually penetrable.

A key vehicle for this breakdown is Isabel's storytelling and music making, performances that are depicted in terms of antebellum occult spectacle. Pierre experiences Isabel's guitar music, for example, as a sort of mesmeric performance: "Isabel seemed to swim in an electric fluid; the vivid buckler of her brow seemed as a magnetic plate"; he takes note of "an extraordinary physical magnetism in Isabel"; she "seemed to swim," the narrator repeats, in "sparkling electricity" (151). Here Isabel occupies the traditionally female role of mesmeric medium, the vehicle through which the "electric fluid" flows. But she also simultaneously assumes the male role of mesmerist, capable of harnessing a powerful "magnetism." And, of course, if Isabel is the mesmerist, then Pierre becomes her medium, a vehicle for female meaning: "Often, in after-times with her, did he recall this first magnetic night, and would seem to see that she then had bound him to her by an extraordinary atmospheric spell—both physical and spiritual—which henceforth it had become impossible for him to break, but whose full potency he never recognized till long after he had become habituated to its sway" (151).

Here, we might once again read *The House of the Seven Gables* as an intriguing intertext for *Pierre*. In particular, Melville seems to gesture toward Hawthorne's—or, rather, Holgrave's—depiction of Alice Pyncheon, the mesmerized victim of the vengeful Matthew Maule. Yet in Melville's depiction Pierre stands in for Alice Pyncheon, while Isabel, now not an "unassuming maid" but rather a "dark, regal being" who commands Pierre to "be silent" in an "imperious . . . tone" (152), recalls Matthew Maule. In Hawthorne's novel, Maule's mesmeric possession of Alice reveals the penetrability, the fragile boundaries of the (female) subject. In *Pierre*, mesmeric penetration also occurs. But here it is the ostensibly impervious male subject who comes to be possessed. While Isabel's mesmeric possession of Pierre thus seems to reverse the sex-gender hierarchy, in fact it merely exposes its problematic terms. She "incorporates" herself into Pierre as the antebellum feme covert does into her husband. In doing so, she weakens rather than fortifies his sense of autonomous selfhood.

In recounting the first part of her story, Isabel tells Pierre that, for her, "there can be no perfect peace in individualness. Therefore I hope one day to feel myself drank up into the pervading spirit animating all things" (119). With her rejection of individualism and its implicit claim to private property, Isabel echoes the narrator of "Hawthorne and His Mosses," the 1850 review Melville wrote for *The Literary World* before he fell from the Duyckinck brothers' critical graces. In "Mosses," Melville's speaker repudiates the idea of individual genius, expressing his desire to "share" the "fullness and overflowing" of intellect with a "plurality of men" (252). But as in "Mosses," where this vision eventually raises the specter of dispossession (Melville describes Hawthorne as a kind of "wizard" whose "wild, witch voice" has "magic[al]," "ravish[ing]" effects [239, 241]), in *Pierre* the repudiation of individualism means, and is much more overtly, a threat to the seemingly secure confines of the possessive individual.[16] Thus, like Mrs. Glendinning, who exercises a "sorcery over his soul" (16), Isabel, too, is depicted as bewitching Pierre. Isabel's "enigmatical story," her guitar's "inexplicable spell," "all this had bewitched him, and enchanted him, till he sat motionless," like a spectral, "mystery-laden visitant, caught and fast bound in some necromancer's garden" (128). It is no wonder that he hurries from their first meeting as if liberated, "burst from . . . sorceries" (128). Both Isabel and Mary Glendinning, in short, come to appropriate and hence spectralize Pierre; but whereas Pierre seems unaware of Mary Glendinning's incursions on his personhood, with Isabel he comes into full knowledge of his own contingency, his internal "confusion and confoundings" (171).

Here the issue is gendered. Pierre's "confoundings" have a great deal to do with his dispossession at the hands of *women*, with the fact that both literal property (the Glendinning estate) and figurative property (Pierre himself) are in female hands. But this disruption rests on a deeper foundation. What is being exposed here, finally, is the dangerous contingency of a self founded on, and constituted by, ownership. According to the logic of possessive individualism, a market-driven logic derived from classic liberal political philosophers such as Hobbes and Locke, human identity "emanates from," "revolves around," and "ceaselessly reaffirms" ownership (Dimock, *Empire for Liberty* 31). But, as Wai-Chee Dimock notes in her analysis of *Pierre*, such a model of selfhood is "perhaps inevitably" a precarious one: "To make ownership the constitutive essence of selfhood," Dimock writes, "is already to commit the self to a theater of eternal warfare, in which everyone, operating as a personified battlefield, is ceaselessly invaded and defended, possessed and dispossessed" (148).

In this context, Pierre's insistence on divesting himself of the relics of his personal and familial past (a divestment that follows on the heels not only of his rejecting his father's hypocrisy and legacy but also of his mother's disinheriting him) suggests a desire to discover an alternative model of selfhood, one that may bypass the precarious circuits of possessive individualism. "Henceforth, cast-out Pierre hath no paternity, and no past," Pierre declares as he strips himself of the objects of his prior identity; "therefore, twice-disinherited Pierre stands untrammeledly his ever-present self!—free to do his own self-will and present fancy to whatever end!" (199). Pierre claims, here, to be fashioning a new, nonproprietary self, a self that is "ever-present" because "twice-disinherited," "untrammeled" and "free" because no longer reliant on property. But in fact, this "new" Pierre is not so much a man who has divested himself of (the desire for) property as he is a man who has learned a lesson from his recent past about the critical role that possession plays in constituting the self. It is in this light that we might best regard Pierre's bizarre decision to come before the world as his half-sister's husband. Pierre may be "twice-disinherited," divested of his paternity and his past, but by claiming Isabel as his wife, he becomes what he had hoped to be with Lucy: the "baron or lord" (to quote Blackstone on laws of coverture) of an ostensibly "inalienable fief." Pierre's "marriage" to Isabel, his appropriation of her as feme covert, functions, thus, as a first step in his efforts to reverse the incursions on his personhood made by Isabel and his mother. But Pierre's authorship, ultimately more reactionary than revolutionary, is the most important instrument in his effort at self-reclamation and reconstruction.

"Wee is the chest that holds the goods of the disowned!" (201), Pierre remarks to his "wife" as they begin the journey to New York City and toward what will become, for Pierre, a new, "truth-telling" authorship. This essay begins with some reflections on the ostensible parallels between the "spectral" author that Melville had become in the eyes of his contemporaries and Melville's own spectralized author-hero, Pierre. But Pierre's spectralization occurs long before he becomes an author. With help from Mary Glendinning, Isabel has authored a transgressive text, unveiling the gothic dynamics of Pierre's own identity. Pierre determines literally to author an alternative text, to create a new narrative bearing witness to his own impregnability. Pierre's authorship, however, signals not his liberation from but rather his reliance on a proprietary model of selfhood. Nor, despite his best efforts, does his authorship effect his escape from the "eternal warfare" that such a model entails (Dimock, *Empire for Liberty* 148).

It is true that from the moment he is ensconced in his writing room, with a "bottle of ink, an unfastened bundle of quills, a pen-knife, a folder, and a still unbound ream of foolscap paper" (270) arrayed before him, Pierre seems capable of exerting a newfound sense of self-possession: in a "steeled and quivering voice," he demands that Isabel "call me brother no more! How knowest thou I am truly thy brother? Did thy mother tell thee? Did my father say so

Figure 1. Elizabeth Shaw Melville. Daguerreotype, ca. 1847. 2.125" x 2.75". Berkshire Athenaeum, Pittsfield, Massachusetts.

Figure 2. Catharine Maria Sedgwick. *The Life and Letters of Catharine Maria Sedgwick*, ed. Mary E. Dewey (New York: Harper & Brothers, 1871).

Figure 3. Alice Cary. *The Poetical Works of Alice and Phoebe Cary* (Boston: Houghton, Mifflin, 1865).

Figure 4. Gail Hamilton. *Gail Hamilton's Life in Letters,* vol. 1, ed. H. Augusta Dodge (Boston: Lee and Shepard, 1901).

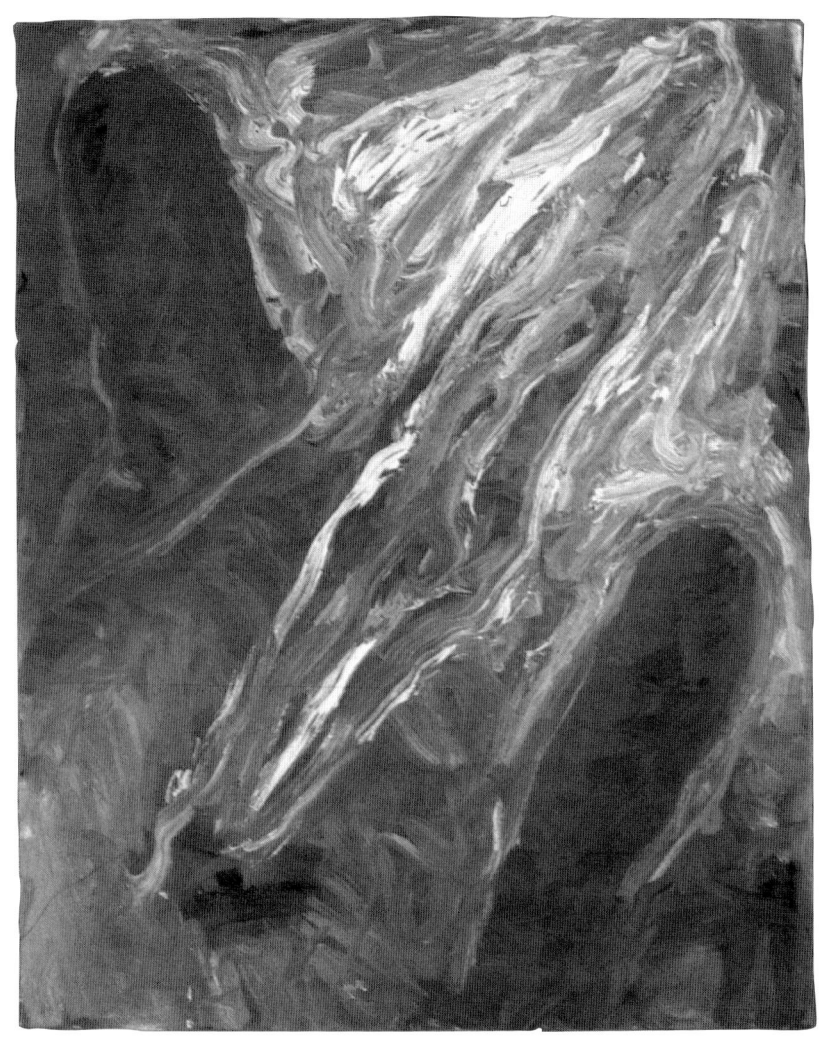

Figure 5. Aileen Callahan. #6 from *The Birth of Moby Dick* series (2002). Oil on canvas. 20" x 16".

Figure 6. Ellen Driscoll. From sketches of *Ahab's Wife* (1998). Ink on paper. 11" x 8.5".

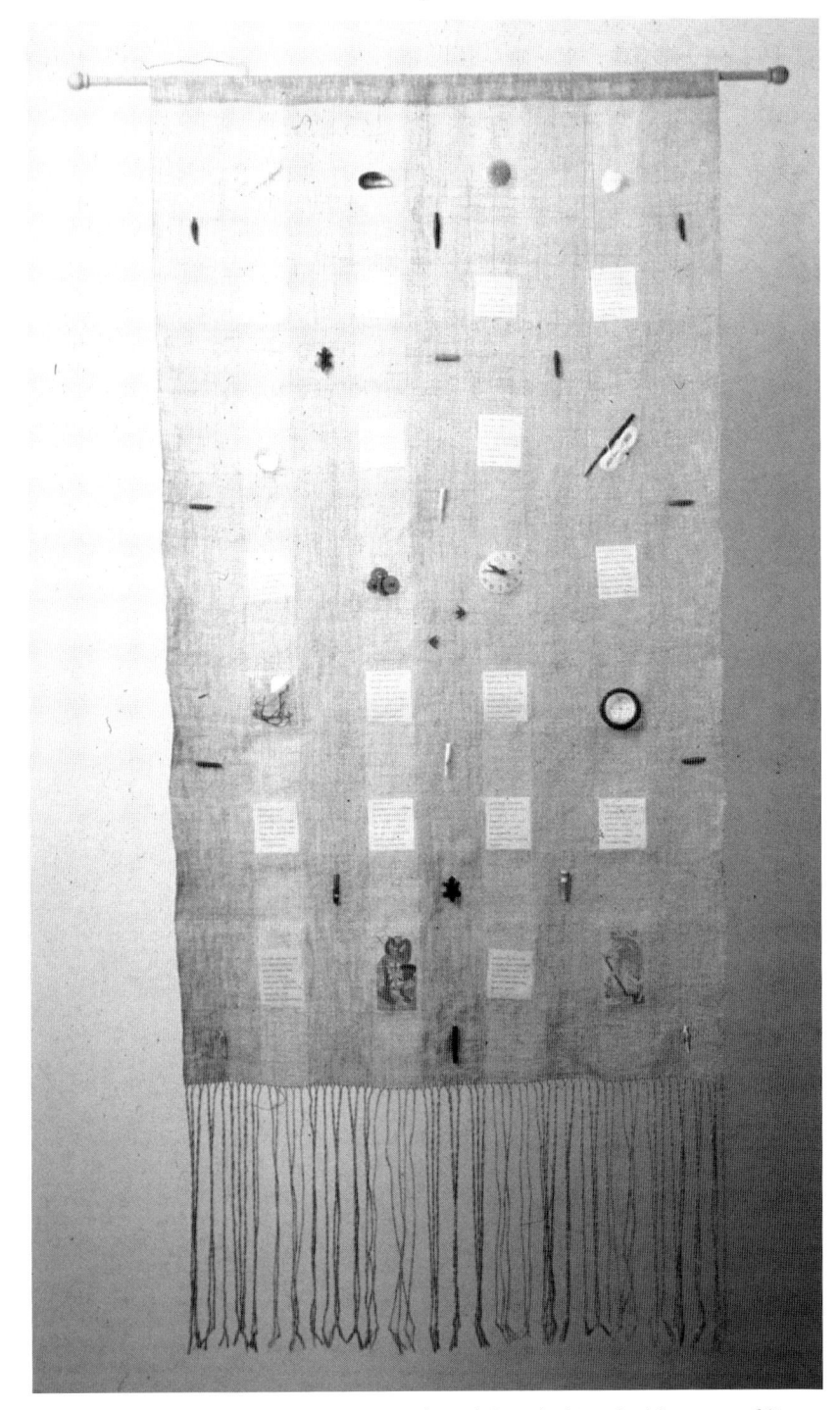

Figure 7. Aimée Picard. *The Loom of Time* (2000). Interlocking double weave of linen, fish line, and found objects, including crab claw, sea urchin, shells, fish hooks, clock, compass parts, Tarot cards, string, and weaving sword. 72" x 32" x 2".

Figure 8. Abby Schlachter Langdon. *Queequeg in Her Coffin II* (1997). Plaster and gauze body cast with ink inscriptions. 62" x 20" x 6.5". Collection of Robert Del Tredici.

to me?—I am Pierre" (273). This claim to autonomous personhood—"I am Pierre"—foreshadows his later sense that the "enthusiasm" Isabel once provoked in him is "no longer so all-potential with him as of yore" (353). Pierre's authorship, then, certainly impels his growing distance from Isabel; if she has heretofore had the capacity to dispossess Pierre of himself, increasingly his authorship seems to reverse this process. Once an author of such sentimental poems as "The Tear" and "The Weather: a Thought," Pierre now attempts a "mature" work in which he hopes "to deliver what he thought to be new, or at least miserably neglected Truth to the world" (283). Pierre's "mature work" is less a work of "neglected Truth," however, than it is a work of self-making, a work by which he tries to write himself out of a female-authored gothic narrative and into a secure(ly) possessive individualism.

The fact that Pierre is doing such proprietary identity work is signaled by Melville's use of plagiarism to describe Pierre's authorship: when we "peep over the shoulder of Pierre, and see what he is writing," we find that "he seems to have directly plagiarized from his own experiences, to fill out the mood of his apparent author-hero, Vivia" (302). As the dissonance in the notion of self-plagiarism suggests—how can one steal from oneself?—Pierre's writing emerges as a rather desperate act of self-reclamation. Priscilla Wald notes that if Pierre has to steal them, then his "*own experiences . . .* evidently do not belong to him. He cannot confer them at will even on his *own* (and *owned*) literary creation" (*Constituting Americans* 130). The "random slips" we read from Pierre's narrative do indeed seem like repossessed bits and pieces from the experiences Pierre is trying to claim as his "own," from "Vivia's" insistence that "I hate the world," to his expressions of utter disillusionment ("to think of the Truth and the Lie!"), to his imprisonment in the "dismal jail" of his writing cell (303). The "Truth" that Pierre tells in his narrative of Pierre-Vivia seems a truth that he himself requires, one that confirms his claims to himself and so frees him from Isabel's gothic trap.

Clearly, that truth has everything to do with secure ownership. In addition to the text the "world" will "read in a very few hours," Pierre is writing another, completely interior text, one "writ down in his soul" for his "own private shelf" (304). He writes a text that is his own private and inalienable property. His power is utterly self-contained; "I fight a duel in which all seconds are forbid," he proclaims when Isabel and Lucy offer to help him in his work (349). Through Vivia, his narrative alter-ego, Pierre gives "life" to a new, enclosed identity that is sui generis, contingent on and possessed by no other. "I am what I am," Pierre declares as the novels (Melville's and Pierre's own) are coming to an end (325). "I render no accounts," he twice repeats (325, 329). Pierre the truth-telling author effects what Pierre the juvenile author could not: he originates a godly self that is ontologically closed ("I am what I am") and seemingly impregnable.[17]

Crucial to this process of self-"invention" is Pierre's ability to contain the sorts of powerfully undermining women who have proven so disruptive to him throughout, to incorporate women, not as women but rather as figures, into his artistic economy. Living (female) bodies, we learn in *Pierre,* are profoundly threatening to the secure (male) self. If Isabel's face first dispossesses Pierre, her magnetic body proves to be even more problematic, awakening him to knowledge of his own sexual appetites and thus, once again, to his own contingency. In charting Pierre's uncontrolled, even enslaving physical response to Isabel (she had, the narrator explains, "bound him to her by an extraordinary atmospheric spell—both physical and spiritual—which henceforth it had become impossible for him to break" [151]), *Pierre* manifests concerns about the risks that sexual desire can pose to (male) selfhood.

In the antebellum period, as Russ Castronovo notes, "anxiety over citizens' sexual behavior" became central to reform movements that sought to demonstrate how men's "[surrender] to carnal impulses" can render them "slaves"; thus, Castronovo notes, "self-reliance as a corporeal principle became a national concern" (63). Although rarely understood as toeing the cultural line on matters of sexuality (Melville's depiction of incest, whether figurative or "actual," was part of what most troubled contemporary critics), *Pierre*'s anxious response to Isabel's and Mary Glendinning's sexual power suggests that the novel may well have a conservative thrust in this regard. Thus, not surprisingly, Pierre frequently engages in converting living bodies into symbols, bodiless figures. When his plans regarding Isabel are barely formed, for example, Pierre, "fearful of ascertaining" the effect those plans will have on Lucy, makes a convenient discursive conversion: "like an algebraist, for the real Lucy he . . . had substituted but a sign—some empty x—and in the ultimate solution of the problem, that empty x still figured; not the real Lucy" (181). Pierre's substitution of the "real Lucy" for an "empty x" seems effective. After this, Lucy conceives of herself as a mere cipher, a "blank" awaiting Pierre's signification; when "thou didst leave me," she writes Pierre, "I . . . felt an utter blank, a vacancy; for wert thou not then utterly gone from me? and what could there then be left of poor Lucy?" (310).

Although Isabel is less easily contained, she, too, comes to function as the mere object of Pierre's representation—a spectral "empty x" in his drama of self-absorbed signification. Incorporating her unsettling narrative into his own ego-driven one, he begins to invert the dynamic of their relation. The more he closets himself in his writing room, "forbidding" all "seconds" in his drama of self-making, the more Isabel is seemingly divested of power.

Whereas once Isabel functioned as a mesmeric artist whose music kept Pierre "fast bound" (128), Pierre now uses that music for inspiration: as Isabel plays the guitar, "Pierre felt chapter after chapter born of its wondrous suggestiveness" (282). Gradually, Isabel's once-threatening desire to be "drank up into the pervading spirit animating all things" becomes the instrument of her own destruction—for she is truly "drank up" by Pierre. Distressed by Lucy's proposal to come live with them at the Church of the Apostles, where she promises to "serve" and "contribute to the welfare of all" (311), Isabel resolves to be fully fashioned by Pierre's originating hand. Divesting herself of any identity except that which comes through Pierre, she depicts herself in terms that strikingly echo those offered by William Blackstone himself. Isabel actualizes her coverture, telling her "husband" that "thy hand is the caster's ladle . . . which holds me entirely fluid. Into thy forms and slightest moods of thought, thou pourest me; and I there solidify to that form, and take it on, and thenceforth wear it, till once more thou moldest me anew" (324). Here, Isabel's effacement as fully divested feme covert signals not covert self-assertion, as it did in her earlier (premarital) mesmeric performances, but rather self-obliteration. The once "imperious" woman who had "unmanned" Pierre by claiming his interiority for her own gives herself over to Pierre's text-making in an act of almost frenzied self-abnegation.

Such self-abnegation is even more disturbingly figured by Isabel's desire to sell her body, or, more specifically, her body parts, on his behalf: "See, I will sell this hair; have these teeth pulled out; but some way I will earn money for thee!" (333). Isabel's willingness to dismember and sell herself merely literalizes the gothic disembodiment she comes at last to experience at the hands (and in the narrative) of Pierre. Her transformation into a figure, a represented image in Pierre's authorial journey, is complete. Fully differentiated now from Mrs. Glendinning, Isabel becomes Lucy's twin. As such, she, like Lucy, is a mere functionary in Pierre's authorial drama, one aspect of the symbolic economy out of which he creates his "comprehensive . . . work" (284). In the end, Pierre is no longer a gothic sign in a feminized symbolic economy; women have become gothic signs in his own.

When Pierre receives the original letter from Isabel that sets the events of the novel in motion, he anticipates needing a kind of defensive posture: what will happen, he wonders, "if once he should permit the distracting thought of Lucy to dispute with Isabel's the pervading possession of his soul?" (106). By the novel's end he has effectively banned *both* women from his soul and so seemingly reclaimed his once-threatened self. Although he is "on either hand clung to by a girl who would have laid down her life for him; Pierre, nevertheless, in his deepest, highest part, was utterly without sympathy from any thing divine, human, brute, or vegetable. One in a city of hundreds of thousands of human beings, Pierre was solitary as at the Pole" (338). Through his acts of representation/appropriation, through his making of a "private" narrative, Pierre has become what he has wanted to be: "untrammeledly his ever-present self" (199). He has written himself out of Isabel's gothic narrative of indeterminacy and spectralization and become the subject whose inalienable self-possession is seemingly confirmed.

But in doing so, Pierre has simply authored another gothic story—one based on the live burial of Lucy and Isabel, on their expropriation, immurement, dismemberment. The gothic is, it seems, inescapable—Pierre invokes it even as he attempts to evade it. In these terms we can make sense of the overtly gothic elements of the novel's final pages. By *Pierre*'s end, only a pile of bodies remains: Pierre has killed Glen Stanly, his cousin and the man who replaced him in the line of inheritance; Lucy dies upon learning that Isabel is Pierre's sister rather than his wife; and both Pierre and Isabel commit suicide. The latter deaths—Lucy's, Pierre's, and Isabel's—take place in the "dungeon of the city prison," where the walls "trickl[e]" with mold (360). The presence of "shadowy figures," "asthmatic turnkeys" (361), a vial of poison, and "pale ghosts" (360) further signals the gothic import of the scene. Such images cast a grim light on the imperial authorial selfhood that Pierre has ostensibly achieved by novel's end, a selfhood akin to that which Melville himself celebrated in a letter he wrote to Hawthorne after reading *The House of the Seven Gables* (and before embarking on the composition of *Pierre*). In the letter, Melville expresses admiration for what he sees as Hawthorne's absolute authorial autonomy, venerating him as a "man who, like Russia or the British Empire, declares himself a sovereign nature (in himself) amid the powers of heaven, hell, and earth" (*Correspondence* 186). Pierre has achieved such sovereignty when he becomes, in his "deepest, highest part," "solitary as at the Pole." But the unabashedly, relentlessly bleak ending of this novel leads us to wonder what *Pierre* might have revealed to Melville himself about the author as an absolute, imperial proprietor.

When Melville first introduces us to Pierre as a "juvenile author," he incorporates a strange fantasy of authorial supremacy that bears on this final scene. Pierre, we learn, can "[let] his body stay lazily at home" and "send off his soul to labor, and his soul would come faithfully back and pay his body her wages. So, some unprofessional gentlemen of the aristocratic South, who happen to own slaves, give those slaves liberty to go and seek work, and every night return with their wages, which constitute those idle gentlemen's income" (261). As an author, then, Pierre is a kind of slave-owner—his authorship ratifying his status as not alienated slave but self-possessed individual. "Yet," the narrator cautions us as if in a gloss on the slavery analogy, "let not such an one be over-confident" (261). Certainly, as Wald writes, "The slave metaphor [in this passage] calls into question how potentially 'free' and assured selfhood ever is" (*Constituting Americans* 152). If a kind of slavery grounds his sovereignty, the author begins to look more and more unstable. He comes indeed to resemble the spectralized slave master that Orlando Patterson describes in *Slavery and Social Death:* "At precisely the point where the master achieves lordship, he finds that he has become dependent on his slave. He cannot be sure even of his own existence, since the reality of his domination rests on the unreality of that which he masters: the slave, whom he has socially killed and rendered non-essential by making him merely an extension of himself" (98). The master, in short, is haunted by the alienation of his slave, in whom the master's own self-possession is precariously vested.

In the end, Pierre's authorship fits precisely this pattern, his "domination" resting on the "unreality"—the now-empty signifiers—of the socially dead Isabel and Lucy. As an author attempting to achieve "mastery," Pierre simply replicates the gothic nightmare from which he has attempted to escape. In perfecting his domination, Pierre has rendered not just Isabel and Lucy gothic subjects but himself as well. His efforts to escape spectralization have led simply to new forms of spectralization, to an inability to "be sure even of his own existence." The final and perhaps most terrifying passage of the novel, in which Pierre's dead body is veiled by Isabel's hair, reveals, in its potent gothic imagery, this uncertainty: "'All's o'er, and ye know him not!' came gasping from the wall; and from the fingers of Isabel dropped an empty vial—as it had been a run-out sand-glass—and shivered upon the floor; and her whole form sloped sideways, and she fell upon Pierre's heart, and her long hair ran over him, and arbored him in ebon vines" (362). Even at the end, Pierre has not revised the gothic narrative of subjective indeterminacy authored by Isabel. Indeed, Isabel's authorship reemerges with a kind of vengeance: just as the end of *The House of the Seven Gables* is given to Alice Pyncheon, "The end of Pierre's story," Gillian Brown has noted, "is not his but Isabel's" (*Domestic Individualism* 165). In *Pierre,* Melville describes one author's effort to recover the self, to fashion a repossessed subject out of its haunted fragments; but that newly fashioned self has, this final image suggests, simply incorporated and interiorized the threats made against it. The "story" Isabel offers in this final scene is not the story of a failed possessive individual, but the story of a perfected one. It is the story of a subject whose work to contain itself and police its confines is always unfinished.

As Pierre's vexed negotiations with his would-be publishers, "Steel, Flint, & Asbestos," remind us, it is impossible not to read Pierre's story of authorship as, at least in part, a meditation on Melville's own. Indeed, as the review in the *Literary World* suggests, readers were drawing parallels between Pierre and Melville from very early on. By recognizing the ways in which *Pierre* registers the unfinished business of possessive individualism, however, the *Literary World*'s treatment of Melville's Pierre-like spectralization takes on new resonance. By drawing attention to the seeming ghostliness of the "author of 'Pierre,'" Melville's "transformation" into a mere "spectre" of his former "substantial" self, the editors of the *Literary World* point to what we might call a half-truth. For what they simultaneously miss *and* inadvertently mark is *Pierre*'s most disturbing truth: constituted as it is by property in (often living) "things," the possessive individual is itself a specter, its boundaries endlessly permeable, frighteningly penetrable. Pierre's story is, then, not only Melville's. It is also the story of the antebellum white man, whose reliance on ownership—in the case of this novel, particularly the ownership of women—leaves him no solid ground on which to stand and, finally, no true escape from the nightmare of his own ghostliness.

Notes

1. According to Jennifer DiLalla Toner, Melville's career manifests an increasing "impatience with [literary] fame and an insistence on biographical oblivion." *Pierre*, she argues, in many respects culminates "Melville's struggle against the ways in which readers and reviewers defined and reified the public authorial self" (238–39). The review of *Pierre* in the *Literary Review*, in Toner's reading, points to Melville's success in achieving what she calls the "unwriting of the biographical subject" (254–55).

2. The extent to which Melville identifies with Pierre-as-author is one of the central critical questions regarding the novel. Perhaps most famously, Brian Higgins and Hershel Parker have argued that *Pierre*'s notorious, even spectacular "failure" is attributable to Melville's "excessively personal sympathy for Pierre's frustrations as an author"—sympathy that leads him, in their formulation, to "lose his grasp" on the narrative as a whole (264, 261). For Higgins and Parker, disappointing reviews of *Moby-Dick*, coupled with demoralizing contract negotiations over *Pierre*, led Melville to shift the novel toward a consideration of Pierre as author. This shift marks a "drastic change in Melville's authorial purpose" (287) and all but dooms the novel, which splits, as a result, into two finally unresolved texts. Michael Rogin argues, similarly, that Melville is gradually taken over by the "conjunction between Pierre's life and his own" and thus "loses himself inside his own fiction" (178). By contrast, Raymond Nelson refuses to read Pierre's story as Melville's: "The novel *works*," he argues, if we take the author of *Pierre* to be "Pierre himself; the staggeringly uneven romance is his. *Pierre* is the book he is writing in his frigid room in the Apostles toward the end of the novel" (202). Nelson echoes the reading of *Pierre* offered by Edgar Dryden, who also attempts to differentiate among Melville, Pierre, and the narrator but who does view the novel as a failure belonging to Pierre himself. Although

Priscilla Wald notes that autobiographical readings of *Pierre* are largely "convincing," she also suggests that such readings have "minimized the thematic treatment of authorship" in the text (*Constituting Americans* 108) and argues for a resituation of scholarship along that line of inquiry. For a recent reading that argues for the instrumentality of Pierre's authorship in the overall conception of the novel, see Silverman.

3. Although less inclined than are Higgins and Parker to denigrate the gothic as "trivial," Newton Arvin takes pains to claim that the "'influence' of the Gothic school" on Melville is only "slight and minor" (33; note that "influence" is in quotation marks, further indicating Arvin's effort to distance Melville from the gothic). Critical treatments of Melville's gothic tend to reflect the general tendency to view the gothic as a debased mode. As Eugenia DeLamotte notes, Pierre's "Gothicism" and its "failure . . . have often been linked either implicitly or explicitly" (92). By contrast with this line of argument, DeLamotte insists that in *Pierre* "Melville turned to the resources of Gothic romance" precisely because the gothic could offer him "a highly developed vocabulary of images, scenes, and plots already associated, in some cases quite subtly, with the theme of knowledge" (65). Wald briefly treats *Pierre* in terms of the gothic, linking its inquiries into "the boundaries of the self"—a concept central to DeLamotte's argument about the gothic in general and to my own analysis in this essay—to Poe's "William Wilson" and Hawthorne's "Young Goodman Brown" (*Constituting Americans* 135–36). For a more recent and thoroughgoing analysis of *Pierre*'s engagement with the ideological foundations of early gothic novels, see Miles.

4. Robert Miles addresses the ideological thrust (and political origins) of the early English gothic and argues that *Pierre* is an "extraordinarily informative interpretation of the relationship between the genre's ideological origins and the genre itself" (157). Melville deploys the gothic in *Pierre* to draw attention not only to the "buried secret of American cultural illegitimacy" (172) but also to the gothic's foundations in what Miles calls the "(mis)appropriation of power and its consequences" (174). Though Miles is more concerned with the ideological origins of the English gothic tradition, his historicist reading of *Pierre*'s gothicism complements my own.

5. See W. Kelley, "*Pierre*'s Domestic Ambiguities." In "Pierre's Blackened Hand," Robert S. Levine draws brief but compelling connections between *House* and *Pierre* on matters of genealogy and race, arguing that these and other texts offer genealogical accounts that stress "cross-racial entanglement" and hence the "ludicrousness of understanding a nation's identity . . . in relation to . . . fictional notions of [racial] purity" (27).

6. In *House*, the deed to the Maine territories that the Pyncheons go to such lengths to find is similarly marked with "the hieroglyphics of several Indian sagamores" (316).

7. For more on the provocative implications of the Glendinnings' slaveholding and the "claims to whiteness" that their slaveholding status ironically undermines, see Levine 30–35. Samuel Otter also takes up the compromised nature of the Glendinning legacy in "The Overwrought Landscape of *Pierre*."

8. Ken Egan sees this exposure of the Glendinning sins as a point of departure in Melville's effort to "carnivalize" the New York epic—a "classic American patriarchal genre"—and as part of Melville's evolving "antipatriarchal theme" (146).

9. For more on Melville's treatment of the antirent movement in *Pierre*, see Brook Thomas 145–47. Like Thomas, but more extensively, Nicola Nixon discusses the ways in which Melville uses the antirent wars to reveal the "Southern" tendencies of Northern antebellum society. Nixon argues intriguingly for reading *Pierre* at least in part as a response to the "ideological fissures in the Union" that were ostensibly (but not effectively) fused by the Compromise of 1850 (720). Also see Otter, "The Overwrought Landscape of *Pierre*" 357–61.

10. Linda Speth provides a useful overview of the Married Women's Property Acts, their

conflicted origins, and the complicated "procedural limbo" in which they left married women. Also see Basch and Salmon.

11. Basch offers a lengthy discussion of Blackstone's extensive influence on the American interpretation of marital law in the eighteenth and nineteenth centuries (43–56).

12. In "Considering Possession in *The Scarlet Letter*," I take up Burnett's remarks by way of meditating on the connections among Hawthorne's novel, the seventeenth-century witchcraft crisis, and the nineteenth-century debate about marital property.

13. It is worth noting, however, that although widows and single women were granted feme sole property rights under the law, they provoked plenty of social and economic discomfort. Indeed, historian Carol Karlsen has argued persuasively for a correlation between witchcraft accusations and anxiety about female ownership. Citing a number of cases, including those of widows such as Katherine Harrison and Anne Hibbins, Karlsen concludes that most accused witches were women who "stood in the way of the orderly transmission of property from one generation of males to another" (116).

14. Gillian Brown sees this as the central problem for Pierre, whose attempts to "refor[m] the sentimental family" depend on his ability to "obviate the role of the mother in reproduction and nurture" (*Domestic Individualism* 156). "In what is perhaps the nineteenth century's most negative portrayal of domestic values," Brown writes, "Melville posits authorship as an annulment of the curriculum vitae supervised by sentimental motherhood and popularized by sentimental literature" (135). At the end of the novel, however, Pierre's suicide—with a vial of "death-milk" kept at Isabel's breast—indicates the triumph of sentimentalism, whose forms of "nurture [block] the writer from start to finish" (165). W. Kelley also explores *Pierre's* engagement with domestic literature and sentimentalism, arguing that Melville seeks (but fails) to "renovate the middle-class household" by turning away from marriage and toward models of "fraternal communion" ("*Pierre's* Domestic Ambiguities" 92).

15. Wald writes that "what Isabel wills, though subtly articulated, replaces what Mrs. Glendinning demands; Pierre simply transfers his allegiance"; thus, she argues, "Isabel does not inaugurate Pierre's break with the past" ("Hearing Narrative Voices" 106). Although Brown reads Isabel as initially allowing Pierre to separate from his mother, she argues that, like Pierre's mother, Isabel ends up making manifest the "maternal containment of the individual" (*Domestic Individualism* 165).

16. I take up these issues at length in "Plagiarism and the Proprietary Self." For an alternative reading of the meanings of incest, authorship, and originality—a reading that seeks to reconcile the seeming contradiction between Melville's appeals to originality and his appeals to literary community in "Hawthorne and His Mosses" and, more particularly, in *Pierre*—see Silverman.

17. Pierre's "successful" self-making also involves his ability to learn that he cannot "climb Parnassus with a pile of folios on his back" (283). Pierre's growth as a writer, then, is marked by his ability to reject his literary fathers, as he rejects Spinoza, Goethe, and Plato in the "random slips" of his writing that we come to read (302–3). This reading of literary "originality" contrasts with the model of fraternal genius that Melville holds out (though not without some anxiety) in "Hawthorne and his Mosses."

Part Four

Women in the Fiction and Poetry

Island Queens

Women and Power in Melville's South Pacific

Juniper Ellis

*E*ach of Melville's first three books—*Typee* (1846), *Omoo* (1847), and *Mardi* (1849)—presents a queen who serves as a synecdoche for the place and people she rules. In Melville's works, examining the queen also means examining the histories and cultures that make her a ruler. Thus, Melville meditates on the tribal imperatives and European interventions that in *Typee* and *Omoo* inform the queen's power. Characteristic of his entire project in these first two books, Melville creates embellished versions of historical figures, establishing through his portraits of the queen the political and cultural condition of the Pacific islands he visits. These figures make visible the damage done by would-be "civilizers"—including French admirals, British missionaries, and U.S. sailors. In *Mardi*, Queen Hautia rules a fictional island, yet her portrayal, too, represents the differing civilizations that claim the Pacific.

Broadly speaking, the queens wield forms of power that can be grouped under the rubrics of culture, politics, and narrative. In each of these categories the queen's bodily presence—and sexuality, in particular—serves as an index of the island she represents. Whether she is exuberantly physical, matronly, or sexually devouring, the queen's displaying or withholding of her body reveals her and her island to be pure or polluted. Melville uses these terms explicitly. The other women of the island (oddly enough, whether they be missionary women or island nymphs) often follow the queen's example, and thus they, too, embody the condition of each Pacific island Melville portrays.

Differing strategies in these books portray the queens' and their islands' power. In *Typee,* Melville depicts the queen using her physical presence to dismiss the French military power, a dismissal that also entails his portraying a pure Pacific culture, untouched by visitors' depredations. In *Omoo,* the queen removes her physical presence from visitors, including Melville's narrator; that strategy encompasses a sustained denunciation of the "degeneracy" (308) that visitors have created in Tahiti. In *Mardi,* Melville depicts the queen's power to end the narrative by ending the narrator's life, a strategy that entails the narrator's fleeing the queen in order to pursue his own story.

The authority thus exerted by these queens encompasses the power of other women on the island, including *Typee*'s unnamed English missionary woman, Fayaway, and Tinor; *Omoo*'s "mickonaree" woman Ideea and the women of Eimeo; and *Mardi*'s Annatoo and Yillah. Melville emphasizes the sources and effects of the women's power (and of their occasional powerlessness), illuminating the circumstances of the Pacific Islands vis-à-vis U.S., English, and French forces. Each of Melville's narrators, as a U.S. traveler in the Pacific, of course brings potential change; the queen's response to the narrator thus underscores the island's political and cultural situation.

Women played important parts historically in giving mariners a place in the Pacific Islands. Establishing relationships with Pacific women was important because mariners were neither entirely separated from nor integrated into the various missionary, military, and trade endeavors run by U.S. and European powers. Melville suggests that the Taipi were isolated from such mariners as himself, many of whom lived with the Marquesans and whose relationships with women were key to the places they secured in the island community. William Ellis's *Polynesian Researches* cites two Marquesans from Fatu Hiva who declare that in 1823 "there were seven white men and two negroes living in their island" (3: 312). Based on his study of ships' logs, Pacific historian Greg Dening provides a six-page list of ships that visited the Marquesas between 1774 and 1842. He notes, "By 1838 there were reported to have been twenty beachcombers on Nukuhiva alone and whalers lost two or three and took on as many each visit" (303). The *Lucy Ann,* the Australian ship that would pick Melville up when he escaped from the Taipi, "had lost eight men and a second officer at Vaitahu on 7 June of the same year" (304). Many of these short-term visitors had temporary liaisons with women. Several sailors, though, such as Jean Baptiste Cabri and Edward Robarts, lived on the islands for years, forming long-term relationships.

The women's power Melville portrays shapes his narrator's ability to observe or participate in events on the island and in discourse about the Pacific. Other U.S. writers before Melville had described the way Pacific women displayed or withheld their bodies, as when the navy captain David Porter justified and the ship's chaplain C. S. Stewart criticized their apparently unrestrained sexuality.[1] What is notable about Melville's accounts is that he explores the fact of women's power in these situations, investigates both the indigenous and imported foundations of that female power in the Pacific, and foregrounds the conventions that govern writing and reading about such power.

The queen of Nuku Hiva appears at the end of Chapter 1 of *Typee* in full bodily glory. Her appearance challenges the military powers that, Melville's narrator Tommo reports, have just claimed the Marquesas Islands for France. (Historically, the French formally claimed Nuku Hiva on June 2, 1842, shortly before Melville arrived at the island and jumped ship. In *Typee*, Melville also modifies strategically the time of his four-week visit to the Taipi, a time he extends to four months.) Her scene is twinned with that of a missionary woman which immediately precedes and introduces the queen's scene. Thus, Melville's opening chapter features Marquesans triumphing over missionary and colonial authorities through the display of a woman's body.

The missionary wife's body is exposed by islanders who wish to determine her sex. Once the islanders determine that the voluminous calico covers a woman's body, "to the horror of her affectionate spouse, she was stripped of her garments, and given to understand that she could no longer carry on her deceits with impunity. The gentle dame was not sufficiently evangelised to endure this, and, fearful of further improprieties, she forced her husband to relinquish his undertaking, and together they returned to Tahiti" (6–7). Involuntarily denuded and rendered powerless, she is by her own standards unable to remain in the Marquesas Islands to serve as an evangelical example.[2] In other words, she no longer has the authority to insist upon the importance of covering the body, in keeping with the sexual modesty and restraint mandated by Victorian and Christian culture. Her nakedness represents, beyond her individual discomfort, the retreat of successive Christian missions from these islands.

Melville follows the fleeing missionaries with a phrase that acknowledges the deliberate parallel of this scene to the queen's: "Not thus shy of exhibiting her charms was the Island Queen herself, the beauteous wife of Mowanna, the king of Nukuhiva" (7).[3] Just as Melville tells of English missionaries leaving the islands, he presents the French military departing hastily from the queen's unexpected physical display. The Island Queen, unlike the missionary wife, displays her own body, thereby routing the French naval officers who believe they hold power.

As Melville's narrator in *Typee* tells it, the king and the Island Queen are invited onto a U.S. man-of-war so that the French may parade their civilizing influence on and for the couple. While the French officers approve of the regal reception the Marquesan couple receives on board the U.S. ship, "picture their consternation," Melville's narrator asks the reader, "when all at once the royal lady, eager to display the hieroglyphics on her own sweet form, bent forward for a moment, and turning sharply round, threw up the skirts of her mantle, and revealed a sight from which the aghast Frenchmen retreated precipitately, and tumbling into their boat, fled the scene of so shocking a catastrophe" (8). These words end Chapter 1; the fleeing French military authorities follow the English missionaries, setting the stage for Melville's narrative.

Missionaries retreat, the French military power flees the scene, but Melville's narrative looks straight at what the Island Queen displays. That gaze is what is shocking about Melville's book—not the scandal of his critique of missionaries, which led him to expunge criticisms in the 1846 revised (U.S.) edition of the book, or the progressive insight that France's claiming of the Marquesas Islands constituted a "buccaneering expedition" (18), but the unfaltering "peep at Polynesian life" that Melville announces in the book's subtitle. Far more effectively than Melville's claims that he has not read the accounts of prior U.S. visitors to the Marquesas Islands, the twinned scenes open space for the narrative. Melville's readers, the narrative promises, will encounter sights otherwise unseen by visitors. Thus, even though the French had the opportunity to see the queen's bare behind, they flee; Melville's narrative gaze, however, remains resolutely (and humorously) focused on even shocking sights.

Prior to displaying her charms, the queen is covered in overelaborate European finery, an ironic measure of the civilizing process the French have introduced (and of Melville's keen sense of incongruity). In the twinned episodes of the missionary wife and the queen, a woman's clothing is an index of culture, of her allegiance to one set of conventions as opposed to another. In other words, some twenty-odd years prior to E. B. Tylor's publication of *Primitive Culture* (1871), which, anthropologists and the *OED* concur, introduced the modern sense of "culture," Melville implies that clothing, tattoos, and women's variously adorned bodies can signify culture.

As Melville tells it, the queen's dignity is apparently less than skin deep and can be thrown off with her clothes as, however, the indelible tattoo designs she displays cannot be. The "charms" that the queen displays when she bends over might be the genitals that the missionary woman hides behind her clothes or might be the rare tattooed girdle that the queen, Vae Kehu, was not shy of showing. Thus, reports Max Radiguet, the secretary to the état-major général on the lead French frigate in the Marquesas, "Some small vertical stripes (rays) at the lips, a kind of insect covering the ear lobe, some mittens and some boots of fine quality were the only apparent tattoos on the body. Later, she saw nothing wrong with showing us with pride a splendid bundle (or flowering) of invention, a veritable masterpiece of inlays which covered her loins [*reins*]."[4] The historical Vae Kehu's girdle circled her loins or lower back in an elaborate design documented by the American anthropologist Willowdean Chatterson Handy.[5] Moreover, in many parts of the Pacific, tattoos could be displayed freely in order to celebrate the beauty of the designs, but a woman's bending over in such a manner could also be a powerful tactic to shame and trump the male viewer: this ultimate exercise of authority reminds the male viewer where he came from.

Here, too, Melville makes strategic modifications to the facts, associating the Island Queen's tattoo with her buttocks by punning on the "agh*ast*" French who flee from the "cat*a*strophe" of her self-display (8).[6] Following Falstaff, Melville points toward the "ass" he does not actually show, satirizing the pretensions of the would-be civilizing powers to confine or control the Island Queen. Part of the sly fun is that the Island Queen reveals that those attempting to exert colonial power make asses of themselves. Rather than revealing the exact location of the tattoo or its cultural significance, the impetus of Melville's episode is to remove the French, to clear the deck of the foreign military presence (if not of U.S. mariners), and to announce that Melville's narrative will be dealing with the indelible, material figures of women's bodies in the Marquesas.

Noting briefly the historical circumstances of the Marquesan queen and king reveals additional strategic modifications Melville makes in presenting the above scenes, modifications that emphasize his elevation of the Island Queen in order to critique the French. In Nuku Hiva, the historical queen was Vae Kehu, wife of Temoana. Vae Kehu, daughter of a Taipi chief, inherited traditional power and, when she married King Temoana, acquired imported status as the queen. Temoana's rule, too, was both inherited according to time-honored traditions and altered by his associations with the French. His grandfather was descended from three or four chiefly lines, and Temoana inherited *haka'iki* status—traditional authority—as a paramount chief.[7] When the French arrived and made Temoana a king, his title changed, but his role as king was founded on his chiefly authority (Dening 226).[8] In other words, Temoana and Vae Kehu united both traditional chiefly and imported monarchical forms of authority. Temoana's elaborate wedding, which similarly combined Marquesan and Christian traditions, was witnessed and described in detail by a missionary (Dening 180).

In *Typee* Temoana and Vae Kehu appear as the characters Mowanna and the Island Queen. Melville focuses on their relationship to French rather than to Nuku Hivan bases of power, thereby underscoring his critique of the French. For instance, where Melville throughout *Typee* emphasizes the traditional practice of polyandry, here he suggests that the monarchy rests on European ideas of marriage. Both chapter subheadings and text describe Vae Kehu as queen, and his narrative depicts the queen variously as the king's "wife," "consort," and "spouse." The association of the pair with European rather than Marquesan practices furthers his portrayal of the royal pair as figureheads established by the French. These associations then heighten the queen's dramatic humiliation of the French.

Similarly, Melville alters the chronology of the Island Queen's visit to the U.S. warship. Historically, such a visit did occur, when Temoana and his wife boarded the naval ship *United States*. That visit, recorded in the ship's journal in October 1843—or sixteen months after the French established a formal claim to the island—notes that the queen was "in a red skirt which reached a few inches below the knee, about 15 years of age, with handsome features, and tattooed on all visible parts" (Anderson, *Journal of a Cruise* 58). The event, as *Typee* depicts it, takes place two to three years after the French had annexed the Marquesas. Melville's telling of the story lengthens the time the French officials have had to "civilize" the royal couple, thereby emphasizing how ineffectual their attempts have been.

The twinned scenes of the missionary woman and the queen frame the narrative of *Typee* both chronologically and structurally. The missionary woman's scene precedes Tommo's adventures with the Taipi, the Island Queen's scene serves as a sequel, and both episode titles introduce these scenes as culturally representative. The "Adventure of a Missionary's Wife among the Savages" (ix) occurs a "short time before my visit to the Marquesas" (6). The "Characteristic Anecdote of the Queen of Nukuheva" (ix) transpires "between two and three years after the adventures recorded in this volume" (7).[9] All of the following events—indeed, the story itself—are read politically and narratively in relation to these paired stories of women. The queen's tattoo scene appears in the first chapter of *Typee* but chronologically closes the story. It enables Melville to write beyond the apparent endings of political and narrative power signaled by the official arrival of colonialism or the temporal conclusion of a story.

Typee's second and third chapters also close with anecdotes of women: the "swimming nymphs" (14) who board Tommo's ship and the English missionary woman who defies the French by continuing to fly a British flag at the mission when the French claim Tahiti. (The flag flown by Mrs. Pritchard, like the queen's tattoos, challenges the French by displaying a sign of another origin.) Chapter 2 closes with Melville's statement that "the 'Dolly' was fairly captured" (15) by swimming Marquesan women. Like the queen, these women display their bodies, in this case in dances that, Melville notes, exhibit an "abandoned voluptuousness in their character which I dare not attempt to describe" (15). In other words, Melville marks his own narrative's strictures. Like the French, then, at some points the narrative, by looking away, looks toward conventions in Melville's own culture.

This point is significant because much of the book focuses on taboos that the narrative attributes to Taipi, several of which relate specifically to women (who are not permitted in canoes, Tommo reports, or allowed to enter the structures that form the meeting area for men). In these instances, however, Melville's narrator notes taboos in the United States, ones that govern what Tommo is able to tell. Tommo may maintain his direct gaze, but the narrative cannot. The reader, however, is well placed to imagine that which Tommo "dare not attempt to describe." Melville is thus ostensibly discreet for his U.S. readers while creating an open space in which nymphs display their bodies in "abandoned voluptuous" dancing.

The image of a ship claimed by island women, in the face of whom the sailors can only acknowledge themselves prisoners, however, leads to Tommo's praise of the "artless," "unstudied," "confiding" women and his denunciation of the sailors' "polluting examples!" (15). The reference to pollution and "the ruin thus remorselessly inflicted upon them by their European civilizers" (15) is likely to venereal diseases that had stricken sailors aboard Melville's ship (two of Melville's *Acushnet* shipmates died from venereal disease[10]; no fewer than five were "ailing & ill of the venereal," attested the captain of the *Lucy Ann*, the ship that Melville signed on after living with the Taipi (Leyda 1: 140; Parker 1: 221). Here, as at the end of Chapter 1, the "civilized" characters are not what they should be.

This scene raises issues of overlapping sexual and narrative power. The island nymphs first capture the ship, taking control of the vessel and the men on board in accordance with their cultural practice, which Melville presents as a sexually innocent abandon. What complicates the situation and its telling, however, is that the sailors are more than willing to be so taken by the women, so the sailors too exercise power in capitulating to the women. Moreover, the Pacific practice of a life-affirming tradition of sexuality becomes deadly due to the venereal diseases the sailors carry and spread in the islands. Melville's narrative is thus decidedly knowing, calling attention to the role of the narrator in presenting the scene that is both innocent and polluted. This self-reflexive narrative offers more than a "mock-serious general condemnation" of the sexual scene (Herbert, *Marquesan* 14). Melville mocks the conventional presentation of the scene to acknowledge the power of both sexuality and disease, innocent vitality and deadly corruption.

In this scene, Melville rewrites a familiar narrative, one told by Stewart, Porter, and Ellis among many others: the ships arrive in the bay, and the women swim out to welcome the sailors. In revising the ship chaplain Stewart's description of this familiar scene, John Samson points out, Melville heightens the mythical overtones of the encounter, referring to the women as nymphs, mermaids, and sylphs. But beyond undermining the "sexual repression" on which Stewart's account rests (Samson 55), Melville also thereby calls attention to the very process of mythologizing or stereotyping women. Women are mythologized in all three visions: Stewart's denunciation of the women for violating proper sexual standards, the sailors' embrace of the women as fulfillment of sexual fantasies, and Tommo's ambiguous reactions to both the sexual encounter and its narratives.

This interplay of mythologies reveals more than scholars have sometimes suggested: "By freeing the implicit sexualization of Stewart's description from its moral censure, Melville simply succeeds in submitting the girls' bodies to another form of the colonial gaze" (Ivison 119). Rather, Melville neither escapes nor reproduces the colonial gaze but calls attention to it, turning the gaze to sexual and textual power. He implies that the very anticipation of intercourse—whether spiritual, physical, or even narrative—may always be both innocent and diseased. The women are both active and passive in this exchange: they initiate the sexual contact, but are the unknowing recipients of the dreams and the contagion that "civilized" people carry.

Typee's women form a narrative and cultural index of the island. The queen, the missionary, and the nymph are recurring characters who encompass almost all women in *Typee* and *Omoo*; they mark the limits of Melville's story, their bodily presence and absence making plain the parameters of the narrator's "peep at Polynesian life" and the accompanying story. Fayaway, the queen, and the swimming women all wield a bodily power. The ways in which individual women characters use their power emphasize the political and cultural situation of the island in question: the queen and the swimming women exemplify Marquesan cultures encountering the dangers of European civilization, while Fayaway embodies the innocence and purity of a precontact state.

In *Typee*, missionary women most often represent not the "feminine heroism" (18) of Mrs. Pritchard, who flies the British flag in the face of the French, but the vanguard of a polluting civilization. "Christianity must precede civilization" (3: 361), declared the missionary William Ellis, one of the sources Melville acknowledges in *Typee* and *Omoo*. The way Melville tells it, that sequence destroys Pacific cultures. Missionary women make fleeting but significant appearances in not only the Marquesas Islands and Tahiti, as already noted, but also Hawaii. In reference to the Sandwich Islands, Melville uses bold irony to convey the debilitating results of missionary work. He describes a missionary woman in Honolulu who makes two Hawai'ian men pull her in a cart, beating them when they are slow in pulling her uphill: the "small remnant of the natives had been civilized into draught horses, and evangelized into beasts of burden" (196). In *Typee* and *Omoo* Hawai'i and Tahiti are portrayed in part to contrast with the condition of the Marquesas Islands, which Melville presents to his readers as a test case of the newly arrived colonial power. Nuku Hiva, in this depiction, is closer to the precontact state and therefore makes visible the effect of visitors.

Fayaway, the female companion to Melville's narrator in *Typee* when her people serve as his hosts or captors, represents the Taipi woman before visitors have inflicted "ruin" upon her or her way of life. She is both the most individualized and the most typical of the nymphs. She is named, described extensively, and notable for the empathy she shows Melville's narrator. But in most ways Fayaway embodies the Taipi woman, Tommo presenting her dress, appearance, and daily habits as representative of an ideal. "Fayaway, with all the other young girls of her age" (86) is Tommo's phrase in depicting her as characteristic regarding, for instance, tattooing.

Significantly, however, Fayaway also allows Tommo to test the limits of the taboo, to try to obtain a special dispensation allowing her into the canoe.[11] One of the most dramatic changes visitors made in Pacific traditions came through violating taboos. When visitors did so with impunity, they shook the foundations of the intricately prescribed and proscribed behavior mandated by taboos. (The concept of *tapu*, rendered as "taboo" in English, is based primarily on the need to separate, in order to protect, that which is sacred.)[12] So Tommo's presentation of Fayaway is paradoxical: she represents the precontact state that exists in the "Happy Valley" (124) prior to changes brought by visitors, but he himself brings some of those changes to her. Melville thus shows his narrator seeking, for his own pleasure, dispensations from Taipi ways. The narrator's placing of Fayaway in a canoe dramatizes the powerful changes mariners helped bring to the Pacific.

Melville also uses the figure of a woman to illustrate the purity of the Taipi. He does so through references not only to the just-cited utopian valley of Samuel Johnson's *Rasselas* but also to Genesis. Putatively, Melville's Taipi valley is the innocent garden, and there women do not work but play. The atypical female character in *Typee* is the mother of Kory-Kory, Tommo's male attendant. "To tell the truth," Tommo declares, "Kory-Kory's mother was the only industrious person in all the valley of Typee" (84). Tinor stands out because she works: in all other cases, it seems, "the penalty of the Fall presses very lightly upon the valley of Typee" (195). Again, the exception emphasizes the rule. In this garden labor is unnecessary. (This presentation of Taipi as the Garden also relies on strategic modifications of reality. As Melville perhaps did not realize fully, harvest and preservation of the staple breadfruit, for instance, required extended periods of concerted labor.) However, women do most of the work out of Tommo's sight, or off the narrative stage, allowing him to assert that they are "exempt from toil" yet able to enjoy "light employments" (147). In enjoying such light labor, *Typee's* women represent the "state of nature" (11) that Melville shows Tommo seeking and finding in these islands, as distinct from the rest of the Pacific. Thus, by depicting them as displaying their sexuality and engaging in play rather than work, Melville represents Nuku Hivan women as largely unaware of the newly arrived French colonialism.

As in *Typee*, women in *Omoo* signal the state of the island. In presenting women in this way, Melville draws on Pacific history to inform his story in *Omoo*, although, as in *Typee*, he strategically departs from historical occurrences in order to dramatize a scene or emphasize the contrast between Pacific and European traditions. From the start of her rule in 1827, the Tahitian queen's political power was derived from traditional practices; Pomare's great-grandfather had first been paramount over Tahiti as a whole. Her inherited rule was also reinforced by English missionary and, later, French military powers. Cultural and political ferment marked Melville's late-September to early-November 1842 visit, leading up to English claims to the island and France's annexing Tahiti outright in November 1843. Ten days prior to Melville's arrival, the same French admiral who had recently claimed Nuku Hiva used his ship, the appropriately named *La Reine Blanche*, "the White Queen," to threaten Pomare's power, training his guns on Pape'ete until she signed an agreement that France would establish a provisional protectorate on Tahiti.[13] Melville depicts the scene with a flourish, altering the chronology to portray his narrator's ship arriving as the bugles blare to announce that while Pomare is away (to give birth and to escape internal battles for political control), the chiefs ratified French intervention in Tahiti. *Omoo*, which picks up the narrative immediately after the narrator has left Taipi valley, tells of Omoo's wanderings through Tahiti and the nearby island of Eimeo (now Mo'orea).

In *Omoo* the queen embodies the decline outsiders have created in Tahiti. She retains control over displaying or withholding herself from display, however, so the narrator gains neither political nor narrative power through his association with her. In her person, the narrative suggests, she represents the combinations of Pacific and European civilization that mark her island fatefully. Like the goods her court collects, the queen herself, as *Omoo* tells it, exemplifies an "assemblage" of European and Tahitian dress and behavior (309). She wears "a loose gown of blue silk, with two rich shawls, one red and the other yellow, tied about her neck" (310). Yet, "her royal majesty was barefoot" (310). Most notable, though, are the foods she chooses to eat and the utensils she declines to use: "surrounded by cut-glass and porcelain, and jars of sweetmeats and confections, Pomaree Vahinee I., the titular Queen of Tahiti, ate fish and poee out of her native calabashes, disdaining either knife or spoon" (310). The scene emphasizes the strangeness of European luxury foods when juxtaposed with Tahitian staples. The queen knows about the European but chooses the Tahitian practice; the passage emphasizes her full title and its incongruous status, founded as it is on both Pacific Islands and European forms of aristocracy.

Most notable about the queen's court, as *Omoo* depicts it, are the material artifacts from all over the world that litter the floor of the court to form a "museum of curiosities" (310). Before Omoo and Long Ghost see the queen, her presence is made clear by the goods on display: "The whole scene was a strange one; but what most excited our surprise, was the incongruous assemblage of the most costly objects from all quarters of the globe. Cheek by jowl, they lay beside the rudest native articles, without the slightest attempt at order" (309–10). The jumbled-together goods that characterize her court stand for the current state of Tahiti: the country and the queen are suspended between civilizations, the most global and the most local juxtaposed and revealed as having equal value.

European goods—and, by extension, European ways, standards, and culture—cannot be translated to a Tahitian setting, *Omoo* reports, without being damaged in the process. All of the goods on display in the museum of curiosities "were more or less injured" (310). Similarly, "probably attributable to her late misfortunes" (310), the queen herself is "care-worn" and looks older than her years (310). The meeting of civilizations damages both the European goods and the good Tahitian queen (as well as the "good news" the missionaries bring). The narrative's devastating assessment of Tahitians' future is nothing short of apocalyptic: "Their prospects are hopeless. . . . Years ago brought to a stand, where all that is corrupt in barbarism and civilization unite, to the exclusion of the virtues of either state; like other uncivilized beings, brought into contact with Europeans, they must here remain stationary until utterly extinct" (192).

Given this impending destruction, the queen's physical power is compromised. She lacks the exuberant bodily authority of *Typee*'s queen: Omoo depicts her body as "matronly" (310) rather than as appealing or shocking. But she retains physical power in another sense. She orders Omoo and his traveling companion to remove themselves from her court and immediately thereafter bans all foreigners from the precincts. In banishing the narrator from her company, the queen exerts her narrative authority; she removes the narrator from her story and herself from his.

Melville, of course, deliberately stages the queen's removing herself from his narrative, in this case choosing not to use hearsay or the stories of Captain Bob and others, as he has done previously in representing her. Pomare practices textual abdication, leaving not her throne but the narrative, thereby marking the limits of both imperial discourse and its critiques. In other words, Melville uses Pomare to critique the French claim to sovereignty over Tahiti; but by having her walk out of his own text, he also indicates that he himself cannot contain her power in his narrative.[14] He thereby acknowledges the bounds of the stories he can and cannot tell. If Pomare poses a political challenge to the French, she also poses a narrative challenge to Melville. Building this challenge into his own story allows Melville to place the story he tells in relation to other, specifically Tahitian stories that he does not tell. Even if the audience does not know what is omitted, that is the point Melville dramatizes when Pomare walks away from the narrator: Omoo cannot follow the queen; content *is* excluded.

Pomare's story occupies two of the final three chapters of *Omoo;* structurally, then, like the queen in *Typee,* the figure of the queen both closes and opens the final parts of the story. The endings provide both closure and disclosure. The queens' and the narratives' power signal one another. Moreover, the episode in *Omoo* anticipates by one chapter the visit to the court and the narrator's banishment.[15] This point is key in terms of structuring the narrative; before meeting the queen, Omoo and his traveling companion had high hopes of finding a place in her court. The desired place is particularly appealing because it would advance the narrator's fortunes at the expense of the French. Finally, presenting this hope for preferment a full fifteen chapters before Omoo's audience with the queen anticipates the drama of seeing "the person of her majesty, the queen" (246) that will form the book's final chapters. This postponement emphasizes her banishing the narrator.

The visit to Pomare's court is anticipated by a story of Pomare told and enacted by the Tahitian character Captain Bob. This episode centers on a struggle for authority between Pomare and her husband, who is defined in relation to her. Her husband is known as Pomare-Tane, which Melville translates as "Pomare's man" but which also means literally Pomare-Man, the title referring to the fact that his wife inherits the Pomare title that

Tahitian paramounts had held for four generations. In his case, then, the phrase can mean both king-man and woman-man. The story, as Captain Bob tells it, involves Pomare-Tane's attempt to resist being subsumed by his wife's political power: the drunken husband beats the "sacred person of Pomaree [sic]" (304). Her power is temporarily called into question by not only the French but also her husband. Her momentary powerlessness when her husband beats her serves only to reinforce the long-term power she exerts over her "prince consort."

To convey this queen's degradation and compromised dignity, Melville creates levels of performativity. Omoo stages Captain Bob's story in a burlesque dramatization: "Captain Bob once told me the story. And by way of throwing more spirit into the description, as well as to make up for his oral deficiencies, the old man went through the accompanying action: myself being proxy for the Queen of Tahiti" (304). When the assault is replayed, the humor challenges the dignity of both the "sacred person" of the queen and her violent husband. (The humor also encompasses the narrator who, in playing "proxy for the Queen of Tahiti," gains none of her political power but receives the reenacted physical blows.) The event is highly staged, with the Tahitian who manages the English consul's jail playing king consort and with Omoo as a momentarily transgendered queen. By distancing the queen's temporary loss of power through humor and transgendering, Melville might appear to trivialize her; but in the context of his representation of the queen and her people, these effects emphasize her decline.

In Melville's portrayal of his narrator's brief glimpse of her, this queen thus represents the state of her island, suspended between Pacific and European practices and damaged in the process. The blows she has received—here, her husband's physical assault, but less damaging by far in Melville's telling than the political depredations inflicted by the French—have aged her prematurely. She wields a different bodily power than her Nuku Hivan counterpart; her power is not that of vitality—sexuality, quick thinking, wit—but rather of a fading dowager for whom sexuality is reduced to domestic violence. Rather than the power of display, she controls the power of withdrawal. She and her court exemplify the changing power of women's bodies in an increasingly Christian Pacific, a change that extends to the other women characters in Tahiti and Eimeo.

Thus, the missionary woman and the nymph, who remain distinct in *Typee*, become combined in *Omoo*'s Tahiti. In *Typee*, the missionary woman's sexuality is based on an elaborately clothed body that remains chaste and the nymph's sexuality is based on an innocent, naked indulgence. In *Omoo* the lovely Ideea is a "mickonaree" woman who, although fully clothed in modest garments and the professed garb of missionary ideals, betrays those ideals by indulging herself sexually. She does so despite knowing that she violates what she says about honoring the Christian church. Ideea is thus a nymph who not only professes to be a missionary woman but who also laughs at the contradiction; seeing her as a figure of hypocrisy, though, Omoo flees from her company.

Omoo visits Ideea in her parents' house and questions her to ascertain the state of the islanders' Christianity. In response, she asserts that she is a Christian in her words but not in other parts: "'Mickonaree *ena*' (church member *here*,)" the young churchgoer confesses, "laying her hand upon her mouth, and a strong emphasis upon the adverb. In the same way, and with similar exclamations, she touched her eyes and hands" (178). Thus, Ideea's self-proclaimed identity as a Christian coexists with her senses and the rest of her body, as Melville's narrator notes before retreating from her confession and her presence "as soon as good-breeding would permit" (178). "She gave me to understand," Omoo declares, "by unmistakable gestures, that in certain other respects she was not exactly a 'mickonaree.' In short, Ideea was 'A sad good Christian at the heart— / A very heathen in the carnal part'" (178). The lines from Alexander Pope's "Epistle to a Lady" allow Omoo to introduce but distance himself from the young woman's "carnal part," her sexuality that is both enticing and disturbing because it is not innocent. Because she knows and violates the Christian and Victorian edicts governing women's sexuality, Ideea fits neither the model of the chaste mid-nineteenth-century woman nor of the innocently sexual Pacific maiden, so the visitors leave her.

Throughout *Omoo*, women indicate the state of the island. Women in the island of Eimeo, in contrast to Tahiti, remain innocent and their sexuality remains appealing. (The narrator also makes running comparisons, both implicit and explicit, between Tahitians and Marquesans, always in favor of the "less civilized" Marquesans.) Describing his later travels in the island of Eimeo, which occupy the second half of *Omoo*, the narrator praises "the young girls, more retiring and modest, more tidy in their dress, and far fresher and more beautiful than the damsels of the coast. A thousand pities, thought I, that they should bury their charms in this nook of a valley" (238). There is, of course, an inherent paradox in the narrative's praise of "fresh" young women who have not been exposed to the perils of civilization. These women are "far fresher" than their coastal counterparts because they have not been exposed to the potential corruption brought by visitors—in other words, such figures as Melville's narrator. The very story in both *Typee* and *Omoo* is predicated on the arrival of just such visitors.

The women embody this deterioration in *Omoo*, from the queen to the "mickonaree" woman to even the decrepit Englishwoman "Old Mother Tot," who runs a house of drinking and gambling and beats her man with the Bible whenever he tries to read that good book. Where *Typee* offers the Taipi in a "state of nature," *Omoo* traces a decline from that original state. "Calculated for a state of nature," the narrator of *Omoo* suggests, using the same terms Melville introduced in *Typee*, "they are unfit for any other. Nay, as a race, they can not otherwise long exist" (190). The books might appear to offer, respectively, an anthropologist's view and a tourist's view of the Pacific. The scandal, however, is not that Tahitian civilization has changed after contact with British, French, and U.S. "civilizers," but that the anthropologist's and the tourist's Pacific are the same place. The pure valley Melville portrays in his first book and the moribund islands he portrays in his second are both part of a continuing fiction in which women embody the visitors' desire for the prelapsarian Pacific.

Melville's Pacific and his queen in *Mardi* are more fictional than historical. Queen Hautia is named after an historical figure, since a man named Hautia did serve as governor of an island near Tahiti. Ellis's *Polynesian Researches* describes Hautia's role historically in putting down rebellious challenges to the new code of law enacted by a previous Pomare at the urging of the missionaries. But Melville's portrayal of the fictional Pacific archipelago, Mardi, begins as a straightforward travel narrative and then veers into vast abstract realms; in the political allegory Melville develops at length in chapters 145 through 169, the entire world becomes part of his archipelago. So it is not a particular Pacific island, culture, or history that Melville delineates and embodies in Queen Hautia but change itself, extending to global and even supernatural dimensions. In keeping with the focus on allegory and allusion, *Mardi*'s women rely far more on narrative conventions than do *Typee*'s or *Omoo*'s; thus the familiar White Maiden/Dark Lady antithesis provides roles for the two major female figures in Melville's third work. The Pacific Islander Annatoo is also associated with literary traditions, particularly of woman warriors and unruly folk.

Like the Nuku Hivan and Tahitian queens, Hautia appears late in the narrative chronologically and becomes associated with the power to end narrative. *Mardi* begins with two travel companions setting out in an open boat in the Pacific. During the realistic first third of the novel, the companions travel with two Pacific Islanders until the island woman is swept overboard. Annatoo hails from "a far-off anonymous island" (68); her non-specific origins permit her role as a conventional shrew, a woman of "Penthesilian qualities," who is even "Calmuc" in nature (90, 91).[16]

Mardi moves into a Romance mode when the three men rescue an intended sacrificial victim from a priest, killing him in the process. The woman they rescue, the pale-skinned Yillah, embodies the dreams and desires of Taji, the narrator; after she disappears, the remainder of the book consists of his search for her throughout the Mardian archipelago. While he seeks her, he is himself sought by the dark Queen Hautia (unmet until the final chapters), who repeatedly sends to him three women bearing her messages and portents.

Mardi's Hautia descends from a line of demonic queens. An ancestor incited all of Mardi to expel the "winged beings, of purer minds, and cast in gentler molds" (642). By banishing these original inhabitants of Mardi, Hautia's ancestor gained the dominion that Hautia now holds. This supernatural conquest does not allow for suspension between cultures: Hautia represents death to the Other.

As Taji reports, Hautia, "through her fixed eyes, slowly drank up my soul," "life ebbing out from me, to her" (652). In other words, she plays the conventional Dark Lady, a dangerous temptress, to Yillah's Blonde Innocence. Melville thus uses standard nineteenth-century literary practices but does so to consider the very basis of narrative and meaning. (In offering two such opposed, iconic figures, Melville also divides *Omoo*'s disturbing Ideea into her component parts.) Here the woman's rather than the narrator's gaze is emphasized, the power of her fixed look threatens life itself. Hautia's gaze overpowers the narrator's. Once again, however, an island queen disrupts Melville's narrative.

Melville uses the queen to point toward that which cannot be represented. At the end of *Mardi*, Hautia impels the narrator to go beyond the ending of the story Melville writes. She shows Taji what appears to be the drowned body of his beloved Yillah, whose disappearance has impelled Taji's journey and therefore spurred the narrative of *Mardi*. Yillah's death removes the need to journey. When Taji still spurns Hautia, preferring even the dead Yillah to the living queen, she apparently sends Yillah's white body outside the reefs of Mardi, and the narrator resolves to follow. The narrative thereby culminates in continual travel beyond the bounds of the Mardian world, calling attention to the narrative's unknown and unknowable, but decisively open, ending.

As conventional literary and iconic antitheses, Hautia and Yillah are connected in several ways. Both women remove the need to journey. The straightforward narrative of a journey with which *Mardi* begins continues until the narrator meets Yillah. At that point, the journey essentially stops: finding Yillah and arriving at a verdant island with her, the narrator has no reason to voyage further. "Sweet Yillah," he declares, "see you not this flowery land? Nevermore shall we desire to roam" (161).

When she is present, Yillah serves as an "earthly semblance" of the narrator's dreams (158), an instantiation of desire. Taji's desire satisfied, the narrative does not move; the quest for meaning ends. Indeed, at the close, the vanished Yillah represents both the ending and the continuing of this quest. When, at the conclusion, the narrator flees Hautia's island and leaves Mardi itself to continue seeking Yillah, he is implicitly ending his life. While to Taji's traveling companions his suicide is a crime, he sees it as necessary to continue his quest for Yillah and wrest from Hautia the power to pursue his own story.

Melville makes this quest larger than Taji's searching for Yillah and fleeing from Hautia; the insistently open ending suggests narrative's desire to move. Just as in *Omoo* Pomare asserted her authority and removed herself from Melville's text, moving beyond the bounds of Melville's story and into (now-altered) Pacific realms, in *Mardi* Melville moves his own narrator beyond the bounds of his story. That paradox ends *Mardi* even as it opens the possibility of endless stories beyond the reach of mortal consciousness.

More broadly, the paradox of his first three books is that in portraying the queen's power, Melville is also testing his own narrative power, writing beyond the apparent endings wrought by colonialism, drastic cultural change, and even death. His island queens, whether displaying or withholding themselves, thus make visible the ends of culture and civilization, of creating narrative and meaning in the Pacific and the world.

Notes

1. T. Walter Herbert's *Marquesan Encounters* does not focus on women but presents an extended comparison of the narratives produced as a result of each writer's visit to the Marquesas—David Porter in 1813, Charles Stewart in 1829, and Melville in 1842.

2. At least one *male* Protestant missionary, John Harris, fled the islands after he found himself subject in 1797 to a similar examination conducted by Marquesan women (Wilson 141–42). The episode is corroborated by similar scenes reported by the Catholic priest, Mathias Gracia, when two separate missionary women were thus inspected in 1833 and 1841 (Gracia cited in Anderson, *Melville in the South Seas* 88, 89).

3. *Island Queen* is the title of Sarah Stickney Ellis's narrative poem, published in the same year as *Typee*, which included material from her husband William Ellis's *Polynesian Researches* and featured Queen Pomare. A prolific early Victorian writer in genres including poetry and conduct books, Stickney Ellis focused on the virtues of English women.

4. Radiguet, cited in Anderson, *Melville in the South Seas* 84–85; translation mine.

5. Willowdean Chatterson Handy, who studied tattoos in the Marquesas Islands as part of the Bayard Dominick expedition in the early 1920s, recorded a rare tattoo design that she identifies as a copy of Vae Kehu's (*Forever the Land of Men* 184). These tattoos in particular mark the queen's signal status in the Marquesas Islands. Like Handy's studies, Alfred Gell's more recent review of scholarship on Marquesan tattoos suggests that, with the exception of Vae Kehu, women were not tattooed on the back.

6. Emphasizing Melville's presentation of this "cata*s*trophe," Hershel Parker notes the connection to "Falstaff's vulgar pun" (*Herman Melville* 1: 275).

7. Temoana's grandfather was Keatonui, the leader Porter knew as Gattanewa when Porter claimed the islands on behalf of the United States in 1813.

8. See also Nicholas Thomas.

9. The episode titles come from *Typee*'s table of contents.

10. Weaver 161; Anderson, *Melville in the South Seas* 34; Leyda 1: 400; Parker 1: 188–89.

11. Since later travelers ascertained that the lake Melville portrays does not exist in the Taipi valley, the canoe story is an added dramatization of Tommo's discovery of women's roles and of his attempt to extend the pleasures of Fayaway's company.

12. E. S. Handy 257.

13. See Colin Newbury 107–8 for the treaty text.

14. Here Pomare embodies a point Gayatri Spivak makes in the very different context of discussing Jean Rhys's novel *Wide Sargasso Sea* in reference to the black Martinican character, Christophine: "She cannot be contained by a novel which rewrites a canonical English text within the European novelistic tradition in the interest of the white Creole rather than the native. No perspective *critical* of imperialism can turn the Other into a self" ("Three Women's Texts" 806–7). Rather than attempting to turn the other into a self in *Omoo,* though, Melville calls attention to the means of creating self and other in the context of imperialism and its discourses.

15. The episode is another in which Melville deliberately modifies even the possibly fictional chronology of events: Captain Bob managed the English consul's jail in which Melville's narrator lived early in the book, yet Melville presents the story in the closing chapters.

16. In Greek myth, Penthesilea was Queen of the Amazons. The term *Calmuc* (now spelled *Kalmuck*) indicates a member of a Mongolian people associated with the Tartars and therefore with violence or intractability.

"Suckled by the sea"

The Maternal in *Moby-Dick*

Rita Bode

In his writing years leading up to the creation of *Moby-Dick*, first in New York and then in the Berkshire countryside, Melville lived in households of women (Parker, "Domesticity" 545).[1] After his marriage to Elizabeth Shaw in August 1847, the newlyweds moved into the home of Melville's mother in Lansingburgh, New York, where Melville's four sisters still resided. A few months later, when Melville and his lawyer brother Allan bought a New York brownstone for themselves and their wives, the Melville females moved in along with them. The pattern continued when Melville purchased his Berkshire farm in the fall of 1850; Arrowhead became home not only to himself and Lizzie and their growing family but also to Melville's mother and three of the four Melville sisters. In this intensely female environment, Melville wrote the whale story that Richard Brodhead has called "outrageously masculine."

In his 1986 "Introduction" to *New Essays on Moby-Dick*, Brodhead writes that "it is a masculine book in the obvious sense that it is all about men and men's activities.... But it is masculine too in its deepest dramatic fantasies: What is the hunt for the enormous sperm whale Moby Dick if not a quest for absolute potency, a quest in which the aggressive assertion of masculine strength calls up a fantastically enlarged version of that strength as its imagined nemesis?" (9–10). Brodhead points to an aspect of the novel that has received comment since the early days of Melville criticism. In 1929,

Lewis Mumford put it this way: "all Melville's books about the sea have the one anomaly and defect of the sea from the central, human point of view: one half of the race, woman, is left out of it" (137). More recently, Leland S. Person offers a concise summary of this critical perspective as a prelude to his exploration of *Moby-Dick*'s masculinism. He writes, "Critics have generally agreed that *Moby-Dick* is a man's book and that Melville's representation of sea-faring manhood inscribes a patriarchal, anti-female ideology that reinforces nineteenth-century gender separatism—a manhood based on differentiation from women" (1).

Melville's personal situation paralleled *Moby-Dick*'s "gender separatism." From the late 1840s on, Melville spent a good part of each day in his New York attic or his Berkshire study, sequestering himself as much as possible from the domestic demands that any smoothly running household entails. In the Berkshires, he made forays for male companionship to his much-admired neighbor, Hawthorne. Laurie Robertson-Lorant concludes about the relationship between Melville and the female co-habitants of his domestic space that "the women of the house treated Melville like a pasha, and he, like *Mardi*'s Donjalolo in his harem, enjoyed being pampered and indulged in his whims. If he sounded brusque or irritable or seemed preoccupied when he was working, they took it as a sign of genius and humored him, as they were flattered to think their 'Typee' might one day be as famous as the great 'Boz'" (117). Melville's women kept their distance, but stayed close by in ready anticipation of his needs. Similarly, although Melville's imaginative and creative energies are focused elsewhere in *Moby-Dick*, women hover on the edges of masculine consciousness, to the ultimate benefit of his artistic achievement.

Critical commentary on *Moby-Dick* has also acknowledged that the feminine keeps asserting itself in various ways, especially through the novel's interest in domesticity—a distinctly feminine realm in the nineteenth century—ranging from the coziness of Ishmael's and Queequeg's marriage bed to Stubb's recipe for cooking whale. More recent criticism has pushed the exploration of the female presence in the novel further.[2] As her title indicates, Elizabeth Schultz locates a "sentimental subtext" in *Moby-Dick* concerned with the situation of women, while Tara Penry explores the various ways in which expressions of a "sentimental fellowship" critique the romantic hero's destructive quest and stand in for values and attitudes deemed feminine by the nineteenth century (Penry 232). Nonetheless, Brodhead's bold statement remains astute, for it articulates the imbalance at the heart of the *Moby-Dick* world that gives the novel a pervading sense of something missing, something lost. While the near-absence of women most obviously conveys this imbalance, the novel's sense of longing focuses more specifically on the maternal.

Despite her abundant gift giving, Aunt Charity is happily forgotten on shore, but yearnings for mother and child inform some of the *Pequod*'s most intense scenes. Not only do Starbuck's "young Cape wife and child" seem to journey with him, imparting their "latent influences" (16) to his whaling thoughts and actions, but maternal images affect Ahab, too: "I see my wife and my child in thine eye" (116, 544), he tells Starbuck just before they begin their three-day chase. The whalers, moreover, remain surprisingly mindful of their mothers. The married Stubb's last thoughts, just before Moby Dick rams the ship, are of his maternal rather than conjugal obligations: "I only hope my poor mother's drawn my part-pay ere this," he exclaims (571). Perhaps the most startling as well as telling indication of the novel's awareness of the maternal occurs in "The Candles" (Chapter 119) when, in the midst of the sea storm, Ahab attempts to reclaim his maternal legacy and calls out for the lost mother. Turning with worshipful attention to "the lofty tri-pointed trinity of flames" (507) that burn at the ship's masts, he cries, "Oh, thou magnanimous! now I do glory in my genealogy. But thou art but my fiery father; my sweet mother, I know not. Oh, cruel! What hast thou done with her?" Ahab's passionate exclamation seems simply to slip out and receives no answer. He turns quickly back to the "fiery father" as his "greater" dilemma, deliberately choosing, it seems, to abandon this "puzzle" of his maternal origins (507–508). But the question hangs in the air, drawing attention to both Ahab's need and evasion. That his cry seems to come out of nowhere is appropriate, for it reflects an emptiness that haunts the whaling enterprise. The absent, missing, unknown mother forces Ahab's momentary public acknowledgment of this emptiness, one to which the novel repeatedly points. The specific presence and absence of the maternal most profoundly expose the inadequacies of the whaling world. Melville repeatedly suggests that the loss and imbalance defined by the maternal are injurious to the human and nonhuman alike. The narrative of the maternal that emerges in the novel challenges the view of *Moby-Dick* as "outrageously masculine," offering an alternative to the aggressive whale hunt as a way of life, an alternative with the potential to preserve and nurture rather than kill.

The dominance of *Moby-Dick*'s masculine imagery is deceptive, for a pattern of transformations emerges in which the masculine gives way to suggestions of the maternal. The *Pequod*'s monkey-rope of Chapter 72, closely associated with the butchering of the whale, recalls the "whale-line," that "thing . . . of true terror" in whaling disasters (280–81), but its use on the *Pequod*, linking men together for life or death, brings an image of intimate human connectedness into the scene of carnage and also looks forward to the life-sustaining "umbilical cord of Madame Leviathan" (388). Spears, lances, towers, and an array of pointed and perpendicular phallic objects are countered by womblike spaces of containment and enclosure. The sperm whale is one such container. Brodhead's symbol of "absolute [male] potency" doubles as a giant womb when Jonah gestates there for three days and three nights before his deliverance into a new life as a better man. Even that part of the sperm whale's head, the case, that contains the spermaceti is turned from tomb into womb by Melville's often-quoted language, serious in content though playful in tone, in Queequeg's rescue of Tashtego in "Cistern and Buckets" (Chapter 78). When Tashtego tumbles into the case, Queequeg's "great skill in obstetrics" comes into play: after having "thrust back the leg," and "by a dexterous heave and toss . . . wrought a somerset" on Tashtego, Queequeg delivers him "in the good old way—head foremost" (343–44). Later, in "The Grand Armada" (Chapter 87), Ishmael perceives leviathanic nurseries during a lull in the ferocious hunt. Melville's maternal at times subsumes his phallic imagery, creating a context for dual possibilities that challenge the whale hunt's aggression and, more importantly, Ahab's monomaniacal vision.

Among Ishmael's many domestic details about sea-usages is his account of the "weary family party" that gathers each day at the cabin table. With patriarchal Ahab presiding over these "solemn meals, eaten in awful silence" (151), the ritual of dinner shows the hierarchy that characterizes every aspect of social relations. While the whale hunt entails a team, individuals working toward a common purpose, the whalemen's positions remain sharply stratified, posing an obstacle to communal experience. Ishmael's three-hundreth lay directly reflects his "degree of importance pertaining to the respective duties of the ship's company" (75). Flask, as an officer, enjoys the privilege of the "first table," but as third mate after Starbuck and Stubb, he must be "the last person down at the dinner, and . . . the first man up. . . . for it is against holy usage for Stubb to precede Flask to the deck" (151); his meal time being strictly limited, Flask is perpetually hungry. Ishmael's account is humorous, but it nonetheless associates hierarchy with not only dissatisfaction but also deprivation.

Scenes throughout *Moby-Dick* counter this hierarchy through an alternative view of relationships often informed by a maternal presence. Schultz has convincingly shown that Melville had an "environmental vision with a conscience" that positions Ishmael as a "proto- environmentalist" ("Environmental Vision" 100; 111–13); but the novel's maternal presence also conveys an early ecofeminist vision, the central tenets of which seem particularly applicable to key scenes in Melville's story. Ecofeminism, as Greta Gaard and Patrick D. Murphy suggest, recognizes the worth of all humans and all living beings and seeks to identify the connections among forms of domination and oppression, including domination over nonhuman nature.

Gaard and Murphy see in ecofeminism a resistance to the absolute difference invoked by binary oppositions while emphasizing interrelationships that acknowledge difference as heterarchy rather than hierarchy; the relational model is the web not the ladder (4). Carolyn Merchant's formulation of "an ethic of partnership among humans and between humanity and nature" clarifies these ideas further. For Merchant, "nature is not created specifically for human use, nor are women and animals seen as helpmates for 'man.'" A partnership ethic involves for humans the acknowledgment of all humans and nonhuman nature as autonomous actors. Central to the ethical perspective of partnership are "ideas of relation and mutual obligation" that lead to mutual benefit for all life forms. A partnership ethic posits equity, moral consideration, and respect for human and biotic life alike, acknowledging their "mutual living interdependence" (220, 26, 223, and passim).

Ishmael's and Queequeg's relationship, the focus of much critical attention, offers a model of partnership among human participants. Robert K. Martin identifies Queequeg with a healing "spirit of community," capable of dispelling Ishmael's isolation, and sees in Queequeg's rescues of two drowning men a "commitment to recognition of human responsibility." He interprets Ishmael's and Queequeg's relationship as characterized by an equity that is the outcome of their equality, citing the instance when, early in their acquaintance, Queequeg "takes out his money and shares it with Ishmael, in a sign that this marriage is to be one of equals." Martin attributes the possibility of their equitable relations to their same-sex coupling, arguing that "inequality . . . would have seemed almost inevitable had the terms of the union been heterosexual" (77, 78, 91). Melville's marriage imagery makes the homoerotic an obvious aspect of Ishmael's and Queequeg's relationship, but their interactions carry other dimensions that suggest the values associated with a partnership ethic. In "The Counterpane," Ishmael, after having settled down to sleep with Queequeg in the same bed, finds himself the next morning with the sleeping Queequeg's arm thrown around him "in the most loving and affectionate manner. You had almost thought I had been his wife" (25). Ishmael's straying thoughts go on to suggest the female role for Queequeg, rather than himself, but in another capacity than the conjugal.

The embrace reminds Ishmael of an incident in his childhood when, early in the day on the longest day of the year, his stepmother confined him to bed as a punishment. He recounts how, upon waking from "a troubled nightmare of a doze" to a darkened room,

> I felt a shock running through all my frame; nothing was to be seen, and nothing was to be heard; but a supernatural hand seemed placed in

mine. My arm hung over the counterpane, and the nameless, unimaginable, silent form or phantom, to which the hand belonged, seemed closely seated by my bedside. For what seemed ages piled on ages, I lay there, frozen with the most awful fears, . . . I knew not how this consciousness at last glided away from me; but waking in the morning, I shudderingly remembered it all, and for days and weeks and months afterwards I lost myself in confounding attempts to explain the mystery. Nay, to this very hour, I often puzzle myself with it. (26)

Ishmael's bewilderment seems misplaced, his reaction out of harmony with the situation. The scene seems comforting, yet Ishmael experiences it as threatening. The owner of the hand remains unidentified, but the indistinguishable form, sitting by the child's bedside and holding his hand, evokes, certainly in nineteenth-century terms, a comforting woman and, more specifically, an image of caring motherhood. Perhaps Ishmael's stepmother has repented of her harshness and comes now to offer solace. Or perhaps Ishmael's true mother, whom we presume to be dead, has reached here from beyond the grave to ease her troubled boy.[3]

Whatever the explanation, the possibility of a maternal presence at this point in the novel, however, does not occur to Ishmael, implying an unconscious dismissal; the female simply does not enter into his considerations. Twelve chapters later, in his search for whaling berths, Ishmael's resistance to the maternal becomes more active when, before settling on the *Pequod*, he deliberately rejects two ships whose names invoke the maternal. He turns from the *Devil-Dam*, which calls up an infernal mother, and he also dismisses the *Tit-bit*. In a novel filled with phallic puns, Melville's choice of "tit," the site of physical, maternal nurturance, for the more common "tid" seems deliberate. The meaning of tidbit, itself, "a tender piece, a sweet morsel," conjures up female associations with fruition and sensuous fulfillment.[4] Stubb's allusion to his tidbit, his "juicy little pear at home" (171) suggests both fondness and relish.

In Ishmael's story of his dreamlike encounter with the "silent form or phantom," moreover, Queequeg assumes the place of the unidentified mother: "Now take away the awful fear," Ishmael recounts, "and my sensations at feeling the supernatural hand in mine were very similar, in their strangeness, to those which I experienced on waking up and seeing Queequeg's pagan arm thrown round me" (26). In their "hearts' honeymoon" (52), Ishmael is "wife" to Queequeg's husband, but the influence that Queequeg exerts on Ishmael is decidedly female. Ishmael's "strange feelings" recur several chapters later when he feels a "melting in me," and declares, "No more my splintered heart and maddened hand were turned against the wolfish world. This soothing savage had redeemed it" (51). Queequeg may appear an unlikely mother figure, but the softening effect that Ishmael attributes to him, along with their mutual attachment, is usually associated, in the nineteenth century, with the maternal, and its absence, through Starbuck's later articulation, is bemoaned: "Oh, God!," cries Starbuck, in "Dusk" (Chapter 38), "to sail with such a heathen crew that have small touch of human mothers in them" (169).[5]

Queequeg's motherliness goes unacknowledged, pointing, like the instance of Ahab's focus on the fiery father in "The Candles" chapter, to the novel's evasion of the maternal. As a "phantom," Ishmael's bedside presence joins the succession of phantoms that Ishmael parades. The phantom whales and phantom ships, the "five dusky phantoms" who make up Ahab's special crew (216), the "demon phantom that, some time or other, swims before all human hearts" (237), and, most significantly, the "one grand hooded phantom" floating in Ishmael's "inmost soul" (7), among others, all seem participants in that "ungraspable phantom of life" (5) that preoccupies Ishmael from the first. Ishmael describes the bedside presence as "nameless, unimaginable, silent" (37). Like the novel's other phantom figures, she is mysterious and unknowable. Like Ahab's missing mother, she remains "a puzzle" (508). For both Ishmael and Ahab, familiarity with the maternal seems limited to the "step-mother world, so long cruel—forbidding" (543). Ishmael's bedside phantom suggests the reluctance to acknowledge the mother while at the same time implying the difficulty of identifying the maternal even when confronted by her.[6]

Throughout *Moby-Dick*, the place of the maternal, both as absence and presence, is closely linked to Melville's representations of the sea. In his whale story, Melville does something that he rarely, if ever, does anywhere else: he writes about the sea in gender-specific terms. His gendering, moreover, is complicated by his evident ambivalence. "The Symphony" presents Melville's sea as masculine: "The firmaments of air and sea were hardly separable in that all-pervading azure; only, the pensive air was transparently pure and soft, with a woman's look, and the robust and man-like sea heaved with long, strong, lingering swells, as Samson's chest in his sleep" (542).

Though he begins by suggesting that female and male are "hardly separable," Melville quickly moves to an elaboration of this binary opposition, deliberately setting "the gentle thoughts of the feminine air" next to "the strong, troubled, murderous thinkings of the masculine sea" (542). Melville's descriptions of the sea itself fall into gendered oppositions. The sea often reflects stereotypically masculine traits of power and physical aggression. It is "omnipotent" (223), "lawless" (143), "savage" (233), and "bold" (542), bearing no seeming indications of the maternal.[7] In the context of a whaling expedition, a masculine sea should not startle, and yet the attribution of masculinity to the sea comes as something of a surprise. Not only is the sea neuter in Melville's other sea stories, but in literature, as well as other disciplines, if the sea is attributed a gender at all, it is usually female. Masculinizing the sea signals an attempt to diminish the female presence. Water has long been recognized as the female element. It is the source, the origin, of all life forms, what Rachel Carson calls the "all-providing, all-embracing mother sea" (8). Indeed, at other points in *Moby-Dick*, Melville acknowledges this traditional gender association for the sea. The sea is "becalmed" (266) and "serene" (482), marked by "stillness" (275) or by "rolling . . . gently rocking" motions (477). "The Town-Ho's Story" points directly to the sea's maternal, nurturing capacity when it refers to Radney, in passing, as at one time having "laid him down on the lone Nantucket beach, to nurse at his maternal sea" (244). More significantly, Ahab identifies the sea as mother when, in Chapter 116, moved by the spectacle of the dying whale, he ponders his maternal ancestry: "born of earth, yet suckled by the sea: though hill and valley mothered me, ye billows are my foster-brothers!" (497).

Ahab's attribution of his origins to the maternal earth and his nurturance to the maternal sea is spontaneous and sincere, celebratory of his maternal legacy; but in the context of the novel's alien and alienating "step-mother world," the maternal sea's positioning as nursing foster mother is problematic. It is a reminder that the maternal in *Moby-Dick* is not always nurturing. The gender oppositions cross over and break down. Starbuck recognizes that the *Pequod*'s "heathen crew" were "whelped somewhere by the sharkish sea" (169). Later in the novel, Ishmael describes a violent, destructive maternal sea that is "a fiend to its own offspring . . . sparing not the creatures which itself hath spawned. Like a savage tigress that tossing in the jungle overlays her own cubs, so the sea dashes even the mightiest whales against the rocks, and leaves them there side by side with the split wrecks of ships" (274). And yet, Ishmael's descriptions of this "universal cannibalism of the sea" (274) occur in the chapter, "Brit," titled after the tiny crustaceans on which the right whale feeds. Brit is a victim of the sea's cannibalism but is also nurturing. The chapter opens with images of fecundity and fruition. Ishmael recounts, "we fell in with vast meadows of brit. . . . For leagues and leagues it undulated round us, so that we seemed to be sailing through boundless fields of ripe and golden wheat" (272). These watery meadows seem closer to "this green, gentle, and most docile earth" that Ishmael privileges at the chapter's end over the "appalling ocean" (274). He has apparently forgotten his explanations at the novel's opening that he goes to sea as "a way . . . of driving off the spleen" of his land encounters (3). The gendered seascapes collapse at times into each other, baffling but not eliminating the emergence of the nurturing, productive maternal presence.

Ishmael's ambivalence about the gender of his seas reflects his ambivalence toward the maternal not only for himself but perhaps also for his creator. Melville's involvement with motherhood was intense. The early deaths of his father and Gansevoort, his older brother and the favored son, made Melville the family's oldest male. He was the tolerated son of a forceful, demanding mother who did not hesitate to burden him with the responsibility of heading the Melville household of women yet persisted in considering the young writer as second best. At the time Melville was writing *Moby-Dick,* his wife was a new mother. *Moby-Dick* was published in October and November, in England and the United States, respectively, in 1851, just around the time of the birth of his second child on October 22. In sharp contrast to the male-dominated whaling ship, populated for the most part by adult males, Melville's daily life in the years leading up to the publication of *Moby-Dick* was filled with pregnant women, births, newborn babes, and mothers, young and old. In *Typee,* the narrator, Tommo, teaches Marheyo only two English words, attesting to their importance, but we are reminded of "Home" and "Mother" at the very moment when Tommo is about to leave behind the paradisiacal but threateningly cannibalistic Typee valley (248).[8] In acknowledging these conflicting feelings and attitudes in his later fiction, Melville's representations of experience became fuller, richer, and more inclusive.

Ishmael's views of the sea in its varied and opposing capacities suggest a movement away from a human-centered perspective, for they grant subject rather than object status to the sea. Whether the sea is nurturing or threatening, Ishmael's observations challenge human beings' self-placement at the top of nature's hierarchy. The gendered sea, furthermore, becomes the most profound site in the novel for foregrounding the destructive effects of an androcentric dominance as well as for enacting the struggle to move toward some kind of equilibrium. It calls for a reassessment of the relations both among humans and between the human and nonhuman. The ambivalent sea is where recognition of the maternal potential is repeatedly forced on the whaling expedition. Thinking they have left the maternal ashore, the whalers continually find her at sea. The masculine aspects of the sea—"wild and distant" (7), "battering" (119), "tumultuous and bursting" (310), and "sledge-hammering" (570)—also, by contrast, suggest, both literally and visually, that the fluid, "watery world" (64) is the female element.

Feminist theoretical explanations of female sexuality and the female body correspond with startling suggestiveness to the moving, changing seas. "That woman-thing," as Luce Irigaray writes about the "'mechanics' of fluids" in her psychoanalytic explorations, *This Sex Which Is Not One,* "is continuous, compressible, dilatable, viscous, conductible, diffusible," with "luminous flow, acoustic waves" (111, 113). In her study of corporeal feminism, *Volatile Bodies,* Elizabeth Grosz argues that Western constructions of the female body see it as "a leaking, uncontrollable, seeping liquid; as formless flow ... not a cracked or porous vessel like a leaking ship, but a formlessness that engulfs all form, a disorder that threatens all order" (203). The real and constant threat of wrecked ships and drowned sailors suggests that the sea, too, always threatens to engulf. As physical entities, woman and sea alike exhibit traits beyond the control of man. Cultural historian Natalie Zemon Davis has shown that "the female sex was thought the disorderly one par excellence in early modern Europe," and her "disorderliness was founded in physiology. As every physician knew in the sixteenth century, the female was composed of cold and wet humours (the male was hot and dry), and coldness and wetness meant a changeable, deceptive and tricky temperament." While medicine abandoned the humour theory, the view of women's disorderliness was adapted to new explanations, since it was based on tradition. Davis writes, "Female disorderliness was already seen in the Garden of Eden, when Eve had been the first to yield to the serpent's temptation and incite Adam to disobey the Lord" (156). The wild sea corresponds to this unruly woman of Western thought who threatens chaos, signals defiance and resistance, and requires containment and confinement. Perhaps Melville's volatile seas are male not only because gender stereotyping sees aggression as masculine but because a masculine sea, no matter how "murderous," is still more familiar, knowable, less threatening for the male whalers than the possibility of female disorder.

Melville's gendering becomes more specific, for his sea transforms into images highly suggestive of the workings of the maternal female body, exuding milk and blood. Twice in the novel, the sea is "milky" (193, 194), but the whale hunt turns the waters bloody. In "Stubb Kills a Whale" (Chapter 61), Ishmael narrates how

> the red tide now poured from all sides of the monster like brooks down a hill. His tormented body rolled not in brine but in blood, which bubbled and seethed for furlongs behind in their wake. The slanting sun playing upon this crimson pond in the sea, sent back its reflection into every face, so that they all glowed to each other like red men. . . . At last, gush after gush of clotted red gore, as if it had been the purple lees of red wine, shot into the frighted air; and falling back again, ran dripping down his motionless flanks into the sea. (285–86)

Although it is the whale and not the sea itself that is wounded, this image of the bloodied ocean suggests, as does "the frighted air," that the injury to nature extends beyond the single act of violence against a specific target. The cruelty and destruction of the whale hunt affect the human and nonhuman alike, tinting them all in shades of red and suggesting as well, perhaps, through the whalers' glowing faces, a tainting with the guilt of violence. The "red men" are morally accountable to the rest of nature. The scene expresses a more subtle and oblique critique of the whaling industry's exploitation of the natural and human world than Ishmael's direct indictments, for the hunted, wounded whale, in physically transforming its surroundings, implies the environmental impact of the hunt. And lest we miss his point, Melville leads the numerous accounts of the wounded whale toward a note in "The Grand Armada" in which Ishmael tells us about the wounded nursing mother whale. Ishmael states, "When by chance these precious parts [the breasts] in a nursing whale are cut by the hunter's lance, the mother's pouring milk and blood rivallingly discolor the sea for rods" (388). Pouring milk and pouring blood resonate disturbingly. The discoloring of the sea suggests another tainting; the discoloring implies a stain on, a damage to nature as a result of the whalers' acts of violence.

The flowing blood in a female sea also suggests menstruation, which Grosz associates "with blood, with injury, with the wound" (205). Melville's bloodied sea suggests the menstruating female body that evokes both creation and a vulnerability to violation. This sea finds a parallel in Annette Kolodny's metaphorical readings of the land in American literature. Kolodny discusses how the initial responses of the early settlers was to see the New World as an Edenic, maternal landscape that promised "a return to the primal warmth of womb or breast." But the settlement of the wilderness required a competitive, self-assertive attitude toward a feminized nature and demanded a different set of metaphors based on sexual domination. For the American frontiersmen, the pristine, fecund land became a female object of conquest, to be raped and violated in the exploitation of her natural resources (*Lay of the Land* 6).[9] Kolodny's virgin land corresponds to Melville's feminine sea. In *Moby-Dick*, the suggestion of the blood of menstruation, with its potential for nurture and reproduction, is fleeting, subsumed by the blood of murderous violence that emphasizes the whale hunt's destructiveness to the mother whale, to nature, and to the very process of the life cycle. It is little wonder that the whaling world usually fails to recognize the maternal, for the whale hunters could not accommodate the implications of such a recognition.

"The Grand Armada" chapter expresses the maternal presence in *Moby-Dick* most forcefully. While *Moby-Dick*'s human women remain ashore, present on the *Pequod* only through the whalers' thoughts, Melville carefully valorizes the females of the nonhuman world, granting them individual subjecthood and reciprocal rather than hierarchical relations with human life. In "The Grand Armada," the *Pequod* encounters one of the sperm whales' extensive herds, the "immense caravans" in which they swim, allowing the whalers to engage directly with the pod of whale mothers and children. The herd dominates the seascape here. The mothers and calves are at the center of the circle of whales into which Queequeg's whaleboat is dragged by a whale he has harpooned. "Our beset boat," recounts Ishmael, "was like a ship mobbed by ice-isles in a tempest, . . . knowing not at what moment it may be locked in and crushed" (385). At the center, however, as they glide "between two whales into the innermost heart of the shoal," they experience an "enchanted calm," while "in the distracted distance . . . the tumults of the outer concentric circles" continue (386–87). More than just calm, the whalers' experience is one of wonder:

> But far beneath this wondrous world upon the surface, another and still stranger world met our eyes as we gazed over the side. For, suspended in those watery vaults, floated the forms of the nursing mothers of the whales, and those that by their enormous girth seemed shortly to become mothers. The lake, as I have hinted, was to a considerable depth exceedingly transparent; and as human infants while suckling will calmly and fixedly gaze away from the breast, as if leading two different lives at the time; and while yet drawing mortal nourishment, be still spiritually feasting upon some unearthly reminiscence;—even so did the young of these whales seem looking up towards us, but not at us, as if we were but a bit of Gulf-weed in their new-born sight. Floating on their sides, the mothers also seemed quietly eyeing us. (387–88)

The whale's maternal presence temporarily de-centers the chaos and carnage. Unlike the violent margins of the hunt, the calm center is womblike, containing and protecting the whalers, and there is no way out until a passage opens up. In this maternal center, the barrier between the human and the nonhuman breaks down. Through the perspective of the newborn calves, the human hunters lose their self-assumed superiority and importance. Their significance, like the gulf-weed's, is determined by their vital relation to other life forms in "mutual living interdependence." The whales' peaceful behavior suggests their presumption of equity for all concerned, since, devoid of aggression, the quiet "eyeing" implies an accepting coexistence.

As his analysis of the whale throughout the novel shows, Ishmael brings multiple perspectives to what he deems important. The significance of the connection between the human and nonhuman is doubly emphasized when he moves from his lyrical account of the wondrous encounter between whales and whalers in the text to the hilarious or, at any rate, absurd suggestions in his odd "strawberries" note in "The Grand Armada." The imagery of maternal injury in this note is embedded in details that suggest the similarity of whale and human maternity. The note's opening statement makes whales less like fish and more like humans: "The sperm whale, as with all other species of the Leviathan, but unlike most other fish, breed indifferently at all seasons." Since mother whales' "gestation . . . may probably be set down at nine months," the length of their pregnancies corresponds to human mothers. Ishmael carries the best known connection (that whales and humans are both mammals, nursing their young from their own breast milk) to outrageous implications when he comments that the maternal whale "milk is very sweet and rich. It has been tasted by man." How could man have tasted this milk if not at the breast of the nursing mother whale? The observation that the milk "might do well with strawberries" reinforces this point since the mamillary projection is physically similar to the fruit (388). Both are "tit-bits." Even though it is relegated to a footnote, the statement on cross-species identification nonetheless makes its point.

A remarkable moment in the novel, indeed, a remarkable moment in nineteenth-century American literature, occurs when Ishmael recounts, "Keeping at the centre of the lake, we were occasionally visited by small tame cows and calves: the women and children of this routed host. . . . Like household dogs they came snuffing around us, right up to our gunwales, and touching them; till it almost seemed that some spell had suddenly domesticated them. Queequeg patted their foreheads; Starbuck scratched their backs with his lance; but fearful of the consequences, for the time refrained from darting it" (387). The contact here between whales and whalers is direct and unmediated. American culture's striving toward an ideal of individual self-sufficiency—the Emersonian dictum, "absolve you to yourself" ("Self-Reliance" 1162)—has no meaning in the face of the whales' assumption of relational recognition. In his discussion of James Fenimore Cooper and other writers of the American Renaissance, Tony Tanner provides the context and furnishes the terminology to pinpoint further the singular aspect of this scene. Tanner writes: "'Waste' was to become a key word in American literature as writers tried to trace out what America has made of its unparalleled resources . . . the 'gifts of the Lord' were quickly changed or trans(de)formed into the commodities of man" (9). For the moment, though, in this scene, the nonhuman whales are no longer means to human achievement, or objects of appropriation and domination. They are no longer commodities. The meeting between whalers and whales, human and nonhuman, is communal, not adversarial. The conquest of the wilderness, be it land or sea, that stimulated the imagination of so many nineteenth-century American writers, including Melville, is momentarily suspended here to the benefit of both human and nonhuman life.

Ishmael, confident that "in the tornadoed Atlantic of [his] being," he still disports "in mute calm ... in eternal mildness of joy," interprets the incident as a taming of the wild (389). But throughout *Moby-Dick,* Melville sees wildness as the male whalers' trait; the wildness that we usually locate in nature and interpret as the opposite of civilization is in the hearts of Ahab and his men; in "Moby-Dick" (Chapter 41), the whalers unite in a "wild, mystical sympathetical feeling" with "Ahab's quenchless feud ... of violence and revenge" (179). And here, in "The Grand Armada," it is clearly not the wild—that is, not the whales—being tamed; rather, they are doing the taming. The *Pequod*'s crew are tamed, domesticated, civilized by the mother whales and their children. Starbuck's fearsome lance becomes a back-scratcher. Queequeg's mighty throwing arm delivers a pat on the head. This is no facile taming. The whalers' fear no doubt restrains their aggression, and it may explain their momentary collaboration with the whales. The circumstances require them to acknowledge their connection and interdependence. But their fear does not explain their receptiveness to the advances of the whale mothers and children. For a brief spell, an ecofeminist perspective dominates; human beings and animals seem to be connected in a common web of life. The whales' relational modeling establishes the nature of the interaction. The presence of these whale cows and calves draws attention to another kind of absence: the absence of the hunt, the absence of death, destruction, and extinction.

Melville's view of nature is not a romantic one. And if he is philosophical, he is also scientific. He does not deny the sometimes harsh and even brutal survival behavior of life forms. The harmonious encounter, reflecting attitudes of mutuality, equity, and respect, is experienced by very few of the *Pequod*'s crew, and their taming does not last. Joyce Sparer Adler has shown the place of "war in Melville's imagination." She finds the "representative of peace, community, and the original latent good in the heart of man" in *Moby-Dick*'s feminine presence (61). If the enchanted moment amidst the whale mothers and children is fleeting, it nonetheless stands in powerful resistance to the warlike hunt. The whale mothers and children oppose the human potential for cruelty that grows sharper, stronger, and increasingly more aggressive in response to the hunt and its results. In "The Grand Armada," Melville dramatically enacts his harsh judgment of the whale hunt by a powerful image that brings death through the hunt into the midst of life. Contemplating an infant whale, "hardly a day old," Queequeg suddenly shouts, "Line! line! ... him fast! ... who line him! Who struck?—Two whale; one big, one little!" Ishmael explains Queequeg's outburst as his confusing the whale line with the "long coils of the umbilical cord of Madame Leviathan, by which the young cub seemed still tethered to its dam." He explains that "not seldom in the rapid vicissitudes of the chase, this natural line, with the maternal end loose, becomes entangled with the hempen one, so that the cub is thereby trapped" (388). This entangling of the human-made line with the vital "natural line" is ominous, for it implies the whale hunt's brutal entanglement with life itself. The "natural line" of sustenance and connection is a reminder that the nursing whale mothers and babies are a life-affirming alternative to the whale hunt; they create, indeed, the novel's counternarrative; the calm waters in which they swim speak of nurturance for all forms of life—nonhuman and human, which the whale hunt destroys.

Melville's condemnations of the hunt, moreover, intensify further as he shows the deadly violence penetrating into the enchanted center. Ishmael recounts that on the frayed edges of the circle, where the other boats continued "drugging the whales," one of the wounded whales breaks "away from the boat, carrying along with him half of the harpoon line" and "the cutting-spade." Ishmael continues, "He was now churning through the water violently flailing with his flexible tail, and tossing the keen spade about him, wounding and murdering his own comrades." The effects are doubly murderous, for the hunters (though inadvertently) turn the wounded whale into a killer of others. The hunt horrifically enlists the whale against its own. The murderous effects keep spreading, encompassing the entire whale population, for the wounded whale's violence generates a panic that causes the whales to "crowd a little, and tumble against each other" in a push into the enchanted center. In the pile-up, "the submarine bridal-chambers and nurseries vanished" (389). Later in the novel, Ishmael wonders "whether Leviathan can long endure so wide a chase, and so remorseless a havoc: whether he must not at last be exterminated from the waters" (460). In the context of this later questioning, the vanished whale cows and calves, the embodiment of propagation, suggest a permanent disappearance.

Near the novel's end, in another encounter with the nonhuman, the *Pequod*'s crew is forced to acknowledge that the grief of lost mothers and children is not limited to humankind. In "The Life-Buoy" (Chapter 126), the whalers are

> startled by a cry so plaintively wild and unearthly—like half-articulated wailings of the ghosts of all Herod's murdered Innocents—that one and all, they started from their reveries, and for the space of some moments stood, or sat, or leaned all transfixedly listening ... while

that wild cry remained within hearing. . . . Those rocky islands the ship had passed were the resort of great numbers of seals, and some young seals that had lost their dams, or some dams that had lost their cubs, must have risen nigh the ship and kept company with her, crying and sobbing with their human sort of wail. (523–24)

The seals' and pups' cries are, perhaps, as dangerous to the whalers as the Sirens' enticing song to Homer's sailors. They enchant the whalers, rendering them, if only briefly, "transfixedly listening." Seals, as Melville tells us, are a source of anxiety for whalers. "Most mariners," Ishmael claims, "cherish a very superstitious feeling about seals, arising not only from their peculiar tones when in distress, but also from the human look of their round heads and semi-intelligent faces, seen peeringly uprising from the water alongside. In the sea, under certain circumstances, seals have more than once been mistaken for men" (524). They voice the sailors' own cries and sorrows. They are a threat, for they invite identification, challenging the hierarchical separation between human and nonhuman that makes the whale hunt possible.[10]

The cries of the seals and pups, moreover, are interchangeable with the "lamentation and bitter weeping" (Jeremiah 31:15) of Rachel crying for her children alluded to just two chapters later when the *Pequod* meets the *Rachel*, whose captain is searching for his missing child. Melville makes the connection unmistakable. The Manxman brings to bear on the lost boy's fate his belief that the "wild thrilling sounds" of the seals are "the voices of newly drowned men in the sea" (523): "'He's drowned with the rest on 'em, last night,' said the old Manx sailor . . . 'I heard; all of ye heard their spirits'" (532). A biblical allusion further elides any distinction between the nonhuman and human experience of anguish. Ishmael first associates the seals' wailing with "the ghosts of all Herod's murdered Innocents" (Matt. 2:16) in Chapter 126 and then, in Chapter 128, moves to "Rachel weeping for her children" (Matt. 2:18), which applies to the *Rachel*'s mourning over the captain's missing child. The *Rachel*'s human face, furthermore, is her captain, a father weeping for his lost boy. He is Rachel.[11] Here Melville's ecofeminism movingly embraces male and female as well as human and nonhuman.

Nonetheless, Melville remains aware of the ambiguity of the maternal. The whaling world's denial of maternal seas may very well be justified, since, as mother, the sea is both the source and the final destination, representing simultaneously both life and death. It is, at once, womb and tomb. The reappearance of Queequeg's coffin at the end is a reminder of the maternal's dual significance. In "Queequeg in his Coffin" (Chapter 110), Queequeg, taken with fever, makes his trial run of death. Creating a little domestic space for himself in his coffin, complete with biscuits, water, and his valued belongings, he tries it out. The "carpenter's box," meant to harbor the dead, might be considered a womblike enclosure for revitalized life, for, after testing it, instead of dying, Queequeg rallies and resumes living. Ironically useless to him, Queequeg's coffin succeeds at sustaining another's life. Requisitioned to replace the *Pequod*'s life-buoy after its loss, the coffin fulfills a new purpose. At the violent end of the *Pequod*'s voyage, Ishmael, the lone survivor, finds himself, in the wake of "the half-spent suction of the sunk ship," drawn toward "the closing vortex." When he reaches the site of destruction, he finds that "it had subsided to a creamy pool," evoking both semen and milk.

Melville's epilogue, with such evocative masculine/feminine ambivalences, concludes by emphasizing the absent mother's return. The potential void of the sunk ship and "black bubble" facing Ishmael transforms into another "vital centre" from which Queequeg's coffin, in a phallic-like eruption, shoots assertively, forcefully, "length-wise from the sea" (573) to save Ishmael from drowning until his rescue by the literal mother ship, *Rachel*. In another maternal transformation, the phallic coffin supports Ishmael until the maternal womb takes in the "orphan" Ishmael, making him one of her children. Melville's whaling story pushes toward death and destruction, foregrounding the imbalance of the whaling world; but at the same time, it offers a counternarrative in which the life-affirming resists the life-denying. Jeremiah introduces Rachel's bitter weeping with the statement "a voice was heard in Ramah." In various manifestations, sometimes muted, sometimes distinct and powerful, the maternal voice is heard as well in *Moby-Dick*, articulating connectedness, care, and interdependence. As the biblical Rachel is the mother not only of individual children but of the Hebrew nation, so Melville's *Rachel* stands for the maternal principle that saves Ishmael. In her "devious cruising" and "retracing search," the persevering *Rachel*, in the novel's final moments, affirms the mother's saving presence.

Notes

1. See also Parker, *Biography* and Robertson-Lorant. Details of Melville's life in the essay come mostly from Roberston-Lorant's biography, which I found most useful to my approach.
2. See Schultz, "Sentimental Subtext." Further relevant studies on female absence/presence in Melville's work include McMaster-Harrison 49–53, 83–86; Joyce W. Warren, chap. 5, "The Masculine Sea" 115–47; Fredricks 41–54.
3. See Leverenz on the phantom figure's possible identity as the stepmother (283, 357n.11). In his note Leverenz quotes Seelye on the phantom as "the spirit of [Ishmael's] dead mother."
4. Both the OED and Webster's (1828) define "tidbit" as interchangeable with "titbit."
5. Catherine Beecher's influential housekeeping book, *A Treatise on Domestic Economy*, is

representative of the period's pervading view of women's influence. She writes: "A woman who is habitually gentle, sympathizing, forbearing, and cheerful, carries an atmosphere about her, which imparts a soothing and sustaining influence, and renders it easier for all to do right, under her administration, than in any other situation" (134). Her general outlook on motherhood is that "the mother writes the character of the future man" (13). Much of nineteenth-century American literature involving mothers reflects the maternal image on which I draw. See also Welter, some of whose ideas, especially on separate spheres, are now being challenged, but whose work nonetheless remains important.

6. In *Pierre*, Melville associates the female presence with phantoms as well when he describes Pierre's feelings after his initial encounter with Isabel: "He felt that what he had always before considered the solid land of veritable reality, was now being audaciously encroached upon by bannered armies of hooded phantoms, disembarking in his soul, as from flotillas of spectre-boats" (49).

7. See Irey for the many descriptive terms that Melville applies to his seas, Gidmark, and Springer's discussion of the sea and American literature in his introduction to *America and the Sea*.

8. However misguided or exaggerated it might be, D. H. Lawrence's designation of Melville's "HOME and MOTHER" as "his damnation" comes to mind. Lawrence writes: "At the age of twenty-five he came back to Home and Mother, to fight it out at close quarters. For you can't fight it out by running away. When you have run a long way from Home and Mother, then you realize that the earth is round, and if you keep on running you'll be back on the same old doorstep—like a fatality. Melville came home to face out the long rest of his life . . . No more paradises . . . A mother: a gorgon. A home: a torture box. A wife: a thing with clay feet" (144, 150).

9. See also Springer's discussion of a feminine sea in American writing. He suggests, however, that "the sea's femininity is different from that so often seen in the 'virgin' (or the 'raped') land by American writers" (19).

10. Melville's writings show his awareness of the sealing industry. He reviewed James Fenimore Cooper's *The Sea Lions, or The Lost Sealers: a Tale of the Antarctic Ocean* for the *Literary World* (28 Apr. 1849); his fictional Captain Delano in *Benito Cereno* commands a sealer; as a nineteenth-century seaman, moreover, he would have been aware, too, of the industry's threat to the seal population suggested by his reference to the seal mothers and cubs, in a context of loss and bereavement. Some restrictions on seal-hunting in different parts of the oceans, because of depletion, were already coming into effect in the first part of the nineteenth century, but then the seal hunt again escalated in the latter half. "As a rule exploitation swiftly followed discovery" of seal breeding grounds (Bonner 60).

11. See Schultz, "Sentimental Subtext": "As captain of the *Rachel*, named for the mother of Joseph and Benjamin, her sons exiled in Egypt, Captain Gardner becomes a grieving maternal figure" (41).

Of Cuttle-Fish and Women

Melville's Goneril in *The Confidence-Man*

Beverly A. Hume

In the degraded social and natural environment of *The Confidence-Man: His Masquerade* (1857), Goneril, ostensible wife of John Ringman, not only satirically dramatizes the androcentric misogyny and racism in mid-nineteenth-century America but serves as a mocking harbinger of the evolution of a new human species in this novelistic April Fool's Day joke with a bite. Submerged deeply in a text that transforms even plot summary into an interpretive enterprise, Goneril surfaces, briefly, as an androgynous variant on the confidence man, one symbolically aligned not only with "women's-rights women" (62), "Indians," boys, and slaves but also with "Dame" or nonhuman nature (108). Along with escalating the fictionality of this snakish narrative, Goneril's story raises significant questions about the chaotic processes of "Nature" depicted in it, while it indirectly speaks to Melville's recognition, as his earlier "The Tartarus of Maids" (1855) attests, that the most troubling, if not deepest, levels of cultural oppression have historically been reserved for women.[1]

Goneril appears to have an "unnatural" or masculine nature that has been made "natural," culturally assimilated, or, to borrow a phrase from Donna Haraway, "reinvented," though not with positive result.[2] Like the nonhuman environs of the Mississippi, the much-discussed invisible "Indians" in this narrative, and other avatars of the confidence man, Goneril touches, jolts, and disrupts the predominantly male "Anacharsis Cloots congress" aboard the *Fidele*, a congress that perpetually muddies its own narrative waters.

She also remains one of the more perplexing inventions in this narrative. Goneril has, for example, been described as possessing an "elusive" and "extreme fictionality" (Van Cromphout 50); as an allegorical figure who retains the "sexual perversity" of her Shakespearean namesake in *King Lear* (Cook 178); as a creature primarily linked to the "touching" scenes in the novel, particularly those involved with economic chicanery (Ramsey 38); as an "Indian-like" female clay-eater who seems designed to reinforce the negative, even subhuman, "connotations of 'Indian' in this book" (Elizabeth Foster 314); as the central character in one of the "interpolated tales" that complicate the narrative (Bryant, "Problem Novel" 320); and as a portrait of a "real" woman, one who reflects Melville's conflicted, if not misogynist feelings about the "mannish" Fanny Kemble (Branch et al. 291).

Though views of the human-nature continuum in Melville's day differed from ours, ecocritical and ecofeminist views offer new insights into Goneril's significance. In his creation of Goneril, Melville arguably anticipates not only ecofeminists, who, as Val Plumwood argues, reevaluate the androcentric "master model" of Western discourse about the "man-nature" continuum from which the "feminine" is seen as a "deviation" (23), but also deep ecologists such as Warwick Fox, who asserts that not only men but "capitalists, whites, and Westerners" have been "far more implicated in the history of ecological destruction than pre-capitalist peoples, blacks, and non-westerners" (232).[3] By 1800, as William Cronon summarizes, deforestation had dramatically changed New England's environment, native populations had been radically diminished, and many areas in the region were "devoid of animals which had once been common" (159–60). Such facts did not, however, transform Romantic poems or narratives about the disappearance of indigenous cultures, forests, or animals into dark warnings about the relationship between human and environmental degradation. In late-eighteenth- and early-nineteenth-century works such as Philip Freneau's "The Indian Burying Ground," William Cullen Bryant's "The Prairies," or James Fenimore Cooper's Leatherstocking tales, the overriding tone remains one of vague, if not sentimental, regret about the disappearance of indigenous cultures, animals, and land. By contrast, Melville's representation of the interlinked oppression of nature, boys, blacks, Indians, and Goneril in *The Confidence-Man* implicates androcentric thinking, whites, Westerners, and capitalists in the intensifying cultural, if not environmental, degradation of his mid-nineteenth-century America. Lawrence Buell defines Melville's "global vision" in *Moby-Dick* as one in which "the chief ingredients" are "imperial enterprise and comparative mythology," ingredients that "produce a cosmopolitan vision" of blurred boundaries between hierarchies of nations, cultures, and species (223). In *The Confidence-Man*, the Cosmopolitan seems a variant embodiment of such a "cosmopolitan vision." He is a figure who is at once human and not-human, one who appears intimately linked to "that multiform pilgrim species, man" aboard the *Fidele* (9), to the Indians or "Indian-like" figures, such as Goneril, mentioned in the text, and to the nonhuman Mississippi and its environs.

"The Mississippi River," as Wyn Kelley observes, "is not an innocent natural element" in *The Confidence-Man* but "part of a fluid urban environment" (243), one "tainted," "contaminated," and "polluted by its associations with cities and their problems" (248). As the surviving, unincorporated manuscript fragment "The River" suggests, the Mississippi has been affected not only by a contaminated urban environment but also by a natural force, by the Missouri river that foams "down on it like a Pawnee from ambush." This Pawnee-like ambush transforms the Mississippi: its "shores are jagged & rent, the hue of the water is clayed," and the "before moderate current is rapid & vexed" (499). Although this fragment was removed from the manuscript of *The Confidence-Man*, it suggests that Melville envisioned an inevitable battle within this narrative in which an "ennobled" father of a "multitude of waters" flowing through a "granary of a continent" has been attacked by a natural but "hostile element," a Pawnee-like "invader" who "freezes the warmth" of such "genial zones" (499). In the printed text, this natural usurpation is committed by the invading and, at times, Indian-linked confidence men who flow onto the *Fidele* in a "confident and cosmopolitan tide" (9) to disrupt and startle, if not "freeze," their predominantly male victims. In the printed text, Melville also sharply restricts third-person descriptions of the Mississippi and its natural environs. Readers learn that the ship is traversing a "swampy and squalid" domain that not only frames the river (129) but pervades the *Fidele*. On board, Melville offers jagged, clayed, and vexed portraits of confidence men claiming to possess an intimate understanding of nonhuman nature, while they are often linked to imagery associated with Indians, including the "Indian"-like, deceased wife, Goneril, allegedly married to one of them.

Goneril's story is told, first, by an avatar of the confidence man (her "husband," John Ringman) to a merchant, Henry Roberts, only after it is "filled out" by another confidence man, a "certain man in a gray coat" (59), who claims to be collecting alms for Seminole widows and orphans. However, before Roberts tells the tale to a third confidence man, John Truman, Melville's narrator cryptically adds that "as the good merchant could, perhaps, do better justice to the man [Ringman] than the story, we shall venture to tell it in other words than his, though not to any other effect" (58). Tracing the "origins" of Goneril's story, the reader discovers that it was told by Ringman to Roberts shortly after the disappearance of Black Guinea, the novel's first confidence man (20). The reader is not told the tale but only informed that, "judging from the auditor's [Roberts's] expression," Goneril's story is one that catches its listener off guard and that at "every disclosure," the merchant's "commiseration" and "alms" grew (21). Her story, then, is designed to be elusive, as well as to elicit an emotional and economic response.

Goneril's full story and later physical description, however, directly align her not only with aggressive women and with Indians but also with cuttlefish and, by metaphoric extension, Medusa.[4] As a squidlike woman who only has to "touch" men to sabotage or freeze their confidence, Goneril is, like earlier dangerous Melvillean women such as Hautia in *Mardi* or Mrs. Glendenning in *Pierre,* credited with the ability to enchant or mesmerize unsuspecting male victims. According to the narrator's revised tale of the merchant, when she was alive, Goneril had an "Indian figure" and a masculine "style of beauty" (60). She also was a mother. Though Roberts sought legally to remove her only daughter from her mother's baneful influence, the cold and devious Goneril gained legal custody. She was notable also for her sustained silences, generated by her need to "thaw" so that she might be on "talking terms with humanity"; during these silent periods, she stared "out of her large, metallic eyes, which her enemies called cold as a cuttle fish" (61) but which she regarded as part of her charm. Such attributes are said to complement her inhuman pleasures of mysteriously "touching" men, tormenting her daughter, "fling[ing] people's imputed faults into their faces," and devouring blue clay, which she "inly . . . chewed" whenever she "saw frankness and innocence tyrannnized into sad nervousness under her spell" (61). Melville's reference to "clay-eaters" at the beginning of the novel (9) may link Goneril to poor, pregnant women who ate clay for sustenance in impoverished nineteenth-century American rural communities. However, in the context of such attributes and of her allegedly inhuman aspect, Goneril's clay-eating, like her other strange pleasures, makes her a monstrous woman who casts spells on or devours others, particularly men.

Although the Medusa archetype has a long, tangled, and unsavory history, Jungian critic Annis Pratt provocatively speculates that in contemporary variations Medusa is, above all, "an archetype of feminine creativity, especially when this creativity is thwarted" (40). Goneril's creativity has been both thwarted and usurped by male stories that have transformed her into a legendary variant on female monstrosity. According to Pratt, the "key to psychological survival as well as to poetic maturity" for both male and female authors is "a face-to-face encounter" with the complexities of Medusa's "personal and archetypal meaning" since only "by looking into her eyes and understanding what lies beneath" can such authors "enter the healing seas of the unconscious" and move toward self-actualization (40). What lies beneath Goneril's "large, metallic eyes" seems to be a narrator and various confidence men who consciously use her physical aspect to frighten, to startle, and to "touch" both misogynist and racist emotions in their primary targets, whether inside or outside the fictive world of this text. Unlike his earlier gorgonlike siren Hautia or devouringly maternal Mrs. Glendenning, however, Melville's Goneril is a richly ironic and ambiguous feminine monster. Despite her ostensibly dispassionate, "calm, clayey, cakey," inhuman nature, Goneril proves more credible than her husband, John Ringman, to a male-dominated mid-nineteenth-century legal system. She not only retains custody of her child by enlisting the aid of "women's-rights women," "able counsel," and "accommodating testimony" (61–62) but nearly manages to have Ringman "permanently committed for a lunatic" when he attempts to make a case for her "mental derangement" (63). Ringman fails to make his case because he cannot explain the peculiar power of Goneril's "mysterious touchings" (63), nor can he evidently explain how such a monstrous woman puts men under her spell. Though the deceased Goneril cannot speak, John Truman (who may also be John Ringman) unexpectedly interrupts and defends her by pointing out that the "description of the lady" appears "more or less exaggerated, and so far unjust" (65). Indeed, Truman (or Ringman) may actually be defending himself at this narrative moment, for Goneril appears by this time to be, like the more critically discussed Black Guinea, one of his possible inventions, if not disguises.

The ambiguity of Goneril's ethnicity supports this perspective. In his creation of Black Guinea, Melville arguably utilizes and satirizes racist masquerades performed in popular American blackface minstrel shows.[5] Goneril is arguably part of this satire. Mid-nineteenth-century American minstrel shows not only engaged in burlesque parodies of Shakespearean theater and depictions of American boasters and hunters but also in the "'carnivalization' of race," including the "Indian" race, and in misogynist burlesques of "women's rights lectures" with their many female impersonators. Such parodies and burlesques were so common that by "the late 1850s, the Woman's Rights issues and Shakespearean burlesques were linked in Dan Gardner's sketch entitled 'Seven Ages of Women,'" a sketch in which Gardner's "cross-dressing" was so successful that "his creation was taken up by other companies in Philadelphia and New York" (Mahar, 196, 7, 45). Even if Melville did not know about Gardner's show, he was doubtless conversant with the frequent cross-dressing in the gender- and race-conscious (and typically racist and misogynist) minstrel traditions in mid-nineteenth-century American popular theater. Although Goneril may be John Ringman's legendary demonized wife, she could, in this context, be one of Ringman's disguises: a cross-dressing, masculine, Indianlike, and "woman's-rights" woman (62) invented primarily to help him elicit sympathy and money, if not "something further," from misogynist and racist fools such as Roberts.

The "touching" scenes in the narrative reinforce the idea that Goneril may be Ringman's invention rather than his bride. Whether they involve the physical, sentimental, emotional, or economic touching of a potential victim, they all point to the *Fidele* as a world "where touch tropes all transactions" (Short 143).[6] John Ringman is the first character to alert readers to the broader implications of such scenes. Melville uses Ringman's tale of mourning regarding the "touching case" of his "deceased wife Goneril" to create an ironic context for understanding "touching" in all its manifestations in the novel. For after learning of Ringman's perceptions regarding Goneril's "mysterious touches," the reader immediately witnesses Ringman's own touchingly personal and economic encounter with an easily duped collegian. Similarly, Ringman claims to know the merchant, Henry Roberts, who insists three times that he does not know him. Such knowledge suggests, as Carolyn Karcher observes, that Roberts does not realize he may already have met Ringman, formerly disguised as Guinea (209). Additionally, it illustrates that Ringman knows how to manipulate, to touch, Roberts's smug and racist certainty.

Ringman then digresses briefly about the problem of memory, informing Roberts that he was "kicked by a horse" and temporarily lost his memory, which eventually led him to the Goneril-like philosophy: "We are but clay, sir, potter's clay, as the good book says, clay, feeble and too-yielding clay" (20). Such a literal or metaphoric horse kick to the head may also have led Ringman to his invention of Goneril, for shortly after he expresses this philosophy, a "writhing expression" (21) steals over Ringman, and he tells Roberts what readers only later learn is Goneril's story. After evoking Roberts's pity with this "touching" story, Ringman accepts Roberts's "alms" almost coldly, crisply confiding to the merchant, before exiting, that the "transfer-agent of the Black Rapids Coal Company" is on board the ship, selling valuable stock (22). In the next chapter, Ringman, assuming a "changed air," throws "off in private the cold garb of decorum, and so giving warmly loose to his genuine heart, seem[s] almost transformed into another being" (25). Such a statement encourages the reader to consider whether Ringman's transformation is the result of "kindness received" from the merchant or the result, as it most likely is, of a deliberately and successfully staged performance (24). Ringman's writhing expression, cold transformation, "touching" behavior, and philosophy about man as "potter's clay" implicitly (if not explicitly) reinforce the impression that his clay-eating "Goneril" is not his deceased demonic wife but either a fictive invention or one of his own clever, cross-dressing disguises.

Why would Melville create such a hidden avatar of the confidence man: a never-present wife who embodies a strange synthesis of cuttle-fish, Indian, and woman? Reconsidering Shakespeare's probable influence on Melville's creation of a female figure whose name does make her seem, as critics have noted, related to the unnatural Goneril in King Lear is useful at this point.[7] As one of the "unnatural hags" in this tragedy, Goneril, like her sisters, represents the antithesis of a female ideal or "*virgo* type." That is, she symbolizes the "familiar *virago* type," who, says Catherine Cox, "would be scorned by an Elizabethan audience" not only for betraying her father (and king) but also for displaying such "masculine" qualities as "assertiveness, courage, [and] self-respect." Although Cordelia is not treacherous, she, like Goneril and Reagan, would also be suspect for her masculine decisiveness and "purportedly unnatural expressions of cross-gendered identity" (146). Like Shakespeare's Goneril, Melville's represents "unnatural" femaleness since his character is also strong, independent, aggressive, and treacherous. Melville's Goneril, however, is also seemingly aligned with conventional *virgo* types, since part of her "touching" deception is to appear submissive and to perform the part of a conventionally domestic and devoted nineteenth-century wife and mother. Yet because of her chuckling, Indianlike, and mannish aggressiveness, Goneril not only fails to convince men of her conventional domesticity, but she remains an atypical Melvillean woman, insofar as aggression in Melville's narratives is, as Richard Brodhead notes, more often linked "to the problem of being a man" ("Melville" 185). During his confidence game with the collegian, Goneril's "husband," John Ringman, observes that he wants confidence "between man and man—more particularly between stranger and stranger" to return. He provocatively adds that he has sometimes thought "that confidence is the New Astrea—emigrated—vanished—gone" (27). Presumably, Ringman's "New Astrea" (or Virgo) would, like his Goneril, paradoxically inspire confidence between men and strangers by giving them a "new" female enemy; that is, a natural woman who is masculine, domestic, and monstrous.[8]

As the confidence man's most silenced and invisible avatar, Goneril is wedded to his machinations as well as to other other nonhuman or natural energies in the text, such as the "Indians" and the clayed waters and banks of the Mississippi. Whether she is a woman pretending to be mannish or Indianlike or a man pretending to be an Indianlike and mannish woman or simply a fictive invention, Goneril remains, finally, an enigma, except perhaps to the confidence man himself. At the same time, the question of Goneril's gender, if not gender identity, can be partially illuminated by another

Melvillean reference to Shakespeare. Directly preceding Goneril's story is a narrative pause of "Only a page or so" (Chapter 11) in which John Truman confides to the merchant, Henry Roberts (who later "tells" Goneril's story), that "Nature . . . in Shakespeare's words, had meal and bran; and, rightly regarded, the bran in its way was not to be condemned" (59). Shakespeare's words about "meal and bran" are spoken by banished Belarious in *Cymbeline* to its cross-dressing female protagonist, Imogen. A male-disguised woman, she responds to the question as to whether she is a "brother": "So man and man should be, / But clay and clay differs in dignity, / Whose dust is both alike" (*Cymbeline* 4.2.3–5). Imogen's ruminations about brotherhood, clay, and man's dignity do not link her directly to *The Confidence-Man*, but Melville's clay-eating (or man-eating) Goneril (whether a man or a woman) would be more at home in the "far fetched" and carnivalesque melodrama of *Cymbeline* than in the dark landscape of *King Lear* (Harrison 1382). Although Melville's confidence man appears to link the quasi-maternal Goneril to the "bran" rather than the substance, or "meal," of nature, the full quotation about "Nature" from *Cymbeline* suggests something more, including a quasi-paternal link: "Cowards father cowards and base things sire base. / Nature hath meal and bran, contempt and grace" (*Cymbeline* 4.2.26–27). "Nature," in its Shakespearean context, is a complex force that fathers both "bran" and "meal," or, in metaphoric terms, "cowards" and their antithesis. In the context of Melville's novel, however, "Nature" engenders a strange new synthesis of its "bran" and "meal" to give birth to the confidence man and his Indian-like bride, Goneril, both of whom appear to be the strangely natural, if not desireable, antidote to the baseness, hypocrisy, greed, distrust, and cynicism on this predominantly male ship of fools.

This paradoxical perception is reinforced by the often-cited narrative digressions in Chapters 14, 33, and 44 that appear to many critics to "frame" *The Confidence-Man* (Branch et al. 309). All three chapters cryptically suggest that the comedy of action in which Goneril and other characters are embroiled is related both to a "comedy of thought" and to the narrator's representation of nature or natural processes (71). In Chapter 14, the narrator implies that the "lesser author" who creates "duck-billed characters" is comparable to "nature" who, to the "perplexity of the naturalists," produces her "duck-billed beavers" (70). Certainly, Goneril might qualify as such a "duck-billed character" since she appears to be authored by the narrator, his confidence men, and Melville himself. At the same time, the narrator observes, "the grand points of human nature" do not change, so that no matter how altered their appearance, humans are the "same-to-day" as they were a "thousand years ago" (70). Although misogynist and "comic" portraits of monstrous women have been around for more than a thousand years, the significance of Goneril's monstrousness has been ironically recontextualized to implicate her male creators in the process. Such a point is reiterated in the novel's next speculative or framing chapter (Chapter 33). Here the narrator asserts that in artistic productions, "people" want "more reality, than real life itself can show," as well as "nature, too . . . nature unfettered, exhilarated, in effect transformed" (183). As a "natural" woman, Goneril is "unfettered, exhilarated, and in effect transformed" as part of an artistic (and gendered) construction—a "woman" who appears, in part, designed to blur the lines between what is natural and what is not, what is masculine and what is not, and what is "Indian" and what is not. Finally, in Chapter 44, the narrator offers speculations not only about the creation of "original" characters but also about generating a "new species," a species that is "almost as much of a prodigy [to fiction], as in real history is a new law-giver, a revolutionizing philosopher, or the founder of a new religion" (239).

Like other avatars of confidence men, Goneril is arguably a member of this invented or new "species," for her quasi-human "story" is relevant to much that precedes and follows it. Shortly before Goneril's story, for example, the reader is offered the story of a "charitable lady" (Chapter 8) who is quickly "touched" (both economically and emotionally) by the man in gray who seems to replace Goneril's husband, John Ringman, as the confidence man. This new avatar pleads for the "Widow and Orphan Asylum recently founded among the Seminoles" (45, 28), but after failing to persuade various male passengers, he moves "laggingly into the ladies' saloon, as in spiritless quest of somebody." There, he spots the "charitable lady," possibly the only "real" woman in this text. This lady has, the narrator observes, an "aspect" which suggests that if she has a "weak point, it must be anything rather than her excellent heart" (43). Finding herself in "an extraordinary way, touched" by the confidence man's professed concern for the Seminoles, she simultaneously reveals her "excellent heart" and "weak point" with the statement: "Poor souls—Indians, too—those cruelly-used Indians" (45).

As a privileged and literate nineteenth-century woman, this "charitable lady" is believably conversant with the fate and exploitation of the Seminoles. In this, she appears typical of most of Melville's readers, who, says Lucy Maddox, "would surely remember the [Second] Seminole War of 1835–1842, in which the U.S. government created a great many Seminole widows and orphans," relocating and transporting them eventually across the Mississippi River. In Maddox's view, Melville omitted more elaborate details regarding this "Asylum" because no writer could hope to "discuss openly such episodes as a messy seven-year war of extermination against the Indians" (83). It seems more likely, however, that Melville's target here is this "charitable lady," who remains unaware that her own widowed state is hardly comparable to that of a Seminole woman devastated by this genocidal war. She remains too self-absorbed, too much a lady, to question whether this confidence man is merely attempting to further exploit well-known accounts "in the popular press" of the Seminoles as victims of war, perhaps most notably of "Andrew Jackson's ruthless military campaign" (Lancaster 5). In addition, the Seminoles, as William Sturdevant explains, "represent a synthesis of various tribal groups, as well as many escaped African slaves," and were so-named in the late eighteenth century "in response to European pressures" since the "tribe is an entirely post-European phenomenon" (103). Like Goneril, the confidence man's Seminole widows arguably represent a cultural synthesis of differing female ethnic groups, a synthesis that comments both indirectly and ironically on the civilized treachery involved in "creating" them.

Goneril's supposed Indianness may also be linked to the "[true] Indian Doctors" (including the herb-doctor) who enter a decaying environment of "sick" male passengers (79) in Chapter 15 to pose interrelated questions about disease, humankind, and nature. The most notable case of this herb-doctor is the much-discussed hard case, Pitch, who seemingly drives him off only to find himself challenged by the final two avatars of the confidence man, the PIO agent and the philanthropist, or Frank Goodman, the Cosmopolitan. Pitch, a land- and boy-owning Missourian who dresses in the skins of animals he has slaughtered, carries a "double-barreled gun" (106) and immediately attempts to argue the case against "Dame Natur" (106) to the herb-doctor, who defends "her" and, by extension, his natural remedies. Although other victims appear drawn to the herb-doctor's marketing rhetoric (and products), Pitch denounces the herb-doctor's idea that he should have confidence in either human or nonhuman nature. In Pitch's view, "Dame Natur" (106) creates disease and can destroy the land and human habitats (107–8).

Claiming to speak with an understanding of the dark relationship between "Dame Natur" and human nature, Pitch's "primitivism" has androcentric, misanthropic, misogynist, racist, and dark economic implications insofar as he wants to control and exploit both this "Dame" and his "boy" or slave laborers. Personifying and anthropomorphizing "Dame Natur" to the herb-doctor, Pitch claims she "embezzled" and "absconded with ten thousand dollars' worth of my property" (108). In fact, Pitch maintains, if this "Dame" is in one of her "passion-fits," she forces any sane man to "bar her out," "bolt her out," or "lint her out" (109). Although Pitch first claims he is not a slaveholder, he reveals himself as a racist who thinks "niggers are . . . freer" than "whites ducking and grinning round for a favor" (112). Later, he tells the PIO agent that he is, in fact, a kind of ultimate slavemaster, since he has purchased many hired boys—"polite boys or saucy boys, white boys or black boys, smart boys or lazy boys, Caucasian boys or Mongol boys—all . . . rascals" (118). The word "boys" arguably refers to the degradation of black male slaves and the exploitation of children.[9]

Again, the confidence man, first as the PIO agent and then as Frank Goodman, attempts, with mixed success, to defend Pitch's victims: boys and "Dame Natur." In so doing, the two pointedly illustrate the pathology of Pitch's contemptuous attitude toward both while indirectly offering a commonplace perception in much ecofeminist discourse: that the androcentric devaluation of land, of nature, is readily mirrored in the devaluation of women, children, and indigenous peoples. The story of Goneril foreshadows this perception. In terms comparable to Pitch's description of "Dame Natur," Goneril is, in the narrator's telling of Henry Roberts's tale, too sexual, too "touching," too maternally malignant, too treacherous, too "Indian," and too animalistic to be human. To Roberts a "woman" like Goneril, is, like Pitch's "Dame Natur" and his boys, inferior, nonhuman, needing to be controlled and dominated. As noted, neither Pitch's attitude toward his boys nor Roberts's toward Goneril is left unchallenged by Melville's confidence men. Like the narrator, they appear to understand how to mirror, manipulate, and mock such muddled androcentricism.

If Goneril, "the woman," has been forgotten by the time the PIO agent attempts to sell confidence to the Missourian, the next Indian segment (the much-discussed "metaphysics of Indian-hating") in the narrative encourages Melville's readers to recall her Indianlike aspect. This final sequence is dominated by a quasi-androgynous Cosmopolitan, who initially appears to a befuddled Pitch as a philanthropist, an effeminate man with a "partihued" and "rather plumagy aspect," complete with "flowered regatta-shirt," "white trowsers of ample duck," and "maroon-colored slippers"—all in all, a "florid show" (131). Pitch subsequently accuses this confidence man of being a "Diogenes masquerading as a cosmopolitan" (138). After aptly describing Diogenes as a philosopher who, "going a step beyond misanthropy, was less a man-hater than a man-hooter" (138), the cosmopolitan denies the charge, despite the fact that he seems, as many critics observe, the "real cynic and misanthrope, the real Diogenes and Timon of this scene and others" (Elizabeth Foster 332). Interestingly, and despite his eccentricities, Diogenes, along with other Cynics, is credited by some environmental writers as being among the "most ecologically minded" of the Greek philosophers insofar as he privileges nature over the "artificial encumbrances of civilization" (Marshall 76). If so, Diogenes was also among the first "ecologically-minded" philosophers to demonstrate the chaotic, amoral, and unpredictable energies of "nature," as suggested by biographical accounts of his eccentric lifestyle and sometimes lewd social conduct. Melville's demonstrable familiarity with this Cynic appears to come from an early biography he "owned, and annotated," Diogenes Laertius's *Lives of Eminent Philosophers* "in the 1853 Bohn edition" (Elizabeth Foster 332). This brief biography is filled with abrupt narrative transitions, crabbed dialogue, and ironic responses by Diogenes regarding civilization and economic systems, and brief reference not only to his belief that he is a "citizen of the world" but also bizarre accounts of his death, presumably from devouring raw octopus (Laertius 79). Although Diogenes is only one of the misanthropic figures to whom Melville's characters refer, his significance, like Goneril's, appears to be his relation to turbulent and transforming "natural" energies in the text.

Whether taking the guise of a black minstrel, the herb-doctor, a Seminole philanthropist, or an Indianlike and mannish cuttle-fish of a woman, the evolving, new, and not clearly human Melvillean species appears to play a natural, if not evolving, role in the affairs of human society. Such a creature appears designed, as the Cosmopolitan describes "him" (or "her") to Mark Winsome, as a "Mississippi Operator" or "Great Medicine" practitioner, as a species best suited to purge and "drain off repletions" among human populations (196). Among those final segments that most directly reinforce the "healing" powers of Melville's invented species are the scenes between the confidence man and his next quarry, Charles Noble, a man inordinately fascinated by men who "hate" Indians. This fascination indirectly recalls Goneril's "Indian" aspect and allegedly hate-filled story. Describing Colonel Moredock's much-discussed "metaphysics of Indian-hating," Noble accurately credits (before substantially modifying Melville's source) the original tale by Judge Hall (Branch et al. 281). According to this "metaphysics," Noble explains to the confidence man, there "can be no biography of an *Indian-hater par excellence,* any more than one of a sword-fish, or other deep-sea denizen," since there is a certain "impenetrability" in the life of a man who spends his life "hating" Indians, alone by himself, deep in the recesses of the wilderness" (150).

Given her Indian, squidlike, and mannish womanliness (or womanly mannishness), Goneril would seem this novel's best example of such an impenetrable "deep-sea denizen," since "she" is credited not only with hating all men, including presumably "Indian" men, but most humans, including her daughter. After this description, Noble's judge states that accounts of the "*Indian-hater par excellence*" have only been reported by "diluted" Indian-haters. Such a "diluted" Indian-hater, after "relaxing" his vows of Indian-hating, "hurries over towards the first smoke, though he knows it is an Indian's" and "embraces him with much affection, imploring the privilege of living a while in sweet companionship." What is "too often the sequel of so distempered a procedure," Judge Hall-Noble concludes, "may be best known by those who best know the Indian" (150). Whether such a "diluted" Indian-hater is accepted, ignored, mocked, or slaughtered remains unanswered. However, men like Hall (and Noble) continue to create wildly fictitious and self-contradictory legends about allegedly undiluted Indian-haters. That is, Indian-haters "par excellence" exist only because of misogynist and racist mythologies or legends recounted by the "diluted" Indian-haters, slave-haters, boy-haters, or, more collectively, "Dame Natur"–haters who thrive among the assorted hunters of fortune, land, boys, slaves, or Indians in this narrative house of mirrors. Goneril's story, like that of Judge Hall-Noble's tale of the Indian-hater "par excellence," can be, as all the avatars of the confidence man understand, commodified, packaged, and sold to such "diluted" haters as well as to those who fail to comprehend its misogynist or racist distortions.

Melville's confidence man not only deals in such metaphorical commodities but does so as an amoral, shape-shifting, and "natural" being. Along with his avatars (including Goneril), the confidence man brings a "Great Medicine," one designed to disrupt racist, misogynist, androcentric, or generally ignorant perceptions regarding relations between man and "Dame Natur" (in "her" various manifestations, human or nonhuman).[10] Whether an Indianlike woman, wife, and mother; a conflicted, cross-dressing man, or a fictive invention; Goneril is thematically significant in this cyclonic narrative. The question of her existence and nature raises questions about the self-deluding folly involved in oppressing or exploiting not only nature but other humans, whether "Dames" or "boys" or "Indians." The predominantly adult male congress depicted in this toxic textual world is one that wages an androcentric and continuously futile war to dominate nature; wilfully enslaves, denigrates, or diddles its fellow man for profit; and ignores deeper ethical questions. "The antithesis to a human community committed to living in sustainable ecological relation to boys, Indians, women, and nature, such a congress, as the final chapter suggests, seems doomed. At the same time, the confidence man and his avatars, including Goneril, may prove part of an unsettling remedy to this darkening textual environment. The only "Something further" that can follow from this "Masquerade" depends, as Melville seems to anticipate, upon its readers.

Notes

1. See Robyn Wiegman's assessment of Melville's critique of patriarchy and "the gendered ideology of the male bond" in "The Paradise of Bachelors and the Tartarus of Maids" (197).

2. Unlike the human-nature-technology continuum more optimistically posited by Haraway, Melville's "reinvention" or innovative synthesis of "nature" and "woman" in the mannish and "Indian-like" Goneril offers an ironic commentary on the man-woman-nature continuum.

3. Although ecofeminists and deep ecologists both generally acknowledge the dangers of anthropocentrism, ecofeminists typically criticize deep ecologists for their failure to "pay attention to the connections between patriarchal power structures" (Littig 38). Conversely, deep ecologists criticize ecofeminists for failing to consider significant factors commonly linked to environmental crisis, such as war, unchecked technological development, and capitalism.

4. In an earlier essay on *Pierre* (1992), I argue that Melville associates the female monstrosity of Mrs. Glendenning with Medusa, as an archetypal or devouring mother. See also discussions of the ambiguity of the Medusa archetype in Dennis Berthold's "Melville's Medusas" and Jelena Sesnic's "Melville and his Medusae."

5. Carolyn Karcher's discussion of Black Guinea's complex role remains among the most illuminating.

6. William Ramsey also links Goneril's physical touching to all the "touching" scenes in this novel; in Ramsey's view, such scenes tend to be economic but can "render the most innocent-looking passages into surprisingly ominous revelations" (38).

7. See, for example, Jonathan Cook's comparison of Melville's Goneril to Shakespeare's in his book-length discussion of the novel.

8. Elizabeth Foster notes that "Astrea," mythic daughter of Zeus and Themis, was driven by human "impiety" to the heavens, where she was "placed among the constellations of the zodiac, under the name Virgo" (305).

9. Karcher, for example, argues that Melville couches this exchange in "bawdy sexual imagery" that "establishes an analogy between sexual and economic exploitation" and reminds readers of "the ugly realities of pederasty, *droit du seigneur,* rape, and prostitution that so blatantly gave the lie to the philosophical and religious pretensions that the master class . . . used to justify slavery" (246–47).

10. William Dillingham persuasively argues that Melville's use of alchemical imagery points to the underlying possibility of such cultural healing.

When Silence Speaks

The Chola Widow

Maria Felisa López Liquete

Through the acknowledged and unacknowledged silences in "Sketch Eighth: Norfolk Isle and the Chola Widow" of "The Encantadas" (1853), especially as they relate to Hunilla, its "heroine," Melville critiques imperialism in general but most particularly that of Spain and the United States. Hunilla, the Chola widow, resists being captured and controlled by a colonizing male narrative voice and view, thereby undermining his author(ity) and exposing his limited vision. In this Sketch, Melville presents and reverses both the colonial and the patriarchal perspectives linked to the story's gendered gaze and its silences. Further, if "postcoloniality" can be understood as a form of contestatory consciousness that fosters processes aimed at revising the norms and practices of colonialism, the narrator of Sketch Eighth also provides a postcolonial perspective of both an exotic land and an exotic character, Hunilla.

Hunilla stands for Spanish America, silent, mysterious, and empowered by stoicism, resistance, and a tortoiselike patience. She is antithetical to Melville's negative portraits of Spaniards in Sketch Tenth and of creoles in Sketch Seventh. A story about a female Robinson Crusoe, Sketch Eighth asks the still much debated question posited by Gayatri Spivak: "Can the subaltern speak?" Who speaks is as important as who is listening and how those sounds are interpreted, but the wish to interpret may distort the acts of writing and reading. Sketch Eighth is a challenging site for debating these issues, for the male North American narrator, because of his own limitations and decisions, as well as Hunilla's silences, proves unable to tell the story of the female South American protagonist in full detail.

Although the relationship of women and silence has a long history, Hunilla's story is unique in linking woman, silence, gender, race, religion, and class all in one. A Chola, the racially mixed Hunilla is a subaltern, oppressed and subordinated in terms of class, caste, and gender. Jorge Klor de Alva usefully points out that racially mixed castes were never colonial subjects but subalterns (245), while Leela Gandhi maintains that "the complex notion of subalternity . . . concerns itself with historically determined relationships of dominance and subordination" (2). Melville, then, in his concern not only with the colonial and imperial past and present but also with the silences and ellipses of historical amnesia, was a forerunner of subaltern studies. In Sketch Eighth Melville probes the imperialism of old Spain in relation to the imperialistic perspective of the new United States. Though both countries face and force themselves on everything and everyone indigenous to the New World, this Sketch is particularly concerned, through Hunilla, the subaltern Chola, with the link between Catholic Spain and the indigenous peoples of America.

Hunilla is presented as an observed object, "colonized" by the white male gaze of the narrator. He seeks to take rhetorical control of her as a metaphorical site in which colonialism is fought out. However, when she is given the opportunity to speak—which she at times uses and at other times prefers not to—she is freed from this totalizing imperial and patriarchal perspective. Since imperialism silences the voices of those it wishes to colonize, and these voices most frequently are those of nonwhite ethnic peoples and of women, Hunilla's silences have performative power, especially considering that her country, Peru, achieved its independence from old Spain in 1821, only thirty-two years before the publication of "The Encantadas." By leaving his narrative incomplete and full of silences, and by respecting Hunilla's resistance to being captured, Melville succeeds in undermining colonialism's discourse.

Melville's choice of the Galápagos Islands as the appropriate setting[1] for a critique of burgeoning U.S. imperialism[2] may have followed Darwin's intent to challenge established ideas. His critique of Spanish colonial imperialism throughout "The Encantadas" in general as well as of its specific endeavors—particularly as evidenced in Sketch Seventh and Ninth—correlates with his critique of the United States's imperialistic actions during the mid–nineteenth century. By using the English names of the islands instead of the Spanish ones in "The Encantadas," Melville demonstrates from the beginning of his story the way in which imperialism controls and silences language. The Buccaneers are not only content to steal Spanish treasures, but they also erase Spanish names as well. Significantly, as is discussed below, Norfolk Isle displaces "Santa Cruz" (Saint/Holy Cross).

Although many concur that the terms "imperialism" and "colonialism" have been applied in dissimilar ways at distinct times to a variety of experiences, all would agree with Klor de Alva's identification of their two foremost and shared attributes. The first of these is primarily intellectual: the exploitation of one corporate group by another. The other "carries . . . political and moral freight. For many, [this] implies unjust social asymmetries, human abuses, and moral imperatives, which call for acts of resistance, demands for justice, and struggles for liberation" (242). Both of these attributes are, in fact, present in Melville's representations of imperialism and colonialism in his first three novels—*Typee, Omoo,* and *Mardi*. They are also apparent in *Moby-Dick*, where Europeans and North Americans alike are shown as claiming superiority over any land or nation that fills their economic or political needs: "What was America in 1492 but a Loose-Fish, in which Columbus struck the Spanish standard by way of waifing it for his royal master and mistress? What was Poland to the Czar? What Greece to the Turk? What India to England? What at last will Mexico be to the United States? All Loose-Fish" (398).[3] Melville's rhetorical queries suggest a historical succession of colonial endeavors, with Spain first in the list and the United States last. Actually, the discovery of America marked a turning point, not only in Spain's claiming and maintaining imperial rights but also by Spain's introducing the idea of empire into Europe, as Frances A. Yates argues.[4] That Melville shows Spain and the United States facing each other in "The Encantadas" reflects a historical reality, and in Sketch Eighth his characterization of Hunilla also works to expose his readers' fears of two exotic subjects or entities, Spain and Catholicism.

Through much of his writing, Melville maintained an interest in Spain and South America alongside his interest in colonialism and imperialism—in *Mardi, Moby-Dick,* "Benito Cereno" (1855), as well as "The Encantadas." In his antipathy toward Spain in "The Encantadas," Melville reflects an attitude prevalent in the United States since the seventeenth century. As Stanley T. Williams points out, the United States had long both envied and hated Spain:

> Hatred of Spain and all of her ways burned deep in the minds of the English colonists of the seventeenth century on the Atlantic seaboard. These pioneers feared the haughty nation whose colonies in America were many times the area of the mother country. They hated her for Catholic tyrannies, which in no unrelated ways had helped to motivate

their exodus from England and Holland, and for her animosity towards the English settlements. They shrank from the legends concerning the terrible Spaniard: his cruelty and craft, his alleged barbarism (embellished by Bartolomé de las Casas) in his colonies, his fanaticism in his dark religion of the Inquisition, and, above all, his firm, prosperous presence in the rich, warm lands of the South. All these boded restraint to the ambitious Englishman. Race, religion, economic rivalry—everything counseled enmity. (3)

Williams argues that following American independence in 1783, "Spanish diplomacy and Spanish greed inspired a hostility rivaling in intensity, especially on the borders of the Mississippi, that felt toward our archenemy, Britain" (23). The narrator's representation of Spaniards as "dastardly," "mercenary," and "retrograde" in Sketch Tenth continues to project this hostile attitude (170–71). In addition, the mid-nineteenth-century ideology of "manifest destiny" upheld the annexation of Spanish territories in America. For example, an 1849 article in the *North American Review* claimed that "very few persons have bestowed any serious observation and thought on the character and resources of these mysterious tropical nations, with whom it is the 'manifest destiny' of our country to be more and more closely connected" ("The Poetry of Spanish-America" 132).[5]

Anti-Catholic movements, active throughout the nineteenth century, also reinforced this hostile attitude toward Spain. J. C. Furnas points out that the nativist Know-Nothing party's favorite target was often the Catholics because the "Pope was allegedly scheming to turn America into a medieval Spain, Inquisition and all" (524). He adds that "among English-speaking Protestants c. 1830 dread of Catholicism was pretty much taken for granted. It was a heritage from centuries of exposure of Britons and Colonists to ... antipapal feeling occasioned by England's post Reformation scuffles with Spain and France." Robert S. Levine contends as well that by the mid-1830s fears of a Roman Catholic conspiracy to gain the American republic as the crown jewel of the papal crown and the threat of conversion had become major subjects of evangelical tracts, revivalist sermons, nativist propaganda, and popular fiction. Furthermore, according to Levine, anti-Catholic discourse had attained a mobilizing power in the cultural life of the U.S., informing both the political millennialism of the 1790s and the Second Great Awakening of the early 1800s, because "many Americans agreed, as Adams wrote Jefferson in 1821, 'that a free government and the Roman Catholic religion can never exist together in any nation or Country'" (*Conspiracy* 106). William Parker presents a similar analysis: "The main bone of contention in the

1850s was religion. Between the Irish and the Catholic Rhineland Germans, the old nonconformist Protestant sects of the United States were about to be swamped by Roman Catholicism. There was talk that the nation would fall to the legions of Rome, to the Grand Army of the papacy" (106).

In addition, economic and social frustrations were linked to the dramatic surge in Catholic immigration, two hundred thousand in the year 1850, mainly Irish and German (Levine 109).[6] Such figures might explain why Samuel Morse warned Americans in *A Foreign Conspiracy Against the Liberties of the United States* (1834) that "an extremely dangerous group of Roman Catholic conspirators, 'despotic, monarchical and aristocratic,' had infiltrated America and now sought nothing less than the corruption of Americans' republican ideals and the geographical conquest of the continent." Morse called them "Jesuitical conspirators . . . skilled in the art of deception" (qtd. Levine 108).[7] In his biography, Hershel Parker maintains that Melville refused to kowtow to his publishers, the Harper brothers. Their nativism might have prevented him from publishing "The Isle of the Cross" with them and have resulted in his sending his stories, including "The Encantadas," to *Putnam's Monthly Magazine* (1: 642).[8] Watson Branch notes that Melville's criticism of Protestant missionary work in *Typee* (1846) and *Omoo* (1847) led to his being regarded by an October 1850 review in the *London Eclectic Review* as a "partisan of popery," one guilty of deliberate and elaborate "misrepresentation" and "a prejudiced, incompetent, and truthless witness" regarding the Protestant missions in Tahiti (12). In fact, Branch believes "The Encantadas" gained literary attention in part because its South Seas setting reminded the reviewers of Melville's first two books, which were listed on the title page of *The Piazza Tales* (35).

Given that pirates were the primary means by which western powers sought to erode Spanish power, "The Encantadas" displays a wide range of pirates, buccaneers, privateers, outcasts, castaways, runaways, renegades, and sea dogs of all kinds.[9] Although the narrator of "The Encantadas" opens his list of sailors with whalemen, the islands' first visitors, buccaneers, appear in most of the sketches, predominantly in Sketch Sixth, "Barrington Isle and the Buccaneers." He tells us that this isle was the resort of Caribbean buccaneers who ravaged the Pacific side of South America and "waylaid the royal treasure ships plying between Manilla and Acapulco" (144). Sketch Seventh, "Charles' Isle and the Dog-King," and Sketch Ninth, "Hood's Isle and the Hermit Oberlus," deal with colonial issues, especially with the difficulties of establishing paradises in this New World.

Whalemen, however, were the main visitors to the Encantadas, for whale oil had become the Pacific's greatest treasure. In 1841, as a whaleman, Melville visited Peru, the last South American country to achieve independence from

Spain, and during his visit perceived vestiges of Peru's colonial past.[10] Chapter 42 of *Moby-Dick*, "The Whiteness of the Whale," paints a devastating portrait of Lima, still suffering from its long colonization: "The strangest, saddest city thou can'st see. For Lima has taken the white veil; and there is a higher horror in this whiteness of her woe. Old as Pizarro, this whiteness keeps her ruins for ever new; admits not the cheerful greenness of complete decay; spreads over her broken ramparts the rigid pallor of an apoplexy that fixes its own distortions" (193).

Lima reappears in Chapter 54, "The Town-Ho's Story," where this white city is subtly connected to the white whale. In *Moby-Dick* Melville notes that the old whale cry "Town Ho" was used to pursue the "Gallipagos terrapin" (242). "The Town-Ho's Story" is one that three white men have tried to keep secret, but they tell it, "with Romish injunctions of secrecy," to Tashtego, the Indian harpooner (242). Tashtego speaks part of it in his sleep, anticipating Hunilla's half-told story in Sketch Eighth. Narrated by Ishmael, this story, like Hunilla's, is also a retelling—"told at the Golden Inn" in Lima to Spanish friends, Don Pedro and Don Sebastian. Ishmael begins by describing the disquieting setting of the Erie Canal: "by rows of snow-white chapels . . . flows one continual stream of Venetianly corrupt and often lawless life. . . . For by some curious fatality, as it is often noted of your metropolitan freebooters that they ever encamp around the halls of justice, so sinners, gentlemen, most abound in holiest vicinities" (249). Melville thereby links whiteness and corruption with Christianity. The Spanish Dons thank the narrator for his "delicacy in not substituting present Lima for distant Venice in your corrupt comparison. Oh! Do not bow and look surprised; you know the proverb all along this coast—'Corrupt as Lima.' . . . churches more plentiful than billiard-tables, and for ever open—and 'Corrupt as Lima'" (249).

In his "Extracts" at the beginning of *Moby-Dick*, Melville includes a statement by Edmund Burke in which Spain is defined as "a great whale stranded on the shores of Europe" (xxiii)—perhaps a "loose fish" to be fastened more securely onto Europe in the turmoil following the French Revolution. Contemporary South American writer Jose de Onís uses a similar metaphor. He claims that "the great American dream would have failed if the United States had not possessed Hispanic America," adding that "Spain—the whale—did not allow Americans to conquer South America as readily as they expected." Startlingly, Onís implies that Moby Dick prevents North Americans from colonizing South America (125).[11]

Certainly, whalers were to play an important role both in the liberation of South America and in the formation of the U.S. empire. Chapter 24 of *Moby-Dick*, "The Advocate," makes clear that, "until the whale fishery rounded Cape

Horn, no commerce but colonial, scarcely any intercourse but colonial, was carried on between Europe and the long line of the opulent Spanish provinces on the Pacific coast. It was the whaleman who first broke through the jealous policy of the Spanish crown, touching those colonies; . . . from those whalemen at last eventuated the liberation of Peru, Chili, and Bolivia from the yoke of Old Spain, and the establishment of the eternal democracy in those parts" (110). Additional analogies between whaling and empire building are made explicit in Chapter 14, "Nantucket": "And thus have these naked Nantucketers, these sea hermits, . . . overrun and conquered the watery world . . .; parcelling out among them the Atlantic, Pacific, and Indian oceans. . . . Let America add Mexico to Texas, and pile Cuba upon Canada; let the English overswarm all India . . . ; two thirds of this terraqueous globe are the Nantucketer's. For the sea is his; he owns it, as Emperors own empires; other seamen having but a right of way through it" (64).[12] While in *Moby-Dick* Melville recognizes the impact of colonization on Mexico, Cuba, and South America, in "The Encantadas" he explicitly refers to Peru's 1821 independence. In Sketch Seventh, "Charles' Isle and the Dog-King," he writes:

> During the successful revolt of the Spanish provinces from Old Spain, there fought on behalf of Peru a certain Creole adventurer from Cuba who . . . advanced himself to high rank in the patriot army. The war being ended . . . Peru had not wherewithal to pay off its troops. But the Creole—I forget his name—volunteered to take his pay in lands. So they told him he might have his pick of the Enchanted Isles, which were then, as they still remain, the nominal appanage of Peru. . . . Charles's Isle is not only the sole property of the Creole, but is for ever free of Peru, even as Peru from Spain. (146–47)

The names of Melville's characters in Sketch Eighth have rich connotations reflecting Spain's impact on them all: "Felipe" resonates with the names of powerful Spanish monarchs, and "Truxill" is that of the second city founded by the Spaniards in Peru, named by Pizarro after his birthplace in Spain. "Hunilla" seems the equivalent of the Spanish Juanilla, a diminutive of Juana, which implies her low social status. Hunilla, the protagonist of Sketch Eighth, is a Chola, "a half-breed Indian woman of Payta in Peru" (152). Abandoned on Norfolk Isle by a French whaler, she is saved by an American one, thanks to "Peruvian pisco [brandy]" provided by a mulatto (152). Although initially accompanied by Felipe, her husband of "pure Castilian blood," and Truxill, her Indian brother, both dearly beloved, following their accidental deaths while fishing, she has lived alone on the island through terrible trials, surviving by her courage, skills, and faith. Love also helps her survive: she is comforted by the memory of her lover/husband's embrace and the little dogs who are her companions in her isolation.

Although colonized indigenous peoples were the voluntary or involuntary recipients of European-introduced forces, such as new technologies, languages, religions, ideologies, diseases, and genes, which had the effect of irreversibly altering them, these processes had the power to create new beings, the Cholos, for instance. The colonial discourse of "The Encantadas," however, does not recognize significant differences among subject peoples, representing all natives as equivalent or interchangable, as shown in Sketch Seventh and Sketch Tenth. Hunilla as a mestiza, racially and ethnically both Indian and Spanish, occupies a difficult social position. Despite exceptions, such as writer Inca Garcilaso, a well-known South American mestizo, historically mestizos were rejected by Indians, Spaniards, and Creoles. Furthermore, "Cholo/a," a Peruvian word, came to be used as a degrading term synonymous for dog, bastard, half-blood, degenerate, or tainted. Melville's frequent use of this term suggests his awareness of the relentlessly degrading impact of colonialism.

America is a feminine term in Spanish, and America has been widely represented by other cultures as a woman, with maps often feminizing the land of America.[13] Jonathan Hart asserts that "the Spanish invasion was, at least metaphorically and materially if not always sexually, a kind of (male) rape of the Indies and mainland America" (101), while José A. de la Puente Candamo claims that in colonial sites "la tierra se hace chola" (the earth becomes chola) (29). Most probably Hunilla, like the chola land, was raped by sailors, although rape, as discussed below, is a subject silenced in the story by the narrator. In "The Encantadas," rape also occurs by a glance. The colonial encounter marks both the colonizer, whose eyes commit an act of violation, and the colonized, who is erased as a unique self by the colonial gaze. The narrator rejects the inhospitable landscapes of the Encantadas, but his gazing on the intriguing Hunilla shows him desiring what must not be desired, Hunilla herself, including her secrets and knowledge. The exemplary Hunilla, however, undermines the desires of the narrator who seeks to define, delimit, and, in part, silence her.

"The Encantadas" in general and Sketch Eighth in particular are full of silences,[14] beginning with silenced names: that of Melville himself, who chose to write these sketches under the pseudonym Salvator R. Tarnmoor,[15] as well as of the Spanish names of the islands, as mentioned above. The name Melville gives to the Galápagos Islands and to his sketches, "The Encantadas or Enchanted Isles," intermingles English and Spanish. Melville's knowledge of

Spanish might have allowed him to perceive the gendered difference between "Encantadas" and "Galápagos." The former, with its "as" ending, points to the feminine gender, which is given in Spanish to all islands as well as to turtles and whales, independent of their sex, whereas the "os" of "Galápagos" is a masculine plural. This gendered choice marks a colonial desire, haunted (enchanted) by the exoticism of America's land or body (body of land). The masculinity of empire came to be superimposed upon the symbolically feminized and conquered geographical space (Gandhi 99).

Norfolk Isle is "sequestered" (151), as is Hunilla, and the island's silenced Spanish name (Saint/Holy Cross) predates both Hunillas's silences and her crosses. Cross, "Cruz" in Spanish, is also a woman's name. This Spanish name bears religious connotations negated by the English one. It also might have encouraged the reader to believe that the island "has become the spot made sacred by the strongest trials of humanity" (151). Furthermore, if Saint/Holy Cross were the island's name instead of Norfolk, the tale would start and finish with the same word, "cross," the paramount sign for Christianity as well as the mark made instead of a signature by a person unable to write. In colonial sites in which the crossing of cultures and civilizations as well as of races produced new identities, in which the introduction of new plants and animals changed the life of the indigenous peoples as well as that of colonists, travelers, and passers by, diverse crosses are apparent. At the conclusion of Sketch Eighth, Hunilla, herself a representative of the crossing of cultures and races, gazes on a cross, part of the harness of the ass on which she is riding. The cross may be at the same time Hunilla herself, and the Christian cross, a source for her courage and patience.

Throughout the sketch, Hunilla is associated with animals. Initially she is associated with the tortoises of the Galapagos—her husband and brother hunt and render them and by their deaths leave to her the oil that, in the end, the American whaling captain sells for her benefit. Her perseverance, patience, and endurance reflect that of these indigenous creatures, while she also resembles them in giving herself up, after 180 recorded days, to timelessness. She shares the island with her dogs, and in the final scene she rides an ass. Both dogs and asses were imported into South America by Spaniards, and both became entirely adapted to their new environment.[16] Asses had become necessary for transport, especially in Perú.[17] In the conclusion of Sketch Eighth, Hunilla on "the small grey ass" with its Spanish "armorial cross" resonates with the image of Jesus riding into Jerusalem—implying not only Hunilla's faith but also her continuing crucifixion by power and injustice.

In telling her story, the narrator suggests that Hunilla endures her isolation, grief, and probable violation on the island by supplementing her Catholic faith with a more primitive submission to a sense of timelessness and fatality. Although he exoticizes both her Catholicism and her Indian stoicism by showing their necessity for her survival, he does not debase them. Thus Hunilla describes her intuitive knowledge of the rescue ship as coming to her "through the air" (158) both fatalistically and (imagines the narrator) as a result of her prayer, "Holy Virgin, aid me!" (156). Although the narrator spies uninvited on her final visit to the grave she has created for her beloved Felipe, his descriptions of the cross she put on his grave and of her own crucifix are moving. Not overtly anti-Catholic, Melville does, however, imply the futility of Christianity in the description of Hunilla's brass crucifix, "worn featureless, like an ancient graven knocker long plied in vain" (161). So while he admires the faithful Hunilla, the narrator condemns "Heaven," justifying his condemnation by saying "they cannot break faith who never plighted it" (155).

Introduced first by her ethnicity as a Chola, Hunilla, secondly, is identified by her gendered social status, "widow," which she is called eight times in the course of the tale.[18] As such, she is placed in a specific, respected social status familiar to Melville's readers, many of whom might have been able to relate directly, emotionally, to the loss of loved ones at sea. To the extent that Hunilla's body is analogous to the body of the New World, her respected widowhood should protect her from the colonizing violation of the "virgin land" so often remarked on by scholars. It does not. Which "rape," literal, metaphorical, or literary, is the greatest crime? The use of the definite article in the title, "The Chola Widow" implies that Hunilla is a representative rather than an individual, although she is given a proper name and addressed as such throughout the tale. According to Alison Findlay, widowhood symbolizes the connection between death and marriage (500). If, as she suggests, "women and female bodies have been a site on which desire and death have frequently been focused, partly because of the analogy between 'mother' and 'earth' that defines her as both womb and tomb," a widow embodies both possibilities: first sex and later death (500).[19] Hunilla survives both events.

Hunilla speaks Spanish, a "strange language" (152). Consequently, for North American readers, the story she tells of her life on Norfolk Isle to the captain of the rescuing whaler must be translated. Thus, her story is not presented from her perspective or in her precise words. The reader is dependent on the voice of the male narrator who not only retells her story after listening to the captain's translation of it but also interrupts it, enters it, and decides what and how it will be told. He presumes to interpret what he designates as "the strange ciphers" on "her soul's lid" (155). He actually puts words in her mouth, indicating her innermost thoughts: "Not yet, not yet; my foolish heart runs on too fast" (156), or "The ship sails this day, today . . . this gives me certain time to stand on; without certainty I go mad. In loose ignorance I have hoped and hoped; now in firm knowledge I will but wait. Now I live and no longer perish in bewilderings. Holy Virgin, aid me! Thou wilt waft back the ship" (156). But if the narrator embellishes and censors, he also assists Hunilla and perhaps rescues the reader from hearing her full anguish. Both a colonial and an imperial sight, Hunilla reflects the narrator's narcissistic observations, and her voice is the voice of the other in him, the colonial other.

Presences and absences,[20] what is seen and overlooked, what is taken for granted or ignored, what is shown and what is omitted, what is silenced and what is spoken exist in Sketch Eighth in an endlessly crisscrossing process. Hunilla's repeated reply to the captain's requests for details of her ordeal, "Señor, ask me not," bears different interpretations: that she does not want to speak openly; that she is not able to express what has already been repressed; that she feels speaking would be an intrusion on intimacy, a violation of her privacy. Since the captain denies Hunilla's repeated petitions not to be asked to speak, her ultimate submission, "Señor, be it as you say" (157), is in fact another way to maintain silence about intimate details while it also silently says, in effect, "the story is of *your* construction, not mine." Once she directly asserts herself by repeating, "I have said, Señor, something came through the air" (158), proving quietly defiant.

Although the narrator claims that her silent suffering makes her highly respected by all sailors, he himself, long before he becomes a narrator and however he excuses it, voyeuristically intrudes on her private life when he follows her through the island, discovering the place where she has interred her husband and describing the scene in detail. Earlier, by contrast, he states explicitly that two events in her ordeal remain untold: "But no, I will not file this thing complete for scoffing souls to quote, and call it firm proof upon their side. The half shall here remain untold. Those two unnamed events which befell Hunilla on this isle, let them abide between her and her God. In nature, as in law, it may be libellous to speak some truths" (157–58). In refusing to reveal these events—the reader may reasonably suspect rape by sailors from passing ships, possibly a miscarriage—the narrator metanarratively discloses and praises his own authorial voice: he lets us know that he knows but chooses not to say.

He does say, though, that Hunilla is the Sketch's "heroine": "Construe the comment of her features, as you might; from her mere words little would you have weened that Hunilla was herself the heroine of her tale" (155). Through his rhetorical tropes he reinforces her heroics, describing her as having "a heart of yearning in a frame of steel" (162) and as one who resists and fights loneliness and despair, struggling "as against the writhed coilings of a snake" (155). Idealizing and idolizing Hunilla rhetorically, the narrator shows his admiration for her patience, endurance, and love and applauds her faith and humility.

There is no objective description of Hunilla in the sketch, for, as should be obvious by now, the narrative is always veiled by the narrator's unconscious desire to see, to understand, to possess. He is a voyeur who enjoys his eye/I, and Hunilla mirrors his desire. The narrator begins his story of her by describing her appearance as if he were producing a portrait: "this woman was a most touching sight; and crayons, tracing softly melancholy lines, would best depict the mournful image of the dark-damasked Chola widow" (152). Calling her "heroine" shows the extent to which the narrator uses his worldview in order to understand her, imposing his standards of self-realization and self-expression and seeking to make the reader sympathetic to his perspective. To him she feels "a Spanish and an Indian grief which would not visibly lament. Pride's height in vain abased to proneness on the rack; nature's pride subduing nature's torture" (161). Such descriptions reveal Melville's sympathies with a mixed-blood woman in addition to preserving the authority of the white, male, American visitor-narrator.

Appropriately, the narrative stages an abundance of erotically ambiguous scenes, showing the seductions of colonial enterprise. The narrator's depictions of Hunilla preserve the patriarchal locus of political power based on prescriptive gender codes of behavior that inscribe the female body as a passive subject. His desire to see more is apparent as he claims: "she showed us her soul's lid, and the strange cipher thereon engraved: all within, with pride's timidity, was withheld" (155). His statement expresses both "a gesture of control and an acknowledgement of the narrator's limits" (Spivak 283). When the narrator looks at her, into her, or through her, he usually adds an equivalent of "but," signaling his awareness of the impossible task of seeing her clearly and fully. His fanciful description of Hunilla's burial of her husband in a "half-conscious, automatic" state (155) and his voyeuristic peering in on her last visit to his grave demonstrate his own and the reader's exoticizing of Hunilla. The scene he draws, with the dark-clad widow "partly prostrate upon the grave; her dark head bowed, and lost in her long, loosened Indian hair" (161), is not only exotic but implicitly erotic.

Silvia Montiglio points out that "precisely because silence is culturally specific, its usage within a given society may be misunderstood by strangers" (3). With specific reference to Melville, Lucy Maddox notes his "fascination with gaps or silences in the American story and with what the discourse could not contain or accommodate without completely undermining itself" (52).[21] According to Montiglio, the rhetorical exploitation of silence or the frequent recourse to *praeteritio* ("I shall not speak about such and such") helps writers shape an ideal image of themselves by showing their preoccupation with the limits of free speech and by asserting their moderation, respectfulness, and calm demeanor (6–7). Thus, silence in Sketch Eighth must also be understood as including the acknowledged silences of the narrator as well as of Hunilla. By overtly mentioning silence, the narrator speaks against it; by distinguishing between things said and things unsaid, he urges the audience to guess what the silence is hiding (156, 157–58). Jenny Franchot suggests that the Melvillean narrator's struggle to provoke silent characters into speech reflects an attempt "to decipher a silence which their author has created and knows all about" (177). Reading Hunilla becomes, at times, reading the male narrator's heart, and leads him as well as the reader to identify with her predicament. However, the narrator's acknowledged silences contrast with hers, validating Franchot's comment that he has "authorial free will to say no" (174).

Although silence may be repressive, as Rigoberta Menchu states, "secrets are, sometimes, the instruments of survival, for they cannot be 'objectified.'"[22] There has been a considerable debate within colonial discourse analysis about the extent to which the silence of the subaltern may carry a transgressive or oppositional weight, assuming that what is important in a work is what it does not say and that silence has its own hegemony. Hunilla and the male narrator's chosen silences may indeed speak about what their culture "prefers not to tell." Thus, in Sketch Eighth, the silences of both the narrator and Hunilla may be considered protective.

All of the silences that appear throughout the tale, whether Melville's, Hunilla's, or the narrator's, mirror literature's most important secret: never close the narrative; leave it open-ended, thereby giving the reader the duty and the privilege of continuing it. Melville starts Sketch Eighth by presenting a white, dominant, imperial gaze that later clashes with a subaltern woman's silence, thereby drawing the reader's attention to the constructs of colonialism that *enable* the suppression of histories of oppression. Violation, in general, is the feeling that fills that silence most of the time—"rape" being a word Hunilla cannot utter. The narrator's decision not to name rape as the violation Hunilla probably experienced exposes his complicity in silence and silencing. He both observes and controls Hunilla's silence; in the narrative only some of it is due to his ignorance ("the half shall here remain untold," 157). The reader's uncertainty regarding the exact nature of Hunilla's violation is not resolved, although her anxiety is displayed during the captain's questioning. Yet it can be argued that the narrator does not behave in an imperialist way when he decides to respect her silence. He does not impose his voice in naming her violation or his vision in describing it; making that choice, he leaves the tale without closure, thereby avoiding the risks of presenting himself as an authoritative representative of the subaltern.

If "to tell the history of another is to be pressed against the limits of one's own" (Suleri, qtd. in Gandhi 10), Sketch Eighth reveals the story of an ambiguous and symbiotic *relationship* between colonizer/oppressor/master narrator and colonized/oppressed/subaltern as well as the colonized's complicity in the colonial condition.[23] As indicated above, despite the conquistador/captain's request, the narrator allows Hunilla's right to secrecy, the writer/reader being complicit in the muting (Spivak 309). In a story filled with sequestration, privacy, silence, and the reality of violation, that Hunilla must display herself from her high rock in order to be rescued by Americans is ambiguously touching and ironic.

The narrator warns the reader in Sketch Eighth that "if he feel not, he reads in vain" (156). In "Norfolk Isle and the Chola Widow," Melville exposes how the other acts as a mirror for readers so that the reflections make their own familiar faces strange. He also demonstrates the degree to which we carry our own preoccupations and preconceptions when we step into other cultures. In choosing Hunilla and the Spanish American empire as his subjects, he reproduces colonialism, imperialism, and racism while challenging those conditions. Through Hunilla the colonial condition is acknowledged and disavowed simultaneously as her character emerges. In this aesthetic process Melville rediscovers the complexity of an individual humanity that transcends racial distinctions even as it marks them. Hunilla, then, represents the victimized, hopeless, and despairing self in need of rescuing, even as this self comes to stand as "sign and symbol" for moral resistance and for imaginative affirmation, for "hopelessly holding up hope in the midst of despair" (*Moby-Dick* 225).

Notes

1. Introducing the ten sketches in "The Encantadas" are epigraphs from Spenser's *Faerie Queene*, which evidence Melville's awareness that Spenser recognized South America as a site of colonialism and imperialism. Actually, at the start of Book 2, Spenser compares his representation of Faerie land to attempts to discover the New World:

And daily how through hardy enterprize,
Many great Regions are discovered,
Which to late age were never mentioned.
Who ever heard of th' Indian *Peru*?
Or who in ventrous vessel measured

> The *Amazons* huge river now found truw?
> Or fruitfullest *Virginia* who did ever view?
> Yet all these were, when no man did them know;
> Yet have from wisest ages hidden beene:
> And later times things more unknowne shall show.
> Why then should witlesse man so much misweene
> That nothing is, but that which he hath seene? (Book 2. sts. 2–3)

According to Hadfield, "The point Spenser is making is that just as explorers discover—or rather, rediscover—Peru and Virginia, so does the poet reveal important truths for the reader." He also mentions that Raleigh in his *Discovery of Guiana* describes it as "a country that had yet her maidenhood," using the familiar colonial description of the land to be colonized as a woman ready to be ravished by the (male) colonizers (30–31).

2. It is ironic that the United States, a former colony, would itself become an imperial colonial power.

3. Robert C. Young's *Postcolonialism* asserts that "the long, violent history of colonialism, which ... began over five hundred years ago, in 1492 ... includes histories of slavery, of untold, unnumbered deaths from oppression or neglect, of the enforced migration and diaspora of millions of peoples." Young adds, "Postcolonial cultural critique involves the reconsideration of this history, particularly from the perspectives of those who suffered its effects" (4).

4. Although she adds that the revival of imperialism by Charles V was a phantom revival, Yates argues that its importance for the idea of empire, for the imperialist hope, and for universal world rule lies precisely in the fact that it was a phantom (1).

5. According to Francisco Morales, "The Monroe doctrine was a challenge of the New World to the Old One" (22), guaranteeing the interventionism of the United States in Hispanic America. Morales also asserts that the Monroe doctrine could not be separated from U.S. imperialism and that a few years after this message, the doctrine of manifest destiny became fully developed (28). Similar accounts are provided by Howard Zinn (221–22) and George Brown Tindall with David E. Shi (468–69).

6. Immigration from the United Kingdom was more than 50 percent of the total in every year, save 1846 and 1854 in the antebellum years. Note also that Ireland and Germany together normally accounted for 65–75 percent of total immigration (W. Parker 106).

7. Echoing Morse, Lyman Beecher's *Plea for the West* (1835) urged Americans to develop Protestant educational institutions as a way of staving off the conspiratorial Roman Catholic church. Fearing the spread of Catholic convents and parochial schools, Beecher in August 1834 had delivered three anti-Catholic sermons in Boston that possibly inspired the burning of Charlestown's Ursuline convent (Levine, *Conspiracy* 109). This event is also mentioned by Hershel Parker (1: 238).

8. This conjecture is mentioned by Levine (*Companion* xviii). The Harpers also supposedly rejected "The Agatha Story," which relates directly to Sketch Eighth, as well as "The Tortoise Hunters," which relates to "The Encantadas." According to Watson Branch, Melville may have used material from "The Isle of the Cross" when he wrote "The Encantadas" (34). Robertson-Lorant also states that Sketch Eighth "seems to incorporate both the Agatha Story and 'The Isle of the Cross'" (338).

9. See Lucena Salmoral.

10. Melville's visit to Peru has been well documented: "On June 23, 1841, the *Acushnet* dropped anchor in the port of Santa, Peru; in July, the cruise continued as far north as the Galapagos Islands" (Hillway 35). Aboard the frigate *United States,* in 1843 Melville visited Callao (Hill-

way 39). Robertson-Lorant mentions Melville's stop at the Galápagos, where his ship lay at anchor off Chatham's Isle for six days while men went ashore in longboats to hunt tortoises as well as a stop at Tumbes, where the captain in Sketch Eighth sells Hunilla's tortoise oil (100). Furthermore, Payta, Hunilla's destination, was the place where the *Acushnet's* first and third mates jumped ship in Peru (106). Another connection with Peru was through Jack Chase, an Englishman Melville met on the *United States,* who apparently deserted a British vessel to join the Peruvian navy in what he thought to be a just cause (Hillway 39; Robertson-Lorant 118).

11. Likewise, Carlos Fuentes identifies Moby Dick as any of the great enemies of North America during each of its major historical periods, as he recently wrote in a Spanish newspaper article entitled "El racista enmascarado."

12. Discovery by Nantucketers of the "Offshore Ground" near Chile and Peru in 1818 inaugurated the "golden age" of New England whaling, which lasted from about 1825 to 1860 (Robertson-Lorant 93).

13. See Hart 99. He adds, "There is no one America, verbal or visual, so that if there were stereotypes of America as a woman, there was no single image above others that prevailed" (98). Furthermore, "There is a kind of moment that often occurred among these multifold images of women in the New World that might have partly to do with the anxiety over the absence of European women, or the desire to justify taking land or women from Native men, or the closeness of European men on these voyages" (100).

14. Melville himself was silenced by his editor at *Putnam's Monthly Magazine,* Charles F. Briggs, who wrote to him after the publication of the third installment of "The Encantadas," explaining, "I will take this opportunity to apologise to you for making a slight alteration in the Encantadas, in the last paragraph of the Chola Widow, which I thought would be improved by the omission of a few words" (Leyda 1: 487). The tales he wrote during the 1850s may be, as Leyda has said, "an artist's resolution of that constant contradiction—between the desperate need to communicate and the fear of revealing too much" (quoted in Branch 32).

15. Salvator R(ose), might be read as "the saviour of the rose," the symbol of the Virgin Mary and of Hunilla, by extension. (The name also alludes to one of Melville's favorite painters, Salvator Rosa.)

16. Melville had already paid attention to the importance of the cross-bred mule as a means of transportation in South America when he described in chapter 59 of *Mardi* "herds of panniered mules driven by mounted Indians along the great road from Callao to Lima" (557).

17. See Puente Candamo.

18. In *Robinson Crusoe,* a widow is Crusoe's best friend (she is stereotyped as faithful, loyal, honest, old, and poor), his main guide, and counselor.

19. Findlay also mentions the Renaissance pun that associates orgasm with death (499).

20. See López Liquete, *Presencia-ausencia.*

21. Maddox's second chapter, "Writing and Silence," analyzes *Typee, Moby-Dick, Pierre,* "Bartleby," "Benito Cereno," and *The Confidence Man* (52–87).

22. "I'm still keeping my Indian identity a secret. I'm still keeping secret what I think no one should know" (Rigoberta Menchu quoted in Spivak 245).

23. That Felipe, Truxill, and Hunilla are complicit in colonial projects is suggested by their search for a valuable commodity, tortoise oil.

Circassian Longings

Melville's Orientalization of Eden

Timothy Marr

"Where a beautiful woman is, there is all Asia and her Bazars." *Pierre* (34).

"Give me the heart that's huge as all Asia." *Mardi* (603).

On the evening of August 9, 1850, Herman Melville—while in the throes of writing *Moby-Dick* and on the same day that he exultantly began "Hawthorne and His Mosses"—dressed up as the Turk. The occasion was a masquerade party thrown by Sarah Morewood at Broadhall, the Pittsfield estate that had previously belonged to Melville's uncle, and the bearded Melville expanded the persona of the "ardent Virginian" he had adopted in "Mosses" by donning flowing robes, a turban, and a makeshift scimitar. Melville's recent biographer Hershel Parker views his night as a Turk ("an exotic predatory infidel") as a displacement of the sexual and artistic arousal he experienced in glorifying Hawthorne, a state of excitability that had also led him that afternoon playfully to abduct a visiting young woman from the local railroad station in what her husband felt was a "Berber fashion."[1] Other evidence of Melville's domestic behavior shows that his orientalist self-fashioning transcended the skylarking of a summer day. Melville later brought a pair of Turkish slippers back from his journey to the eastern Mediterranean in 1857. Their flat heels are proof of regular use, and the fact that Melville later hung them beside his chimney at Arrowhead (along with a tomahawk pipe) dramatizes their symbolic importance. Melville's granddaughter disapprovingly recalled his wearing of loose "Constantinople" pajamas around the house, even when the family was receiving company.[2]

These vestiges from Melville's own life demonstrate what is clear in his fiction: that he was invested in the multivalent conventions of nineteenth-century Islamic orientalism, including its resources for romanticizing the privileges of patriarchy. In his 1856 short story called "I and My Chimney," for example, Melville personifies the same chimney upon which he hung his slippers as a sultanic presence: a "grand seignior" so identified with his narrator's sense of authority as to become the "back-bone" of his domestic ego. Through this story, Melville's narrator keeps his demanding wife at bay by constructing an inviolate den of male leisure comprised of himself and his two "cronies"—his chimney and his pipe—with whom he is "indolently weaving [his] vapors" as "wicked old sinners" (*Piazza Tales* 353, 365, 367, 372).

It was out of such figurative "vapors" that Melville condensed a prodigious body of literature celebrating an imaginative liberation from the conventional virtues of nineteenth-century domesticity. During his residence in the Berkshires, Melville struggled to align a romantic pursuit of happiness with the compromising cultural demands of the masculine work ethic and the feminized moralization of the home. He called his authorship of *Redburn* and *White-Jacket* in 1849 "two *jobs,* which I have done for money—being forced to it, as other men are to sawing wood" (*Correspondence* 138). He complained in a letter to Hawthorne that "Dollars damn me" and that he longed for "the silent grass-growing mood in which a man *ought* always to compose," which he feared could "seldom be mine"(*Correspondence* 191). The fact that Arrowhead served as the center of his literary production engendered tensions in a busy household that included at various times his wife, mother, sisters, servant, and young children. Melville's reliance on the labor of his sisters and wife as copyists, and his decreasing economic success as an author, contributed to an antagonistic relationship with the literary marketplace, represented in such works as *Pierre* (1852), "Bartleby, the Scrivener" (1853), and "The Paradise of Bachelors and the Tartarus of Maids" (1855). In the last story, the bucolic Berkshires are figured instead as a withering space of industrial despotism, a "Tartarus" or hellish pit, that exploits its female workers. Melville allegorically links economic and procreative systems of labor in this story, noting that "machinery—that vaunted slave of humanity—here stood menially served by human beings, who served mutely and cringingly as the slave serves the Sultan" (*Piazza Tales* 328). As this more malignant strain of orientalism attests, the burdens of paternity reminded

Melville of the penalty of the fall with its bondage to labor, suffering, and death. Employing the fertile power of his imagination to challenge this fatal sentence, he authored a countervailing literary dominion that empowered him to sustain the gallant glamour of masculine prerogative, even in the midst of a domestic situation whose financial and psychological economies made it at times anything but romantic. By recalibrating notions of paradise, leisure, and love in ways that sustained both his critical rebellion and his male authority, Melville was able to prolong his passionate dedication to literary creation to the end of his life.

This essay examines a central modality of Melville's female figuration by focusing on how he consistently sought throughout his long career as a writer—from his first "Fragments" in 1839 to the poetry he was assembling at his death in 1891—to evoke a generative vision of woman as an angelic Eve who retained a symbolic connection with the freshness and youth of creation. This artistic aspiration created an exalted vision of woman that drew on cultural scripts depicting "the fair sex" as ministering angels from a heavenly realm; as pure spirits (muses and goddesses) persisting from the golden ages of pagan simplicity; and, above all, as romantic embodiments of oriental beauty. Melville transfigured female beauty from a standard of fashion into a primal symbol of sublime paradise purified from the toils and woe of earthly evil, and it served as an important inspiration for his continuing artistic composition.

The images of Adam and Eve in Melville's writing underline his allegiance to a vision of the divine freedom to love without guilt that characterized life in Eden. Following Milton's lead, Melville elevated humans to a celestial status through their descent from their parents in paradise, though *Moby-Dick*'s Ishmael mischievously calls them the "the two orchard thieves" (6). "The sons of God did verily wed with our mothers, the irresistible daughters of Eve," the narrator of *Mardi* (1848) asserts; "thus all generations are blended: and heaven and earth of one kin." The imperial quest of demi-gods seeking the image of perfection expresses the reach of Melville's desire to intimate a more human and egalitarian view of heaven where "at last, our good, old, white-haired father Adam will greet all alike, and sociality forever prevail" (12–13). Allying himself with the ideal of a celestial Adam, Melville aimed to recreate a paradise within the realm of his fictive imagination expressed as a dream of sensual consummation with a beautiful woman. He celebrated the natural energies of human desire by inventing a symbolic Eve as a muse in whom the corporeal and the heavenly were blended. Seeing the source of sensual intimacy in the very design of creation empowered him to transgress the stifling cultural dogmas of original sin and the work ethic, as well as the confining propriety of ostensible female passionlessness.

Melville's imaginative involvement with women as, what Bruce Eardley Mitchell has called "conduits to knowledge," however, was a constant creative struggle between sustaining a heavenly image of women who celebrated pleasure, beauty, and agency and acknowledging the earthly realities of female sexuality, suffering, and subjugation (2). For Eve left a divided symbolic legacy: she represented not only the sybilline freshness of celestial companionship but also the Lamian implications of seduction with its miseries of exile in this world.[3] Melville represents these contending valences in his two other primary motifs of female experience: one is the seductive enchantments of Circean syrens (Hautia in *Mardi*, Isabel in *Pierre*, and a presumptive Venetian beauty in "In a Bye-Canal") and the other the dignity of female fortitude in a fallen world of woe (the Chola Widow in "The Encantadas," Marianna in "The Piazza," Delly Ulver in *Pierre*, and the young women in "The Tartarus of Maids").

At the center of Melville's titanic struggle to "realize the unreal" (*Clarel* 1.27.71) were his literary attempts to incarnate the sweet passion of Edenic love in the physical form of a woman. Fred Pinnegar concluded in his dissertation on Melville's women that "Melville always reinforces with vigor and delight the central importance of the sexual element in human relations" (52, 6). But negotiating Eros through literary expression posed particular difficulties that Melville found challenging to surmount even as they stimulated his creativity. The moral economies of Melville's age condemned open expression of sexuality outside the privacies of monogamy. Melville, a publishing writer and therefore affected by these cultural restrictions, eluded their power by sublimating sensual desire into the realm of creative imagination. Exalting women to a realm of ideality enabled him to define women as inspiring muses of platonic love and thereby to "wrestle with the angel—Art" (*Poems* 270). While Leland Person Jr. has noted that for Melville "the achievement of a 'genuine masculinity' meant affirming a creative relationship with women," he also suggests that such an end could be stymied by the alienation resulting from "projecting [women] into devitalizing aesthetic form[s]" (75, 87). Melville's desire to integrate these opposites was fraught with danger: if a woman was too ethereal her inspiration would be infertile; but once dragged into what Melville called "the downward way," she could no longer engender redemptive reminders of guiltless joy and stood instead as an abiding exemplar of the punitive bondage of the fall ("Lamia's Song," *Poems* 266).

Melville's metaphor of female millworkers as slaves serving the sultan demonstrates that his orientalism was also multivalent. One of the ways he employed its conventions was to launch critical barbs at what he derisively called the "triumph of the insincere / Unanimous Mediocrity."[4] Melville employed orientalist rhetoric to satirize the pretenses of gendered conventions that comprised the tyranny of the majority. In *Mardi*, for example, he ridicules the idolatry of fashion in his depiction of the female Tapparians from the island of Pimminee who have created their own society based on the dictates of artificial propriety—indeed they are named for the cloth that they love so much (398–413). Melville parodies the matronly woman of society by calling her a "Begum" (or Muslim lady) and judges her ludicrously insular constellation of values to be a "masquerade of vapidities" (409). In the "Schools and Schoolmasters" chapter of *Moby-Dick*, Melville associates a pod of whales with both an Ottoman harem and a parade of fashionable American women (391–94). He wittily criticizes the custom of wearing whalebone corsets by lauding a female whale with a "comparatively delicate" waist of eighteen feet (391).

If Melville focused on this valence of orientalism to humorously lampoon the constrictions of female fashion and gendered convention, he also employed more liberatory aspects to release women from such bondage into the more permissive latitudes of the east. Melville further used the generic resources of orientalism to figure female models whose exoticism enabled him to relish the natural ethos of desire without being censored by his publishers or censured by his readers. During the years of Melville's growth into an author, Islam and its cultures were frequently figured as an anti-christian and despotic opposition to the project of American republicanism. But with the declining power of the Ottoman Empire after 1830, more romantic dimensions of Islam emerged, drawing on the influential heritage of *The Thousand and One Arabian Nights*—first available in Europe at the beginning of the eighteenth century—with its beguiling female narrator, Scheherezade. One element of this trend was the image of Muslim paradise as a renegade realm of love that allowed everlasting access to beautiful females known as *houris* and *peris*. Houris are luxurious virgins awarded to the righteous in Islam's heaven. "Companions with beautiful, big, and lustrous eyes," they are described in the Qur'an as "reclining on green Cushions and rich Carpets of beauty."[5] While many Christians viewed Qur'anic metaphor as evidence of Muhammad's treachery in luring his followers to faith with promises of sensual rewards, more adventurous Westerners such as Melville (who wrote to Hawthorne that he refused to believe in a "Temperance Heaven" [*Correspondence* 191]) were attracted by this romantic vision of opulent consummation, seeing in its orientalized pleasures a return to the prelapsarian paradise of Eden. At several moments in his writing, Melville expresses admiration for Muhammad for both the robustness of his patriarchal leisure and his attraction to perfumes and essences.[6] Peris, according to an 1847 article in *The Literary World*, lived in Peristan, located in the Caucasus and conceptually based on the paradise of Eden. These beings subsist on the fragrance of flowers and are "idealized as incarnations of love at its highest and purest."[7]

Melville's juvenile education in classical and romantic literature had equipped him to project his longings onto visions of orientalized women. This is evident in the Byronic depictions of his first publications, the "Fragments from a Writing Desk," which he wrote in 1839 while still a teenager. The narrator of the "First Fragment" exults in "seraphic visions" of female loveliness—one of whom possesses "a little of the roseate hue of the Circassian"—that transported him "to the land of Dreams, where lay embodied, the most brilliant conceptions of the wildest fancy." Melville's narrator passionately turns Turk in the service of a more sensual vision than that offered by a Christian heaven, one motivated by some hope of achievable intimacy with an angelic embodiment of oriental beauty: "If the devout and exemplary Mussulman who dying fast in the faith of his Prophet, anticipates reclining on beds of roses, gloriously drunk through all the ages of eternity, is to be waited on by Houris such as these: waft me gentle gales beyond this lower world . . . !"[8] (*Piazza Tales* 194–95). This intemperate devotion is replicated in the "Second Fragment," which relates the narrator's mysterious journey to a splendid and secluded villa "as beautiful and enchanting as any described in the Arabian Nights," one filled with "delicious perfumes" and art depicting scenes from classical Arcadia.[9] The cynosure of sensual attraction is Inamorata, a voluptuous odalisque described as having "Andalusian eyes" and "Turkish sleeve," who is unable to reciprocate his voluble passion because she is dumb and deaf (*Piazza Tales* 202–4). Thus, at the outset of his literary career, Melville realized that despite the fact that his portrayal of female beauty posited an unattainable romantic ideal, such a feminized space of oriental imagination provided a powerful impetus to his own transgressive artistic expression.

Throughout his life as an author, Melville often figured women as spiritual symbols whose beauty and fragrance intimate celestial purity. His first book, *Typee* (1846), etherealizes the smoking Fayaway as she is "languishingly giving forth light wreaths of vapor from her mouth and nostrils" to which, like a peri, "her rosy breath added a fresh perfume" (133). Twice in Melville's works, in *Redburn* and in a poem he began composing in the mid 1870s, "Naples in the Time of Bomba," his narrators fleetingly encounter beautiful women portrayed as peris. The former features Redburn's encounters during a Sunday excursion into the Liverpool countryside with three "ravishing charmers" who appear to him as "Peris" or "Houris" (213–15). In the poem, the poet is accosted in his coach by a flowergirl who pins a rose on his lapel and is described as "a buoyant nymph on odorous wing" and "a flying Peri" with "titillating fingers" (*Poems* 385). In an 1872 letter to his cousin Kate, Melville refers to a variety of angels that "leave behind them a fragrance as of violets," that he called in *Clarel* (1876) the "perfumed spell / Of Paradise-flowers invisible" (1.29.24–26) (*Correspondence* 424). It is clear even from these short examples that for Melville female beauty often brought with it the redolence of heavenly paradise that he conveyed through the vehicle of his orientalist imagination.

Melville consistently fleshed out his subversive vision of an Eastern heaven with references to the classical pastoral as well as to biblical and romantic convention. His Circassian vision was clearly influenced by the tradition of British romantic orientalism that included Spenser, Coleridge, Keats, Shelley, Southey, Byron, and Thomas Moore. Melville's imagination of paradise celebrated what he often called the "ruddiness" of nature by associating it with the bucolic beauty of the ancients. To supplement the idyll of Adam and Eve in Eden, where sensual love preceded the curse, Melville drew on such locations as the vales of Arcadian simplicity in Virgil's *Eclogues,* Chronos's kingdom during the Golden Age of Saturn, Cupid's paradise where Psyche was whisked by the Zephyrs, and the vale of Enna where Persephone gathered blooms before being dragged by Hades down to the underworld. The legend of Venus as goddess of sensual love appears frequently in Melville's writings. For example, the epicurean Lesbian in *Clarel* sings a song of this "Arcadian time" when "Love and peace went hand in hand," describing an era of joyful mirth and revel when "Venus burned both large and bright, / Honey-moon from night to night" (3.20.28, 2, 7–8). Melville's poem about the Aegean island of "Syra" likewise reminisces about "Saturn's prime / When trade was not, nor toil, nor stress, / But life was leisure, merriment, peace, / And lucre none and love was righteousness" (*Poems* 291).[10]

What I call Melville's "Circassian longings" updates and goes beyond the pastoral visions of the classical past and refers specifically to the land in the Caucasus that was known best in Melville's time both as the cradle of female beauty and the valued source of light-skinned women for the Sultan's harem in Istanbul. Johann Friedrich Blumenbach in 1795 construed the Caucasian as the original and most beautiful human archetype from which his other four "races" had degenerated through distance and modification.[11] The purest specimens of the Caucasian were said to abide in the territory of Circassia, which was described in the 1797 *Encyclopedia Britannica* as a country long "celebrated for the extraordinary beauty of its women." The concept of Circassia as a rarified locus of romantic consummation flourished throughout Europe and the United States in the mid–nineteenth century. When George Leighton Ditson became the first American to visit Circassia in the 1840s, he brought with him the expectation that Circassians were "incomparable paradigms of all that is admirable and fascinating in feminine form and loveliness" (378).

By inventing a Caucasian cradle, Westerners were able to think of racial whiteness as coeval with the creation of the human species. Circassia was remote both in time and place: it was the original site of the rebellion of Prometheus that was also contiguous with the geographical coordinates of Eden—"a garden eastward" that was home to the primal human beings. By relocating his envisioned promised land within Circassia, Melville preserved both the pristine source of beauty and the genetic vitality of whiteness from the traffic of human greed and guilt that tainted its purity. While Toni Morrison has read Melville's obsession with whiteness in *Moby-Dick* as his recognition that the purported superiority of white racial ideology was dangerously savage and inhuman, his longings for a Circassian paradise can be seen as an attempt to recover a pure racial identity free of the evils accomplished in its name ("Unspeakable" 16–18). Melville attempted to transcend the burdens of sin and guilt by abducting the white woman from her infidel earthly seraglio and symbolically resituating her in a pristine paradise of chivalrous love.

Such a process is evident in the hyperbolic beginning of *Pierre*, where his youthful protagonist rhapsodizes about a natural paradise that he calls "this summer world of ours" (32). Melville then expands beyond the cycle of the seasons into a wider temporal and spatial cosmos in which the paradise of the past is projected into the future through the rhetoric of his orientalist imagination. "Out of some past Egypt, we have come to this new Canaan; and from this new Canaan, we shall press on to some Circassia. Though still the villains, Want and Woe, followed us out of Egypt, and now beg in Canaan's streets: yet Circassia's gates shall not admit them; they, with their sire, the demon Principle, must back to chaos, whence they came" (33).[12] Melville here provides a schematic view of the evolution of humanity from its origins in chaos toward a vision of a future heaven, shorn of the "demon Principle" and its offspring "Want and Woe."[13] He transposes the myth of Edenic paradise onto a vision of a Circassia of the future (which he calls "a fairer world than this to come" [32]). Melville's paradise is figured as a migratory pilgrimage eastward out of the earthly estate of Canaan through the "gates" of Circassia, a place that inherits the unmaterialized promise of a land of "milk and honey." His transgressive vision restores the pure delight of Eden by relocating (or as he suggests "translating" [33]) it to Circassia, the pure matrix of human love symbolically preserved from the evil associated with the garden of Genesis.[14]

The vagueness of the description of Circassia's actual coordinates and its confusion with the classical pastoral certifies that it was not a land that Melville was able to find in his travels; like Queequeg's Kokovoko, it "is not down in any map; true places never are" (*Moby-Dick* 55). Yet Melville frequently pictured himself as gaining a symbolic paradise in the oriental lands east of the Holy Land. On board the *Southampton* during his 1849 trip to Europe, he became captivated with planning a "glorious Eastern jaunt" whose "grandness" resonated in his mind throughout the passage (*Journals* 7–9). In 1851 he told Hawthorne that writing *Moby-Dick* had made him feel "in my proud, humble way, —a shepherd-king, —I was lord of a little vale in the solitary Crimea" (*Correspondence* 212). Two months later Melville explored this spiritual geography in a letter to Sophia Hawthorne by narrating a journey that leads east through the Black Sea toward "some Circassia": "Life is a long Dardenelles. My Dear Madam, the shores whereof are bright with flowers, which we want to pluck, but the bank is too high; & so we float on & on, hoping to come to a landing-place at last—but swoop! we launch into the great sea! Yet the geographers say, even then we must not despair, because across the great sea, however desolate & vacant it may look, lie all Persia & the delicious lands roundabout Damascus" (*Correspondence* 220). In his canto on "The Prodigal" in *Clarel*, Melville connects these "lands about Damascus" with the imagery of the healing waters of the streams of paradise: "grace and pleasure there, / In Abana and Pharpar's streams / (O shady haunts! O sherbet-air!) / So twine the place in odorous dreams" (4.26.119–22).[15] Circassia in its various forms stood as a visionary paradise into which Melville projected the fulfillment of his desires: an allusive realm of imaginative resolution where—like the vales and bowers of romantic poetry—love and leisure were the only lords.

The most fundamental basis for Melville's imagination of paradise, however, rested in his own experience of travel. Melville drew regularly on his revealing visits to the fertile islands of the Pacific, as well as on traditions of pagan and orientalist paradises, to gain the latitude he desired for both cultural criticism and artistic creativity. Robert Milder recently reminded us that it was "Melville's particular fate . . . to have experienced a paradise that most Romantics could only theorize about" ("Avenging" 252). Melville's sojourn in the permissive beauty of the South Seas formed the instigating force for his literary enterprise, impressing him with powerful visions of an earthly Eden that he sustained throughout his literary career. In *Typee,* Tommo's enchantment with the unspoiled valleys of the Marquesas provokes him to announce, "Had a glimpse of the gardens of Paradise been revealed to me I could scarcely have been more ravished with the sight" (49).[16] Melville registers this powerful memory of encountering a worldly paradise at the end of his lecture on "The South Seas" (1858–59) in which he pleads for the preservation of "these Edens of the South Seas" (*Piazza Tales* 420) and in his later poetry, such as in the poem "To Ned," which recalls the "Authentic Edens in a Pagan sea" where the "pleasure-hunter ... breathed primeval balm / From Edens ere yet overrun; / Marvelling mild if mortal twice, / Here and hereafter, touch a Paradise" (*Poems* 238–39). Rolfe in *Clarel,* representative of Melville's earnest adventurer, is likewise prompted by a palm tree in Palestine to lapse into "Sylvan reveries" of the island paradise he once visited; he castigates himself for ever having "abjure[d its] simple joy," which he claims was "much as man might hope and more than heaven may mean" (3.29.37, 74, 63). Melville had thus experienced his own paradise and lost it before he began his serious career as a writer of fiction and poetry. But he did not allow his seraphic visions of Pacific beauty to degenerate into mere nostalgia for his own youthful exploits. This experience also served as an abiding memory of unencumbered freedom and hope and a sustaining vision of ideal love amidst the many challenges of his family and professional life.

Readers were attracted to Melville's Polynesian adventures by the fresh energies of encounters with unspoiled cultures, especially in the form of their beautiful women. His depictions of Fayaway in *Typee* and Yillah in *Mardi* dramatize his creative uses of orientalism to intimate the erotic liberation he experienced in his Pacific travels. Melville translated the paradise of the South Seas into Eastern metaphor as a way of celebrating its free sensuality of "naked houris" (*Typee* 5). Indeed, his description of the Typeean paradise as a "heaven of bread-fruit, cocoa-nuts and young ladies" is little more than the Islamic afterworld transposed into the lush land of the South Seas. "In that happy land," Melville gloried, "best of all, women far lovelier than the daughters of the earth were there in abundance" (172–73). In the "Typee Manuscript," where Melville originally described Tommo's consummate joy at the "luxurious operation" of being massaged by a number of Marquesan maidens, he imagined himself as the amorous highwayman of John Gay's *The Beggar's Opera,* relishing the sensations of an oriental paradise: "With Captain Macheath in the opera I could have sung 'Thus I lay like a Turk with my doxies around,' for never certainly was effeminate ottoman in the innermost shrine of his seraglio attended by lovelier houris with more excess of devotion than happened to me on these occasions I have mentioned.—Sardanapalus might have experienced such sensations—but I dou[b]t whether any of the Sultans ever did."[17] The fact that Melville chose to excise this passage before publishing *Typee* (and his feminizing of the male who experienced these pleasures) demonstrates how the sensual enjoyment of female bodies, even if they were orientalized, remained a transgressive act to antebellum American readers. When publishing his first book, then, Melville learned of the need to sublimate sensual desire within his literary expression. The creation of his Circassian ideal with its oriental latitudes of leisure enabled Melville to both etherealize and universalize female sensuality without sacrificing all of its libidinal energies.

Melville employs a complex confluence of biblical, classical, and romantic strategies to sublimate Tommo's erotic encounter with Fayaway in his original Pacific paradise, drawing on such fictional models as diverse as Milton's "Eden" (*Paradise Lost*), Spenser's "Bower of Bliss" (*The Faerie Queen*), Samuel Johnson's "Happy Valley" (*Rasselas*), and Byron's island idylls with Neuha ("The Island") and Haidee ("Don Juan"). Fayaway is *Typee*'s Eve who wears what Melville twice calls "the garb of Eden" (87, 181).[18] Despite his contention that his depiction of Fayaway was "drawn from the most vivid recollections of the person delineated," he nevertheless describes the lines of her face "as perfectly formed as the heart or imagination of man could desire" (86, 85). Melville sidesteps the taboo against literary eroticism by sublimating the valley of Typee (especially the imaginary lake where he bathes with the female beauties) as a "land of spirits," a "fairy region," where the women lose their flesh and become "mermaids" and "river nymphs" (132–34). By making Fayaway into the "very perfection of female grace and beauty" and comparing her with models of classical beauty such as Venus de' Medici, Melville smuggles both Fayaway's nakedness and her racial difference into the parlors of his readers (85, 161). In his lecture on "The South Seas" he compares Marquesan women's loveliness to the beauty of another popular statue of a naked woman, Hiram Powers's "The Greek Slave," which toured the United States at the same time that Melville's initial fame was being established: "I have seen among them as graceful a young girl's foot and as delicately-turned ankle as those of the Grecian girls whose duplicate statues adorn the galleries of Europe" (*Piazza Tales* 419). Tommo's claim that Fayaway has "the most bewitching ankle in the universe" (135)—a fetishizing of the part of the female body with the best chance of being revealed under conventional Western dress—is a direct attempt to outdo Byron, who describes Haidee in "Don Juan" as having "the prettiest ankle in the world" (Canto 3, Stanza 72).

Melville's most thorough fictional evocation of his female muse from the "land of Dreams" is Taji's obsession in *Mardi*: the sublime white captive, Yillah. Melville's narrator imagines his escape from the monotony of ship life in one of the *Arcturian*'s whale-boats as equivalent to a "dashing young Janizary . . . run[ning] off with a sultana from the Grand Turk's seraglio" (20). Having succeeded, the narrator—in a move symbolizing the expansion of *Mardi* from travelogue into romantic allegory—"strikingly improve[s]" his costume by "making it free, flowing, and eastern" to the extent that he announces, "I looked like an Emir" (127), and then adopts the title Taji (perhaps from the

Arabic word *taj,* meaning crown). From then on Taji pursues with abandon the white maiden Yillah, apparently a brainwashed Anglo woman whom he rescues by killing her captor, the "dusky" prince Aleema (142). Yillah's name invokes both the purity of the Lily and the Muslim invocation of God: "la ilaha il Allah" (There is no God but God).[19]

Yillah's beauty is more essence than substance, and Taji's progressive descriptions of her emphasize her angelic insubstantiality as houri and peri. She exemplifies Mohja Kohf's description of the romantic paradigm of the Muslim woman as "an angelic paragon of numinous feminine nothinghood, a shimmering fetish object for both the competing males within the narrative and the projected male reader" (152). She is initially portrayed as a beautiful girl cowering in her tent, but her mystery is expanded by her status as a sacrificial victim with "snow-white skin; blue, firmament eyes: Golconda locks . . . [and] gauze-like robe"(136).[20] Yet she is so sublimated as to become barely discernible: her hand in Taji's "seemed no hand, but a touch" (144), and the human substance of her beauty is expressed only by allusions to fleeting flushes of nature and reducible to the rose pearl that she wears on her breast.[21] Yillah assumes for Taji, as the seraphic maiden of Melville's first "Fragment" had for its narrator, the status of a barely earthly manifestation of heaven. Taji avers, "Often I thought that Paradise had overtaken me on earth, and that Yillah was verily an angel, and hence the mysteries that hallowed her" (193). The story that Yillah relates of her genesis tells of a being whose essence was condensed from a flower blossom's "rosy mist" that "exhaled away in perfumes" (137–38). Motivated by an unattainable dream of blissful union with Yillah, Taji searches through the allegorical islands of Mardi (the Persian word for "manhood") as obsessively as Ahab would later pursue the white whale.

Taji's search for Yillah throughout the realms of Mardi, which include the Near East as the mythical land of Orienda, testifies to Melville's enduring quest for an earthly Eden. Melville figures the lush interior of a Pacific island, circled around by dangerous reefs, as an embodiment of paradise, with its "green flowery field within, [which] lies like a rose among thorns; and hard to be reached as the heart of a proud maiden. Though once attained, all three—red rose, bright shore, and soft heart—are full of love, bloom, and all manner of delights" (82). The confluence of geography, gender, and nature (embodied by the mystical beauty of the rose) served as a powerful paradigm in Melville's imagination and helps explain how the distant Pacific continued to inform his Circassian longings.[22] It appears in the Tamai episode of *Omoo* where the narrator encounters the dances of the Tahitian women (238–42) and when Ishmael in *Moby-Dick* counsels his reader never to push off from that "one insular Tahiti, full of peace and joy" (274). In his poems "Times Long Ago!" and "The Enviable Isles," Melville relishes the halcyon peace of inland island refuges, where "Slow-swaying palms salute love's cypress tree" (*Poems* 242), and "all is green, / And wins the heart that hope can lure no more" (419).

Melville's own blasphemy, indicated by his comment in his *Journals* that "J. C. should have appeared in Taheiti [sic]" (154), is that he allows himself to be seduced like Taji by a Circassian paradise of love more passionate than that allowed by Christian sentimentality. While Melville takes up the conventional romantic rhetoric of flower language and oriental maidens, he also—Ishmael-like—identifies himself with its rebellious ramifications. Assuming the guise of an oriental infidel who violates the moral constraints of the lingering Calvinism of his time, Melville refabricates an enchanting Eve to whom he is the gallant and chivalrous suitor. Together, they reassume their mystic regime of celestial love and demigodly wisdom and thereby both redeem the failure of humanity and spite the punitive God who had ousted them from paradise. As had the gnostics, Melville subversively redefined original sin to signify not Adam and Eve's disobedience to God but rather the unjust banishment of them into the realm of labor and death because of their love for each other and their desire to awaken to knowledge. (In his poem "The New Rosicrucians," for example, Melville claims that "For all the preacher's din / There is no mortal sin— / No, none to us but Malice" [*Poems* 337].) By authoring his own orientalized literary dominion, Melville invented a Circassian paradise where, like other Promethean artists in his poem "Hearts-of-Gold," he thrives as one of the "Dexterous tumblers eluding the Fall" (428). Refusing to be condemned as "Eden's bad boy," he testifies instead that "No Past pertains to Paradise" (311, 391). Melville sought to reestablish his heavenly credentials by effacing the Fall through a redemptive transgression of love, leisure, and literature.

The transfiguration of mundane femininity into the ideal of a heavenly consort served as the real attraction of Melville's Circassian vision. Following his evocations of female beauty in his fiction set in the South Seas, Melville continued in his conflicted attraction to the ideal of love as he wrote literature set on land. The importance of two other major female characters, Lucy and Ruth, is symbolized by their betrothal to the protagonists, Pierre and Clarel. Melville explains when lauding Lucy in *Pierre* that "a lovely woman is not entirely of this earth" but rather "a visible semblance of the heavens," and he also asserts that "heaven [has no] blessing beyond her earthly love" (24, 34). Although these potential matches seem more lasting than Tommo's dalliance with Fayaway and Taji's mystical quest to recover Yillah, the fact that these fiancées meet their end in death rather than marriage is further evidence of the unattainable ideality of Melville's Circassian vision.

Lucy Tartan is the last of Melville's pristine female idealizations in his prose, and Pierre describes her as nothing short of a "holy angel," the "most celestial of all innocents," even "bait set in Paradise" from whose face and cheek came "the fresh fragrance of her violet young being" (40, 28, 33). Compared to "a Bird from Arabia," Lucy is described as such a prize that "the Grand Turk, and all the other majesties of Europe, Asia and Africa to boot, could not, in all their joint dominions, boast as sweet a girl as [she]" (24, 26). Pierre's paeans to female beauty are so extensive as to betray such cultural ideals as the sanctity of life and the primacy of Christ. He hyperbolically claims that a "true gentleman in Kentucky would cheerfully die for a beautiful woman in Hindostan, though he never saw her; . . . he would turn Turk before he would disown an allegiance hereditary to all gentlemen, from the hour that their Grand Master, Adam, first knelt to Eve" (24). However, Lucy's tragic death, like the disappearance of Yillah, foreshadowed by their replacement in their narrators' consciousnesses by the alluring sexuality of Isabel and Hautia, ultimately signals Melville's difficulty in representing love's capacity to counter sin and suffering in his fictional worlds.

The romantic subplot in his long poem about pilgrims in the Holy Land travels much the same road. *Clarel*'s American Jewish maiden, Ruth, is as heavenly as Lucy and Yillah: she is an "angel succorer" (1.22.98) whose eyes are "Pure home of all we seek and prize" (1.23.67). Ruth has "the grace of Nature's dawn: an Eve-like face" (1.16.163–66), and she "looked a legate to insure / That Paradise is possible / Now as hereafter" (1.27.18–19). Together, Clarel and Ruth embody the hope that "the light / Of love could redeem the trace / Of grief" (1.39.5–7). But this love, as well as Ruth's father's Zionist dream of the redemptive glories of Jerusalem, is shattered first by his death at the hands of the Arabs and then by Ruth's grief, ritual seclusion, and untimely death. The expiration of Lucy and Ruth, whose names respectively mean light and companion, symbolize the evaporation of Melville's dream of materializing his Circassian ideal. With their deaths, Melville's Circassian vision of celestial companionship seems no more than a mirage.

Cast out from the Eden of his aspirations, Melville was forced to lower his standard of attainable felicity, a realization represented by the shift in his writing from prose to poetry and his change of career from professional author to customs house officer in New York City, a job that he worked at for almost twenty years. After he finished *Moby-Dick*, Melville had imagined himself trying on "the crown of India" that was delivered him through "the good goddess's bonus" of Hawthorne's praise, even if it did fall down on his ears (*Correspondence* 212). Almost a quarter of a century later, however, Melville declined an offer to be met when his boat docked up the Hudson, saying, "When the Shah of Persia or the Great Khan of Tartary comes to Albany by the night-boat—*him* meet on the wharf and with salvoes of artillery—but not a Customs House Inspector" (*Correspondence* 429). Melville acknowledged (in a poem included in *Timoleon, Etc.* [1891] called "C's_____ Lament," in which he had penciled in and then erased "Coleridge") that although youthful romance had allowed him to rise upward and view the earth as an insubstantial "Aladdin-land" (*Poems* 271), his painful wisdom had caused him to realize, as he did when he dedicated *Pierre* to Mt. Greylock and *Israel Potter* (1857) to the Bunker Hill Monument, the abiding futility of viewing earth as anything but a mineral tomb.[23] This was the devastating lesson he learned from his own journey in 1856–57 to the eastern Mediterranean: that the Holy Land and the romantic orient was in reality a stony and barren landscape full of what he called the "unleavened nakedness of desolation" (*Journals* 83).[24]

While Melville experientially apprehended the ungraspability of his ideal, he wisely comprehended the continuing need for the dreaming spirit of youth. Refusing to submit to silence and despair, he condemned the Fall and its bitter sentence of irredeemable desire, perpetual toil, and earthly death in a short unpublished poem that interlaces with the sartorial imagery central to both *Redburn* and *White-Jacket*, as well as the oriental guises he gave to Omoo (as turbaned "Bashaw with Two Tails") and Taji (as robed "Emir"):

> My jacket old, with narrow seam—
> When the dull day's work is done
> I dust it, and of Asia dream,
> Old Asia of the sun!
> There other garbs prevail;
> Yea, lingering there, free robe and vest,
> Edenic Leisure's age attest
> Ere work, alack, came in with Wail. (*Poems* 426)[25]

The expansion from dust, boredom, and constriction (see Melville's pun "alack" as "a 'lack'") to free and opulent expansiveness alludes to the symbolic space he was able to create for himself through his authoring of an orientalized paradise, a space where his word was made to counteract both "work" and "Wail." The poem also represents the liberation that Melville felt at being able to lay aside his daily customs house duties and resume his literary passions. He explained his contempt for the Protestant work ethic in an 1877 letter to his cousin Kate: "Whoever is not in the possession of leisure can hardly be said to possess independence. They talk of the *dignity of work*. Bosh. True Work is the *necessity* of poor humanity's earthly condition. The dignity is in leisure" (*Correspondence* 464).[26]

With his retirement from the customs house on the last day of 1885, Melville finally found himself in possession of the leisure he had longed for, and he used the years before his death in 1891 to compile and create three collections of poems: *John Marr and Other Sailors* (1888), *Timoleon, Etc.,* and the incomplete *Weeds and Wildings Chiefly, with a Rose or Two,* as well as his unpublished novella *Billy Budd, Sailor (An Inside Narrative)*. Melville's Circassian vision survived the demise of his fictional incarnations in this poetry that he assembled late in life. Especially in his poems about roses from *Weeds and Wildings,* Melville embodied his vision, not as he had earlier by etherealizing women into an unapproachably sublime ideal, but rather by grounding their beauty in the "simple grace" of natural flowers, whose rebirth in spring ("A lowlier Eden mantling in her face") intimated the connection with the cycle of creation for which he had for so long aspired.[27] "The visible world of experience," Melville had written in *Pierre,* is "that procreative thing which impregnates the muses" (259).

Melville dedicated *Weeds and Wildings* to "Winnefred," known to be his wife, Elizabeth, and its poems evoke simple memories of the early years of their marriage in the Berkshires as well as his eventual contentedness with married life. He realized that even if he had penetrated the illusions of youth, he had to tend its dreaming spirit against the onslaughts of hopelessness. "Grain by grain the Desert drifts / Against the Garden-Land," acknowledged Melville in a short poem, advising, "Hedge well thy Roses, heed the stealth / Of ever-creeping Land" (*Poems* 336). Melville used his pen to stave off the desert of despair. By tending his gardens of both real and figurative roses, he acknowledged the psychological necessity of a "the Paradise of the Fool" by claiming that "hope [did] frequent share / The mirage when despair / Overtakes the caravan."[28] He inscribed *John Marr* to "the most precious things I know of in this world—Health and Content," and on the frontispiece of *Weeds and Wildings* he included a quotation from Hawthorne's *The Dolliver Romance*: "Youth is the proper, permanent, and genuine condition of man" (*Poems* 196, 299). The phrase "Keep true to the dreams of thy youth!" that Melville kept on a card in his writing desk was his own personal motto (Metcalf 384).

Billy Budd's florid name also symbolizes this desire to embody youth, but the displacement of his fate into the past and his sacrifice within the martial rigor of naval life ensures that he lives only in memory. Melville manifested a more viable spirit of youth in his poetry by evoking the female through the form of the generative flower. He wrote in his poem "Rip Van Winkle's

Lilac" that women, by "inheriting more of the spirit of Paradise than ourselves," are capable of recognizing the spirit of youth in everything (*Poems* 326). Melville's spiteful condemnation of the expulsion from Eden and the continuing value he bestowed on heavenly images of women is perhaps clearest in his poem "The Devotion of the Flowers to Their Lady" narrated by "handmaidens"—personified as flowers in Shushan—who long for the pastures of paradise of which they remain the purest trace. "We are natives of Eden," they sing, "Sharing its memory with you."[29] The resumption of this primeval order of natural sensuality symbolized by the union of Adam and Eve stokes Melville's dreams, of which the flowers stand as the surest "voucher." Importantly, it is woman—the "daughter of far descent"—who remains "blessed in banishment," her Edenic allegiance affirmed and still worthy of devotion.[30] This "secret desire / For the garden of God" (*Poems* 341–42) is also highlighted in Melville's poem "The Lover and the Syringa-Bush," in which love proves so be such a "heightening power" to the lover-poet that a simple shrub (named after the Greek word for the pipe of Pan) transports him to "Eden's gate" where he lingers, "Love's tryst to keep with truant Eve" (312). William Bysshe Stein has suggested that it is "not until Eve is lured out of the stagnant garden that she actually realizes herself in complete womanhood."[31] This desire for a romantic consummation—one that actualizes the lover by making her angelic presence accessible in nature—forms the core of Melville's Circassian longings in his latter days.

The poem "After the Pleasure Party" from *Timoleon* dramatizes Melville's abiding desire for what he calls "love's stronger reign" (*Poems* 257). Speaking through a female persona, Urania—the virgin muse of astronomy (and Milton's muse in *Paradise Lost*)—Melville challenges God's division of humanity into two sexes when Eve was fashioned from Adam's rib. The poem condemns the Fall from "the glade / Wherein Fate sprung Love's ambuscade" (255) and continues the complaint by reflecting on Aristophanes's discourse on love from Plato's "Symposium":

Why hast thou made us but in halves—
Co-relatives? This makes us slaves.
If these co-relatives never meet
Selfhood itself seems incomplete
And such the dicing of blind fate
Few matching halves here meet and mate.
What Cosmic jest or Anarch blunder
The human integral clove asunder
And shied the fractions through life's gate? (257)

In its portrayal of Urania's disillusioned dismay as she confronts the reign of repressed sexual desire, Melville's poem acknowledges the wisdom that "never" can "Art inanimate for long / Inspire." Melville echoed this perception in "In the Hall of Mirrors" where he confessed that "primal fervours all displaced / Our arts but serve the clay" (*Poems* 420). Yet by inhabiting his virgin female muse and making her voice the volcanic power of human desire, Melville's "Amor" animates his own creation and accomplishes the fertile integration of art and life for which Urania longs.[32] In "Michaelmas Daisies," he implicitly contrasts Urania's unsatisfying quest to study the stars in the heavens with animated fields of autumnal asters that peep up from earth with inscrutable eyes that "No star-gazers scrutinize" (315). By integrating the male and female genders in "After the Pleasure Party," Melville partakes of the process he suggested in his poem "Art": that to embody the dream and "pulsed life create, / What unlike things must meet and mate" (*Poems* 270).[33]

In his poems "Pontoosuce" and "The Rose Farmer, " Melville attests to the lasting viability of his Circassian vision—the abiding assurance of a feminized idealization of youth—as both a fertile motive for his continuing literary creation and as the reward of death. The former, named after a lake near Melville's home in Pittsfield, begins with the narrator beset by the knowledge that the pastoral beauty of the scene is merely transient, despairing that "evanescence will not stay! . . . All dies!" Bemoaning "death's ancient wrong" and the impermanence of even stars and mountains which "tell / Of havoc ere our Adam fell," the narrator suddenly experiences a mystical visitation of a floating sylph. She counsels him of the everlasting cycles of rebirth and balance in nature: "Since light and shade are equal set / And all revolves, nor more ye know; . . . Let go, let go!" The poem ends with their sensual embrace through which the natural and the heavenly cohere:

> With that, her warm lips thrilled me through,
> She kissed me, while her chaplet cold
> Its rootlets brushed against my brow,
> With all their humid clinging mould.
> She vanished, leaving fragrant breath
> And warmth and chill of wedded life and death.

"Pontoosuce" embodies Melville's abiding vision of the peri, who is here possessed of "fragrant breath" and "arrayed / As in the first pale tints of morn— / So pure, rose-clear, and fresh and chill" (*Poems* 431–34).[34] His consort is comprised of the New England earth that Melville glorified in the Saddle Meadows overture to *Pierre* and celebrated in "Hawthorne and

His Mosses" when he claimed that "this Vermont morning dew is as wet to my feet, as Eden's dew to Adam" (*Piazza Tales* 246). She imparts heavenly wisdom by her kiss as signified by the warmth of her lips. However, the poem is also a vision of the appearance of death with its cold and clinging earth. For Melville the flower that symbolized "bridal blossoms from love's bowers" also betokened the remembrance of the individual (and of his own artistic creation) after death.[35]

"The Rose Farmer" from *Weeds and Wildings* also attests that "down in heart youth never dies" (*Poems* 346) and that Melville's Circassian vision persisted during his later years with his wife, Lizzie, when he finally possessed the "silent grass-growing mood" (*Correspondence* 191) he had longed for years before. A "corpulent grandee of the East" bequeaths to the poem's narrator a rose farm located in a "pleasure-ground" near Damascus, laved by the healing rivers Abana and Pharpar (344). The poem's language reflects Melville's acknowledgment in a letter that after his retirement he had "come into possession of unobstructed leisure" and now "husband[s]" his "vigor" for writing (*Correspondence* 519). The substance of the poem consists of the new farmer's musings as to whether he should enjoy the roses in bouquets or distill them into attar (the Arabic word for perfume). Throughout the poem the roses are personified as a harem of virgins whose fate lies in the balance. Advised by both a Persian florist and a Parsee perfumist, the narrator eventually sides with the former and concludes "The flower of a subject is enough" (349). The Persian gentleman farmer explains to him, with words that flatter the roses, his "Angelic sweethearts":

This evanescence is the charm!
And most it wins the spirits that be
Celestial, sir. It comes to me
It was this fleeting charm in show
That lured the sons of God below,
Tired out with perpetuity
Of heaven's own seventh heaven aglow;
Not Eve's fair daughters, sir; nay, nay,
Less fugitive in charm are they:
It was the rose. (347–48)

"The Rose Farmer" conveys Melville's final reckoning of the limits of his art and the impossibility of recapturing the "fugitive" essence of paradise in prose. Yet, as humble bouquets, the poems of *Weeds and Wildings* also memorialize the redolent intimation of paradise's presence amidst the dumb matter of earth. Having given up his "painstaking throes" to "crystallise the rose" through the alembic of fiction, Melville, through his jocular rose farmer, came into possession of the very paradise he desired.[36] "There is nothing like the bloom," Melville would confirm in another unpublished poem, ironically entitled "The Vial of Attar" (*Poems* 338). In 1852, Melville had imagined life as "a long Dardenelles" with steep banks preventing the plucking of the beautiful flowers on its shores. By the end of his life, though, he had gathered his flowers in the delicious lands of his Circassian imagination. Eloquently testifying to the reward of his long journey is the conclusion of his poem "Pebbles":

> Healed of my hurt, I laud the inhuman Sea—
> Yea, bless the Angels Four that there convene;
> For healed I am even by their pitiless breath
> Distilled in wholesome dew named rosmarine. (*Poems* 244)

It was by manifesting his vision of paradise and female beauty in the evanescent spirit of the earthly flower that Melville was able to become a resident of a Circassia with "celestial grass that is forever tropical."[37] The humble damask roses, through the medium of the narrator's poetry, blossom into the houris of paradise and become the seraphic sweethearts of his celestial seraglio.

Dedicated to the memory of Dorothee Metlitzki Finkelstein and Brian Short.

Notes

1. Parker, *Biography* 1: 760–61; Leon Howard, an earlier biographer, refused to accept that Melville was this abductor (159).

2. Metcalf 217; Robertson-Lorant, *Melville* 571.

3. The Lamia, celebrated by Keats and by Melville's poem "Lamia's Song," was a female vampire so obsessed with her dead children that she vengefully lured young people to their destruction (*Poems* 266).

4. "Immolated," *Poems* 411. Melville invokes the angel in his poem "Angel O' the Age" to "sprinkle, do, some drop of grace, / Nor polish us into commonplace" (*Poems* 422).

5. Qur'an, trans. Abdullah Yusuf Ali, 44:54, 52:20, 56:22, 55:76. In a book review, Melville comments on "the pleasant spirit of the Mahometan ... who rewards all true believers with a houri" (*Piazza Tales* 236). The poet Botargo in *Mardi* dreams, "in merry fancies," of his poems "being thrilled by the blessed houris in paradise" (396).

6. *White-Jacket* 268; *Pierre* 94.

7. S. B. H., "Of the Mythology and Superstitions of the Arabian Nights, and other Eastern Tales," *The Literary World* 59 (18 Mar. 1847): 123–24. The association of peris with heaven was popularized by Thomas Moore's tale "The Paradise and the Peri" in his widely read *Lalla Rookh* (1817). See Finkelstein, *Melville's Orienda* 208–14.

8. Melville's brother Gansevoort had been similarly ravished by the Muslim heroine of Byron's "The Bride of Abydos," calling her in his journal of 1834 "the most sweetly beautiful female character that I have ever met with in Poetry, so gentle, affectionate, amiable, & ingenuous in disposition, so simply beautiful in her ideas, and so happy in expressing them, and appearing to possess every quality of heart and mind, calculated to make those around her happy, joined with a person, which would realize all the ideas that the Mahometan has of the beauty of the Houris, those dark eyed girls of Paradise, all conspire to make a woman as near perfection, as is possible for her to attain" (Leyda 1: 60).

9. Melville would return to such a supercharged orientalist space, although one with more ominous metropolitan overtones, in his depiction of the London den of pleasure in *Redburn* called "Aladdin's Palace" (227–36).

10. Melville was particularly attracted by the pastoral landscapes of the French painter Claude Lorraine, whose work he felt "haunt[ed] the Arcadian woods in haze." Commenting on Lorraine's style while visiting Rome, Melville wrote, "All their effect is of atmosphere. He paints the air" (*Journals* 109). In a 6 July 1859, letter to Daniel Shepherd, Melville punned on his correspondent's name and invited him to visit the pastoral "Arcady" of the Berkshires (*Correspondence* 337–39).

11. Blumenbach's representative "Caucasian" was Mahommed Jumla, a Vizier of Mogul Emperor Aurungzeb (pictured in Greene, *The Death of Adam* 225).

12. See Melville's poem "The New Zealot of the Sun" for an instance of how the release of chaos from a figurative "Persian"—whom he associated with "Calvin's last extreme"—was an element of his orientalist imagination (*Poems* 264–65).

13. Although the Marquesas might seem an earthly approximation of paradise, the valley Melville finds himself in proves not to be the hoped-for Happar. The Typee valley is stained with the "demon Principle" in the evils of cannibalism and incipient imperialism, just as Melville's own text of *Typee* is riddled with serpent imagery.

14. Melville imagines heaven not only as a place "where want and misery come not" but as a community "peopled with heretics and heathens" and "almost entirely made up of the poor and despised" (*Mardi* 428, 487). Melville wrote in the midst of his own pilgrimage to the Holy Land in 1857, "Hapless are the favorites of heaven" (*Journals* 91).

15. "Are not Abana and Pharpar, rivers of Damascus, better than all the waters of Israel? May I not wash in them, and be clean?" (2 Kings 5:12). The waters of these "rivers of Damascus" are mentioned as sources of healing in *Omoo* (27).

16. This experience was one that Melville shared with Richard T. Greene, the "Toby" with whom he escaped, who likewise became "seized with the romantic" when he entered the harbor at Nukuheva and "saw its almost unearthly beauties break, as if by magic, on our bewildered eyes" (Leyda 1: 129).

17. This part of the "Typee Fragment" is quoted in Parker, *Biography* 1: 364–65. This paragraph would have been on pages 110–11 of *Typee*.

18. In *Omoo*, Melville concurs with the French naming of Tahiti as the "New Cytherea," quoting Louis-Antoine de Bougainville as saying, "Often I thought I was walking in the garden of Eden" (66).

19. See Finkelstein 221–22, 204.

20. Golconda refers to legendary diamond mines near Hyderabad, India.

21. Melville's mystic portrayal of Yillah as houri was parodied in a lampoon in *The Man in the Moon* of May 1849: "Yillah basks beside me—her great black eyes, lustrous and full-orbed, the doors through which angels and spirits float into her being from that heaven which is higher than the seventh heaven seen by the camel-driver [i.e. Muhammad] in his vision" (Branch, *Critical Heritage* 160).

22. Melville's narrator in *Mardi* is inspired to abandon ship in the middle of the Pacific by a sublime vision from the masthead of the "entire western horizon high piled with gold and crimson clouds; airy arches, domes and minarets; as if the yellow, Moorish sun were setting behind some vast Alhambra." Such an orientalist vista leads him into a trance "leading to worlds beyond" in which "the cadence of mild billows laving a beach of shells, the waving of boughs, and *the voices of maidens*, and the lulled beating of my own dissolved heart, all blended together" (7–8; emphasis mine).

23. "Matter in end will never abate / His ancient brutal claim," wrote Melville in "Fragments of a Lost Gnostic Poem of the Twelfth Century" (*Poems* 272).

24. Ruth's Jewish ethnicity and Clarel's failure to consummate his relationship with her perhaps represents Melville's inability to gain access to any embodiment of oriental female beauty during his visit, with the exception of brief glimpses of women in Turkey (*Journals* 57, 63). In *Clarel*, Melville is thus forced to represent the eroticism of Eastern femininity in his description of Zar, the wondrous mare of the Druze guide, Djalea. For the effects of Melville's Near Eastern journey on his romantic oriental visions, see Marr, "Mastheads and Minarets."

25. During his own trip to Europe in 1849, Melville wore a conspicuous green jacket, which elicited a "mysterious hint" and "play[ed] the devel [sic] with my respectability" (*Journals* 12, 40). Upon returning to New York, he exultantly donned it to promenade out to the Battery to look at the stars (Melville to Evert A. Duyckinck, 7 Mar. 1850, *Correspondence* 159).

26. Ishmael categorically rejects the punishment of work at the beginning of *Moby-Dick* when he criticizes "the universal thump" ("who ain't a slave?"[6]) and retorts that he "abominate[s] all honorable toils, trials and tribulations of every kind whatsoever" (5).

27. "A Ground Vine," *Poems* 335. In another poem "The Late-Comer," Melville personifies the coming of spring as the longed-for appearance of an "errant and young" maiden bringing blooms as she arrives from the south (*Poems* 305–7).

28. "A Spirit Appeared to Me," *Poems* 423; "Pausilippo," *Poems* 282.

29. Shushan, or Susa, was the ancient capital of Persia and is the setting for the Bible's Book of Esther. Such orientalization of Eden is also evident in *Timoleon*'s "Syra" where Melville directly links "orient finery" with Eve's sacred hands (*Poems* 289–91).

30. Melville protects himself from the possible blasphemy of this vision (the confusion of Mary with Eve) by attributing "The Devotion of the Flowers to Their Lady" to a monk from the eleventh century, who eventually retired "for an unrevealed cause" to a monastery from "the gay circles where he had long been a caressed favourite" (*Poems* 341).

31. Stein, *The Poetry of Melville's Late Years* 162.

32. Laurie Robertson-Lorant explores how Melville "achieved a harmonious marriage between the male and female sides of his own nature" in her article "Melville's Embrace of the Invisible Woman" (410).

33. The philosopher Babbalanja in *Mardi* describes the gendered dialectic of Melville's creativity: "And what, if he pulled down one gross world, and ransacked the etherial spheres, to build up something of his own—a composite:—what then? matter and mind, though matching not, are mates; and sundered oft, in his Koztanza they unite:—the airy waist, embraced by stalwart arms" (597).

34. Cf. Freibert, "Weeds and Wildings" and Dillingham, *Melville and His Circle* (192n.89).

35. See "Thy Aim, Thy Aim!" and "Immolated," *Poems* 415, 411.

36. Interestingly, the bequest was granted because the narrator had fixed a "chowder" for the grandee during his Ramadan fast; these references look back to the trusting and playful

companionship of Ishmael and Queequeg on Nantucket in "The Ramadan" and "Chowder" chapters of *Moby-Dick* and intimate that Melville's own fictional labor did indeed have its symbolic rewards.

37. Melville to Hawthorne, June 1851, *Correspondence* 191.

Bibliography

Adler, Joyce Sparer. *Dramatization of Three Melville Novels.* Lewiston, NY: Edwin Mellen Press, 1992.

———. "Introduction: Women in Melville's Art." *Melville Society EXTRACTS* 65 (Feb. 1986): 2–3.

———. "Melville and Misogyny?" *Melville Society EXTRACTS* 98 (Sept. 1994): 11–12.

———. *War in Melville's Imagination.* New York: New York UP, 1981.

Anderson, Charles Roberts. "The Genesis of *Billy Budd.*" *American Literature* 12.3 (Nov. 1940): 329–46.

———. *Melville in the South Seas.* 1939. Rpt. New York: Dover, 1966.

———, ed. *Journal of a Cruise to the Pacific Ocean, 1842–1844, in the Frigate* United States. Durham, NC: Duke UP, 1937.

Arvin, Newton. *Herman Melville.* The American Men of Letters Series. New York: William Sloane Associates, 1950.

———. "Melville and the Gothic Novel." *New England Quarterly* 22 (Mar. 1949): 33–48.

Avallone, Charlene. "Calculations for Popularity: Melville's *Pierre* and *Holden's Dollar Magazine.*" *Nineteenth-Century Literature* 43 (1988): 82–110.

———. "The *Kunstlerroman* Comes to America: The 'Domestic' Fictions of Caroline Chesbro, Herman Melville, and Fanny Fern." *Melville Society EXTRACTS* 100 (Mar. 1995): 4–5.

———. "What American Renaissance? The Gendered Genealogy of a Critical Discourse." *PMLA* 112.5 (Oct. 1997): 1102–20.

Barber, Patricia. "What If Bartleby Were a Woman?" *The Authority of Experience: Essays in Feminist Criticism.* Ed. Arlyn Diamond and Lee R. Edwards. Amherst: U of Massachusetts P, 1977.

Barker-Benfield, G. J. *The Horrors of the Half-Known Life: Male Attitudes toward Women and Sexuality in Nineteenth-Century America.* New York: Harper and Row, 1976.

Basch, Norma. *In the Eyes of the Law: Women, Marriage, and Property in Nineteenth-Century New York.* Ithaca, NY: Cornell UP, 1982.

Batsleer, Janet, et al. *Rewriting English: Cultural Politics of Gender and Class*. New Accents. Ed. Terence Hawkes. New York: Methuen, 1985.

Baym, Nina. *Novels, Readers, and Reviewers: Responses to Fiction in Antebellum America*. Ithaca, NY: Cornell UP, 1984.

———. *Woman's Fiction: A Guide to Novels by and about Women in America, 1820–1870*. Ithaca, NY: Cornell UP, 1978.

Beecher, Catherine. *A Treatise on Domestic Economy*. 1841. Rpt. New York: Source Book, 1971.

Bercaw, Mary K. *Melville's Sources*. Evanston, IL: Northwestern UP, 1987.

Bergmann, Johannes D. "Melville's Tales." *A Companion to Melville Studies*. Ed. John Bryant. New York: Greenwood, 1986. 241–78.

Berthold, Dennis. "Charles Brockden Brown, Edgar Huntly, and the Origins of the American Picturesque," *William and Mary Quarterly*, Third Series, 41.1 (1984): 62–84.

———. "Durer 'At the Hostelry': Melville's Misogynist Iconography." *Melville Society EXTRACTS* 95 (Dec. 1993): 1–8.

———. "Melville's Medusas." *Melville "Among the Nations": Proceedings of an International Conference, 1997*. Ed. Sanford E. Marovitz and A. C. Christodoulou. Kent, OH: Kent State UP, 2001. 287–96.

Bickley, R. Bruce, Jr. *The Method of Melville's Short Fiction*. Durham, NC: Duke UP, 1975.

Birdsall, Richard D. "William Cullen Bryant and Catharine Sedgwick—Their Debt to Berkshire." *New England Quarterly* 28.3 (1955): 349–71.

Blackstone, William. *Commentaries on the Laws of England*. Ed. Stanley N. Katz. 4 vols. Chicago: U of Chicago P, 1979.

Bonner, W. Nigel. *Seals and Man: A Study of Interactions*. Seattle: U of Washington P, 1982.

Branch, Watson G. *Melville: The Critical Heritage*. London: Routledge and Kegan Paul, 1974, 1985.

———, Hershel Parker, Harrison Hayford, and Alma Parker. "Historical Note." *The Confidence-Man: His Masquerade*. Evanston, IL: Northwestern UP and Newberry Library, 1982.

Braswell, William. "The Satirical Temper of Melville's *Pierre*," *American Literature* 7 (1936): 424–38.

Breinig, Helmbrecht. "The Destruction of Fairyland: Melville's 'The Piazza' in the Tradition of the American Imagination." *English Literary History* 35.2 (1968): 254–83.

Bremer, Fredericka. *The Homes of the New World: Impressions of America*. Trans. Mary Howitt. 2 vols. New York: Harper's, 1853.

Broderick, John C. "Melville and the Missionaries: Once More." *Melville Society EXTRACTS* 67 (Sept. 1986): 15–16.

Broderick, Warren F. "Melville's First Five Poems." *Melville Society EXTRACTS* 92 (Mar. 1993).

Brodhead, Richard. *Hawthorne, Melville, and the Novel*. Chicago: U of Chicago P, 1973.

———. "Introduction." *New Essays on* Moby-Dick or, The Whale. New York: Cambridge UP, 1986.

———. "Melville; or Aggression." *Melville's Evermoving Dawn: Centennial Essays*. Ed. John Bryant and Robert Milder. Kent, OH: Kent State UP, 1997. 181–92.

Brooks, Peter. *The Melodramatic Imagination: Balzac, Henry James, Melodrama, and the Mode of Excess*. New Haven, CT: Yale UP, 1976.

Brown, Gillian. *Domestic Individualism: Imagining Self in Nineteenth-Century America*. Berkeley: U of California P, 1990.

———. "The Empire of Agoraphobia." *Herman Melville: A Collection of Critical Essays.* Ed. Myra Jehlen. Englewood Cliffs, NJ: Prentice-Hall, 1994.

Bryant, John. "*The Confidence-Man:* Melville's Problem Novel." *A Companion to Melville Studies.* Ed. John Bryant. Westport, CT: Greenwood, 1986. 315–50.

———. *Melville and Repose: The Rhetoric of Humor in the American Renaissance.* New York: Oxford UP, 1993.

———. "Ordering the Rose: Melville's Poetic Revisions," *Melville Society EXTRACTS* 117 (July 1999): 17–18.

———. "Toning Down the Green: Melville's Picturesque." *Savage Eye: Melville and the Visual Arts.* Ed. Christopher Sten. Kent, OH: Kent State UP, 1991. 145–61.

Buell, Lawrence. *Writing for an Endangered World: Literature, Culture, and Environment in the U.S. and Beyond.* Cambridge, MA: Harvard UP, 2001.

Butler, Judith. *Bodies That Matter: On the Discursive Limits of "Sex."* New York: Routledge, 1993.

Cahir, Linda. *Solitude and Society in the Works of Herman Melville and Edith Wharton.* Contributions to the Study of American Literature, No. 3. Westport, CT: Greenwood, 1999.

Carson, Rachel. *The Sea around Us.* 1950. Rev. ed. New York: Oxford UP, 1961.

Cary, Alice. "Uncle Christopher's." *Clovernook Sketches and Other Stories.* Ed. Judith Fetterley. New Brunswick, NJ: Rutgers UP, 1987.

Castronovo, Russ. *Necro Citizenship: Death, Eroticism, and the Public Sphere in the Nineteenth-Century United States.* Durham, NC: Duke UP, 2001.

Catalogue of Books in the Library of the Young Men's Association of the City of Albany. Albany, NY: 1848.

Chapone, Hester. *Letters on the Improvement of the Mind Addressed to a Young Lady.* 1773.

Mrs. Chapone's Letters and Dr. Gregory's Legacy. London: J. Walker, 1810.

Charvat, William. "Melville and the Common Reader." *Studies in Bibliography* 12 (1959): 41–57.

———. *The Profession of Authorship in America, 1800–1870: The Papers of William Charvat.* Ed. Matthew J. Bruccoli. Columbus: Ohio State UP, 1968.

Chase, Richard. *Herman Melville: A Critical Study.* New York: Macmillan, 1949.

Child, Lydia Maria. "The Hindoo Anchorite." *The Union Magazine* (Apr. 1848): 151–53.

Chodorow, Nancy. *The Reproduction of Mothering.* Berkeley: U of California P, 1978.

Chow, Rey. "'It's you, not me': Domination and Othering in Theorizing the Third World." *American Feminist Thought at Century's End.* Ed. Linda Kauffman. Oxford, UK: Blackwell, 1993.

Coffler, Gail. *Melville's Allusions to Religion: A Comprehensive Index and Glossary.* Westport, CT: Greenwood, 2004.

———. *Melville's Classical Allusions: A Comprehensive Index and Glossary.* Westport, CT: Greenwood, 1985.

Cohen, Hennig, and Donald Yannella. *Herman Melville's Malcolm Letter: "Man's Final Lore."* New York: Fordham UP and New York Public Library, 1992.

Colatrella, Carol. "Home Improvement: Melville's Narratives and Domestic Culture." *Melville Society EXTRACTS* 100 (Mar. 1995): 5–6.

———. *Literature and Moral Reform: Melville and the Discipline of Reading.* Gainesville: UP of Florida, 2002.

Coleridge, Samuel Taylor. *Poetical Works*. Ed. Ernest Hartley Coleridge. Oxford, UK: Oxford UP, 1912, 1978.

Cook, Jonathan A. *Satirical Apocalypse: An Anatomy of Melville's* The Confidence-Man. Westport, CT: Greenwood, 1996.

Coultrap-Quinn, Susan. *Doing Literary Business: American Women Writers in the Nineteenth Century*. Chapel Hill: U of North Carolina P, 1990.

———, ed. *Gail Hamilton: Selected Writings*. New Brunswick, NJ: Rutgers UP, 1992.

Cowen, Walker. "Melville's Marginalia." 11 vols. Diss. Harvard, 1965.

Cox, Catherine S. "'An excellent thing in woman': Virgo and Viragos in *King Lear*." *Modern Philology* 96 (Nov. 1998): 143–157.

Cronon, William. *Changes in the Land: Indians, Colonists, and the Ecology of New England*. New York: Hill and Wang, 1983.

Damon-Bach, Lucinda, et al. "Chronological Bibliography of the Works of Catharine Maria Sedgwick." *Catharine Maria Sedgwick: Critical Perspectives*. Ed. Lucinda Damon-Bach and Victoria Clements. Boston: New England UP, 2003. 295–13.

Dante Alighieri. *The Divine Comedy of Dante Alighieri*. Trans. Rev. H. F. Cary. New York, NY: Lovell, Coryell and Co., 1814.

Davidson, Cathy N., ed. *Reading in America: Literature and Social History*. Baltimore: Johns Hopkins UP, 1989.

———. *Revolution and the Word: The Rise of the Novel in America*. New York: Oxford UP, 1986.

Davis, Merrell R. "The Flower Symbolism in *Mardi*." *Modern Language Quarterly* 2 (1941): 625–38.

———, and William H. Gilman, eds. *The Letters of Herman Melville*. New Haven: Yale UP, 1960.

Davis, Natalie Zemon. "Women on Top." *Society and Culture in Early Modern France*. Palo Alto, CA: Stanford UP. Rpt. *Feminism and Renaissance Studies*. Ed. Lorna Hutson. New York: Oxford UP, 1999. 156–85.

DeLamotte, Eugenia. *Perils of the Night: A Feminist Study of Nineteenth-Century Gothic*. New York: Oxford UP, 1990.

Dening, Greg. *Islands and Beaches: Discourse on a Silent Land: Marquesas 1774–1880*. 1980. Rpt. Chicago: Dorsey, 1988.

de Staël, Germaine. *Corinne, or Italy*. Trans. and ed. Avriel H. Goldberger. New Brunswick, NJ: Rutgers UP, 1987.

Dewey, Mary E. *The Life and Letters of Catharine Maria Sedgwick*. New York: Harper's, 1872.

Dillingham, William B. *Melville and His Circle: The Last Years*. Athens: U of Georgia P, 1996.

———. *Melville's Later Novels*. Athens: U of Georgia P, 1986.

Dimock, Wai Chee. *Empire for Liberty: Melville and the Politics of Individualism*. Princeton, NJ: Princeton UP, 1989.

———. "Ethics of Care in Law and Science." *Feminist Studies* 21.2 (Summer 2001): 510–13.

Direnç, Dilek. "What Do These Women Want? *Pierre* and the New World of Gender." *Melville "Among the Nations": Proceedings of an International Conference, 1997*. Ed. Sanford E. Marovitz and A. C. Christodoulou. Kent, OH: Kent State UP, 2001. 384–93.

Ditson, George Leighton. *Circassia; or, A Tour to the Caucasus.* New York: Stringer and Townsend; London: T.C. Newby, 1850.

Djelal, Juana Celia. "Melville's Bridal Apostrope: Rhetorical Conventions of the Connubium." *Melville Society EXTRACTS* 110 (Sept. 1997): 1–5.

Dobson, Joanne. "Sex, Wit, and Sentiment: Frances Osgood and the Poetry of Love." *American Literature* 65.4 (Dec. 1993): 631–50.

Doenges, Richard E. "The Blizzard and Tulips of '88: Clues for Dating Melville." *Melville Society EXTRACTS* 56 (Nov. 1983): 11–12.

Douglas, Ann. *The Feminization of American Culture.* New York: Alfred A. Knopf, 1977. Rpt. New York: Anchor/Doubleday, 1988.

Downing, Andrew Jackson. *The Architecture of Country Houses.* New York: D. Appleton, 1850. Rpt. New York: Dover, 1969.

Dryden, Edgar. *Melville's Thematics of Form: The Great Art of Telling the Truth.* Baltimore: Johns Hopkins UP, 1968.

Duberstein, Larry. *The Handsome Sailor.* Sag Harbor, NY: Permanent, 1998.

Egan, Hugh. *Proceedings of the naval court-martial in the case of Alexander Slidell Mackenzie (1844: A Facsimile Reproduction).* Delmar, NY: Scholars' Fascimiles and Reprints, 1992.

Egan, Ken. *The Riven Home: Narrative Rivalry in the American Renaissance.* Selinsgrove, PA: Susquehanna UP, 1997.

Egan, Phillip J. "Isabel's Story: The Voice of the Dark Woman in Melville's *Pierre.*" *American Transcendental Quarterly,* New Series 1.2 (1987): 99–110.

Ellis, William. *Polynesian Researches during a Residence of Nearly Eight Years in the Society and Sandwich Islands.* 4 vols. London: Bohn, 1853.

Emerson, George [B]. *A Lecture on the Education of Females.* Boston: Hillard, Gray, Little, and Wilkins, 1831.

———. *Reminiscences of an Old Teacher.* 1875. Rpt. Boston: Alfred Mudge and Son, 1878.

Emerson, Ralph Waldo. "Self-Reliance." *The Norton Anthology of American Literature, 1820–65.* Vol. II. Ed. Nina Baym et al. 6th ed. New York: Norton, 2003. 1160–76.

Evans, Lyon, Jr. "Inaccuracies and Discrepancies in Herman Melville's 'To Winnefred.'" *Melville Society EXTRACTS* 95 (Dec. 1993): 13–14.

Fetterley, Judith. "Entitled to More than 'Peculiar Praise': The Extravagance of Alice Cary's *Clovernook.*" *Legacy* 10.2 (1993): 103–19.

———. "Preface to *Clovernook; or, Recollections of Our Neighborhood.*" *Clovernook Sketches and Other Stories.* New Brunswick, NJ: Rutgers UP, 1987.

———. *Provisions: A Reader from 19th-Century American Women.* Bloomington: Indiana UP, 1985.

———. *The Resisting Reader: A Feminist Approach to American Fiction.* Bloomington: Indiana UP, 1977.

Fiedler, Leslie. *Love and Death in the American Novel.* New York: Dell, 1960, 1969.

Findlay, Alison. "Women and Drama." *A Companion to English Renaissance Literature and Culture.* Ed. Michael Hattaway. Oxford, UK: Blackwell, 2000.

Finkelstein, Dorothee Metlitsky. *Melville's Orienda.* New Haven, CT: Yale UP, 1961.

Foley, Barbara. "From Wall Street to Astor Place: Historicizing Melville's 'Bartleby.'" *American Literature* 72.1 (Mar. 2000): 87–116.

Foster, Elizabeth, ed. *The Confidence-Man.* New York: Hendricks House, 1954.

Foster, Hannah. *The Boarding School; or, Lessons of a Preceptress to her Pupils: Consisting of Information, Instruction, and Advice, Calculated to Improve the Manners, and Form the Character of Young Ladies. To Which Is Added, a Collection of Letters, Written by the Pupils to Their Instructor, Their Friends, and Each Other.* Boston: Thomas and Andrews, 1798.

Fox, Warwick. "The Deep Ecology-Ecofeminism Debate and Its Parallels." *Environmental Philosophy: From Animal Rights to Radical Ecology.* Ed. Michael E. Zimmerman. Englewood Cliffs, NJ: Prentice-Hall, 1993. 227–44.

Franchot, Jenny. "Melville's Travelling God." *The Cambridge Companion to Herman Melville.* Ed. Robert S. Levine. Cambridge, UK: Cambridge UP, 1998, 1999. 157–85.

Fredricks, Nancy. "Melville and the Woman's Story." *Studies in American Fiction* 19 (1991): 41–54.

Freibert, Lucy M. "Herman Melville: The Feminine Dimension." *Melville Society EXTRACTS* 65 (Feb. 1986): 9–11.

———. "Weeds and Wildings: Herman Melville's Use of the Pastoral Voice." *Essays in Arts and Sciences* 12 (1983): 61–83.

Fryer, Judith. *The Faces of Eve: Women in the Nineteenth-Century American Novel.* New York: Oxford UP, 1976.

Fuentes, Carlos. "El racista enmascarado" ("The Masked Racist"). *El País,* martes, 23 de marzo de 2004.

Fuller, Margaret. "American Literature: Its Position in the Present Time and Prospects for the Future." 1846. Rpt. in *Margaret Fuller: Essays on American Life and Letters.* Ed. Joel Myerson. New Haven, CT: College and University P, 1978. 381–400.

———. Rev. of *Typee.* New-York *Daily Tribune,* 4 April 1846.

Furnas, J. C. *The Americans: A Social History of the United States 1587–1914.* New York: G. P. Putnam's Sons, 1969.

Gaard, Greta, and Patrick D. Murphy, eds. *Ecofeminist Literary Criticism: Theory, Interpretation, Pedagogy.* Urbana: U of Illinois P, 1998.

Gandhi, Leela. *Postcolonial Theory: A Critical Introduction.* Edinburgh: Edinburgh UP, 1998.

The Gansevoort-Lansing Collection. The New York Public Library.

Garcia, Wilma. *Mothers and Others: Myths of the Female in the Works of Melville, Twain, and Hemingway.* New York: Peter Lang, 1984.

Garside, Peter. "Picturesque Figure and Landscape: Meg Merrilies and the Gypsies." *The Politics of the Picturesque: Literature, Landscape and Aesthetics since 1770.* Ed. Stephen Copley and Peter Garside. Cambridge, UK: Cambridge UP, 1994.

Gell, Alfred. *Wrapping in Images: Tattooing in Polynesia.* Oxford: Clarendon, 1993.

Gidmark, Jill B. *Melville Sea Dictionary: A Glossed Concordance and Analysis of the Sea Language in Melville's Nautical Novels.* Westport, CT: Greenwood, 1982.

Gilbert, Sandra M., and Susan Gubar. *The Madwoman in the Attic: The Woman Writer in the Nineteenth-Century Literary Imagination.* New Haven, CT: Yale UP, 1979.

Gilligan, Carol. *In a Different Voice: Psychological Theory and Women's Development.* Cambridge, MA: Harvard UP, 1982.

Gilman, William H. *Melville's Early Life and Redburn.* New York: New York UP, 1951.

Gilmore, Michael. *American Romanticism and the Marketplace.* Chicago: U of Chicago P, 1985.

Gilmore, Michael T. "The Book Marketplace I." *The Columbia History of the American Novel.* Ed. Emory Elliott. New York: Columbia UP, 1991. 46–71.

Goddu, Teresa. *Gothic America: Narrative, History, and Nation.* New York: Columbia UP, 1997.

Graves, Mrs. A. *Woman in America. Being An Examination into the Moral and Intellectual Condition of American Female Society.* Harper's Family Library No. 166. New York: Harper and Brothers, 1844.

Greene, John C. *The Death of Adam: Evolution and Its Impact on Western Thought.* Ames: Iowa State UP, 1959.

Greenwood, Grace. "Letter from the Author of Typee," "Copyright, Authors, and Authorship" series, *Saturday Evening Post,* 9 Oct. 1847. Rpt. in *Greenwood Leaves: A Collection of Sketches and Letters.* Boston: Ticknor, Reed, and Fields, 1850. 294–96.

Grosz, Elizabeth. *Volatile Bodies: Toward a Corporeal Feminism.* Bloomington: Indiana UP, 1994.

H., S. B. "Of the Mythology and Superstitions of the Arabian Nights, and other Eastern Tales." *The Literary World* 18 (Mar. 1847): 123–24.

Haberstroh, Charles. *Melville and Male Identity.* Rutherford, NJ: Fairleigh Dickinson UP, 1980.

Hadfield, Andrew. *The English Renaissance: 1500–1620.* Oxford, UK: Blackwell, 2001.

Hale, Sarah. "The Bell and the Bleu." *Sketches of American Character.* Boston: Putnam and Hunt, and Carter and Hendee, 1829.

Hall, David D. "Readers and Reading in America: Historical and Critical Perspectives." *Proceedings of the American Antiquarian Society* 103 (1993): 337–57.

Hamilton, Gail. "The Murder of Philip Spencer." *Cosmopolitan Magazine* 7.134 (June 1889): 133–41, 248–54, 345–54.

———. "A Spasm of Sense." *Atlantic Monthly* 11.66 (Apr. 1863): 407–20.

Handy, E. S. Craighill. *The Native Culture in the Marquesas. Bernice P. Bishop Museum Bulletin* 9. Honolulu: Bishop Museum, 1923. Rpt. New York: Kraus, 1971.

Handy, Willowdean Chatterson. *Forever the Land of Men: An Account of a Visit to the Marquesas Islands.* New York: Dodd, Mead, 1965.

———. *Tattooing in the Marquesas. Bernice P. Bishop Museum Bulletin* 1. Honolulu: Bishop Museum, 1922.

Hanson, Elizabeth I. *The American Indian in American Literature: A Study in Metaphor.* New York: Edwin Mellen, 1988.

Haraway, Donna. *Simians, Cyborgs, and Women: The Reinvention of Nature.* New York: Routledge, 1991.

Hardwick, Elizabeth. *Herman Melville.* New York: Viking, 2000.

Harris, Susan K. *19th-Century American Women's Novels: Interpretive Strategies.* Cambridge, UK: Cambridge UP, 1990.

———. "But is it any *good?* Evaluating Nineteenth-Century American Women's Fiction." *American Literature* 63.1 (Mar. 1991): 43–61. Rpt. in *The (Other) American Traditions: Nineteenth-Century Women Writers.* Ed. Joyce W. Warren. New Brunswick, NJ: Rutgers UP, 1993. 263–79.

———. "Responding to the Text(s): Women Readers and the Quest for Higher Education." *Readers in History: Nineteenth-Century American Literature and the Contexts of Response.* Ed. James L. Machor. Baltimore: Johns Hopkins UP, 1993. 259–82.

Harrison, G. B. "Introduction." *Cymbeline. Shakespeare: The Complete Works.* Ed. G. B. Harrison. New York: Harcourt Brace and World, 1968.

Hart, Jonathan. *Columbus, Shakespeare, and the Interpretation of the New World.* New York: Palgrave Macmillan, 2003.

Hawthorne, Nathaniel. *The Scarlet Letter.* The Centenary Edition of the Works of Nathaniel Hawthorne. Ed. William Charvat et al. Vol. 1. Columbus: Ohio State UP, 1962.

———. *A Wonder Book and Tanglewood Tales.* The Centenary Edition of the Works of Nathaniel Hawthorne. Ed. William Charvat et al. Vol. 7. Columbus: Ohio State UP, 1972.

Hayford, Harrison. *The Somers Mutiny Affair.* Englewood Cliffs, NJ: Prentice-Hall, 1959.

———, and Merton M. Sealts, Jr., eds. *Billy Budd: The Genetic Text.* Chicago: U of Chicago P, 1978.

Hedrick, Joan D. *Harriet Beecher Stowe: A Life.* New York: Oxford UP, 1994.

Heflin, Wilson L. "New Light on the Cruise of Herman Melville in the *Charles and Henry*." *Historic Nantucket* 22.2 (Oct. 1974): 6–27.

Henderson, Andrea. "'An Embarrassing Subject': Use Value and Exchange Value in Early Gothic Characterization." *At the Limits of Romanticism: Essays in Cultural, Feminist, and Materialist Criticism.* Ed. Mary A. Favret and Nicola J. Watson. Bloomington: Indiana UP, 1994. 225–45.

Herbert, T. Walter. *Dearest Beloved: The Hawthornes and the Making of the Middle-Class Family.* Berkeley: U of California P, 1993.

———. *Marquesan Encounters: Melville and the Meaning of Civilization.* Cambridge, MA: Harvard UP, 1980.

Herzog, Kristin. *Women, Ethnics and Exotics: Images of Power in Mid–Nineteenth Century American Fiction.* Knoxville: U of Tennessee P, 1983.

Higgins, Brian, and Hershel Parker, eds. *Critical Essays on Melville's* Pierre; or the Ambiguities. Boston: G.K. Hall, 1983.

———. "The Flawed Grandeur of Melville's *Pierre*." *Critical Essays on Melville's* Pierre; or, the Ambiguities. Boston: G. K. Hall, 1983. 240–66.

Hillway, Tyrus. *Herman Melville.* Boston: Twayne, 1979.

Hobbs, Catherine. "Introduction: Cultures and Practices of U.S. Women's Literacy." *Nineteenth-Century Women Learn to Write.* Charlottesville: U of Virginia P, 1995. 1–33.

Holy Bible. King James Version.

Howard, Leon. *Herman Melville: A Biography.* 1951. Rpt. Berkeley: U of California P, 1977.

Howes, Jeanne C. "Melville's Sensitive Years." *Melville and Hawthorne in the Berkshires: A Symposium.* Ed. Howard P. Vincent. Kent Studies in English. Kent, OH: Kent State UP, 1968. 22–41.

Hume, Beverly A. "Of Krakens and Other Monsters: Melville's *Pierre*." *American Transcendental Quarterly* 6:2 (June 1992): 95–108.

Irey, Eugene F., ed. *A Concordance to Herman Melville's* Moby-Dick. 2 vols. New York: Garland, 1982.

Irigaray, Luce. *This Sex Which Is Not One,* 1977. Rpt. Trans. Catherine Porter with Carolyn Burke. Ithaca, NY: Cornell UP, 1985

Ivison, Douglas. "'I saw everything but could comprehend nothing': Melville's *Typee*, Travel Narrative, and Colonial Discourse." *American Transcendental Quarterly* 16.2 (2002): 115–30.

Jehlen, Myra. *American Incarnation: The Individual, the Nation, and the Continent.* Cambridge, MA: Harvard UP, 1986.

———, ed. *Herman Melville: A Collection of Critical Essays.* Englewood Cliffs, NJ: Prentice-Hall, 1994.

Kakutani, Michiko. "Biography Becomes a Blood Sport." *New York Times Book Review,* 20 May 1994. B1, B6.

Karcher, Carolyn. *Shadow over the Promised Land: Slavery, Race, and Violence in Melville's America.* Baton Rouge: Louisiana State UP, 1980.

Karlsen, Carol. *The Devil in the Shape of a Woman: Witchcraft in Colonial New England.* New York: Vintage Books, 1989.

Keats, John. *The Letters of John Keats.* 2 vols. Ed. Hyder E. Rollins. Cambridge, MA: Harvard UP, 1958.

———. *The Poems of John Keats.* Ed. Jack Stillinger. Cambridge, MA: Harvard UP, 1978.

Kelley, Mary. "'A More Glorious Revolution': Women's Antebellum Reading Circles and the Pursuit of Public Influence." *New England Quarterly* 71 (June 2003): 163–96.

———. "Reading Women/Women Reading: The Making of Learned Women in Antebellum America." *Reading Acts: U.S. Readers' Interactions with Literature, 1800–1950.* Ed. Barbara Ryan and Amy M. Thomas. Knoxville: U of Tennessee P, 2002. 53–78.

———. *Private Woman, Public Stage: Literary Domesticity in Nineteenth-Century America.* New York: Oxford UP, 1984.

Kelley, Wyn. "'I'm Housewife Here': Herman Melville and Domestic Economy," *Melville Society EXTRACTS* 98 (Sept. 1994): 7–10.

———. *Melville's City: Literary and Urban Form in Nineteenth-Century New York.* New York: Cambridge UP, 1996.

———. "'My Literary Thirst': Augusta Melville and the Melville Family Correspondence." *Resources for American Literary Study* 25.1 (1999): 46–56.

———. "*Pierre*'s Domestic Ambiguities." *The Cambridge Companion to Herman Melville.* Ed. Robert S. Levine. Cambridge, UK: Cambridge UP, 1998. 91–113.

Kellner, Robert Scott. "Slaves and Shrews: Women in Melville's Short Stories." *University of Mississippi Studies in English* 5 (1984/1987): 297–310.

———. "Toads and Scorpions: Women and Sex in the Writings of Herman Melville." Diss. U. of Massachusetts, 1977.

Kennedy, Joyce, and Frederick Kennedy. "Additions to *The Melville Log.*" *Melville Society EXTRACTS* 31 (Sept. 1977): 4–8.

———. "Elizabeth and Herman." *Melville Society EXTRACTS* 33 (Feb. 1978): 4–11.

———. "Elizabeth and Herman. (Part II)." *Melville Society EXTRACTS* 34 (May 1978): 3–8.

———. "Elizabeth Shaw Melville and Samuel Hay Savage, 1847–1853." *Melville Society EXTRACTS* 39 (1979): 1–7.

Kier, Kathleen. *A Melville Encyclopedia: The Novels.* New York: Whitsand Publishing, 1990.

Kirkland, Caroline. *Holidays Abroad; or, Europe from the West.* 2 vols. New York: Baker and Scribner, 1849.

Kittay, Eve Feder, and Diana T. Meyers, eds. *Women and Moral Theory*. Totowa, NJ: Rowman and Littlefield, 1987.

Klor de Alva, J. Jorge. "The Postcolonization of the (Latin)American Experience: A Reconsideration of 'Colonialism,' 'Postcolonialism,' and 'Mestizaje.'" *After Colonialism. Imperial Histories and Postcolonial Displacements.* Ed. Gyan Prakash. Princeton: Princeton UP, 1995.

Kohf, Mohja. *Western Representations of the Muslim Woman: From Termagant to Odalisque.* Austin: U of Texas P, 1999.

Kolodny, Annette. *The Land Before Her: Fantasy and Experience of the American Frontiers, 1630–1860.* Chapel Hill: U of North Carolina P, 1984.

———. *The Lay of the Land: Metaphor as Experience and History in American Life and Letters.* Chapel Hill: U of North Carolina P, 1975.

Kring, Walter Donald, and Jonathan S. Carey, "Two Discoveries Concerning Herman Melville." *Proceedings of the Massachusetts Historical Society* 87 (1975): 11–15.

Kuebrich, David. "Melville's Doctrine of Assumptions: The Hidden Ideology of Capitalist Production in 'Bartleby.'" *New England Quarterly* 69.3 (Sept. 1996).

Laertius, Diogenes. *Lives of Eminent Philosophers.* Vol. 2. Trans. R. D. Hicks. Cambridge, MA: Harvard UP, 1958.

Lancaster, June. *Removal Aftershock: The Seminole Struggle to Survive in the West, 1836–1866.* Knoxville: U of Tennessee P, 1994.

Lauter, Paul. "Melville Climbs the Canon." Rpt. in *From Walden Pond to Jurassic Park: Activism, Culture, and American Studies.* New Americanists Series. Ed. Donald E. Pease. Durham, NC: Duke UP, 2001. 199–220.

Lawrence, D. H. *Studies in Classic American Literature.* 1923. Rpt. Harmondsworth, UK: Penguin Books, 1971.

Leverenz, David. *Manhood and the American Renaissance.* Ithaca, NY: Cornell UP, 1989.

Levine, Robert S. *Conspiracy and Romance: Studies in Brockden Brown, Cooper, Hawthorne, and Melville.* Cambridge, UK: Cambridge UP, 1989.

———. "Pierre's Blackened Hand." *Leviathan* 1.1 (1999): 23–44.

———, ed. *The Cambridge Companion to Herman Melville.* Cambridge, UK: Cambridge UP. 1998, 1999.

Lewis, Paul. "'Lectures or a Little Charity': Poor Visits in Antebellum Literature and Culture." *New England Quarterly* 73.2 (June 2000): 246–73.

Leyda, Jay. *The Melville Log: A Documentary Life of Herman Melville, 1819–1891.* 2 vols. New York: Harcourt Brace, 1951. Rpt. with supplementary material. New York: Gordian, 1969.

Litman, Vicki Halper. "The Cottage and the Temple: Melville's Symbolic Use of Architecture." *American Quarterly* 21.3 (1969): 630–38.

Littig, Beate. *Feminist Perspectives on Environment and Society.* New York: Prentice-Hall, 2001.

The London Carcanet. Containing Passages from the Most Distinguished Writers. From the Second London Edition. New York: Peabody, 1831.

López Liquete, Maria Felisa. "Melville's Failure and Success." *Reden* 9 (1995): 45–53.

———. *Presencia-ausencia de la mujer en la obra de Melville.* Bilbao: Universidad del País Vasco, 1996.

Lorant, Laurie Jean. "Herman Melville and Race: Themes and Imagery." Diss. New York U, 1972.

Lucena Salmoral, Manuel de. *Piratas, bucaneros, filibusteros y corsarios en América*. Madrid: Mapfre, 1992.

Macherey, Pierre. *Literature in the Modern World: Critical Essays and Documents*. Ed. Dennis Walder. New York: Oxford UP, 1990

Machor, James L. "Historical Hermeneutics and Antebellum Fiction: Gender, Response Theory, and Interpretive Contexts." *Readers in History: Nineteenth-Century American Literature and the Contexts of Response*. Baltimore: Johns Hopkins UP, 1993. 54–84.

Macpherson, C. B. *The Political Theory of Possessive Individualism: Hobbes to Locke*. London: Oxford UP, 1962.

Maddox, Lucy. *Removals: Nineteenth-Century American Literature and the Politics of Indian Affairs*. New York: Oxford UP, 1991.

Mahar, William J. *Behind the Burnt Cork Mask: Early Blackface Minstrelsy and Antebellum American Popular Culture*. Urbana: U of Illinois P, 1999.

Mailloux, Steven. *Interpretive Conventions: The Reader in the Study of American Fiction*. Ithaca, NY: Cornell UP, 1982.

———. "Misreading as a Historical Act: Cultural Rhetoric, Bible Politics, and Fuller's 1845 Review of Douglass's *Narrative*." *Readers in History: Nineteenth-Century American Literature and the Contexts of Response*. Ed. James L. Machor. Baltimore: Johns Hopkins UP, 1993. 3–31.

———. *Rhetorical Power*. Ithaca, NY: Cornell UP 1989.

Markels, Julian. "The *Moby-Dick* White Elephant." *American Literature* 66 (Mar. 1994): 105–22.

Marovitz, Sanford E. "Ahab's 'Queenly Personality' and Melville's Art." *Melville Society EXTRACTS* 65 (Feb. 1986): 1–9.

Marr, Timothy W. "Mastheads and Minarets: Islamic Architecture in Melville's Writings." *Melville "Among the Nations": Proceedings of an International Conference; Volos, Greece, July 2–6, 1997*. Ed. Sanford E. Marovitz and A. C. Christodoulou. Kent, OH: Kent State UP, 2001. 472–84.

Marshall, Peter. *Nature's Web*. Armonk, NY: M. E. Sharpe, Inc., 1966.

Martin, Robert K. *Hero, Captain, and Stranger: Male Friendship, Social Critique and Literary Form in the Sea Novels of Herman Melville*. Chapel Hill: U of North Carolina P, 1986.

Martínez Díaz, Nelson. *La independencia hispanoamericana*. Madrid: Biblioteca Historia 16, 1989.

McFarland, Philip. *Sea Dangers: The Affair of the Somers*. New York: Schocken Books, 1985.

McMaster-Harrison, June. "'What Hast Thou Done With Her?' Analogical Clues to the Lost Feminine." *Canadian Woman Studies/Les Cahiers de la Femme* 8.1 (1987): 49–53. Rpt 11.3 (1991): 83–86.

———. *Billy Budd, Sailor: An Inside Narrative*. Ed. Harrison Hayford and Merton M. Sealts Jr. Chicago: Chicago UP, 1962.

———. *Journal of a Visit to London and the Continent: 1849–1850*. Ed. Eleanor Melville Metcalf. Cambridge, MA: Harvard UP, 1948.

———. *Moby-Dick; or, The Whale*. Ed. Luther S. Mansfield and Howard P. Vincent. New York: Hendricks House, 1952.

Melville, Herman. *Billy Budd, Sailor: An Inside Narrative.* Ed. Harrison Hayford and Merton M. Sealts Jr. Chicago UP, 1962.

———. *Journal of a Visit to London and the Continent: 1849–1850.* Ed. Eleanor Melville Metcalf. Cambridge, MA: Harvard UP, 1948.

———. *Moby-Dick: or, The Whale.* Ed. Luther S. Mansfield and Howard P. Vincent. New York: Hendricks House, 1952.

———. *Poems.* New York: Russell and Russell, 1963.

———. *Weeds and Wildings, Chiefly; with a Rose or Two, by Herman Melville: Reading Text and Genetic Text.* Ed. Robert Charles Ryan. Evanston, IL: Northwestern UP, 1967.

———. *The Writings.* Ed. Harrison Hayford, Hershel Parker, and G. Thomas Tanselle. Evanston, IL: Northwestern UP and the Newberry Library. 1968–. [So far, including *Typee; Omoo; Mardi; Redburn; White-Jacket; Moby-Dick; Pierre; Israel Potter; The Piazza Tales and Other Prose Pieces, 1839–1860; The Confidence-Man; Clarel; Correspondence; Journals.*]

The Melville Collection. The Newberry Library, Chicago.

The Melville Family Papers. The New York Public Library.

Memoirs of Anne C. L. Botta. Written by her Friends. With Selections from Her Correspondence and from her Writings in Prose and Poetry. New York: J. Selwin Tait and Sons, 1894.

Merchant, Carolyn. *Reinventing Eden: The Fate of Nature in Western Culture.* New York: Routledge, 2003.

Metcalf, Eleanor Melville. *Herman Melville: Cycle and Epicycle.* Cambridge, MA: Harvard UP, 1953. Rpt. Westport, CT: Greenwood, 1970.

Milder, Robert. "Melville and the Avenging Dream." *The Cambridge Companion to Herman Melville.* Ed. Robert S. Levine. Cambridge, UK: Cambridge UP, 1998. 250-78.

———. "Melville Criticism in the 1970s; or, Who's Afraid of Wellek and Warren." *Melville Society EXTRACTS* 43 (Sept. 1980): 4–7.

———. "Old Man Melville: The Rose and the Cross," *Melville Society EXTRACTS* 117 (July 1999): 15–16.

Miles, Robert. "'Tranced Griefs': Melville's *Pierre* and the Origins of the Gothic." *ELH* 66 (1999): 157–77.

Miller, Angela. "Everywhere and Nowhere: the Making of the National Landscape." *American Literary History* 4.2 (1992): 207–29.

Miller, Edwin Haviland. *Melville: A Biography.* New York: George Braziller, 1975.

Mitchell, Bruce Eardley. "Women and the Male Quester in Herman Melville's *Typee, Mardi,* and *Pierre.*" Diss. Northwestern U, 1979.

Mitchell, Donald Grant (Ik Marvel). *Reveries of a Bachelor; or, A Book of the Heart.* New York: Baker and Scribner, 1851.

Montiglio, Silvia. *Silence in the Land of Logos.* Princeton, NJ: Princeton UP, 2000.

Moore, Richard S. *That Cunning Alphabet: Melville's Aesthetics of Nature.* Amsterdam: Rodopi, 1982.

Morales Padrón, Francisco. *Historia de España: América Hispana. Las Nuevas Naciones.* Madrid. Editorial Gredos, 1986.

More, Hannah. *Strictures on Women's Education. The Works of Hannah More.* Vol. 1. New York: Harper Bros., 1848.

Morrison, Toni. *Playing in the Dark: Whiteness and the Literary Imagination.* Cambridge, MA: Harvard UP, 1992.

———. "Unspeakable Things Unspoken: The Afro-American Presence in American Literature." *Michigan Quarterly Review* 28 (1989): 1–34.
Mumford, Lewis. *Herman Melville: A Study of His Life and Vision.* New York: Harcourt, Brace and World, 1929. Rev. ed. London: Secker and Warburg, 1963.
Murray, Henry A. "Introduction." *Pierre; or, the Ambiguities.* Ed. Henry A. Murray. New York: Hendricks House, 1949. xiii–ciii.
Mushabac, Jane. *Melville's Humor: A Critical Study.* Hamden, CT: Archon Books, 1981.
Naslund, Sena Jeter. *Ahab's Wife; or, The Star-Gazer.* New York: William Morrow, 1999.
Nelson, Dana. *National Manhood: Capitalist Citizenship and the Imagined Fraternity of White Men.* Durham, NC: Duke UP, 1998.
Nelson, Raymond J. "The Art of Herman Melville: The Author of *Pierre.*" *Yale Review* 59 (1970): 197–204.
Newbury, Colin. *Tahiti Nui: Change and Survival in French Polynesia, 1767–1945.* Honolulu: U of Hawai'i P, 1980.
Newbury, Michael. *Figuring Authorship in Antebellum America.* Palo Alto, CA: Stanford UP, 1997.
Newman, Lea Bertani Vozar. "Marginalia as Revelation: Melville's 'Lost' Copy of Dante and a Private Purgatorial Note." *Melville Society EXTRACTS* 92 (Mar. 1993): 4.
———. "Melville's 'Bell-Tower' Revisited: A Story of Female Revenge." *Melville Society EXTRACTS* 65 (February 1986): 11–14.
———. *A Reader's Guide to the Short Stories of Herman Melville.* Old Tappan, NY: Macmillan, 1986.
Nichols, Elisabeth B. "'Blunted Hearts': Female Readers and Printed Authority in the Early Republic." *Reading Acts: U.S. Readers' Interactions with Literature, 1800–1950.* Eds. Barbara Ryan and Amy M. Thomas. Knoxville: U of Tennessee P, 2002. 1–28.
Nixon, Nicola. "Compromising Politics and Herman Melville's *Pierre.*" *American Literature* 69 (1997): 719–41.
Oates, Joyce Carol. Introduction. *American Gothic Tales.* New York: Penguin, 1996. 1–9.
O'Malley, Therese. Introduction. *Treatise on the Theory and Practice of Landscape Gardening.* By Andrew Jackson Downing. Washington, DC: Dumbarton Oaks, 1991. v–xii.
Onís, Jose de. *Melville y el mundo hispánico (Melville and the Hispanic World).* Puerto Rico: Editorial Universitaria de Puerto Rico, Colección UPREX, 1974.
Osborne, Frances Cuthbert Thomas. "Family Reminiscences." *The Early Lives of Melville: Nineteenth Century Biographical Sketches and Their Authors.* Ed. Merton M. Sealts Jr. Madison: U of Wisconsin P, 1974.
Otter, Samuel. "The Eden of Saddle Meadows: Landscape and Ideology in *Pierre.*" *American Literature* 66.1 (1994): 55–81.
———. *Melville's Anatomies.* Berkeley: U of California P, 1999.
———. "The Overwrought Landscape of *Pierre.*" *Melville's Evermoving Dawn: Centennial Essays.* Ed. John Bryant and Robert Milder. Kent, OH: Kent State UP, 1997. 349–74.
Paglia, Camille. "*Moby-Dick* as Sexual Protest." *Moby-Dick.* Ed. Hershel Parker and Harrison Hayford. New York: Norton, 2002. 697–701.
Parker, Hershel. *Herman Melville: A Biography.* 2 vols. Baltimore: Johns Hopkins UP, 1996, 2002.
———. "*Moby-Dick* and Domesticity." *Critical Essays on Herman Melville's* Moby-Dick. Ed. Brian Higgins and Hershel Parker. New York: G. K. Hall, 1992. 545–62.

———. *Reading* Billy Budd. Evanston, IL: Northwestern UP, 1990.

———, ed. *Pierre; or, the Ambiguities: The Kraken Edition*. Illus. Maurice Sendak. New York: HarperCollins, 1995.

Parker, William N. *Europe, America, and the Wider World: Essays on the Economic History of Western Capitalism*. Vol. 2. Cambridge, UK: Cambridge UP, 1991.

Pattee, Fred Lewis. *The Feminine Fifties*. New York: D. Appleton-Century, 1940.

Patterson, Orlando. *Slavery and Social Death: A Comparative Study*. Cambridge, MA: Harvard UP, 1982.

Patterson-Black, Gene. "On Herman Melville." *American Novelists Revisited: Essays in Feminist Criticism*. Boston: G. K. Hall, 1982. 107–42.

Penry, Tara. "Sentimental and Romantic Masculinities in *Moby-Dick* and *Pierre*." *Sentimental Men: Masculinity and the Politics of Affect in American Culture*. Ed. Mary Chapman and Glenn Handler. Berkeley: U of California P, 1999. 226–43.

Person, Leland S. *Aesthetic Headaches: Women and a Masculine Poetics in Poe, Melville, and Hawthorne*. Athens: U of Georgia P, 1988.

Person, Leland S., Jr. "Melville's Cassock: Putting on Masculinity in *Moby-Dick*." *ESQ: A Journal of the American Renaissance* 40.1 (1994): 1–26.

Petruilionis, Sandra Harbert. "Re-Reading 'Bachelors and Maids': Melville as Feminist?" *Melville Society EXTRACTS* 110 (Sept. 1997): 1, 5–10.

Pinnegar, Fred. "Women, Marriage, and Sexuality in the Work of Herman Melville: A Cultural/Gender Study." Diss. U of Arizona, 1990.

Plumwood, Val. *Feminism and the Mastery of Nature*. New York: Routledge, 1993.

Poe, Edgar Allan. "Catharine Maria Sedgwick." "The Literati of New York City" (1846). *Edgar Allan Poe: Essays and Reviews*. Ed. G. R. Thompson. New York: Library of America, 1984. 1201–4.

"The Poetry of Spanish America." *North American Review*. 68.142 (Jan. 1849): 129–60.

Porter, David. *Journal of a Cruise*. 1815. Annapolis, MD: Naval Institute Press, 1986.

Post-Lauria, Sheila. *Correspondent Colorings: Melville in the Marketplace*. Amherst: U of Massachusetts P, 1996.

Pratt, Annis. *Dancing with Goddesses: Archetypes, Poetry, and Empowerment*. Bloomington: Indiana UP, 1994.

Pratt, Louise. *Imperial Eyes: Travel Writing and Transculturation*. London: Routledge, 1992.

Price, Martin. "The Picturesque Moment." *From Sensibility to Romanticism*. Ed. Frederick W. Hilles and Harold Bloom. New York: Oxford UP, 1965. 259–92.

Puente Candamo, José A. de la. *La independencia del Perú*. Madrid: Mapfre, 1992.

Puett, Amy Elizabeth. "Melville's Wife: A Study of Elizabeth Shaw Melville." Diss. Northwestern U, 1969.

Pulsifer, Janice Goldsmith. "Gail Hamilton, 1833–1896." *Essex Institute Historical Collections*. Salem, MA: Essex Institute Press, 1968. 165–217.

Ra'ad, Basem L. "'The Encantadas' and 'The Isle of the Cross': Melvillean Dubieties, 1853–54." *American Literature* 63.2 (June 1991): 317–23.

Radway, Janice A. "Reading Is Not Eating: Mass-Produced Literature and the Theoretical, Methodological, and Political Consequences of a Metaphor." *Book Research Quarterly* 2 (Fall 1986): 7–29.

———. *Reading the Romance: Women, Patriarchy, and Popular Literature*. Chapel Hill: U of North Carolina P, 1984.

Ramsey, William M. "'Touching' Scenes in *The Confidence-Man*." *ESQ: A Journal of the American Renaissance* 25.1 (1979): 37–62.

Razack, Sherene H. *Looking White People in the Eye: Gender, Race, and Culture in Courtrooms and Classrooms*. Toronto: U of Toronto P, 1998.

Renker, Elizabeth. "Herman Melville, Wife-Beating, and the Written Page." *American Literature* 66 (Mar. 1994): 123–50.

———. *Strike Through the Mask: Herman Melville and the Scene of Writing*. Baltimore: Johns Hopkins UP, 1996.

Reynolds, David S. *Beneath the American Renaissance: The Subversive Imagination in the Age of Emerson and Whitman*. New York: Knopf, 1988.

Roberts, Audrey J. "The Letters of Caroline M. Kirkland." Diss. U of Wisconsin-Madison, 1976. Ann Arbor: UMI, 1976.

Roberts, Terry. "Ishmael as Phallic Narrator." *Studies in American Fiction* 20 (1992): 99–109.

Robertson-Lorant, Laurie. *Melville: A Biography*. New York: Clarkson Potter, 1996. Rpt. Amherst: U of Massachusetts P, 1998.

———. "Melville's Embrace of the Invisible Woman." *The Centennial Review* 34 (Summer 1990): 401–11.

Robillard, Douglas, ed. *The Poems of Herman Melville*. Kent, OH: Kent State UP, 2000.

Robinson, Sidney K. *Inquiry into the Picturesque*. Chicago: U of Chicago P, 1991.

Rogin, Michael Paul. *Subversive Genealogy: The Politics and Art of Herman Melville*. Berkeley: U of California P, 1979. Rpt. New York: Knopf, 1983.

Romero, Lora. "A Society Controlled by Women: An Overview." *Home Fronts: Domesticity and Its Critics in the Antebellum United States*. New Americanists Series. Ed. Donald E. Pease. Durham, NC: Duke UP, 1997. 11–34.

Rosenblatt, Louise M. *Literature as Exploration*. New York: Noble and Noble, 1968.

———. *The Reader, the Text, the Poem: The Transactional Theory of the Literary Work*. Carbondale: Southern Illinois UP, 1978.

Rourke, Constance. *American Humor: A Study of the National Character*. New York: Harcourt, Brace, 1931.

Ruskin, John. *Modern Painters*. Vol. 4. New York: Lovell, n.d.

Ryan, Barbara, and Amy M. Thomas, eds. *Reading Acts: U.S. Readers' Interactions with Literature, 1800–1950*. Knoxville: U of Tennessee P, 2002.

Salmon, Marylynn. *Women and the Law of Property in Early America*. Chapel Hill: U of North Carolina P, 1986.

Samson, John. *White Lies: Melville's Narratives of Facts*. Ithaca, NY: Cornell UP, 1989.

Sandberg, Robert Allen. "Melville's Unfinished 'Burgundy Club' Book: A Reading Edition." Diss. Northwestern U, 1989.

[Sanders, Elizabeth Elkins.] *Remarks on the "Tour around Hawaii," by the Missionaries, Messrs. Ellis, Thurston, Bishop, and Goodrich in 1823*. Salem, MA: 1848.

Sattelmeyer, Robert, and James Barbour. "The Sources and Genesis of Melville's 'Norfolk Isle and the Chola Widow." *American Literature* 50 (1978): 398–417.

Schneidman, Edwin S. "Some Psychological Reflections on the Death of Malcolm Melville." *Suicide and Life-Threatening Behavior* 6 (1976).

Schultz, Elizabeth. "Feminizing *Moby-Dick:* Contemporary Women Perform the Whale." *"Ungraspable Phantom": Essays on Moby-Dick*. Ed. John Bryant, Mary K. Bercaw Edwards, and Timothy Marr. Kent, OH: Kent State UP, 2006. 305–20.

———. "Melville's Environmental Vision in *Moby-Dick*." *ISLE: Interdisciplinary Studies on Literature and Environment* 7 (2000): 97–113.

———. "The Sentimental Subtext of *Moby-Dick:* Melville's Response to the 'World of Woe.'" *ESQ: A Journal of the American Renaissance* 42 (1996): 29–49.

———. "Visualizing Race: Images in *Moby-Dick*." *Leviathan*. 3.1 (Mar. 2001): 31–60.

Sealts, Merton M., Jr. *The Early Lives of Melville: Nineteenth-Century Biographical Sketches and Their Authors*. Madison: U of Wisconsin P, 1974.

———. *Melville's Reading*. Rev. ed. Columbia: U of South Carolina P, 1988.

Sedgwick, Catharine Maria. "The Country Cousin." *The Token*. Ed. S. G. Goodrich. Boston: Carter and Hendee, 1829. Rpt. *Stories of American Life*. Ed. Mary Russell Mitford. Vol. 1. London: H. Colburn and R. Bentley, 1830. 97–140.

———. *Hope Leslie, or, Early Times in the Massachusetts*. New York, 1827; rpt. New Brunswick, NJ: Rutgers UP, 1987.

———. *Le Bossu. Tales of Glauber-Spa*. Ed. William Cullen Bryant. New York: J. J. J. Harper, 1832. 25–108.

———. *The Linwoods; or 'Sixty Years Since' in America*. 1835. Rpt. New York: Harper and Brothers, 1873.

———. *Means and Ends, or Self-Training*. 1839. 4th. ed. Boston: Marsh, Capen, Lyon, and Webb, 1839.

———. *A New-England Tale*. 1822. Rpt. New York: Oxford UP, 1995.

———. "Old Maids." 1834. Rpt. *Old Maids: Short Stories by Nineteenth-Century U.S. Women Writers*. Boston: Pandora, 1984. 8–26.

———. *The Poor Rich Man, and the Rich Poor Man*. New York: Harper and Brothers, 1836.

———. *Stories for Young Persons*. New York: Harper and Brothers, 1841.

Sedgwick, Eve. *Epistemology of the Closet*. Berkeley: U of California P, 1990.

Seelye, John. *Melville: The Ironic Diagram*. Evanston, IL: Northwestern UP, 1996.

Sesnic, Jelena. "Melville and His Medusae: A Reading of *Pierre*." *Leviathon* 7.1 (2005): 41–54.

Sewall, Richard B. *The Life of Emily Dickinson*. New York: Farrar, Straus, and Giroux, 1980.

Shakespeare, William. *Cymbeline. Shakespeare: The Complete Works*. Ed. G. B. Harrison. New York: Harcourt, Brace, and World, 1968.

Shelley, Percy Bysshe. *Shelley: Poetical Works*. Ed. Thomas Hutchinson and G. M. Matthews. London: Oxford UP, 1979.

Shifrin, Susan, ed. *Women as Sites of Culture: Women's Roles in Cultural Formation from the Renaissance to the Twentieth Century*. Aldershot, UK: Ashgate, 2002.

Short, Bryan. *Cast by Means of Figures: Herman Melville's Rhetorical Development*. Amherst: U of Massachusetts P, 1992.

Sicherman, Barbara. "Reading and Middle-Class Identity in Victorian America." *Reading Acts: U.S. Readers' Interactions with Literature, 1800–1950*. Ed. Barbara Ryan and Amy M. Thomas. Knoxville: U of Tennessee P, 2002. 137–60.

———. "Sense and Sensibility: A Case Study of Women's Reading in Late-Victorian America." *Reading in America: Literature and Social History*. Ed. Cathy N. Davidson. Baltimore: Johns Hopkins UP, 1989. 201–25.

Silverman, Gillian. "Textual Sentimentalism: Incest and Authorship in Melville's *Pierre*." *American Literature* 74.2 (June 2002): 345–72.

Simpson, Eleanor E. "Melville and the Negro: From *Typee* to 'Benito Cereno.'" *On Melville: The Best from American Literature*. Ed. Louis J. Budd and Edwin H. Cady. Durham, NC: Duke UP, 1988.

Smith, Elizabeth Oakes. "The Seven Travellers." *Emerson's Magazine and Putnam's Monthly* 7 (Nov. 1858): 452–63.

Spark, Clare. *Hunting Captain Ahab: Psychological Warfare and the Melville Revival*. Kent, OH: Kent State UP, 2001.

Speth, Linda E. "The Married Women's Property Acts, 1839–1865: Reform, Reaction, or Revolution?" *Women and the Law*. Vol. 2. Ed. D. Kelly Weisberg. Cambridge, UK: Schenkman Publishing, 1982. 69–91.

Spivak, Gayatri C. "Can the Subaltern Speak?" *Colonial Discourse and Post-Colonial Theory*. Ed. Patrick Williams and Laura Chrisman. New York: Columbia UP, 1988. 66–111

———. *A Critique of Postcolonial Reason: Toward a History of the Vanishing Present*. Cambridge, MA: Harvard UP, 1999.

———. "Three Women's Texts and a Critique of Imperialism." *Feminisms: An Anthology of Literary Theory and Criticism*. Ed. Robyn R. Warhol and Diane Price Herndl. New Brunswick, NJ: Rutgers UP, 1997. 798–814.

Springer, Haskell, ed. *America and the Sea: A Literary History*. Athens: U of Georgia P, 1995.

———, ed. "Bartleby, the Scrivener." <www.ku.edu./~zeke/bartleby/index.html./>

Stanton, Elizabeth Cady, Susan B. Anthony, and Matilda Joslyn Gage, eds. *History of Woman Suffrage, Volume I: 1848–1861*. 1881. New York: Arno and *New York Times*, 1969.

Stein, William Bysshe. *The Poetry of Melville's Late Years: Time, History, Myth, and Religion*. Albany: SUNY P, 1970.

Sten, Christopher. "Melville and the Visual Arts: An Overview." *Savage Eye: Melville and the Visual Arts*. Ed. Christopher Sten. Kent, OH: Kent State UP, 1991.

Stewart, Charles S. *A Visit to the South Seas, in the Ship* Vincennes, *During the Years 1829 and 1830*. New York: Sleight and Robinson, 1831.

Stilgoe, John. *Borderland: Origins of the American Suburb, 1820–1939*. New Haven, CT: Yale UP, 1988.

Sturdevant, William C. "Creek into Seminole." *North American Indians in Historical Perspective*. Ed. Eleanor Burke Leacock and Nancy Oesterich Lurie. New York: Random House, 1971. 100–109.

Sweeting, Adam. *Reading Houses and Building Books: Andrew Jackson Downing and the Architecture of Popular Antebellum Literature, 1835–1855*. Hanover, NH: UP of New England, 1996.

Tanner, Tony. *Scenes of Nature, Signs of Man*. Cambridge, UK: Cambridge UP, 1987.

Taylor, Mark Lloyd. "Ishmael's (m)Other: Gender, Jesus, and God in Melville's *Moby Dick*." *The Journal of Religion* 72.3 (1972): 325–50.

Thomas, Brook. *Cross-Examinations of Law and Literature: Cooper, Hawthorne, Stowe, and Melville*. Cambridge, UK: Cambridge UP, 1987.

Thomas, Nicholas. *Marquesan Societies: Inequality and Political Transformation in Eastern Polynesia*. Oxford: Clarendon, 1990.

Tindall, George Brown, with David E. Shi. *America: A Narrative History*. Vol. 1. New York: Norton, 1992.

The Titus Munson Coan Papers. The New-York Historical Society.

Tolchin, Neal L. *Mourning, Gender and Creativity in the Art of Herman Melville.* New Haven, CT: Yale UP, 1988.

Tompkins, Jane. *Sensational Designs: The Cultural Work of American Fiction, 1790–1860.* Oxford, UK: Oxford UP, 1985.

Toner, Jennifer DiLalla. "The Accustomed Signs of the Family: Rereading Genealogy in Melville's *Pierre.*" *American Literature* 70 (1998): 237–63.

Tuthill, Louisa C. *The Boarding-School Girl.* Boston: Crosby and Nichols, 1848.

———. *I Will Be a Lady: A Book for Girls.* Cambridge, MA: Metcalf, 1844.

Tylor, E. B. *Primitive Culture: Researches into the Development of Mythology, Philosophy, Religion, Art, and Custom.* 2 vols. London: J. Murray, 1871.

Van Cromphout, Gustaaf. "*The Confidence-Man:* Melville and the Problem of Others." *Studies in American Fiction* 21 (Spring 1993): 37–50.

Wald, Priscilla. *Constituting Americans: Cultural Anxiety and Narrative Form.* Durham, NC: Duke UP, 1995.

———. "Hearing Narrative Voices in Melville's *Pierre.*" *boundary 2* 17.1 (1990): 100–132.

Wallace, James D. "Hawthorne and the 'Scribbling Women' Reconsidered." *American Literature* 62.2 (June 1990): 201–22.

Warner, Anna B. *Susan Warner ("Elizabeth Wetherell").* New York: Putnam's and Knickerbocker P, 1909.

Warren, Joyce M. *The American Narcissus: Individualism and Women in Nineteenth-Century American Fiction.* New Brunswick, NJ: Rutgers UP, 1984.

Warren, Robert Penn, ed. *Selected Poems of Herman Melville.* New York: Random House, 1967.

Watson, E. L. Grant. "Melville's Pierre." *New England Quarterly* (Apr. 1930): 195–234.

Weaver, Raymond M. *Herman Melville: Mariner and Mystic.* New York: George H. Doran, 1921.

Weidman, Bette S. "Women in Melville's Art: The Reader's Education in Feeling." *Melville Society EXTRACTS* 65 (Feb. 1986): 3–6.

Weinauer, Ellen. "Considering Possession in *The Scarlet Letter.*" *Studies in American Fiction* 29 (2001): 93–112.

———. "Plagiarism and the Proprietary Self: Policing the Boundaries of Authorship in 'Hawthorne and His Mosses.'" *American Literature* 69 (1997): 697–718.

Weinstein, Cindy. *The Literature of Labor and the Labors of Literature: Allegory in Nineteenth-Century Fiction.* Cambridge, UK: Cambridge UP, 1995.

———. "Melville, Labor, and the Discourses of Reception." *Cambridge Companion to Herman Melville.* Ed. Robert S. Levine. Cambridge, UK: Cambridge UP, 1998. 202–23.

Weiss, Philip. "Herman-Neutics." *The New York Times Magazine,* 15 Dec. 1996. 60–65, 70–72.

Welles, Orson. *Moby Dick—Rehearsed.* New York: Samuel French, 1965.

Welter, Barbara. *Dimity Convictions: The American Woman in the Nineteenth Century.* Athens: Ohio UP, 1976.

Wenke, John. "Complicating Vere: Melville's Practice of Revision in *Billy Budd.*" *Leviathan* 1.1 (Mar. 1999): 83–88.

———. "Melville's Indirection: *Billy Budd,* the genetic text, and 'the deadly space between.'" *New Essays on* Billy Budd. Ed. Donald Yannella. New York: Cambridge UP, 2002. 114–44.

Wheeler, Lawrence. "Documents: The Minutes of the Edgeworthalian Society, 1840–1844." *Indiana Magazine of History* 46 (June 1950): 179–202.

Widmer, Edward L. *Young America: The Flowering of Democracy in New York City.* New York: Oxford UP, 1999.

Wiegman, Robyn. "Melville's Geography of Gender." *American Literary History* 1.2 (1989): 735–53. Rpt. *Herman Melville: A Collection of Critical Essays.* Ed. Myra Jehlen. Englewood Cliffs, NJ: Prentice-Hall, 1994. 187–98.

Willard, Emma. *The Advancement of Female Education; or, a Series of Addresses in Favor of Establishing at Athens, Greece, a Female Seminary, especially designed to Instruct Female Teachers.* Troy, NY: Norman Tuttle, 1833.

Williams, Patrick, and Laura Chrisman, eds. *Colonial Discourse and Post-Colonial Theory.* New York: Harvester Wheatsheaf, 1993.

Williams, Stanley T. *The Spanish Background of American Literature.* 2 vols. Hamden, CT: Archon Books, 1968.

Wilson, James. *A Missionary Voyage to the Southern Pacific Ocean, 1796–1798.* 1799. Facsimile ed. Graz, Austria: Akademische Druck, 1966.

Winslow, Richard E., III, and Mark Wojnar. "Melville Reviews and Notices." *Melville Society EXTRACTS* 124 (Feb. 2003): 1–2, 12–17.

Woodson, Thomas. "'Hawthornesque Shapes': The Picturesque and the Romance." *Studies in the Novel* 23.1 (1991): 167–82.

Wright, Nathalia, ed. *Mardi and a Voyage Thither.* Putney, VT: Hendricks House, 1990.

———. *Melville's Use of the Bible.* Durham, NC: Duke UP, 1949.

Yannella, Donald, and Hershel Parker. *The Endless, Winding Way in Melville: New Charts by Kring and Carey.* Glassboro, NJ: Melville Society, 1981.

Yanella, Donald, ed. *New Essays on Billy Budd.* New York: Cambridge UP, 2002.

Yates, Frances A. *Astraea: The Imperial Theme in the Sixteenth Century.* London: Ark Paperbacks, 1975.

Young, Philip. *The Private Melville.* University Park: Pennsylvania State UP, 1993.

Young, Robert. *Postcolonialism: An Historical Introduction.* Oxford: Blackwell, 2001.

Zboray, Ronald J. *A Fictive People: Antebellum Economic Development and the American Reading Public.* New York: Oxford UP, 1993.

———, and Mary Saracino Zboray. "'Have You Read . . . ?': Real Readers and Their Responses in Antebellum Boston and Its Region." *Nineteenth-Century Literature* 52 (1997): 139–70.

Zelnick, Stephen. "Melville's 'Bartleby, The Scrivener': A Study in History, Ideology, and Literature." *Marxist Perspectives* 2 (Winter 1979/80): 74–92.

Zinn, Howard. *A People's History of the United States 1942-Present.* 1980. Rpt. New York: HarperCollins, 1995.

Zwarg, Christina. "Reading before Marx: Margaret Fuller and the *New-York Daily Tribune.*" *Readers in History: Nineteenth-Century American Literature and the Contexts of Response.* Ed. James L. Machor. Baltimore: Johns Hopkins UP, 1993. 228–58.

Contributors

Charlene Avallone, an independent scholar, co-chaired the Fourth International Melville Conference, Lahaina, Hawaii, in 2003. In addition to articles on Melville, she has published studies of Margaret Fuller, Elizabeth Palmer Peabody, Catharine Maria Sedgwick, and the American "Renaissance" critical tradition.

Peter Balaam teaches American literature at Carleton College. He is at work on a study of loss and theodicy in nineteenth-century American literature titled, in Melville's phrase, *Misery's Mathematics*.

Rita Bode is assistant professor of English literature at Trent University in Canada. She has research interests in American and British authors of the nineteenth and early twentieth centuries and has published in *Conradiana, SEL, ESQ,* and other journals.

Aileen Callahan, who teaches at Boston College, has exhibited her paintings at the National Academy of Arts, Letters Invitational, and, recently, at the New Bedford Art Museum. Her series paintings include *The Birth of Moby Dick* and *Furnace Mouth—Moby Dick*. She has received important grants and awards for her work.

Ellen Driscoll has been awarded distinguished commissions and has had numerous solo exhibitions since the 1970s. Her works in multiple media and genres have also appeared in group exhibitions and are in many public and private collections. Presently she teaches at the Rhode Island School of Design.

Juniper Ellis is associate professor of English at Loyola College in Maryland. She has written published and forthcoming articles on U.S. and Pacific literature for *PMLA, Arizona Quarterly,* and *Ariel*.

Wendy Stallard Flory is professor of English at Purdue University She has published *Ezra Pound and the Cantos: A Record of Struggle* (1980) and *The American Ezra Pound* (1989) as well as several essays on Melville. She is working on a manuscript that concerns "a new American Romance criticism."

Beverly A. Hume is associate professor of English and linguistics at Indiana

University-Purdue University in Fort Wayne, Indiana. She has written articles on nineteenth-century authors, including Melville, and is currently working on a book-length study of "the dark economy of nature" in Poe and Melville.

Wyn Kelley is a member of the literature faculty at the Massachusetts Institute of Technology. She is author of *Melville's City: Literary and Urban Form in Nineteenth-Century New York* (1996), editor of Blackwell Publisher's *Companion to Herman Melville* (2006), and associate editor of the Melville Society journal *Leviathan*. She has also published in a number of collections focused on Melville.

Maria Felisa López Liquete is the senior lecturer in American literature at the University of the Basque Country (Spain), where she specializes in gender and postcolonial studies. Her book *Presencia-ausencia de la mujer en la obra de Herman Melville (Presence-Absence of Women in Melville's Work)* was published in 1996. Her present research concerns Melville and Spain.

Timothy Marr is assistant professor in the curriculum of American studies at the University of North Carolina, Chapel Hill. He is the author of *The Cultural Roots of American Islamicism* (2006) and editor of essays in *The Oxford Historical Guide to Herman Melville* (2005) and *Leviathan*. He is co-editor of *"Ungraspable Phantom": Essays on* Moby-Dick (2006).

Aimée Picard is an award-winning, Chicago-based weaver who has shown her work in numerous solo exhibitions and group shows throughout the United States. She has often worked collaboratively with poets, and she specializes in weaving for religious organizations.

Kathleen Piercefield is a painter and printmaker who lives in Kentucky. She finds inspiration for her imagery in both literature and natural history, as is reflected in her recent series of works inspired by *Moby-Dick*.

Laurie Robertson-Lorant is the author of *Melville: A Biography* (1996, 1998) and *The Man Who Lived among the Cannibals: Poems in the Voice of Herman Melville* (2005). She is currently a visiting lecturer in the education department at the University of Massachusetts-Dartmouth.

Abby Schlachter Langdon, while raising a family in Ohio, experiments with a variety of media in her artwork. Her most recent experiment involved textiles.

Elizabeth Schultz, professor emerita at the University of Kansas, is a founding member of the Melville Society Cultural Project and curator of several Melville exhibitions. She is the author of *Unpainted to the Last:* Moby-Dick *and Twentieth-Century American Art* (1995), *Shoreline: Seasons at the Lake* (2001), and articles on American and Japanese writers.

Haskell Springer is professor emeritus at the University of Kansas. He has published books, articles, and on-line editions in American literature, including *America and the Sea* (1995) and a hypertext "Bartleby, the Scrivner." He is co-editing the new Longman's Critical Edition of *Moby-Dick*.

Ellen Weinauer is associate professor of English at the University of Southern Mississippi. She co-edited *American Culture, Canons, and the Case of Elizabeth Stoddard* (2003) and has published articles on Hawthorne, Melville, and Stoddard, among others.

Index

abandonment: and female characters of Melville, 67; of Isabel (*Pierre*), 145; of narrator in "Uncle Christopher's," 87; of women, 64

abuse, domestic, 82, 83; in *Omoo*, 175

Acushnet, 169, 228n10

Adam: images of in writing by Melville, 231; banishment as unjust, 241; union of with Eve, 245

Adler, Joyce Sparer, 9, 14; dramatizations of, 13; on feminine presence in *Moby-Dick*, 194

"After the Pleasure Party" (Melville), 4, 8, 6, 245–46

"Agatha Story, The" (Melville), 227n8

Albany Female Academy, 44

Albany Young Men's Association: and women writers, 51, 58n19

American Literature, 8

American Novelists Revisited (Patterson-Black), 7

American Renaissance: artists of, 6; male scholars of reading Melville, 7

Anderson, Charles Roberts, 101–4, 116nn5, 13

Anderson, Laurie, 13

"Angel O' the Age" (Melville), 248n9

Anthony, Susan B., 4

"Apple-Tree Table, The" (Melville), 5

Architecture of Country Houses, The (Downing), 60

Arcturian (whaleship) (*Mardi*), 239

Armstrong, Clarissa Chapman: on *Typee*, 48

Arrowhead: as center of literary production of Melville, 230; life at for Melville family, 20, 27, 28, 106, 181; renovations of, 61, 62. *See also* Berkshires

Arvin, Newton, 7; on gothic and Melville, 159n4; on Isabel (*Pierre*), 149

authorship: female, 7; male, 6, 7; in *Pierre*, 141–42, 152, 153, 160n15; of Pierre and Melville, 158n3; possessive individualism of Pierre through, 156–57; self-actualization of authors, 202–3; as theme in *Pierre*, 133, 136–37, 140n12; trials of, 125–26; and writing of Gail Hamilton, 105

Bachelor (ship): Pacific island women aboard, 4

Bailey, Gamaliel: as employer of Hamilton, 105

Baillie, Joanna, 51

Barber, Patricia, 94, 97n11

"Bartleby, the Scrivener" (Melville): anxieties of lawyer-narrator, 85, 94–95; Bartleby as wage slave, 89; compared to "Uncle Christopher's," 82, 83, 84; death of Bartleby, 85, 95, 96; feminization of Bartleby,

273

"Bartleby, the Scrivener" (*cont.*)
    67, 94, 95; Ginger Nut, 89; homosexuality, 97n11; hypocrisy of lawyer-narrator, 86–87, 92; lawyer-narrator and Bartleby, 92, 93, 96, 97n5; literary marketplace, 239; Nippers, 86–87, 89; office, 84; paternal, 86–87, 89; sentimentality, 96; starvation, 92, 93, 97n4; treatment of employees, 89, 90; Turkey, 86, 87, 89, 90, 92; use of gothic, 142
Basch, Norma, 160n12
Battle of the Books, The (Hamilton), 107
Battle-Pieces (Melville), 6, 20
Beecher, Catherine: on maternal, 56n1, 197–98n5
Beecher, Lyman: and fear of Catholicism, 227n7
Beggar's Opera, The (Gay), 238
Bellipotent (ship), 65, 108, 110
"Bell-Tower, The" (Melville), 9
Bellows, Henry Whitney, 15, 30, 31
"Benito Cereno" (Melville): colonialism, 215; feminization of Benito, 67; imperialism, 215; reinterpretation of in art, 13; sealing industry, 198n10; use of gothic, 142
Bennett, James Gordon, 102, 103
Bentley, Richard, 122
Bercaw, Mary K. *See* Edwards, Mary K. Bercaw
Berkshires, 60, 68, 181, 230; and domestic style, 63; landscape of in *A New-England Tale*, 71; Melville at, 79n10; and picturesque scenery, 64; settlement of, 69. *See also* Arrowhead.
Berthold, Dennis, 9
Bible: allusions, 63, 231, 235, 241, 243, 245, 249n22
Billy Budd, Sailor (An Inside Narrative) (Melville), 9, 13, 33, 100, 244; Billy Budd, 5, 110, 115, 244; Captain Edward Fairfax Vere, 98, 99, 100, 103, 110, 115; Claggart, 99, 102, 110; compared to "The Murder of Philip Spencer," 98, 100, 101, 103, 107, 110, 112–13; ethic of care, 110, 115; and feminist ethics, 110; femininity in man, 99, 100; female intercession, 110, 111–12; irony, 113; and masculinist justice, 110, 112, 115; masculinity, 98; maternal, 108, 110, 112; paternal, 110; Red Whiskers, 108–9; revisions of, 99, 100–101, 115, 116n2; sources of, 104–5; unreliability of texts and words, 114–15

"Birth-mark, The" (Hawthorne), 5
Blackstone, William, 145–46, 149, 152, 155, 160n12
Blaine, James G., 105
blasphemy: and Melville, 241, 251n47
Blumenbach, Johann Friedrich, 235, 249n18
Boarding-School Girl, The (Tuthill), 46
body, female: display of in *Typee*, 169; as passive subject, 224; presence and absence of, 170; as sign of power, 165, 175; threatening to male self in *Pierre*, 154; in works of Melville, 167
Bowles, Caroline, 51
Branch, Watson G., 217, 227n8
Bremer, Fredericka, 79n3
"Bridegroom Dick" (Melville), 112
"Bride of Abydos, The" (Byron), 249n14
Briggs, Charles F., 228n14
Broderick, Warren F., 35n12
Brodhead, Richard, 148, 181, 182, 184, 205
Brown, Gillian, 9, 148, 157, 160nn 15, 16; on Bartleby, 94, 97n4, 97n13
Bryant, John: on Melville and picturesque, 72–73
Bryant, William Cullen, 79nn3, 8, 200
buccaneers: stealing of Spanish treasures by, 214–15
Buell, Lawrence, 200–201
Burke, Edmund, 218
Burnett, Jonathan, 146–47
Butler, Sharon, 13
Byron, Lord: influence on Melville, 234, 235, 239

Cabri, Jean Baptiste, 164
Callahan, Aileen, 13
Calvinism, 64, 69, 70, 71
Camōens, Luis de: poetry of, 31
capitalism, 82, 85, 90
Carax, Leos, 13–14
Carson, Rachel, 188
Cary, Alice, 4, 82, 83, 88, 89, 96n1. *See also individual titles.*
Cary, Phoebe, 4
Castle of Otranto, The (Walpole): as influence on *Pierre*, 144, 149
Castronovo, Russ, 154
Catholicism, 214–17, 222, 227n7
Caucasus, 235
Channing, William Ellery, 47
Charvat, William, 43

274   Index

Chase, Richard, 7
Chesbro, Caroline, 59n26
Child, Lydia Maria, 48, 52, 56n1
Chola/Cholo, 213, 214, 219, 220
Christianity, 106, 115, 221, 233; as culture of modesty, 165; and democracy, 82; ethic of care, 110; influence of in the Pacific, 175; linked to whiteness and corruption, 218; in *Omoo*, 175–76; and sentimentality, 241; and sexuality of Ideea (*Omoo*), 175–76; view of heaven, 234; William Ellis and, 170
Circassia, 235, 236–37, 241–42, 244
Clarel (Melville), 6, 31, 235; Eastern femininity, 250n40; Rolfe's visit to island paradise, 238; Ruth, 241–42
class: in *Clovernook*, 96n3; consciousness of, 82, 85, 86–87; and Hunilla, 214; inequities of, 82, 83; and "The Piazza," 76, 77; and relationships, 86
Clovernook (Cary), 83, 96n3
Coan, Titus Munson, 37n57
Coffler, Gail, 8
Coleridge, Samuel Taylor, 131, 243; influence on Melville, 235
colonialism, 227n3; in "The Encantadas," 213, 214, 215, 226; impact of, 220; and imperialism, 215; in *Omoo*, 171, 173, 175; and queen in *Typee*, 167; in *Typee*, 165, 168, 170, 171, 172; in writing of Melville, 179, 217
Commentaries on the Laws of England (Blackstone), 145–46
Confidence-Man: His Masquerade, The (Melville), 5, 201, 206–8, 210–11; Black Guinea, 201–2, 203, 204, 212n5; charitable lady, 207, 208; clay-eating, 200, 202; Cosmopolitan, 201, 208, 209; environment of, 199, 208; *Fidele*, 199–200, 201, 204; Goneril, 199–209, 210, 211, 212n2; Henry Roberts, 201, 204, 209; John Ringman, 199, 203–5, 207; John Truman, 201, 203; Judge Hall, 210–11; nature, 199, 201, 211; oppression, 200; Pitch, 208–9; and racism, 199; satire, 199, 203; sexuality, 200; "The Indian Hater" as influence on, 59n24; True Indian Doctor, 208; touching scenes, 200, 202, 204, 207; vision of, 201
Cooper, James Fenimore, 46, 53, 193, 104–5, 200

Corinne (de Staël), 52
"Country Cousin, The" (Sedgwick), 53–54
coverture, 30, 145, 146, 152, 155
Cowen, Walker, 16
Cox, Catherine, 205
creativity, 126–27; as feminine, 9, 202; and poverty, 121; questioned by Melville in *Pierre*, 52, 126, 127; as way of overcoming cultural restrictions, 232
Cronon, William, 200
cross-dressing: in minstrel shows, 203–4
cross-gender: in *Pierre*, 66; in "The Paradise of Bachelors and the Tartarus of Maids," 66
Cult of True Womanhood, 4, 91, 94
Curtis, George William 79n3

Damascus, waters of in *Omoo*, 247, 249n25
Damon, S. Foster, 134
Dana, Richard Henry, 104–5
Dante Alighieri: influence on Melville, 33; use of in *Pierre*, 137–38
Darwin, Charles: influence on Melville, 214
Davidson, Cathy N., 56n3
Davis, Merrell, 46
Davis, Natalie Zemon, 190
DeLamotte, Eugenia, 159n4
De Marco, John, 35n9
Dening, Greg, 164
de Staël, Madame, 4, 52
Devil-Dam: ship in *Moby-Dick*, 186
"Devotion of the Flowers to Their Lady, The" (Melville), 245, 251n47
Dewey, Mary, 61
Dickens, Charles, 19, 50
Dickinson, Emily, 49
Dillingham, William, 139n3, 212n10
Dimock, Wai Chee, 9, 104, 151
Direnç, Dilek, 8
Ditson, George Leighton, 235–36
Divine Comedy, The (Dante): Melville's copy of, 33
domesticity, 9, 63, 75, 85, 59n26; in "Bartleby, the Scrivener," 94; conventions of, 230; Downing on, 76; and Goneril, 205; ideology of, 31; and individualism, 88; and landscapes, 69; and Melville, 229, 230–31; in *Moby-Dick*, 182; in "The Murder of Philip Spencer," 108; in *A New-England Tale*, 70; on *Pequod*, 184, 194; in *Pierre*, 160n15; rural, 74, 79n3; and Sedgwick, 60–62; in "A

Index   275

domesticity (cont.)
  Spasm of Sense," 105–6, 107; in *White-Jacket*, 26
"Don Juan" (Byron): use of by Melville, 239
Douglass, Ann, 7
Dow, Jane, 19
Downing, Andrew Jackson, 60–61, 62, 76, 77, 78n2, 79n3
Driscoll, Ellen, 13
Dryden, Edgar, 158–59n3
Duberstein, Larry, 37n48
Duyckinck, Evert and George, 23, 24, 27, 79n10, 141; and Melville, 53, 141, 151
Dwight, Timothy, 47

Eckert, Rinde, 13
ecofeminism, 184–85, 196, 212n3; in *The Confidence-Man*, 209; and significance of Goneril, 200; and whale encounter in *Moby-Dick*, 194
Eden: orientalization of, 251n46; as paradise, 236; Peristan based on, 233–34; in South Seas, 237–38; visions of by Melville, 237
Edwards, Mary K. Bercaw, 8, 35n11, 103
Egan, Hugh, 113
Egan, Ken, 149, 159n9
Egan, Phillip, 148
Ellis, Sarah, 43
Ellis, William, 45, 170, 177
Emerson, George B., 21, 45, 57n8
Emerson, Ralph Waldo, 21; influence on American culture, 193
"Encantadas, The" (Melville): ambiguity of erotic scenes, 224; buccaneers, 217; colonialism, 213, 214, 215, 220, 226; English and Spanish in names, 220–21; epigraphs of, 226n1; imperialism, 215; rape, 220; sent to *Putnam's Monthly Magazine*, 217; "Sketch Eighth: Norfolk Isle and the Chola Widow," 4, 8, 67, 213–15, 219–26, 228n23; "Sketch Ninth: Hood's Isle and the Hermit Oberlus," 214, 217; "Sketch Seventh: Charles' Isle and the Dog-King," 213, 214, 217, 219, 220; "Sketch Sixth: Barrington Isle and the Buccaneers," 217; "Sketch Tenth," 213, 216, 220; Spanish power, 217; symbols of Eve, 232; writing of, 227n8
"Enviable Isles, The" (Melville), 241
"Epistle to a Lady" (Pope): in *Omoo* (Melville), 176
ethic of care, 109, 110, 114, 115

Euridice, 6
Eve, 34, 231, 241; female disorderliness of in Garden of Eden, 190; images of in writing of Melville, 231; as muse, 231; symbolism of, 231, 232

Faerie Queen, The (Spenser), 226n1; Melville's use of, 239
Falstaff (Shakespeare), 167, 180n6
Fatu Hiva: sailors living on, 164
Fayaway, 238; parody of, 48
femininity, 7, 46–47, 56n1, 66, 95, 146, 230; in "Bartleby, the Scrivener," 94; in *Billy Budd, Sailor*, 99, 100, 108, 110; and Circassian vision of Melville, 241; and de Staël, 52; and domestic ideology, 31; in *Clarel*, 250n40; in *Moby-Dick*, 182, 194; of moon in "The Piazza," 75; in *Pierre*, 147, 148, 150; in *Omoo*, 174–75; in deleted passages from *Typee*, 238
feminism, 8, 66–67
Fern, Fanny, 105, 107
Fetterley, Judith, 57n8, 83, 96n2, 96n3
Fiedler, Leslie: on *Pierre*, 134
Fields, James T., 107
"Figure-Head, The" (Melville), 33
Findlay, Alison, 222, 228n19
Finkelstein, Dorothee Metlitzki, 9, 248
"First Fragment" (Melville), 234
flowers: fragrance of in Eden, 233–34; in *Mardi* (Melville), 240; use of by Melville, 244, 245
Foley, Barbara, 97n14
Folger (née Morrel), Mary, 5
Forester, Fanny, 57n9
Foster, Elizabeth, 8, 212n8
Fox, Warwick, 200
"Fragments from a Writing Desk" (Melville), 5, 52, 231, 234
"Fragments of a Lost Gnostic Poem of the Twelfth Century" (Melville), 250n39
Franchot, Jenny, 225
Fredericks, Nancy, 9
French, the, 165, 175; claim the Marquesas Islands, 165, 166; claim Nuku Hiva, 165; claim Tahiti, 168–69, 250n29; departure of in *Typee*, 165–66; effect of on the Pacific, 177; Melville's critique of, 167–68, 174; military forces of, 164, 172
Freneau, Philip, 200
Freud, Sigmund, 7, 134, 135

Fuentes, Carlos, 228n11
Fuller, Margaret, 4, 48, 53, 57n9
Furnas, J. C., 216

Gaard, Greta, 184–85
Galápagos Islands, 214, 220–21
Gandhi, Leela, 214
Gansevoort, Catherine "Kate" (cousin), 16, 18
Gansevoort, Catherine von Schaick (grandmother), 17
Gansevoort, Guert (cousin), 101, 102, 103, 109–10, 115, 116n5
Gansevoort, Herman (uncle), 22
Gansevoort, Peter (grandfather), 125
Garcia, Wilma, 7
Garcilaso, Inca, 220
Gardner, Augustus Kinsley, 36n33
Gardner, Dan, 203–4
Garside, Peter, 80n15
Gay, John, 238
Gell, Alfred, 179n5
gender, 9, 116, 214, 232–33; in "After the Pleasure Party," 245–46; in "Bartleby, the Scrivener," 82, 94–95; in *Billy Budd, Sailor*, 98, 103, 104, 114; and Circassian longings of Melville, 240; effect of on reading practices, 42–43; and literacy, 45; and Melville's works, 10, 67; in *Moby-Dick*, 182, 187; in *Omoo*, 175; and patriarchy, 49; in *Pierre*, 148–51; of sea, 189; in "Sketch Eighth," 224; stereotypes of, 24, 124–25; in *The Confidence-Man*, 207; in "The Murder of Philip Spencer," 99, 103, 114; in "The Paradise of Bachelors and the Tartarus of Maids," 212n1; in "The Piazza," 76, 77; in "Uncle Christopher's," 82–83; of words, 220
Gifford, Ellen, 47
Gilligan, Carol, 103–4, 116
Gilman, William, 35n7
Gilmore, Michael, 85
Glendinning, Mary (*Pierre*), 126, 136, 143, 147, 151; differentiated from Isabel, 155; and gothic, 152; masculinity of, 147; as maternal, 147–48, 203; and Medusa, 212n4; as monster, 147; and ownership, 145, 147; rejection of by Pierre, 152; sentimentality and, 148; sexual power of, 154; symbolism of, 125; as termagant, 7
Glendinning, Pierre (*Pierre*), 130–31, 135–36,
156–57; on Adam and Eve, 242; authorship of, 133, 153, 156–58, 160n18; betrothal to Lucy, 241–42; creativity, 127–28; dependence on women, 97n8; difficulties in writing, 132–33; dilemma of as writer, 122; effect of Isabel on, 128–29, 138, 148–49, 154; femininity of, 147, 148, 150; financial circumstances, 122, 132; and gender consequences of submission, 149; gendered confusion, 151; as gothic subject, 157; and identity, 143–44, 151–52, 152–53; incestuous lust for Isabel, 124; loss of property, 151; on Lucy, 149, 242; marriage to Isabel, 152; moods of, 139nn5, 6; and the muse, 126; as outcast, 124; and paternal, 124, 137, 151, 152; poverty, 124; publishers, 124; sexual relationship with Isabel, 121, 123, 126, 129–30, 133, 134, 135, 136; response to sexual power, 154; sexuality of, 154; similarity to Melville, 123, 124, 127, 143, 152, 153, 158; spectralization of, 142, 148, 149–50, 151, 152, 157, 158; suicide of, 156; truth-telling by, 141–42, 152, 153
Goddu, Teresa, 142
Godey's Ladies Book, 50, 145
Goneril (Shakespeare): as termagant, 205
gothic: and Isabel, 155; and Melville, 159n4; in *Pierre*, 142, 144, 149, 152, 153–54, 156, 157
Gracia, Mathias, 179n2
Graham, Sylvester, 24
Graveling, Captain (*Moby-Dick*), 108
"Greek Slave, The" (Powers), 239
Greene, Richard T., 249–50n27
Greenwood, Grace, 48, 57n9
Griggs, George, 19
Grosz, Elizabeth, 190, 191

Haberstroh, Charles, 7
Hadfield, Andrew, 226–27n1
Hale, Sarah, 44
Hamilton, Gail, 103, 105–7; on gendered spheres, 105–6; influence on Melville, 98, 100, 101, 102, 112; on Philip Spencer, 99–100, 104; ethic of care, 114; voice of, 115–16
Handy, Willowdean Chatterson, 167, 179n5
Haraway, Donna, 199–200, 212n2
Hardwick, Elizabeth, 9
Harper brothers, 217
Harpers, 53, 59, 59n24, 65, 67, 227n8
Harper's New Monthly Magazine, 29

Index   277

Harris, John, 179n2
Harris, Susan K., 57n8
Hart, Jonathan, 220, 228n13
Hautia (*Mardi*), 7, 163, 177, 178, 179, 203
Hawaii, 50–51; in *Omoo*, 171; in *Typee*, 171
Hawthorne, Julian, 6–7
Hawthorne, Nathaniel, 6, 26, 151, 156, 229, 233, 237; and *Godey's Lady Book*, 50; influence on Melville, 140n12; as inspiration for *Moby-Dick*, 26; on *Moby-Dick*, 140n12; "neutral territory," cf. piazza of Melville, 79n4; relationship with Melville, 35n6; on Sedgwick, 53, 79n10
Hawthorne, Sophia, 29, 46, 237; conflict with James T. Fields, 107; on Melville, 29, 46
"Hawthorne and His Mosses" (Melville), 47, 160n18, 246–47
Hayford, Harrison, 99, 100, 115, 116n6
Hearts and Homes (Ellis), 43
"Hearts-of-Gold" (Melville), 241
Hemstreet, Charles, 96n1
Henderson, Andrea, 142–43
Herbert, T. Walter, 179n1
Herman Melville: A Biography (Howard), 34–35n6
hermeneutics, 42
hierarchy, 150, 184; in *Moby-Dick*, 200–201; in nature, 189; social, 69
Higgins, Brian, 142, 158n3
Hoadley, John, 20
Holidays Abroad (Kirkland), 52
Holmes, Oliver Wendell, Jr, 29
Home (Sedgwick), 65
Home Journal: on *Typee*, 47
homosexuality, 35n6; in "Bartleby, the Scrivener," 97n11; of Ishmael and Queequeg, 97n11; in *Moby-Dick*, 182, 185, 186
Hope Leslie (Sedgwick), 59n23
Horth, Lynn, 8
houri, 234, 248; description of, 233; in Muslim paradise, 233; in *Redburn*, 234; in South Seas, 238; in "The Bride of Abydos," 249n14; in "Typee Manuscript," 238; Yillah as, 240, 250n34
House of the Seven Gables, The (Hawthorne): influence on *Pierre*, 144, 150, 157, 159n6; Melville on, 156; and picturesque, 80n19; silence, 150
Howard, Leon, 248n1
Hunter, Augusta Whipple, 22

"I and My Chimney" (Melville), 5, 230
identity: based on ownership, 151; and change of marital property rights, 146–47; in *Pierre*, 147
imagery: British Romantic, 131; feminine, 183–84, 186, 187, 190–91, 194–95; feudal, 149; gothic, 157; marriage, 185; masculine, 183–84, 187, 188, 197; maternal, 184, 190, 193, 195, 197; phallic, 33, 88, 147, 148, 184, 197; phantom, 186, 187; vulvic, 33
immigration, 227n6
imperialism, 214–15, 227n4; critique of by Melville, 213, 214; in *Moby-Dick*, 200–201; in *Omoo*, 50, 180n14; of Spain, 214; in "The Encantadas," 215, 226; in *Typee*, 50, 249n22; of U.S., 214
"In a Bye-Canal" (Melville), 232
incest: in *Pierre*, 124, 133, 134, 135, 136, 154
Indian hating: in *The Confidence-Man*, 199–200, 201, 209, 210–11
individualism, 88; idea of from Emerson, 193; of men, 143; in *Pierre*, 150, 153, 156–57; possessive, 142, 151, 152, 156–57; rejection of by Isabel, 150–51
"In the Hall of Mirrors" (Melville), 246
Irigaray, Luce, 189–90
Irving, Washington, 34, 53, 79n3
Isabel (*Pierre*), 4, 53–54, 97n8, 124, 134, 155; coverture, 155; abandonment of, 145; as dispossessed, 143; effect on Pierre, 128–29, 148–49, 154, 155; face of, 127, 131, 135, 137, 138; and Glendinning line, 148; and gothic, 149, 152, 155, 157; as imagination, 121, 124, 125, 126–28, 131, 139n3; imagery of Dante, 138; marriage to Pierre, 152; masculinization of, 150; and the maternal, 137; as muse, 124; and Pierre's authorship, 153; as Pierre's imagination, 123, 124, 127, 132–33, 136; playing guitar, 132, 150, 151; as prototype of evil, 7; readings of, 121–22, 133; rejection of individualism, 150–51; relationship with Pierre, 123, 126, 129, 130, 138, 148, 150–51; relationship with Pierre as sexual, 121, 126, 133, 134, 135, 136; sexual power of, 154; as sexual "Dark Lady," 124; spectralization of, 149–50; suicide, 156; and silence, 136; as symbolic character, 121, 124, 133, 137; guitar of, 130–31
Isabel ("The Country Cousin"), 53–54
Islam, 233, 238
"Island, The" (Byron), 239

Island Queen (Sarah Ellis), 179n3
"Isle of the Cross, The" (Melville), 217, 227n8
isolation: in "Bartleby, the Scrivener," 84; in "Uncle Christopher's," 93
Israel Potter (Melville), 5, 243
Ivanhoe (Scott), 5

Jehlen, Myra, 9
John Marr and Other Sailors (Melville), 112, 116n6, 244
Johnson, Barbara, 9
Johnson, Samuel, 239
justice: in *Billy Budd, Sailor*, 98, 103, 104, 114; and ethics, 104; feminist, 99, 100, 101, 102, 116; masculinist, 107, 110, 111, 112, 115

Kakutani, Michiko, 15
Karcher, Carolyn, 9, 204, 212nn5, 9
Karlsen, Carol, 160n14
Keats, John, 248n6; influence on Melville, 125, 131–32, 136, 139n10, 235
Kelley, Wyn, 9, 26, 45, 144, 160n15, 201
Kennedy, Joyce and Frederick, 21
Kier, Kathleen, 8
King Lear (Shakespeare), 80–81n25, 200, 205
Kirkland, Caroline, 48, 49, 57n9, 58n16
Klor de Alva, Jorge, 214, 215
Kohf, Mohja, 240
Kolodny, Annette, 191
Kring, Walter Donald, 15
"Kubla Khan" (Coleridge), 131
Kuebrich, David, 85

Ladies' National Magazine, 50
Laertius, Diogenes, 209–10
LaFarge, John, 4
Lamé-Fleury, Françoise (aunt), 17
Lamia, the: celebrated by Keats and Melville, 248n6
"Lamia's Song" (Melville), 248n6
Lansing, Abraham, 18
La Reine Blanche (ship), 172
"Late-Comer, The" (Melville), 250n43
law: influence of Blackstone on, 160n12; and masculinist ethic, 104; of women's rights of ownership, 145, 160nn11, 13, 14
Lawrence, D. H., 198n8
Le Bossu (Sedgwick), 64
Lemieux, Margo, 13
Leslie, Eliza, 52

Letters on the Improvement of the Mind (Chapone), 44
Levine, Robert S., 216
Lewis, Paul, 56n1
Leyda, Jay, 34–35n6
"Lilac Land" (Melville), 34
Linwoods, The (Sedgwick), 19, 53, 55
literacy: effect of education on, 45; and gender, 45
Literary Review: review of *Pierre*, 158n1
Literary World, The, 23, 53, 141, 142, 151, 158, 233–34
Litman, Vicki Halper, 78n2
London Eclectic Review, 217
Longfellow, Fanny Appleton, 22, 48
Lorraine, Claude, 249n17
Love and Death in the American Novel (Fiedler), 134
"Lover and the Syringa-Bush, The" (Melville), 245
Lucy ("The Country Cousin"), 53–54
Lucy Ann (whaleship), 164, 169
Lynch, Ann, 44, 45, 48, 57n9
Lynch, Patty, 13

Macbeth (Shakespeare), 6, 19
MacDougall, Alma A., 8
Mackenzie, Alexander Slidell (Captain) 99, 101, 102–3, 109–10, 111, 113–14, 116n9
Macready, William, 19
Macpherson, C. B., 142
Maddox, Lucy, 207–8, 224–25, 228n21
Mailloux, Steven, 56n3
manifest destiny, 216
Marble Faun, The (Hawthorne), 28
Mardi, 20, 24–25, 27, 46, 50, 177, 215, 233; Annatoo, 7, 24, 164, 177; Donjalolo, 182; houris, 249n12; image of queen, 163; narrative focus of, 177, 178–79; narrative power of queen, 164, 177, 178, 179; orientalism, 250n36; parody, 233; Queen Hautia, 7, 163, 177, 178, 179, 203; as romantic allegory, 239–40; symbols of Eve, 232; Taji, 164, 177–79, 231, 239–40, 241–42, 243; Yillah, 7, 164, 177–79, 238, 240, 242, 250n34
Markels, Julian, 47
Marquesan Encounters (Herbert), 179n1
Marquesas Islands, 164, 165, 166, 179nn1, 2, 5; culture of, 170; in *Omoo*, 171, 176; queen and king of, 167–68; in *Typee*, 165, 171

Index   279

marriage, 78; and autonomy, 66; commentary on, 65; companionate, 44; conventional, 46; European ideas of, 168; loss of identity, 145, 146–47; Lucy (*Pierre*) as perfect type for, 149; meaning of in *Pierre*, 152

Martin, Robert K., 87, 97n13, 185

masculinity, 24, 41, 65, 67, 92, 147, 232; in *Billy Budd, Sailor*, 98; and domestic ideology, 31; in *King Lear*, 205; of lawyer-narrator ("Bartleby, the Scrivener"), 95; in *Moby-Dick*, 181; in *Pierre*, 148, 150; and socialization of women, 49; in *The Confidence-Man*, 199, 200, 202, 207; in "The Murder of Philip Spencer," 103; of words, 221; of work ethic, 230; in work of Melville, 66, 230–31

maternal, 65, 95, 183, 196, 198n5; in *Billy Budd*, 112; in *Pierre*, 128, 136, 137, 143, 145, 147–48, 151–52, 160nn15, 16; presence and absence of in whaling world, 183; in *Moby-Dick*, 182, 183, 188, 189, 191–92, 197; stepmother as, 20; in *The Confidence-Man*, 209; in "The Murder of Philip Spencer," 99, 108, 109, 110–11, 114

Mathews, Cornelius, 27

McIlroy, Daniel, 21

Medusa, 9, 202, 212n4

melodrama, 55; in *Pierre*, 52, 123, 126, 134, 138

Melvill, Allan (father): death of, 17–18, 189

Melvill, Julia Maria (cousin), 18, 20, 47

Melvill, Kate (cousin), 235, 243–44

Melvill, Maria Gansevoort (mother), 20, 44; criticism of Elizabeth Shaw Melville, 26, 27; relationship with Melville, 17, 22, 33, 189

Melvill, Mary (aunt), 47

Melvill, Robert (cousin), 25

Melvill, Thomas (grandfather), 17

Melvill, Thomas (uncle), 17–18

Melville, Allan (brother), 19, 22, 25, 181

Melville, Augusta "Gus" (sister), 18, 19–20, 31, 35n9, 44, 47; as copyist/ proofreader for Melville, 27, 93–94, 97n7, 106; correspondence of, 45; reading of 49

Melville, Elizabeth "Bessie" (daughter), 31–32, 93–94

Melville, Elizabeth "Lizzie" Shaw (wife), 16, 22, 25–28, 30–31, 34, 97n7, 138; as copyist for Melville, 93–94; education of, 21, 44, 45; finances of, 32–33; and Helen, 19, 21; influence of on *Mardi*, 46; letter to Sarah Morewood, 29–30; like Desdemona, 21; marriage of, 15, 22, 29–30, 33, 244, 247; on married life, 22, 23, 25; and moods of Melville, 18; physical abuse of, 29, 37n49; reading habits, 47, 105, 106; relationship with friends and family, 19, 20, 32; relationship with Melville, 21–22; romances of, 21; sexuality of, 24; sympathy of, 106; in *Weeds and Wildings*, 33–34, 244

Melville, Frances "Fanny" (daughter), 31, 32, 93–94

Melville, Gansevoort (son), 17, 19, 33, 45, 58n19, 189, 249n14

Melville, Herman, 30, 47, 158, 232–33; accused of insanity, 123; on birth of son, 31; blasphemy of, 241, 251n47; and Byron, 239; change of career, 242; Circassian longings/vision of, 217, 236–37, 239, 240–41, 244, 245, 246; Civil War poems of, 6, 20, 30; contempt for Protestant work ethic, 243–44; correspondence with Hawthorne, 61, 62, 230, 233, 237; on creative imagination, 138; criticism of fashion, 233; cultural restrictions of as writer, 232; dilemma of as writer, 122, 125, 126; and domesticity, 16–17, 229, 230–31; and Duyckinck brothers, 141, 151; escape of from the Taipi, 164, 249–50n27; ambivalence toward maternal, 189; father, death of, 17–18, 66; femininity in works, 46–47, 66, 234; finances of, 16, 25, 29, 30, 32–33, 65–66, 122, 230–31; and gender, 95, 125, 186, 232–33; and the gothic, 142, 159n4; Hamilton as influence, 98, 100, 101, 102, 112; Hawthorne as influence, 26, 144, 150, 151, 156, 157, 159n6, 229; heavy drinking of, 15, 29; and human evolution, 236; and imperialism, 214; influences on, 5, 34, 41–42, 45, 46, 51–52, 77, 80–81n25, 201, 205, 214, 231, 234, 235, 239; life after retirement, 244, 247; life at Arrowhead, 27–28; life in works, 35n11, 62, 63, 64; like Lear, 34; like Othello, 21; literary education of, 234; longevity of writing career, 231; male authority of, 231; marginalia of, 16; marriage of, 16–17, 22, 29–30, 33, 181, 244, 247; masculinity in work, 65, 66, 230–31; Milton as influence on, 245; and misogyny, 7, 16, 35n6, 200; moods of, 18, 29, 31, 139n6; muse of, 66; narrative power of, 179; at Nuku Hiva, 165; orientalism, 229, 230, 232–33, 235–38, 241, 243, 249n21; as outcast, 124; Pacific

280 *Index*

experience as influence on, 164, 165, 169–70, 172, 179n1, 238; and patriarchy, 159n9; piazza of, 60, 61, 62, 66, 79n5; and *Pierre*, 53, 122, 126, 129, 135, 137–38, 139n8, 140n12, 153, 241; on portrayal of female beauty, 218, 234; and publishers, 65, 217, 230; punctuation practices of, 27; reading of women's writing, 41, 42, 43, 51, 52, 56; readers of, 41–42, 47, 78, 233; relationship with contemporaries, 9, 28–29, 35n6, 37n48, 182, 237; relationship with family, 3, 22, 31–33, 189; romances of, 35n12; satire of, 232–33; and Sedgwick, 55, 64–66, 70, 79n7, 10; sexuality, 24, 232; similarity to Donjalolo (*Mardi*), 182; similarity to Pierre, 123, 124, 126, 127, 143, 152, 153, 158; Smith, H. D., as influence on, 101, 102, 116n6; South Seas fiction and life, 24, 51, 188, 237–38, 241; and spectralization, 152, 158; struggle for happiness, 230; symbolism of flowers, 218, 237, 244, 247; travels as influence on, 237; treatment of Elizabeth and Frances, 31; truth from narrative, 115; vision of paradise, 218, 237; as whaler, 217–18; Walpole as influence on, 144, 149; and women, 3–4, 16–18, 27, 67, 94, 164–65, 181, 189, 230–32, 234, 235; and women of the family, 3, 9, 24–25, 27–28, 182, 230; writing of *Moby-Dick* 61, 62, 181, 189, 229, 242–43. *See also individual titles.*

Melville (Griggs), Helen Maria (sister), 37n49, 44–45, 47, 53; as copyist/proofreader for Melville, 19, 27, 93–94, 106; education of, 18–19, 44; relationship with Melville, 19, 21

Melville (Hoadley), Catherine "Kate" (sister), 20, 44, 47, 94

Melville, Malcolm (son), 30, 31, 33, 37n52, 107, 116n12

Melville, Maria "Milie" Gansevoort (niece), 25

Melville, Sophia Thurston (sister-in-law), 22, 25, 27

Melville, Stanwix "Stannie" (son), 31, 116n12

Melville (Thomas), Frances "Fanny" Priscilla (sister), 17, 20, 31, 32, 44, 45, 47, 94

Melvillean imagination, 123, 127

Melville family: correspondence of, 16; documentation of, 30; dominated by women, 34; library of, 57n9; women of, 18, 27, 35n9, 97n7

Melville Revival, 7, 8, 123, 134

Melville Society, 14

Melville's Sources (Edwards), 139n10
Memoirs of the Literary Ladies of England, 45
Menchu, Rigoberta, 225
Merchant, Carolyn, 185
Metcalf, Eleanor Melville (granddaughter), 8, 32, 35n10, 36n35, 37n49
"Michaelmas Daisies" (Melville), 246
Milder, Robert, 42, 237
Miller, Edwin Haviland, 16, 35n6, 86
Milton: as influence on Melville, 231, 239, 245
minstrel shows, 203–4
misogyny, 6, 57n8, 199, 207; of burlesques, 203; and Melville, 35n6, 200; of Melville in marginalia, 16; of minstrel shows, 203–4; in *The Confidence-Man* (Melville), 199, 203
Mitchell, Bruce Eardley, 231–32
Mitchell, Donald Grant, 79n3
Mitford, Mary Russell, 53–54
Moby-Dick (Melville), 13–14, 19, 20, 27, 46–47, 219; absence and presence of maternal, 187; Ahab, 66, 67, 183–84, 187–88, 240; allusions to women, 5–6, 139n9; associations of whale pod, 233; Aunt Charity, 183; Circassian longings in, 240–41; colonialism, 215, 219; and commerce, 218–19; critique of the whaling industry, 191, 194, 195; Duyckinck brothers on, 141; ecofeminism, 184; evasion of the maternal, 187; female absence, 181–82; feminine presence through domesticity, 182; feminine imagery, 191, 197; Flask, 184; gendering of the sea, 187–88; Hawthorne as inspiration for, 26, 140n12; imperialism, 200–201, 215; Ishmael, 97n11, 182, 184–86, 188–89, 190–93, 195, 197, 218, 231, 250n42, 251n54; masculine imagery, 181, 182, 183, 197; maternal presence, 182, 183, 184, 187–88, 190–93, 197; mythology, 200–201; patriarchy of, 182; phantom imagery, 186, 187; portrait of Lima, 218; Queequeg, 97n11, 182, 184–87, 193, 194–95, 196–97, 236–37, 251n54; reviews of, 29, 124, 158n3; sentimentality in, 56n1; silence, 184; Starbuck, 183, 184, 187, 188, 193, 194; Stubb, 182–84, 186; symbolism of sea, 196; "The Town-Ho's Story," 218; writing of, 26, 61, 62, 181, 189, 229
Mohammad, 233
Montiglio, Silvia, 224, 225
Moore, Thomas, 235, 249n13
Morales, Francisco, 227n5

Index 281

Morewood, Sarah, 26–28, 29–30, 37n48, 46–47, 139n8, 229
Morrison, Toni, 9, 236
Morse, Samuel, 217
Mosses from an Old Manse (Hawthorne), 47
Mount Greylock, 28, 64
Mumford, Lewis, 7, 181–82
"Murder of Philip Spencer, The" (Hamilton): Captain Alexander Slidell Mackenzie, 99, 101, 102–3, 109–10, 111, 113–14, 116n9; compared to *Billy Budd, Sailor*, 98, 101, 103, 107, 110, 112–13; feminist themes, 99, 100–103, 110, 116; female intercession, 111–12; masculinist themes, 110, 111, 112; maternal, 99, 108, 109, 110–11; sentimentality, 103, 107–8, 112; sources of, 98, 99, 102, 104, 112
Murray, Henry A., 35n6, 134, 140n13
Murphy, Patrick D., 184–85
Murillo, 80n20
muse, 124–26, 231–32, 239, 244, 245, 246
"Mutiny on the Somers, The" (Smith), 102, 103, 104
mythology: interplay of 170; in *Moby-Dick*, 200–201

"Naples in the Time of Bomba" (Melville), 234–35
Naslund, Sena Jeter, 13
Native Americans. *See* Indians
nativism, 50–51, 164, 165, 167, 168–69, 216–17, 220
nature, 209–10; and Circassian longings of Melville, 240; in *King Lear*, 206; in *A New-England Tale*, 75; in *The Confidence-Man*, 206, 209; in "The Piazza," 75; questioned by True Indian Doctor (*The Confidence-Man*), 208
Nelson, Dana, 9, 158n3
Neversink (ship), 65
New Criticism, 8
New-England Tale, A (Sedgwick), 66, 69, 70, 74; Calvinism, 64, 69, 70, 71; Crazy Bet, 70, 71, 78, 80n15; domesticity, 69, 71–72; Jane Elton, 69–71, 72, 73, 78; Mary and Jane Oakley, 72, 73; picturesque, 64–65, 68–71; similarity of to "The Piazza," 64, 70, 74–75
New Historicism, 9
Newman, Lea Bertani Vozar, 8, 9
"New Rosicrucians, The" (Melville), 241
Nixon, Nicola, 159n10

"Norfolk Isle and the Chola Widow" (Melville), 226
North American Review, 216
Nuku Hiva / Nukuheva, 5, 165, 167–68, 171, 172, 175

Oates, Joyce Carol, 66–67
"Ode to Psyche" (Keats), 131, 136, 139n10
"Ode to Melancholy" (Keats), 131–32
"Old Maids" (Sedgwick), 57n8
Omoo, 5, 22, 48, 50, 170, 172, 176–77, 250n29; banishment of narrator, 174; Captain Bob, 174–75, 180n15; Circassian longings of Melville, 240–41; colonialism, 171, 173, 175, 215; criticism of missionary work, 217; Ideea, 164, 175–76, 178; image of queen, 163, 164, 173–74, 175; imperialism, 180n14, 215; narrative gaze, 174, 180n15; nativism, 164; omission of chapters, 35n12; Omoo, 174, 175, 176, 243; Pomare-Tane, 174–75; Queen Pomare, 172, 173–75, 179, 179n3; symbolism of women, 172, humor, 175; waters of Damascus, 249n25
Onís, Jose de, 218
"On the Slain Collegians" (Melville), 6
Orienda, land of, 240
orientalism, 33, 229–30, 232–33, 234–38, 240, 241, 249nn15, 21, 250n36
Osborne, Frances Cuthbert Thomas (granddaughter), 32, 37n49
Osgood, Fannie, 45–46
Otter, Samuel, 135
ownership: in the gothic, 144; in *Pierre*, 142, 144, 147–49, 150, 151, 158; and settlement, 69; and truth, 153; women's rights of, 145, 160n11, 160n13, 160n14

Pacific Islands, 163–64, 170–71, 172–73, 175, 177
Paglia, Camille, 9
paradise, 34, 231, 233; Circassian, 241; experience of Melville with, 238; in New World, 217; orientalism of, 238
Paradise Lost (Milton), 239, 245
"Paradise of Bachelors and the Tartarus of Maids, The" (Melville), 5, 82, 66–67, 94, 199, 230, 232
Parker, Hershel, 79n6, 133, 134, 140nn12, 13, 142, 180n6; and Melville, 9, 15, 138, 158n3, 217, 229
Parker, William, 216–17

282   *Index*

Parmalee, Mary, 35n12
parody: in *Mardi*, 233; Melville and, 66; the gothic in *Pierre* as, 142
paternal, 65; in *Billy Budd,* 103, 110; and orientalism, 230; in *Pierre,* 127, 129, 137, 145, 151, 152; in *The Confidence-Man,* 201; in "The Murder of Philip Spencer," 108; in "Uncle Christopher's," 86–87, 89, 95
patriarchy, 114, 212n1, 233; and gender, 49; of Islamic orientalism, 230; and Melville, 159n9, 182; in "Paradise of Bachelors," 66–67; in "Sketch Eighth," 213, 214, 224; in "The Piazza," 65; in "Uncle Christopher's," 84, 85–86, 87, 90, 94
Patterson-Black, Gene, 14
Patterson, Orlando, 157
"Pebbles" (Melville), 248
Peebles, Anthony Augustus, 20
Penry, Tara, 182
Pequod (ship) (*Moby-Dick*), 65, 183, 186, 191–92, 194
peri, 247; association with heaven, 249n13; description, 233–34; fragrant breath of, 246; in Muslim paradise, 233; in "Naples in the Time of Bomba," 234–35; in "Pontoosuce," 246; in *Redburn,* 234
Persephone, 6
Person, Leland S., 9, 182, 232
Peru, 214
Peters, Bill, 13
piazza: as expression of its inhabitant, 60; symbol of in "The Piazza," 62–63
"Piazza, The" (Melville), 62–63, 73, 77; Downing as source, 80n22; Marianna, 62, 65, 67, 73, 76, 77–78; narrator of, 62, 73–76, 77–78; patriarchy, 65; picturesque, 64–65, 76; references to *Le Bossu,* 64; similarity to *A New-England Tale,* 64, 70, 74–75; symbol of Eve in, 232; symbol of piazza, 62–63
Piazza Tales, The (Melville), 62, 217
Picard, Aimée, 13
picturesque, 67–69, 72–73, 74, 78, 78n1, 135; imitation of, 79n12; in *A New-England Tale,* 64–65, 70; and *The House of the Seven Gables,* 80n19; in "The Piazza," 64–65, 76
Pierre; or, the Ambiguities (Melville), 52, 53–55, 67, 121, 128, 236; allusions to Keats in, 125, 131–32, 136, 139n10; ambiguity, 122, 135–36; Anne Marie Priscilla (cousin) as inspiration for Isabel, 17; authorship, 136–37, 141–42, 156, 160n15; Beatrice Cenci, 5; Danae, 5; Delly Ulver, 5, 97n8, 125–26, 132, 147; domesticity, 160n15; Enceladus, 135; feudal imagery, 149; Glendinning line, 144, 145, 147–48, 151; the gothic in, 142, 144, 149, 152, 153–54, 156, 157, 159nn4, 5; identity in, 147; importance of authorship in, 152, 153; importance of sexuality in, 132–33; importance of women in, 121; incest in, 59n26, 124, 133, 134, 135, 136, 154; individualism in, 150–51; interpretations of, 121, 123, 132–33, 134–35, 140n13, 159n3; Isabel, *see under individual entry;* Lucy Tartan, *see under individual entry;* Mary Glendinning, *see under individual entry;* masculinity, 147; maternal, 160n15; melodrama, 123, 134, 138; ownership of land and people in, 144; Pierre Glendinning, *see under individual entry;* poverty, 125; readers of, 48; reinterpretation of, 13–14; responses to, 123; reviews of, 29, 50, 141, 158, 158n1; as a romantic novel, 122; sensationalism, 122, 134; sentimentality, 122, 160n15; sexual power, 154; sexual reading of, 134; spectralization in, 142, 143, 151; spiritualism in, 48–49; success of, 55; symbolic reading of, 122, 123, 130–31, 139n3, 232; sympathy with women in, 94; *The House of the Seven Gables* as influence on, 150, 157, 159n6; use of Dante, 137–38; writing style, 123, 131, 135, 139n8, 140nn11,12, 13
Pinnegar, Fred, 7, 9, 232
Plumwood, Val, 200
Poe, Edgar Allan, 50, 53, 142
Polynesian Researches (Ellis), 164
"Pontoosuce" (Melville), 246–47
"Poor Man's Pudding, and Rich Man's Crumbs" (Melville), 55, 64, 106
Poor Rich Man, and the Rich Poor Man, The (Sedgwick), 55, 64, 65
Pope, Alexander, 176
Porter, David, 164–65, 170, 179n1
Porter, Jane, 51, 58n19
Post-Lauria, Shelia, 9, 46
poverty: awareness of by Melville, 72; in "Bartleby, the Scrivener," 93; of characters in *Pierre,* 124, 125; and women, 94
power, 82, 90, 164, 167, 179; challenged by queen in *Typee,* 165; forms of, 163; of men over women in *Pierre,* 149; narrative, 168–70, 174, 177, 178, 179; physical, 173–74, 175;

Index 283

power (cont.)
    political, 168, 172, 174, 175; sexual:, 154, 169, 170, 175; on side of males, 67; of women in works of Melville, 164
Powers, Hiram, 239
Pratt, Annis, 202–3
Price, Martin, 67, 72–73
Primitive Culture (Tylor), 166
"Prodigal, The" (*Clarel*), 237
property: marital, 145; ownership of, 145, 160nn11, 12, 13, 14; ownership of in *Pierre*, 147; as reminder of the gothic in *Pierre*, 144
Puente Candamo, José A. de la, 220
Putnam's Monthly Magazine, 29, 30, 217, 228n14

Queen Elizabeth I, 5
Queen Anne, 5
queens: forms of power, 163, 164; physicality and sexuality, 163, 179; symbolism of in *Omoo*, 172–73
Quincy, Edmund, 22
Qur'an, 233

Rachel (ship): meets *Pequod* in *Moby-Dick*, 196; as maternal in *Moby-Dick*, 197
racism: in Circassian paradise, 236; of minstrel shows, 203–4; in "Sketch Eighth," 226; in *The Confidence-Man*, 199, 203
Radcliffe, Ann, 5
Radiguet, Max, 166–67
Radway, Janice, 56n3
Ramsey, William, 212n6
rape: in "The Encantadas," 220; types of, 222; as word Hunilla cannot say, 225
Rasselas (Johnson), 171, 239
reader-response criticism, 42
Redburn (Melville), 4–5, 19, 35n11, 43, 50, 80n20; houris and peris, 234; Orientalism, 249n15; Redburn, 234; sartorial imagery, 243; writing of, 25
Redwood (Sedgwick), 59n23
religion, 51, 63, 214. *See also specific forms of*
Reliques (Percy), 33
Renker, Elizabeth, 9, 15, 37n52, 94, 97n7
"Review of the Proceedings of the Naval Court Martial" (Cooper), 102, 103
Reynolds, David S., 80n14
Rhys, Jean, 180n14
"Rime of the Ancient Mariner, The" (Coleridge), 139n9

Rights of Man (ship), 108, 109, 115
"Rip Van Winkle's Lilac" (Melville), 244–45
"River, The" (Melville), 201
Robarts, Edward, 164
Robertson-Lorant, Laurie, 9, 182, 227n8, 228n10, 251n49
Robinson, Sidney K., 67–68
Rogin, Michael Paul, 9, 85, 97n13, 148, 158n3
Rosa, Salvator, 73, 80n21, 228n15
"Rose Farmer, The" (Melville), 246, 247–48
Rosenblatt, Louise, 56n3
Rourke, Constance, 8
Rowland, Beryl, 8
Rowson, Susannah, 52
Ruskin, John, 73, 74
Ruth Hall (Fern), 107

sailors: influence of on the Pacific, 171; relationships of with Pacific women, 164; sexuality of, 169–70
Samson, John, 170
Sanders, Elizabeth Elkins, 50–51, 59n26
San Dominick (ship) ("Benito Cereno"), 5
Savage, Samuel Hay (brother-in-law), 15, 20, 30, 37n49
Scheherezade (*The Thousand and One Arabian Nights*), 233
Schlachter, Abby Langdon, 13
Schultz, Elizabeth, 9, 56n1, 182, 184
Scollay, Priscilla (paternal grandmother), 17
Scott, Sir Walter, 5, 70
"Scout Toward Aldie, The" (Melville), 6
sea: in American writing, 198n9; as bloody, 190–91; as feminine, 188, 189, 190, 191, 198n9; as masculine, 187–88, 189, 190; as maternal in *Moby-Dick*, 188, 189, 196
Sealts, Merton M., Jr., 57n9, 99, 100, 115, 116n6
"Second Fragment" (Melville), 234
Sedgwick, Catharine Maria, 4, 19, 26, 56n1, 57n9, 65, 80nn15, 17; added piazza to house, 60, 61; cultural shifts in writing, 69; on Crazy Bet (*A New-England Tale*), 70; on Downing, 60, 79n3; and domesticity, 60–62; and Hawthorne, 53; influence on American novels, 44–45, 66; influence on Melville, 55; misnaming of, 59n22; novels of domestic manners, 46; and "The Piazza," 80n17; use of picturesque, 73; writing style, 52
Sedgwick, Elizabeth: school of, 18–19, 44–45

284   *Index*

Sedgwick, Eve Kosofsky, 9, 110, 116n9
Seminoles, 207–8
sensationalism, 51, 122, 126, 134, 135
sentimentality, 9, 50, 52, 54, 55, 58n16, 69, 200; in books read by men and women, 46; in *Billy Budd, Sailor,* 99, 112; as Christian, 241; of Mary Glendinning (*Pierre*), 148; in *Moby-Dick,* 56n1, 182; in *Pierre,* 122, 135, 153, 160n15; in "The Murder of Philip Spencer," 103, 107–8, 112; in "Uncle Christopher's," 95, 96; in *White-Jacket,* 26
sexuality, 9; female, 231–32; expression of in time of Melville, 232; of Ideea (*Omoo*), 175–76; in *Pierre,* 121, 124, 125, 126, 132–34, 154; of men in antebellum period, 154; of Pacific women, 164–65; of island queens, 163; in *The Confidence-Man,* 200, 209; in *Typee,* 169–70; in Victorian era, 24; of women, 172, 175, 176
Shakespeare, 21, 34, 54, 74, 200, 203; and *Moby-Dick,* 5–6; influence on Melville, 205–6; recited by Melville, 28; and *Typee,* 167, 180n6; work of as source of Crazy Bet (*A New-England Tale*), 70. See also titles of works.
Shaw, Elizabeth. *See* Melville, Elizabeth "Lizzie" Shaw
Shaw, Hope Savage (mother-in-law), 20, 37n49
Shaw, John (brother-in-law), 20
Shaw, Lemuel (father-in-law), 19, 20, 22
Shaw, Lemuel, Jr. (brother-in-law), 20
Shelley, Mary, 131, 235
Shepherd, Daniel, 249n17
silence, 150, 214; in *Billy Budd,* 110; as culturally specific, 224; and eating in *Moby-Dick,* 184; of Goneril (*The Confidence-Man*), 202; in *Pierre,* 136, 150; in "Sketch Eighth," 213, 225; in "The Encantadas," 220; in "Uncle Christopher's," 89, 90, 94
Simpson, Eleanor E., 9
Slater, Judith, 8
slavery, 4–6, 82–97, 230–32; wage slavery 82, 83, 87, 89
Smart, Christopher, 71, 80n18
Smith, Charlotte, 51
Smith, Elizabeth Oakes, 48–49, 57n9
Smith, Lieutenant H. D., 101–4, 116n6
Somers mutiny, 98, 99, 101, 112, 113
"Song to David, A" (Smart), 71
South Seas lecture (Melville), 51, 237–38, 239

Southworth, E. D. E. N., 44, 52
Spain: feared by readers of "The Encantadas," 215; hostile attitude toward, 215–16; imperialism, 213, 214; introducing idea of empire to Europe, 215; invasion of Americas by, 220; power of in "The Encantadas" (Melville), 217; whale metaphor of, 218
Spark, Clare, 9
"Spasm of Sense, A" (Hamilton), 105–6, 107
spectralization: in the gothic, 142–43; of Isabel (*Pierre*), 149–50; of Melville, 152; of Pierre, 148, 149–50, 151, 152, 156; as theme in *Pierre,* 142, 143
Spencer, Philip, 98–99, 101, 104, 108, 110–11, 113–14, 160n11, 235
Spies, JoAnne, 13
Spivak, Gayatri, 180n14, 213
Springer, Haskell, 198n9
Stanton, Elizabeth Cady, 4, 146
Steel, Flint, & Asbestos (*Pierre*), 158
Stein, William Bysshe, 245
Stewart, Charles S., 164–65, 170, 179n1
Stone, Lucy, 4
Sturdevant, William, 208
subaltern, 213, 214, 225, 226
"Syra" (Melville), 251n46

Tahiti, 176; claimed by the French, 168; in *Omoo,* 164, 171, 173; political power of queen, 172; in *Typee,* 171; women in, 175–76
Taipi, 164, 165, 167–69, 171, 172
Tanaquil, 5
Tanner, Tony, 193
Tartan, Lucy (*Pierre*), 4, 53–54, 147, 152; betrothal to Pierre, 241–42; death, 156; dependence of Pierre on, 97n8; as "Fair Maiden," 124, 134; foreshadowing of death of, 242; as gothic subject, 157; on Pierre, 154; as prototype of good, 7–8; sufferings inflicted on by Pierre, 136; symbolism of, 125, 242; as twin of Isabel, 155
Temoana, 167–68, 180n7
Thomas, Brook, 144
Thousand and One Arabian Nights, The (Scheherezade), 233
"Times Long Ago!" (Melville), 241
Timoleon, Etc. (Melville), 6, 33, 243, 244, 250n39, 251n46
Tit-bit (ship) (*Moby-Dick*), 186

Index 285

Todd, John, 36n33
Tolchin, Neal L., 79n11
"To Ned" (Melville), 237–38
Toner, Jennifer DiLalla, 158n1
"Tortoise Hunters, The" (Melville), 227n8
Tylor, E. B., 166
Typee (Melville), 22, 61, 175, 189, 217; colonialism, 165, 168, 170, 215; female characters in, 170; Fayaway, 4, 164, 170–71, 234, 238–39; the French in, 5, 164, 168–69; image of queen, 163, 167, 173–74; imperialism, 215, 249n22; island queen, 5, 165, 167–68; Kory-Kory, 171; missionaries in, 50; modifications of facts in, 167–68, 172; Mowanna, 167–68; Mrs. Pritchard, 5, 164, 165, 168–69, 170; narrative gaze, 166, 167, 168, 169–70, 172; narrative power, 169, 170; nativism, 164, 165, 167, 168–69; physical presence of queen in, 164, 165, 166, 167; power of women in, 170; restoration of Hawaiian government in, 50–51; reviews of, 20, 47; sexual power, 169, 170; source of characters, 167–68; symbolism of women, 171, 172; taboos, 171; Tinor, 164, 171, 172; Tommo, 169–71, 189, 237–39, 241–42; visitors to island in, 176, 177; William Ellis as source for, 170
"Typee Manuscript" (Melville), 238

"Uncle Christopher's" (Cary), 91; Andrew, 88, 89, 90, 91, 95; and domesticity, 85; isolation, 93; Mark, 88, 90–93, 95–96; narrator, 86, 87–88, 89, 90–93; sentimentality, 95, 96; silence, 89, 90, 94; patriarchy, 84, 85–87, 88, 89, 90, 94; Uncle Christopher, 85–91, 93, 95, 96
United States (frigate), 35n8, 102, 168, 228n10
United States, 58n19; effect on the Pacific, 164, 177; hostile attitude toward Spain, 215–16; imperialism, 213, 214, 227n2; role of whalers in formation of empire, 218; taboos of, 169; in "The Encantadas," 215
United States Magazine and Democratic Review, 145

Vae Kehu, 166–67, 179n5
Vedder, Elihu, 6
Venus: legend of in Melville's writings, 235
"Vial of Attar, The" (Melville), 248

Wald, Priscilla, 148, 153, 157, 159nn3, 4, 160n16
Walpole, Horace, 144, 149
Warner, Susan, 46
Warren, Joyce M., 7
Watson, E. L. Grant, 139n3
Weaver, Raymond, 7
Weeds and Wildings, Chiefly; with a Rose or Two (Melville), 16, 33–34, 244, 247
Weinstein, Cindy, 9
Welles, Orson, 13
Wenke, John, 100, 116n2
whales: encounter with crew of *Pequod* (*Moby-Dick*), 192, 194; as nursing mothers in *Moby-Dick*, 191, 192, 195; sperm, 184
whalers: 194, 196, 217–19
White-Jacket (Melville), 5, 19, 25, 26, 50, 58n16, 61, 243
White Lady of Avanel (*The Monastery*), 5
Whitman, Sarah, 48–49
Wide, Wide World, The (Warner) 52
Wide Sargasso Sea (Rhys), 180n14
Wiegman, Robyn, 9, 212n1
Willard, Emma, 57n8
"William Wilson" (Poe), 159n4
Williams, Stanley T., 215–16
Willis, Nathaniel Parker, 79n3
Wilson, Ann, 13
Wilson, Gilbert, 13
women, 82, 160n12, 163, 177, 202, 239, 240; abandonment of, 64; bodies of, 189, 190, 191, 238; artists, 13; as clay-eaters, 202; cultural oppression of, 199; as "Dark Lady" or "Fair Maiden," 124; education of, 21, 44, 45; fiction of, 69; as houris, 233; identity, 145, 146–47, 176; influence on Melville, 47; interaction with sailors in the Pacific Islands, 164; in life of Melville, 9, 16; men's ownership of , 142, 158; metaphor of as slaves, 232; misogynist portraits of, 207; missionary, in Pacific, 171; as muses, 124–25, 232; as monsters, 207; narrative power of, 164; Pacific, 164–65; parody of, 233; power of in works by Melville, 164; as readers, 41–44, 46, 47–48, 49, 56, 57n6, 58n13; rights of ownership of, 145, 160nn11, 13, 14; in *Moby-Dick* performances and revisions, 13; as scholars of Melville, 9, 10, 14; and sea, 190; sympathy of Melville with, 94; writing style, 52

286 *Index*

"Women, Marriage, and Sexuality" (Pinnegar), 5
Wonder Book, A (Hawthorne), 79n10
Wright, Nathalia, 8

Yanella, Donald, 15
Yates, Frances A., 215, 227n4
Yillah (*Mardi*), 7, 164, 177–79, 238, 240, 242, 250n34

"Young Goodman Brown" (Hawthorne), 159n4
Young, Robert C., 227n3

Zelnick, Stephen, 87
Zwarg, Christina, 57n8

Index   287